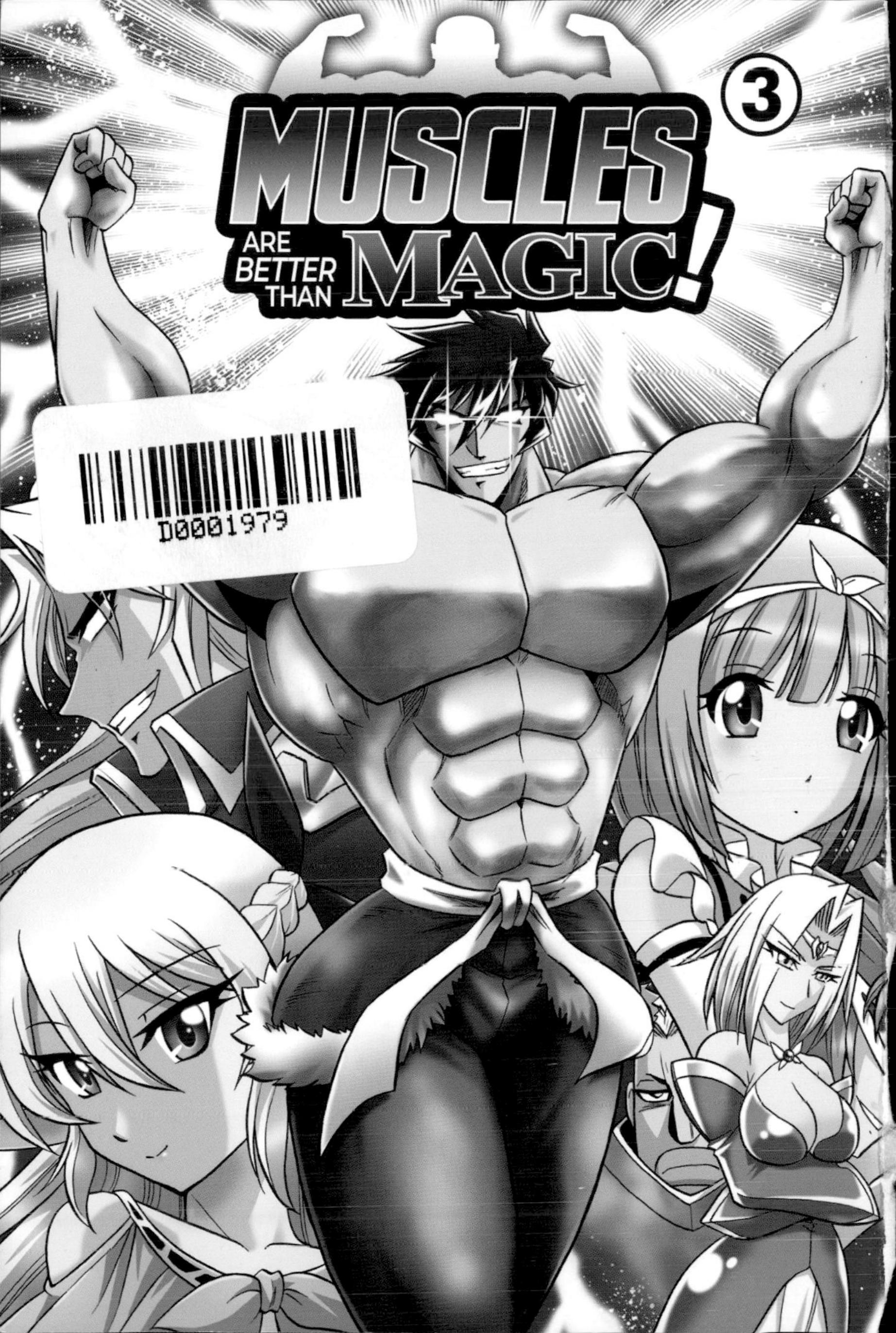
3
MUSCLES ARE BETTER THAN MAGIC!

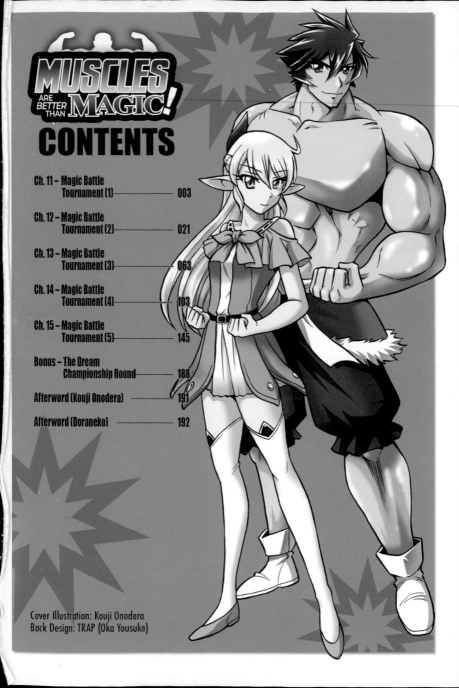

MUSCLES ARE BETTER THAN MAGIC!

CONTENTS

Cover Illustration: Kouji Onodera
Back Design: TRAP (Oka Yousuke)

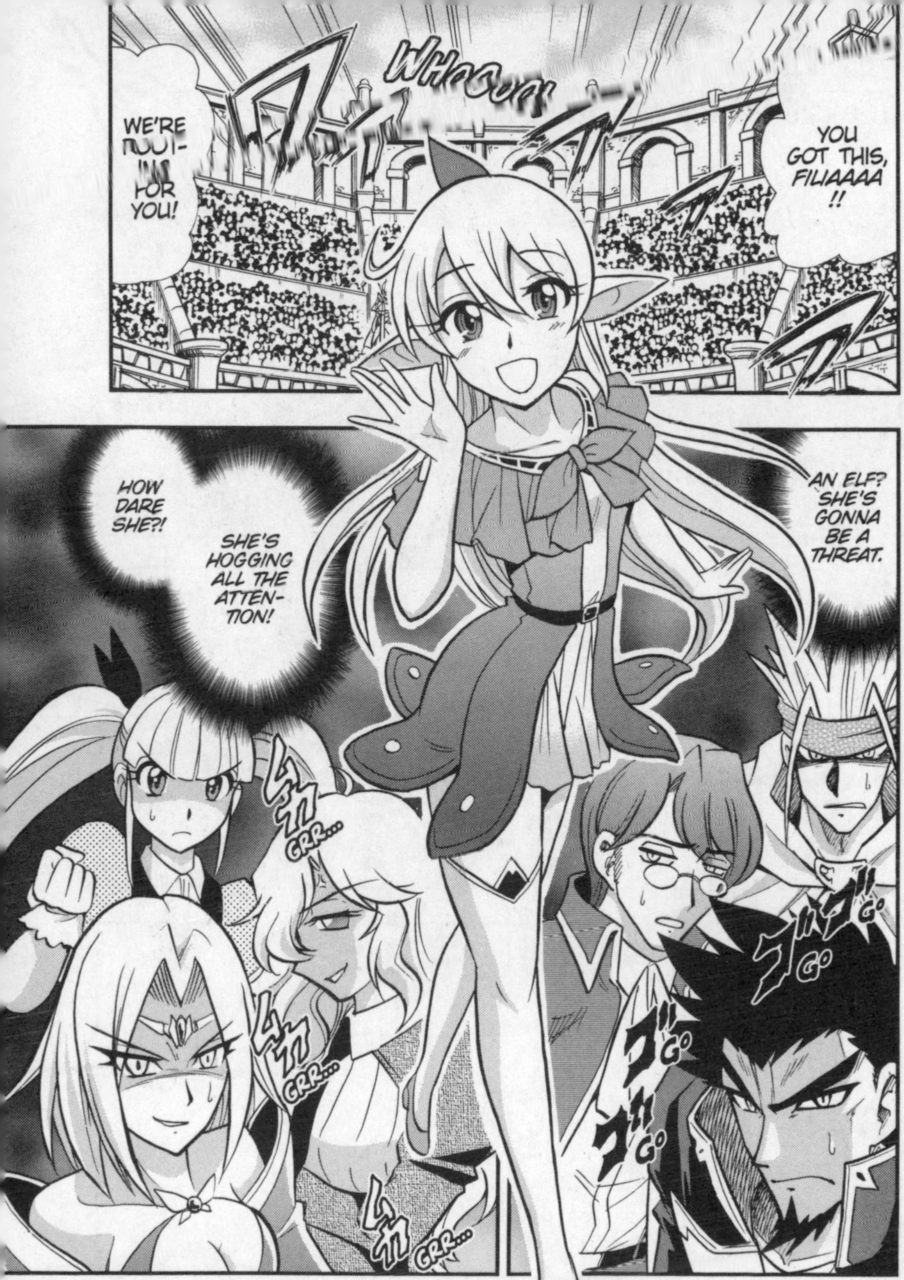
YOU GOT THIS, FILIAAAA!!
WHOOOOO!!
WE'RE
FOR YOU!
AN ELF? SHE'S GONNA BE A THREAT.
HOW DARE SHE?!
SHE'S HOGGING ALL THE ATTEN-TION!
GO
GO
GO
GO
GRR...
GRR...
GRR...

CHAPTER 11
Magic Battle Tournament (1)

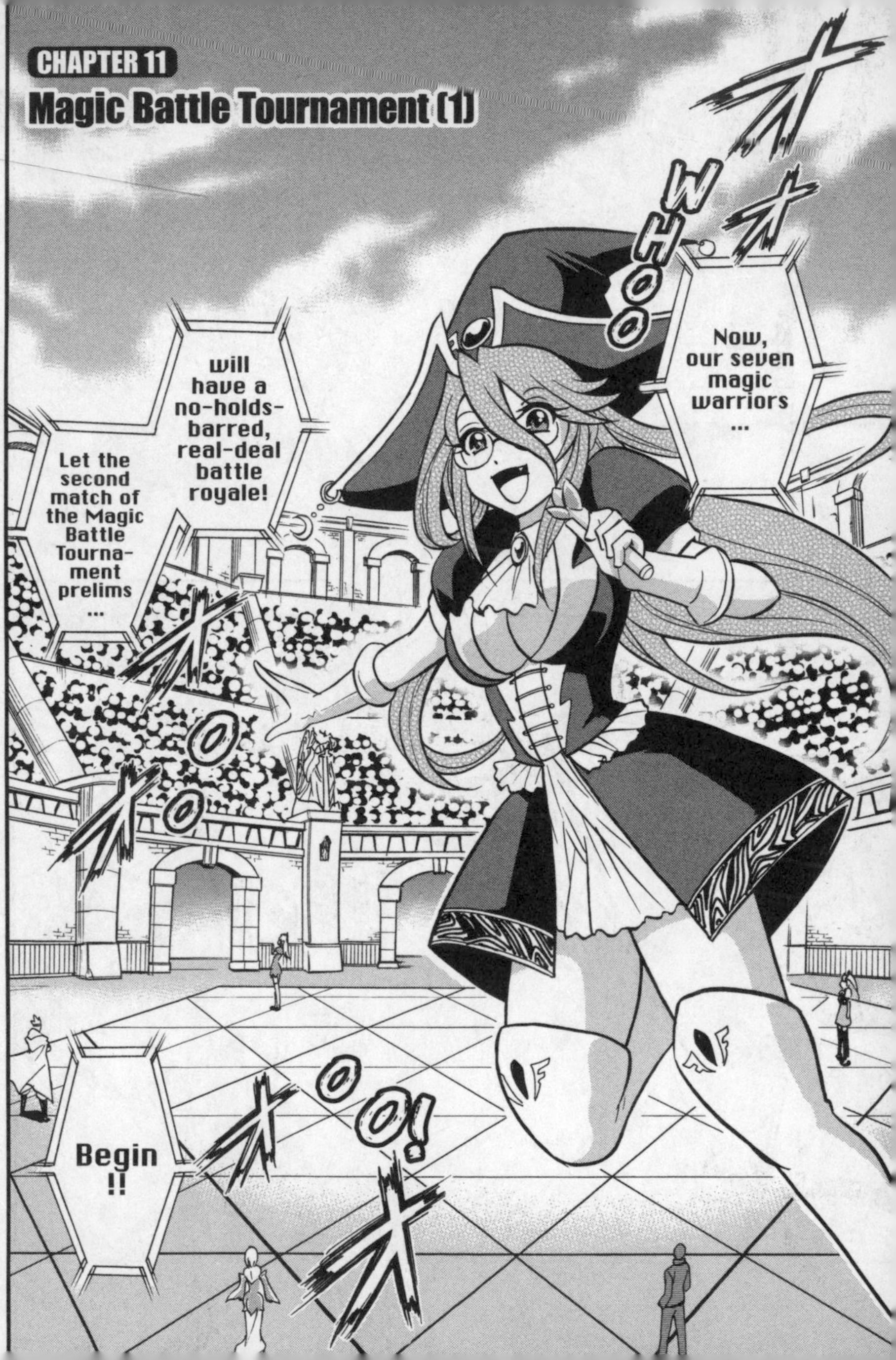
WHOOOO
Now, our seven magic warriors ...
will have a no-holds-barred, real-deal battle royale!
Let the second match of the Magic Battle Tournament prelims ...
OOOO!
Begin !!

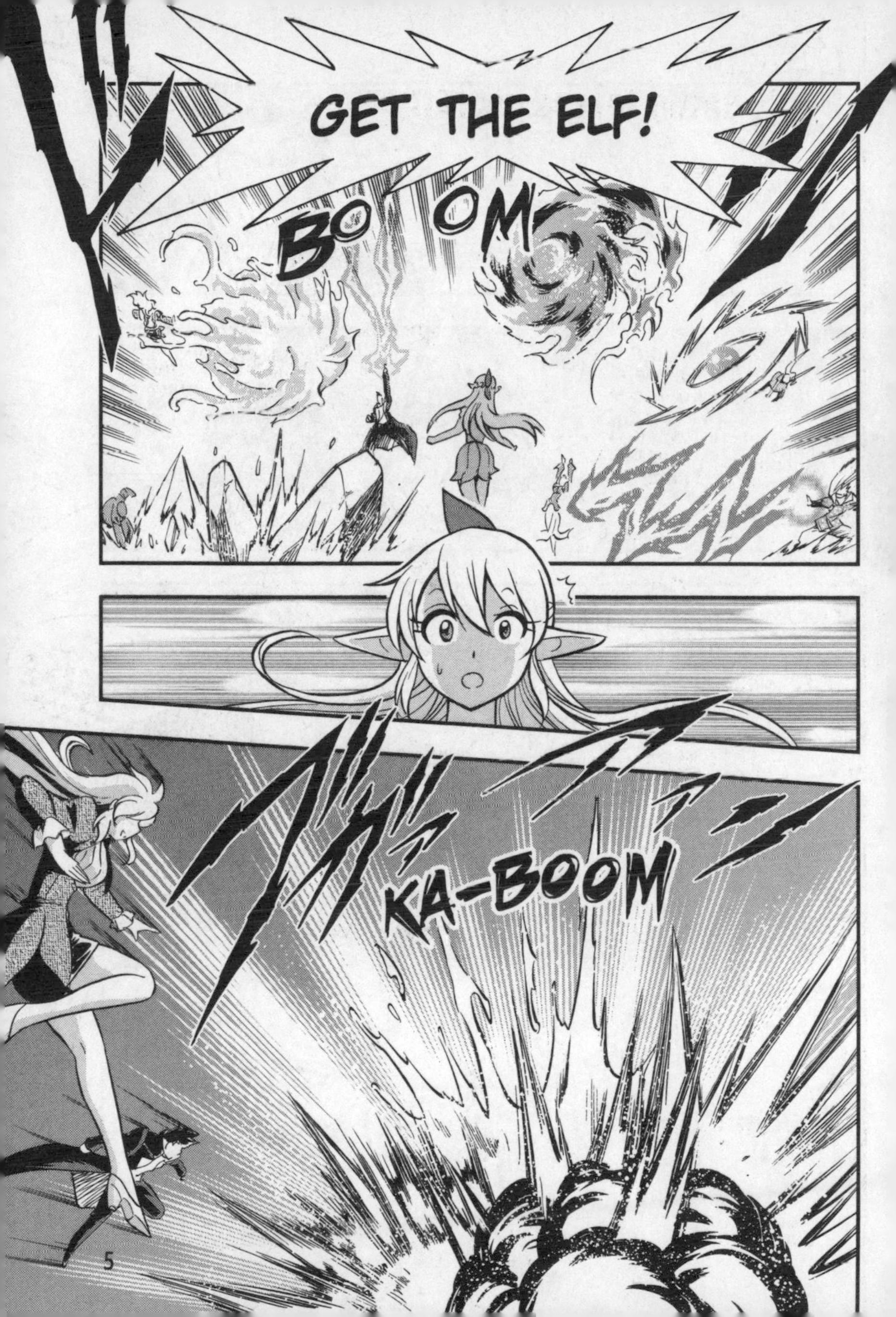
GET THE ELF!
BOOM
KA-BOOM

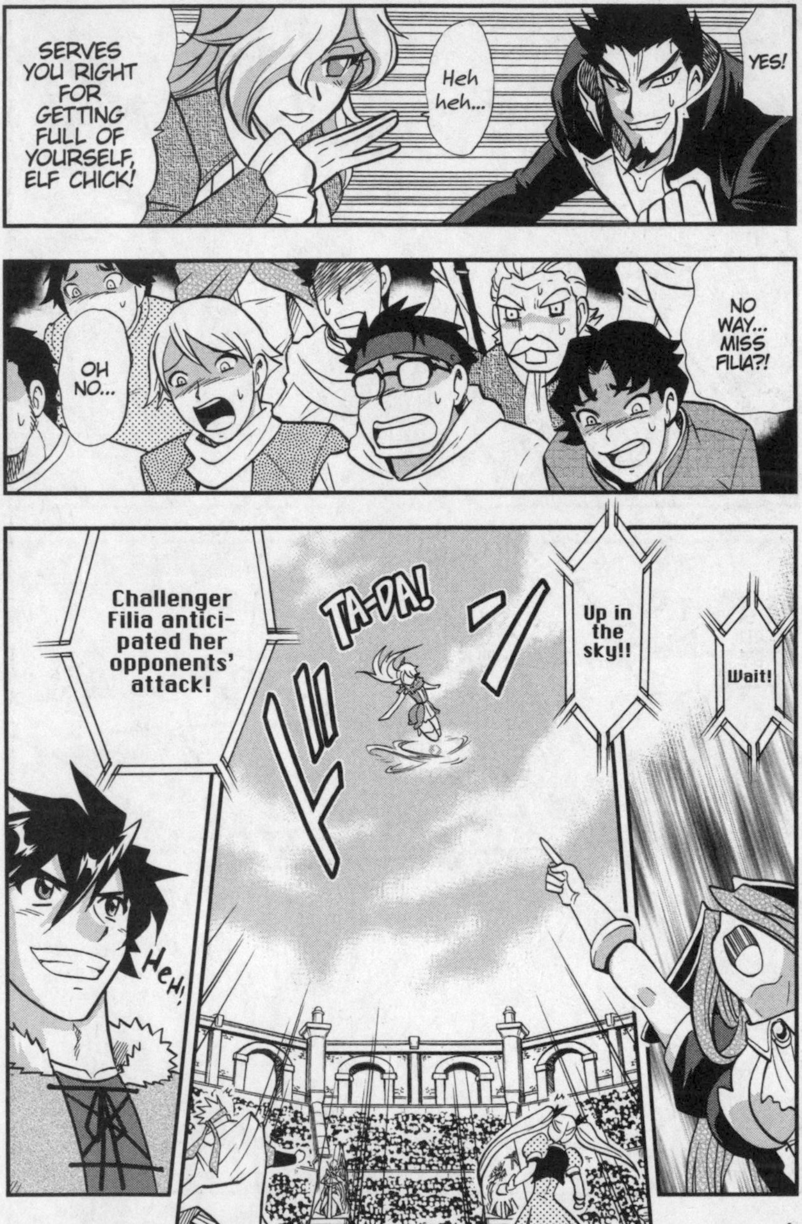
YES!
Heh heh...
SERVES YOU RIGHT FOR GETTING FULL OF YOURSELF, ELF CHICK!
NO WAY... MISS FILIA?!
OH NO...
Wait!
Up in the sky!!
TA-DA!
Challenger Filia antici-pated her opponents' attack!
HEH!

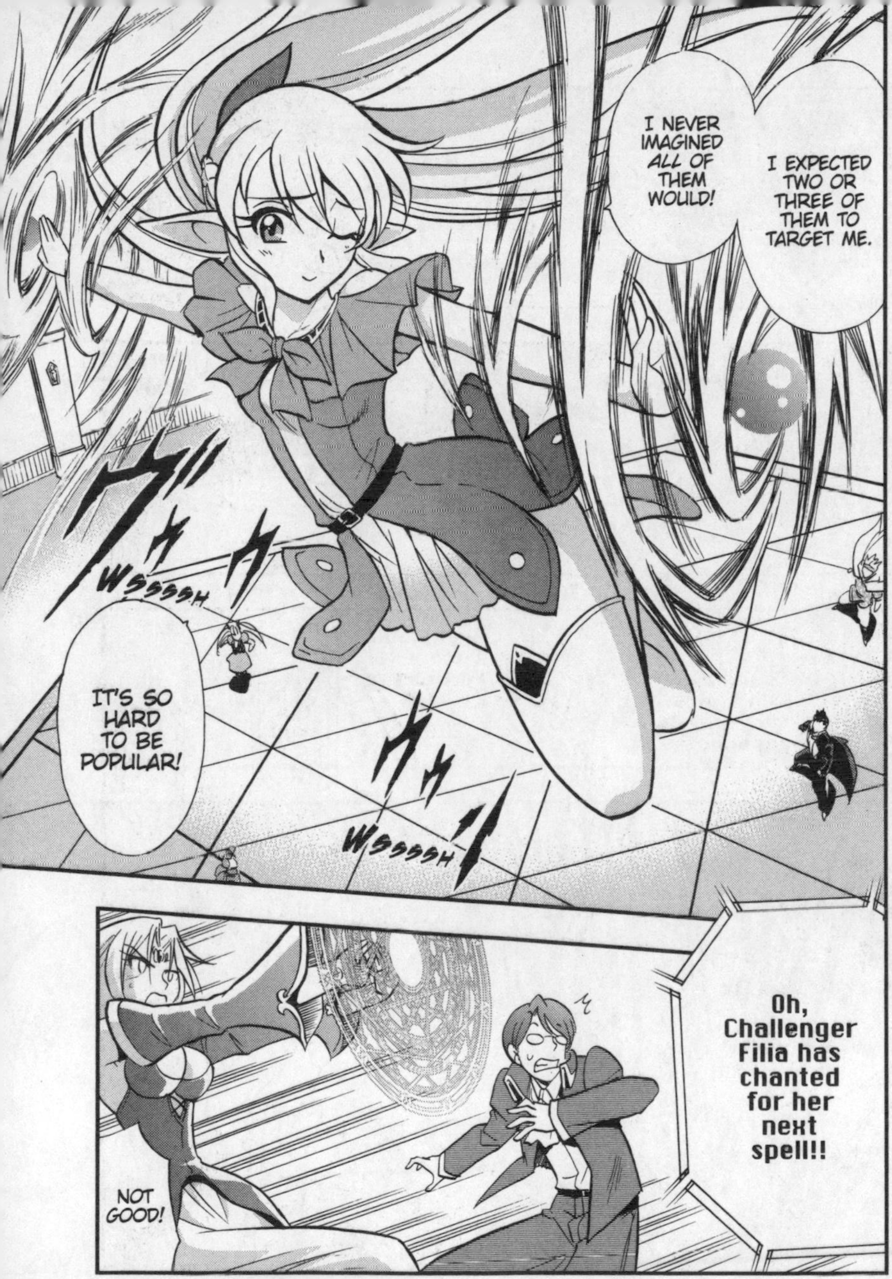
I EXPECTED TWO OR THREE OF THEM TO TARGET ME.
I NEVER IMAGINED ALL OF THEM WOULD!
WSSSSH
IT'S SO HARD TO BE POPULAR!
WSSSSH
Oh, Challenger Filia has chanted for her next spell!!
NOT GOOD!

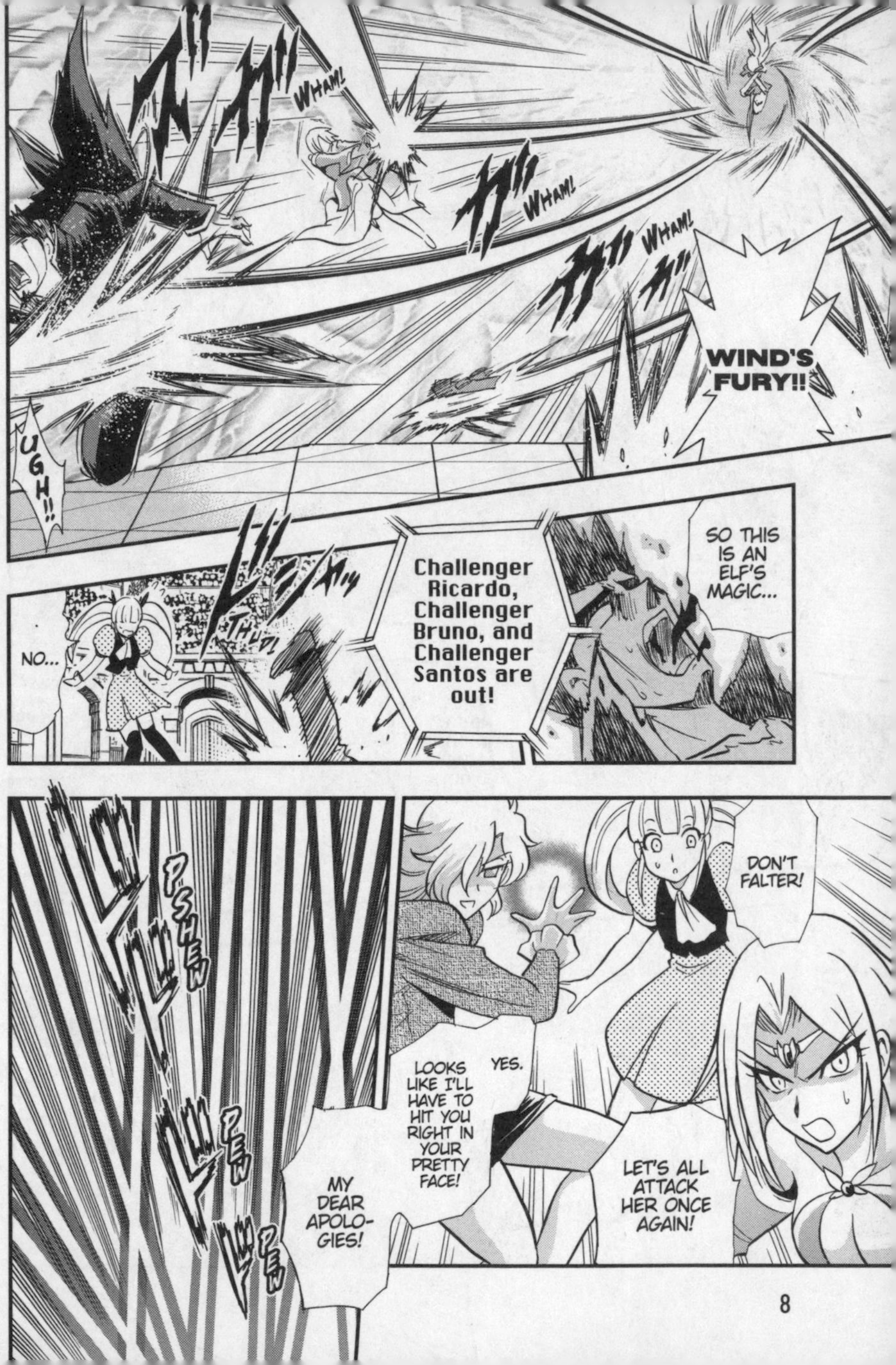
WHAM!
WHAM!
WHAM!
WIND'S FURY!!
UGH!!
SO THIS IS AN ELF'S MAGIC...
Challenger Ricardo, Challenger Bruno, and Challenger Santos are out!
THUD!
NO...
DON'T FALTER!
LET'S ALL ATTACK HER ONCE AGAIN!
YES.
LOOKS LIKE I'LL HAVE TO HIT YOU RIGHT IN YOUR PRETTY FACE!
MY DEAR APOLOGIES!
PSHEW
PEW
PEW

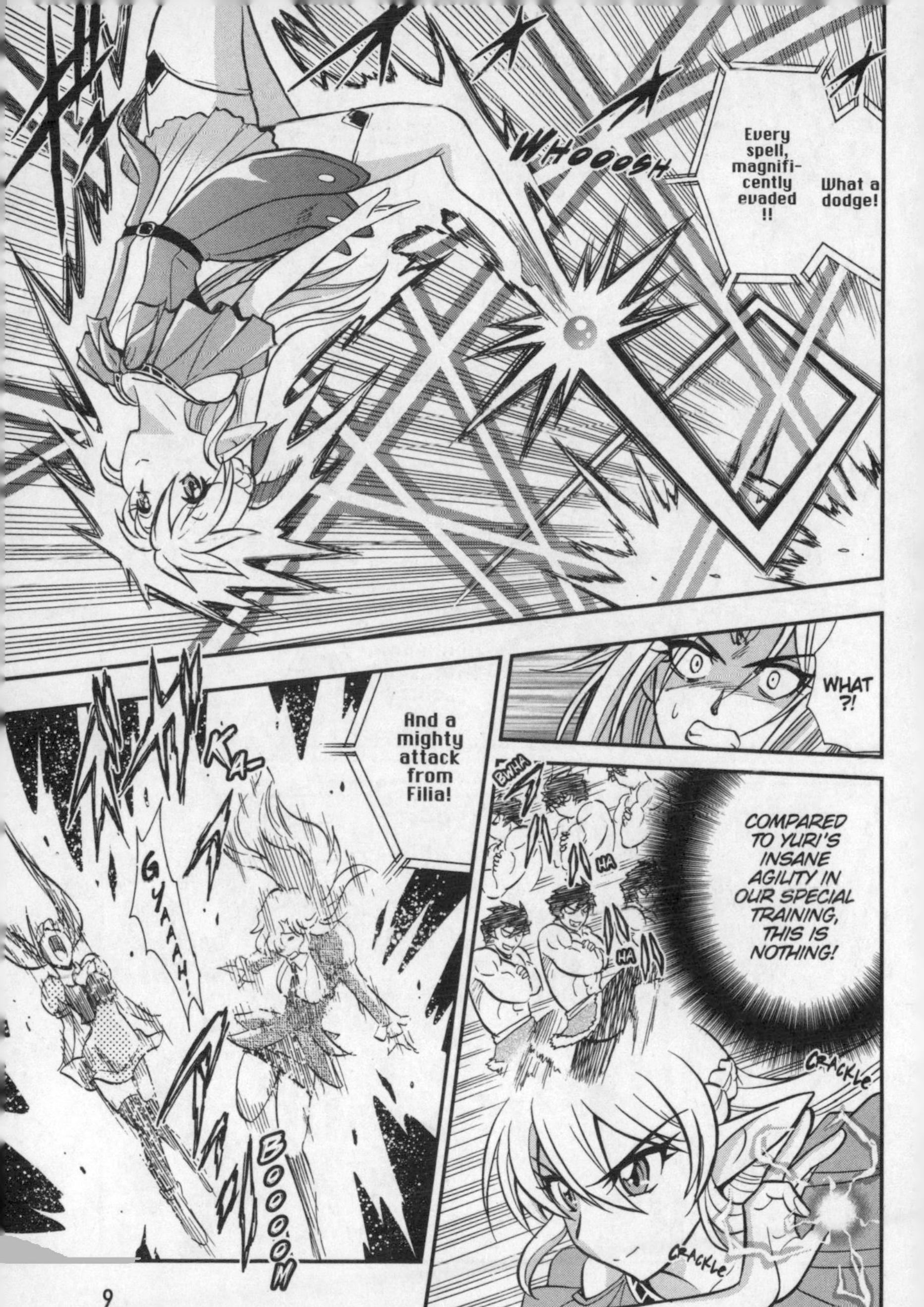
WHOOOOSH
What a dodge!
Every spell, magnificently evaded!!
WHAT?!
BWHA
HA
HA
COMPARED TO YURI'S INSANE AGILITY IN OUR SPECIAL TRAINING, THIS IS NOTHING!
CRACKLE
CRACKLE
And a mighty attack from Filia!
KA-
GYAAAH!!
BOOOOOM

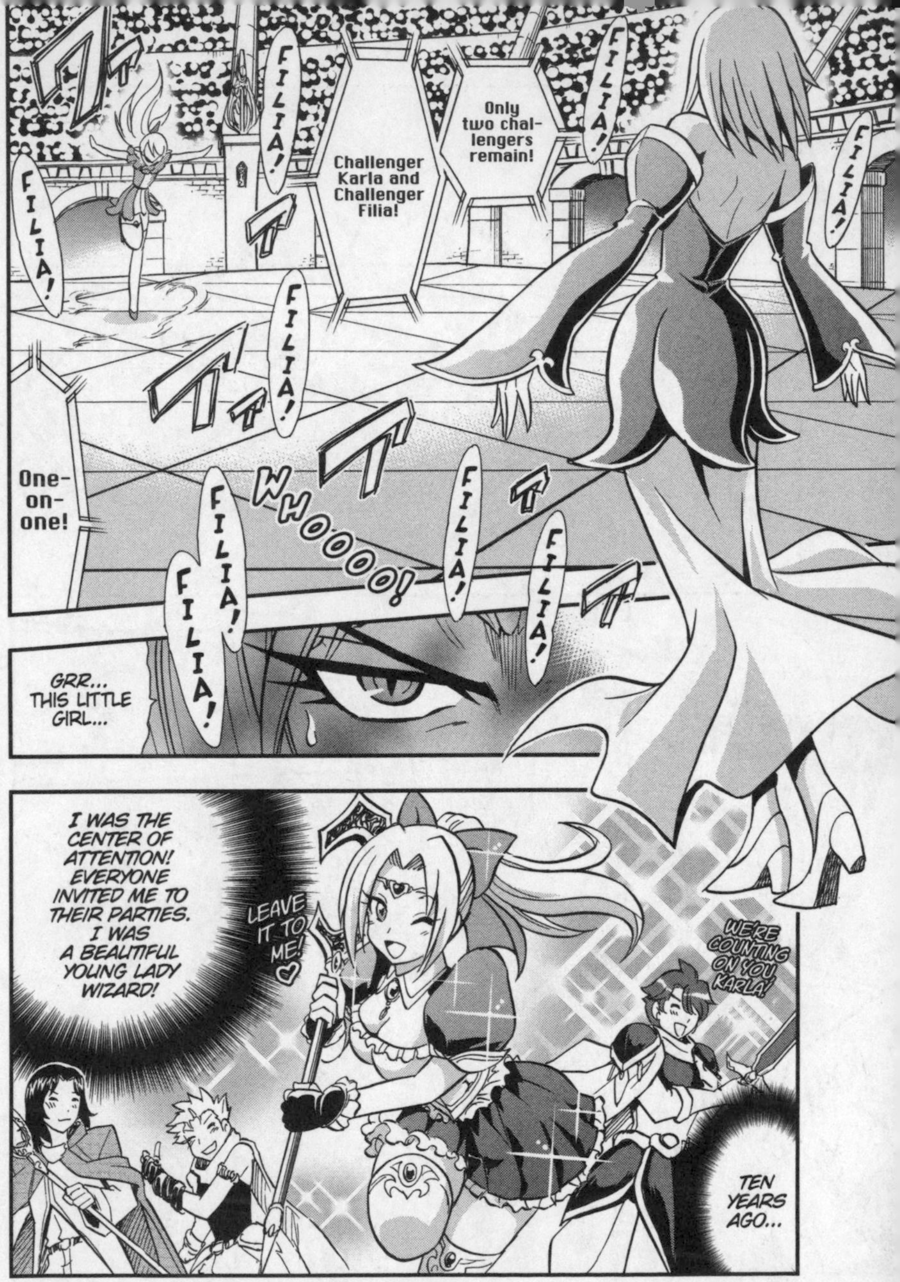
FILIA!
FILIA!
Only two challengers remain!
Challenger Karla and Challenger Filia!
FILIA!
FILIA!
FILIA!
FILIA!
FILIA!
WHOOOOO!
FILIA!
FILIA!
One-on-one!
GRR... THIS LITTLE GIRL...
WE'RE COUNTING ON YOU KARLA!
LEAVE IT TO ME! ♥
I WAS THE CENTER OF ATTENTION! EVERYONE INVITED ME TO THEIR PARTIES. I WAS A BEAUTIFUL YOUNG LADY WIZARD!
TEN YEARS AGO...

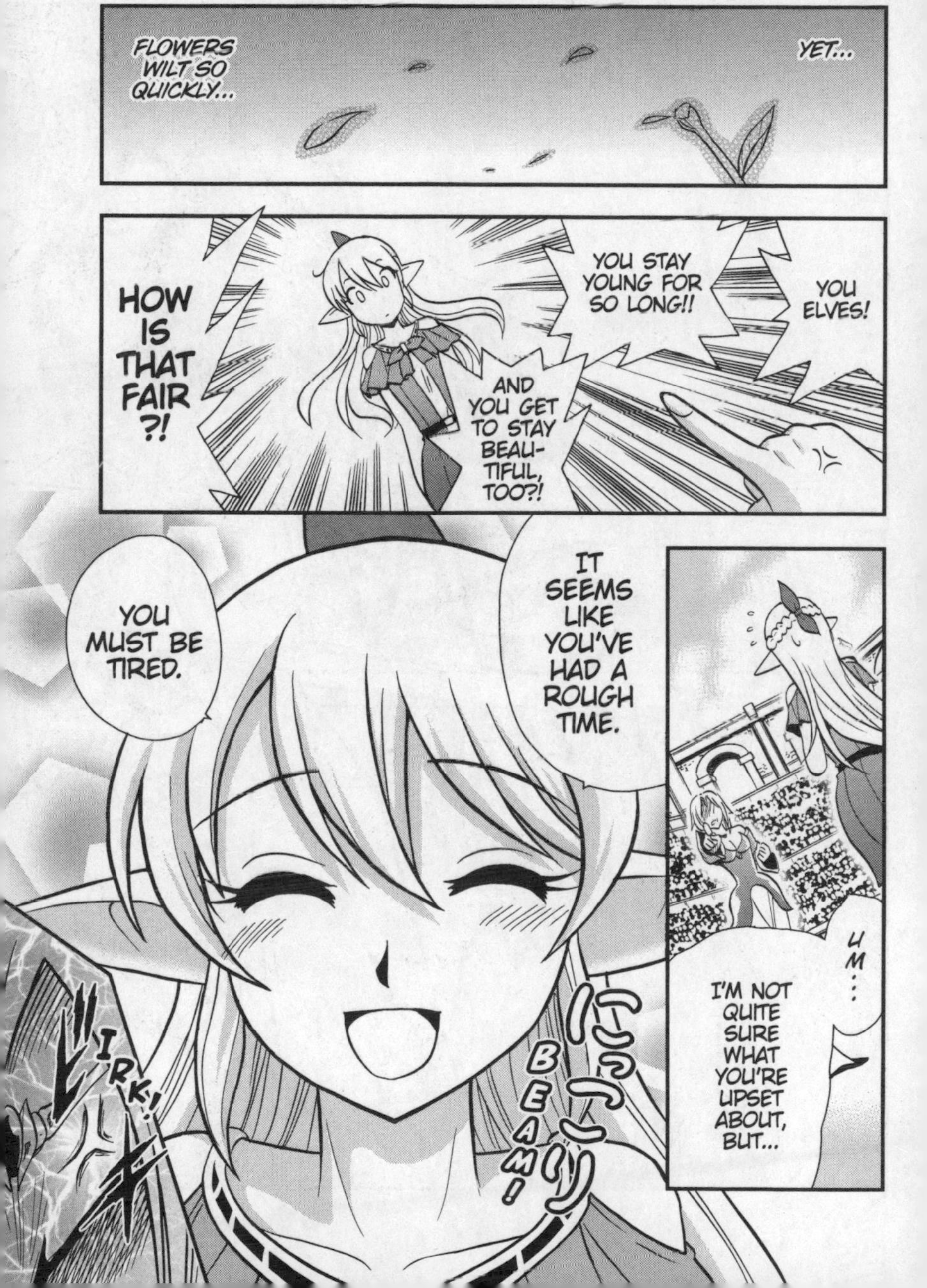
FLOWERS WILT SO QUICKLY...
YET...
YOU ELVES!
YOU STAY YOUNG FOR SO LONG!!
AND YOU GET TO STAY BEAU-TIFUL, TOO?!
HOW IS THAT FAIR?!
UM...
I'M NOT QUITE SURE WHAT YOU'RE UPSET ABOUT, BUT...
IT SEEMS LIKE YOU'VE HAD A ROUGH TIME.
YOU MUST BE TIRED.
BEAM!
IRK!

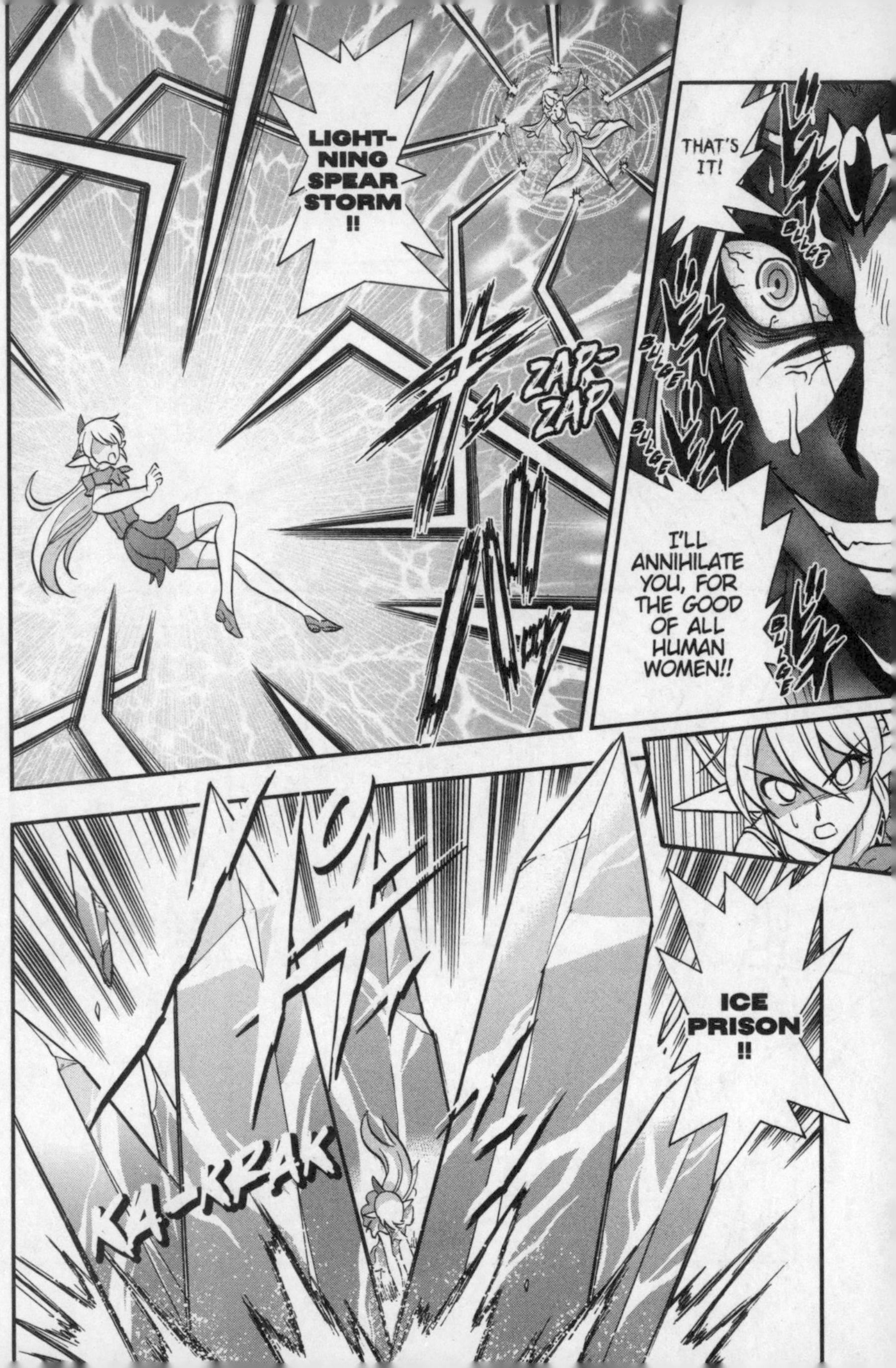
THAT'S IT!
BULGE
BULGE
BULGE
BULGE
I'LL ANNIHILATE YOU, FOR THE GOOD OF ALL HUMAN WOMEN!!
BULGE
LIGHT-NING SPEAR STORM!!
ZAP-ZAP
ICE PRISON!!
KA-KRAK

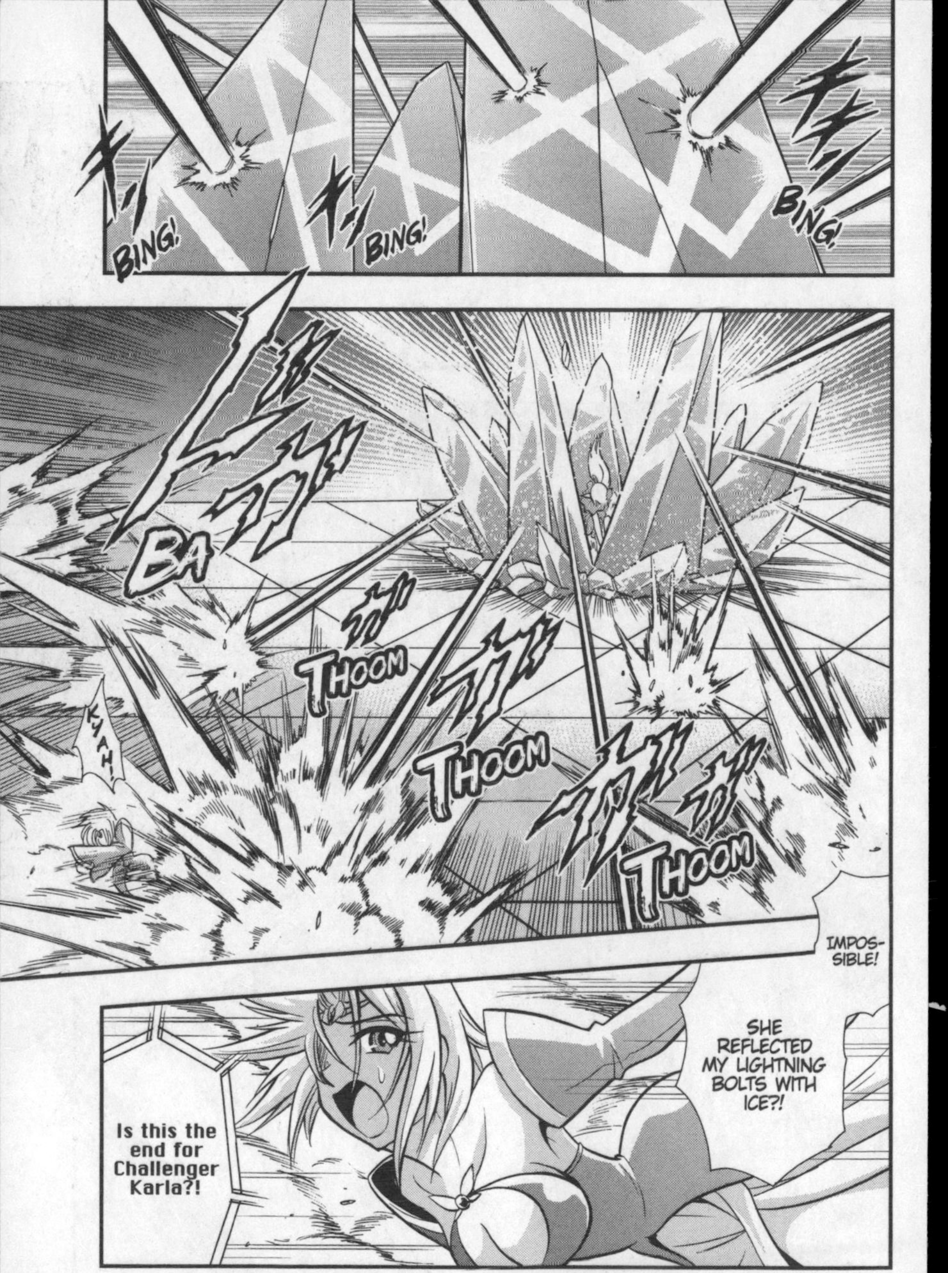
BING!
BING!
BING!
THOOM
THOOM
THOOM
BA
KYAH!
IMPOSSIBLE!
SHE REFLECTED MY LIGHTNING BOLTS WITH ICE?!
Is this the end for Challenger Karla?!

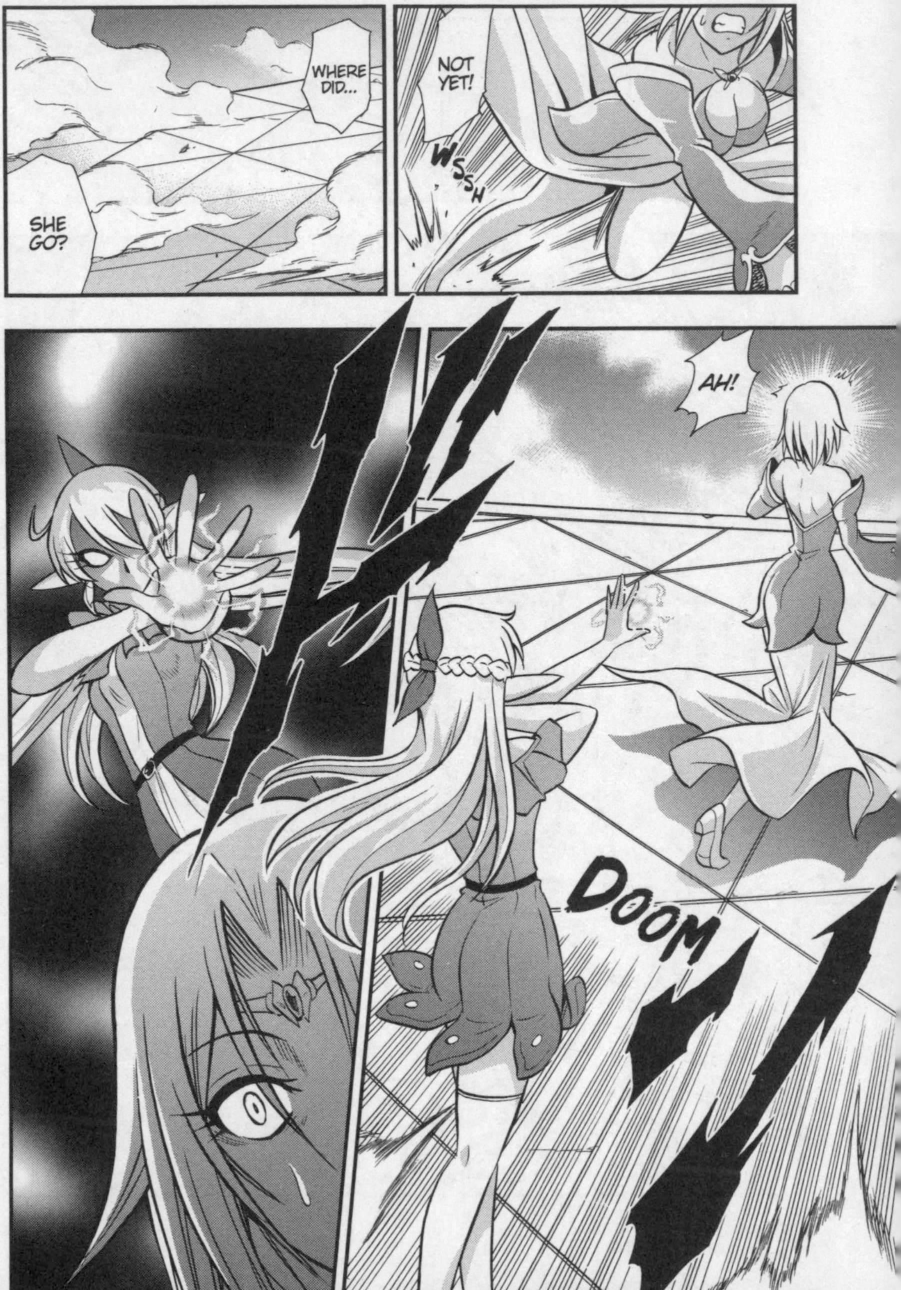
NOT YET!
WSSSH
WHERE DID...
SHE GO?
AH!
DOOM

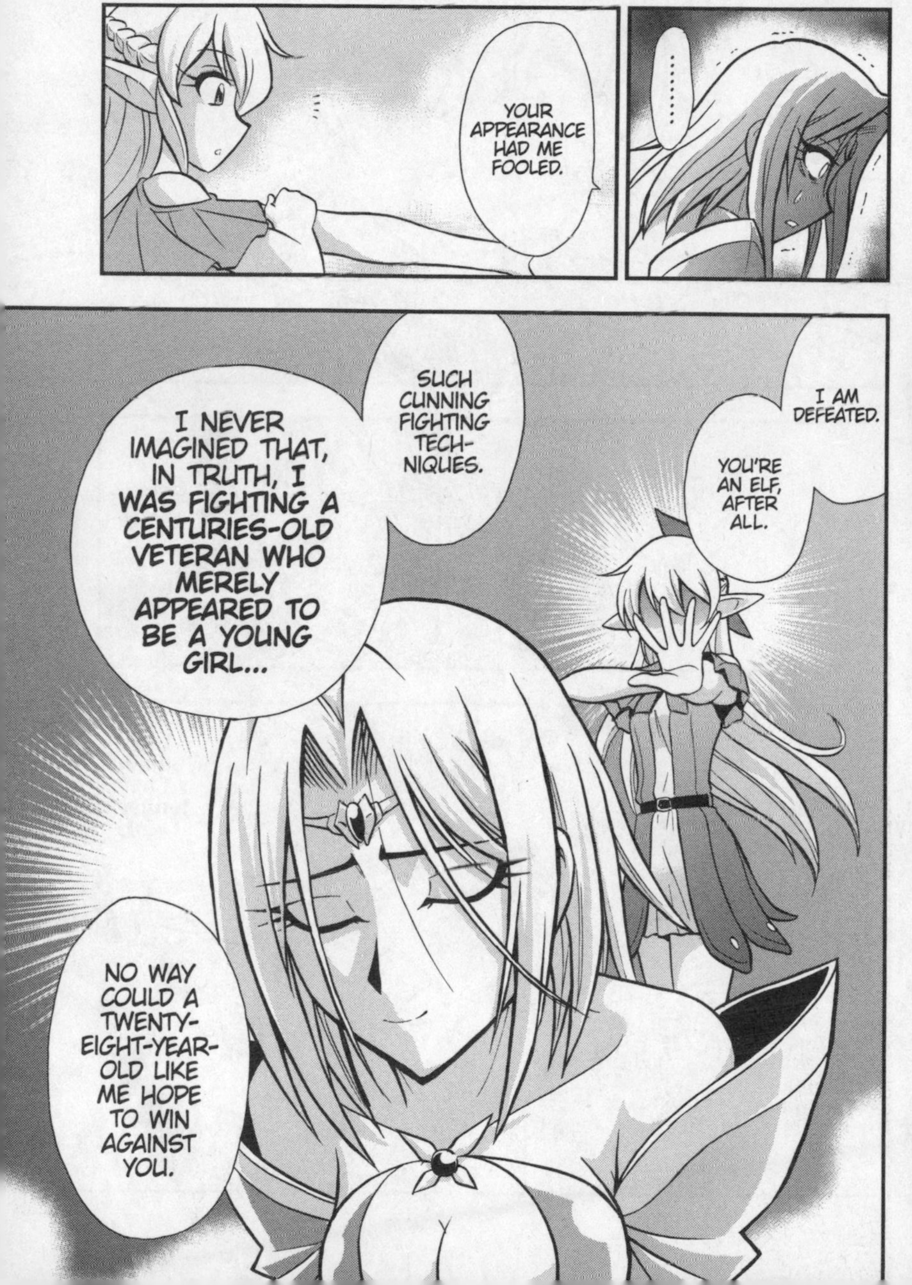
......
YOUR APPEARANCE HAD ME FOOLED.
I AM DEFEATED.
YOU'RE AN ELF, AFTER ALL.
SUCH CUNNING FIGHTING TECH-NIQUES.
I NEVER IMAGINED THAT, IN TRUTH, I WAS FIGHTING A CENTURIES-OLD VETERAN WHO MERELY APPEARED TO BE A YOUNG GIRL...
NO WAY COULD A TWENTY-EIGHT-YEAR-OLD LIKE ME HOPE TO WIN AGAINST YOU.

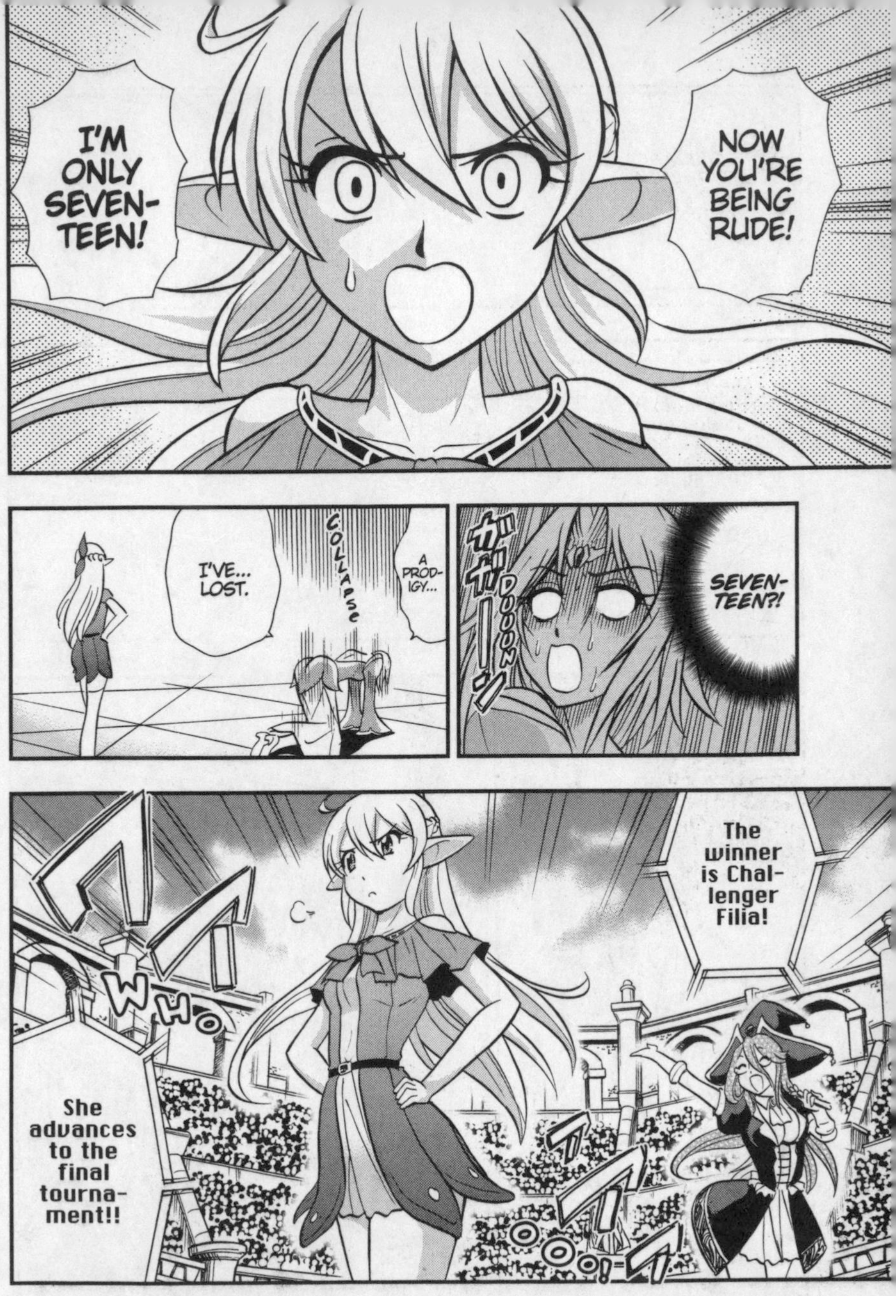
NOW YOU'RE BEING RUDE!
I'M ONLY SEVEN-TEEN!
SEVEN-TEEN?!
DUOON
A PROD-IGY...
COLLAPSE
I'VE... LOST.
The winner is Chal-lenger Filia!
She advances to the final tourna-ment!!
WHO
OOOO!

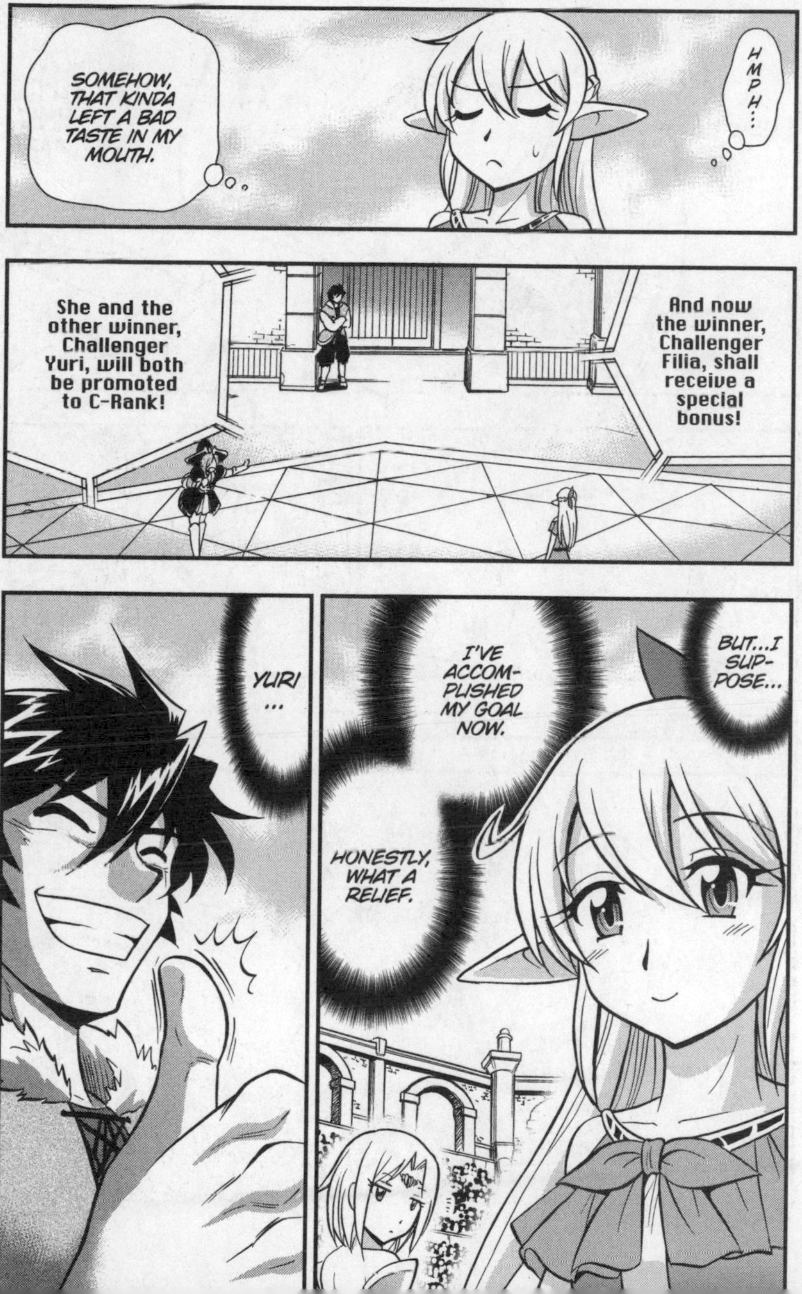
HMPH...
SOMEHOW, THAT KINDA LEFT A BAD TASTE IN MY MOUTH.
And now the winner, Challenger Filia, shall receive a special bonus!
She and the other winner, Challenger Yuri, will both be promoted to C-Rank!
BUT...I SUPPOSE...
I'VE ACCOMPLISHED MY GOAL NOW.
HONESTLY, WHAT A RELIEF.
YURI ...

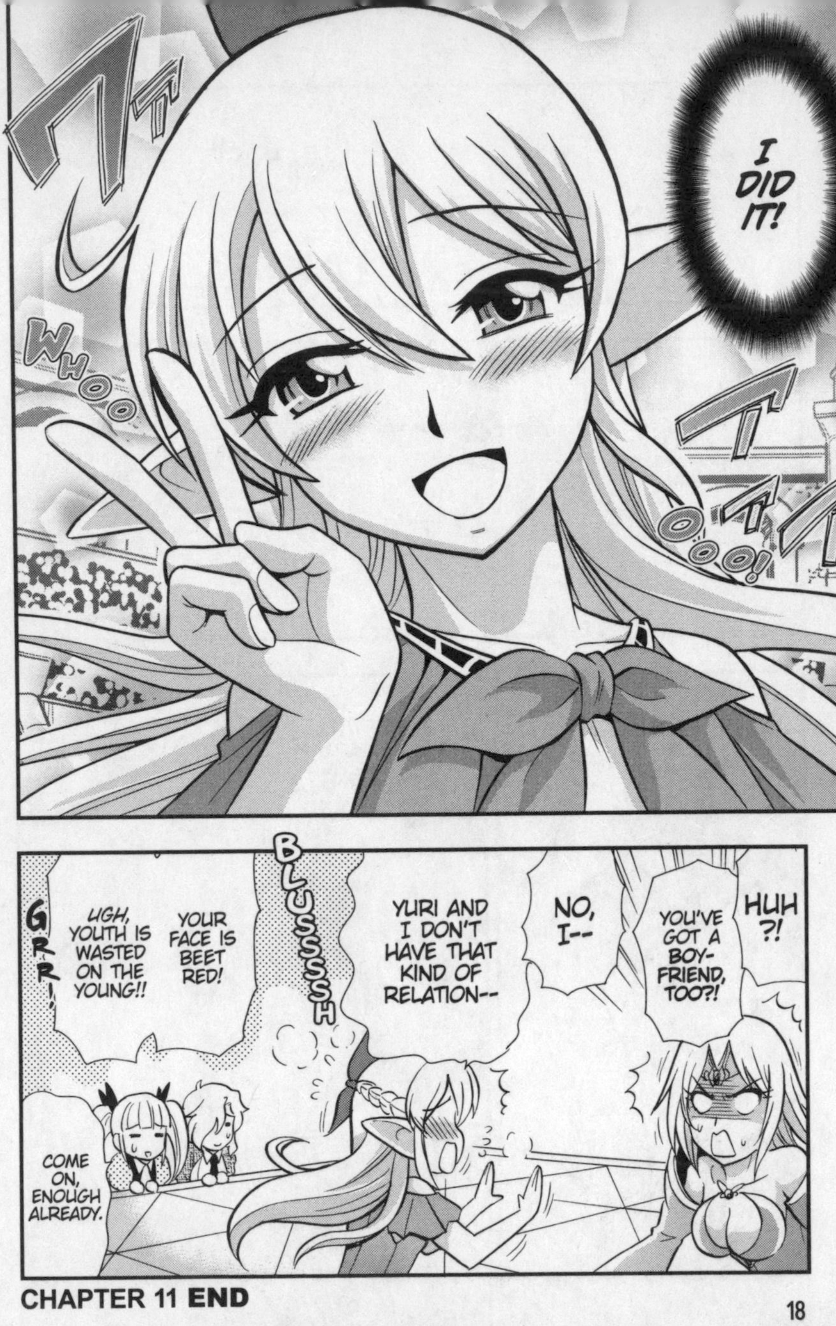
I DID IT!
OOOO!
WHOOO
HUH?!
YOU'VE GOT A BOY-FRIEND, TOO?!
NO, I--
YURI AND I DON'T HAVE THAT KIND OF RELATION--
BLUSSSH
YOUR FACE IS BEET RED!
UGH, YOUTH IS WASTED ON THE YOUNG!!
GRR!
COME ON, ENOUGH ALREADY.

CHAPTER 11 END

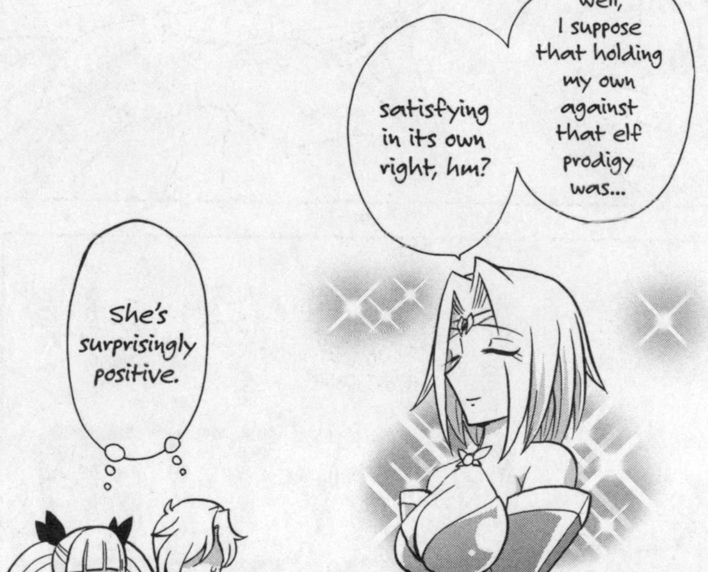
Well, I suppose that holding my own against that elf prodigy was...
satisfying in its own right, hm?
She's surprisingly positive.

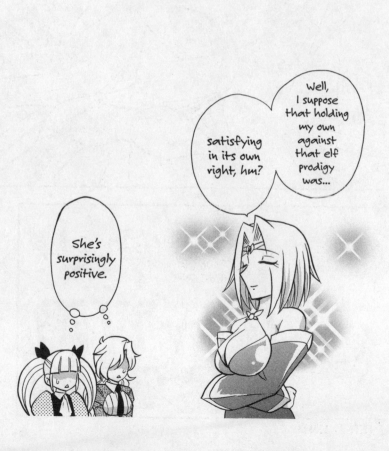

MUSCLES ARE BETTER THAN MAGIC!

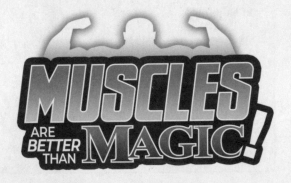

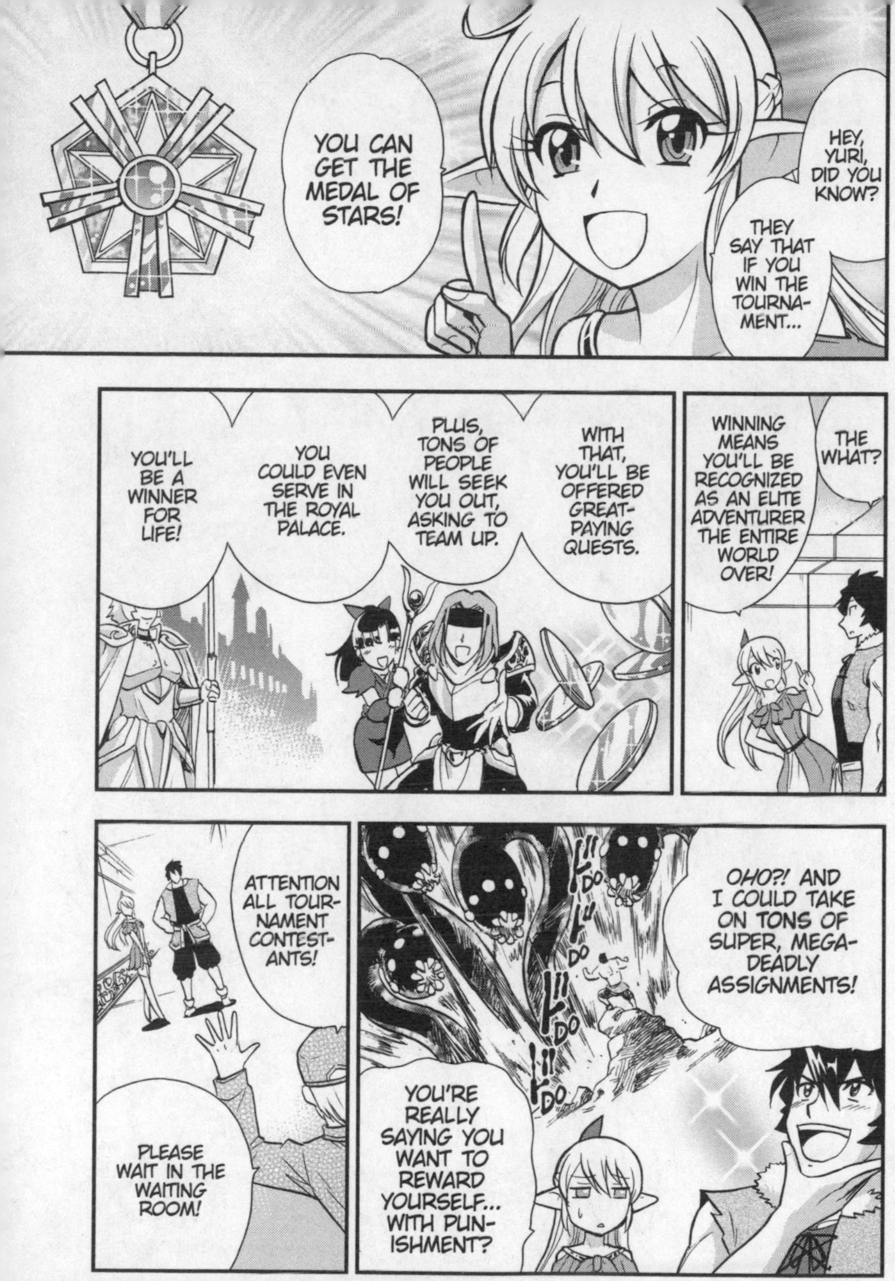
HEY, YURI, DID YOU KNOW?
THEY SAY THAT IF YOU WIN THE TOURNA-MENT...
YOU CAN GET THE MEDAL OF STARS!
THE WHAT?
WINNING MEANS YOU'LL BE RECOGNIZED AS AN ELITE ADVENTURER THE ENTIRE WORLD OVER!
WITH THAT, YOU'LL BE OFFERED GREAT-PAYING QUESTS.
PLUS, TONS OF PEOPLE WILL SEEK YOU OUT, ASKING TO TEAM UP.
YOU COULD EVEN SERVE IN THE ROYAL PALACE.
YOU'LL BE A WINNER FOR LIFE!
OHO?! AND I COULD TAKE ON TONS OF SUPER, MEGA-DEADLY ASSIGNMENTS!
DO
DO
DO
DO
YOU'RE REALLY SAYING YOU WANT TO REWARD YOURSELF... WITH PUN-ISHMENT?
ATTENTION ALL TOUR-NAMENT CONTEST-ANTS!
PLEASE WAIT IN THE WAITING ROOM!

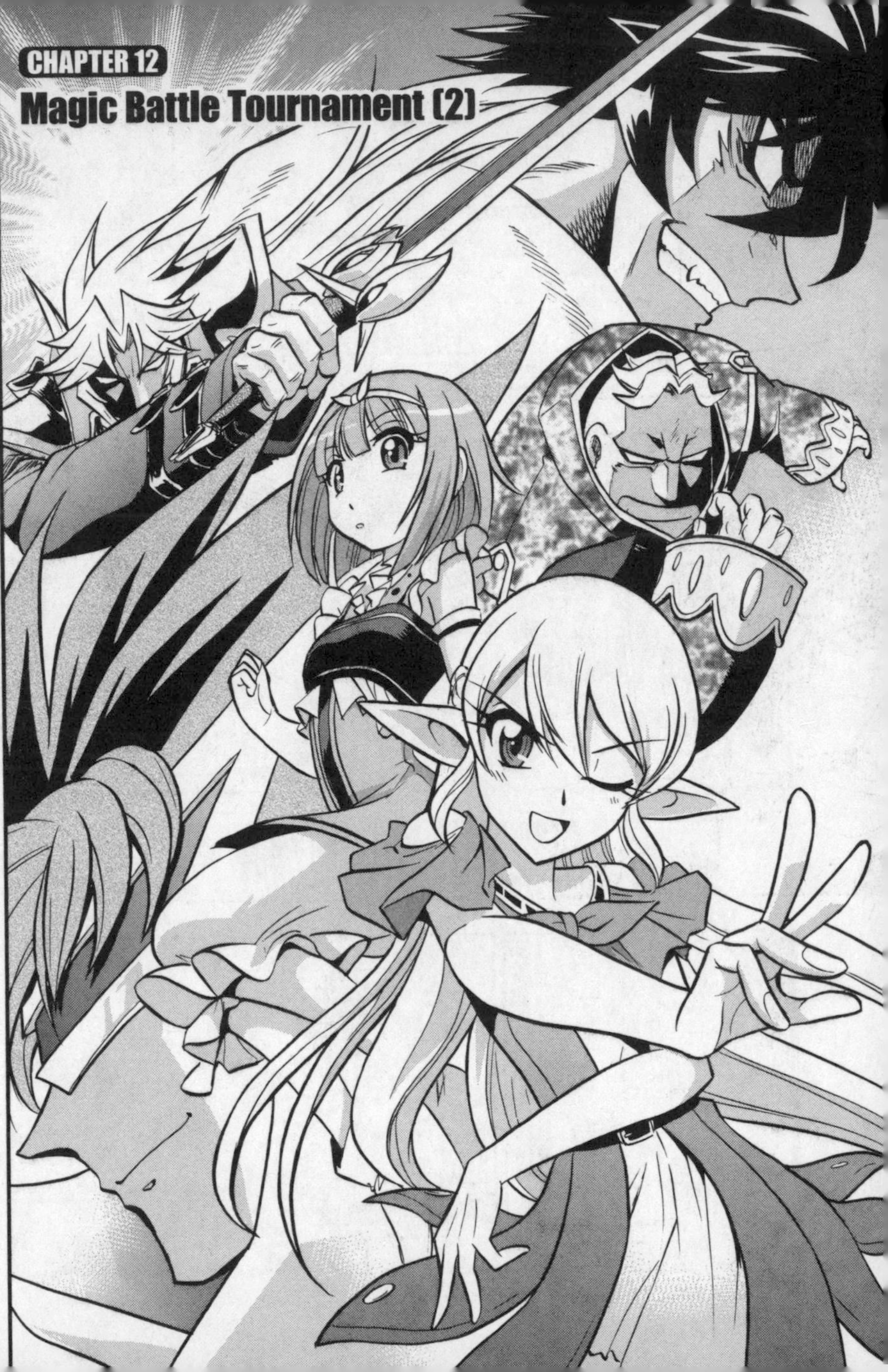
CHAPTER 12
Magic Battle Tournament (2)

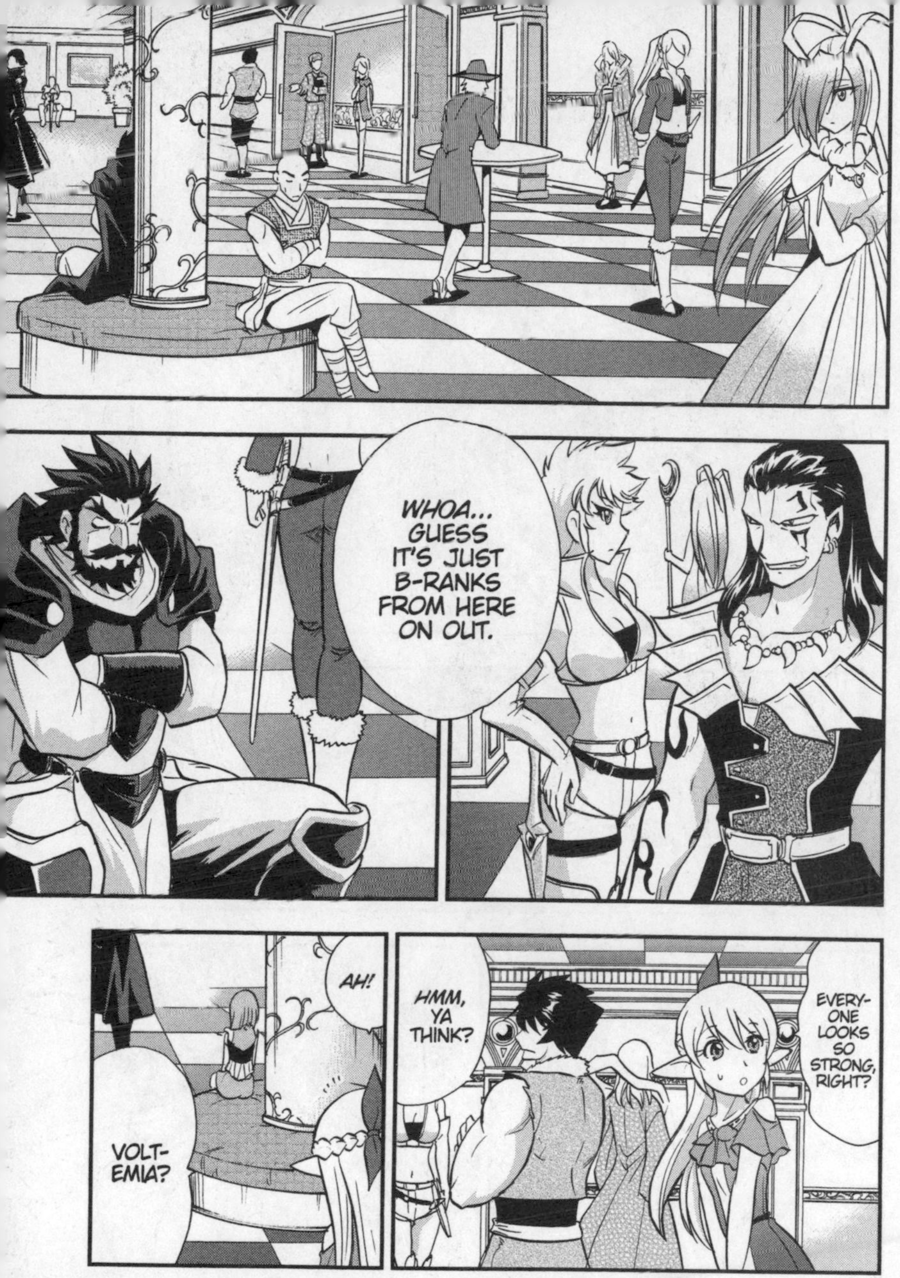
WHOA... GUESS IT'S JUST B-RANKS FROM HERE ON OUT.
EVERY-ONE LOOKS SO STRONG, RIGHT?
HMM, YA THINK?
AH!
VOLT-EMIA?

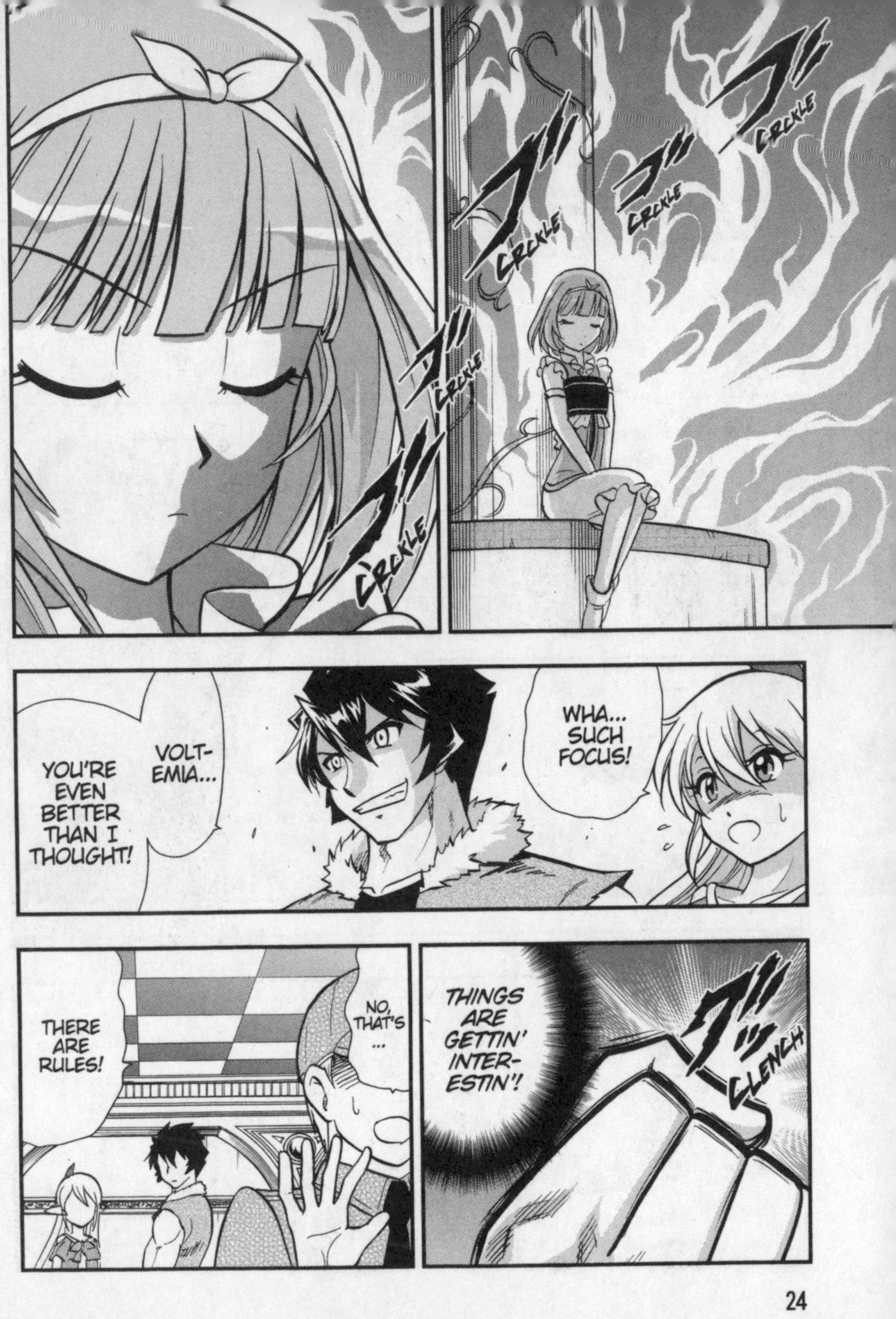
CRCKLE
CRCKLE
CRCKLE
CRCKLE
CRCKLE
WHA... SUCH FOCUS!
VOLT-EMIA...
YOU'RE EVEN BETTER THAN I THOUGHT!
THINGS ARE GETTIN' INTER-ESTIN'!
CLENCH
NO, THAT'S ...
THERE ARE RULES!

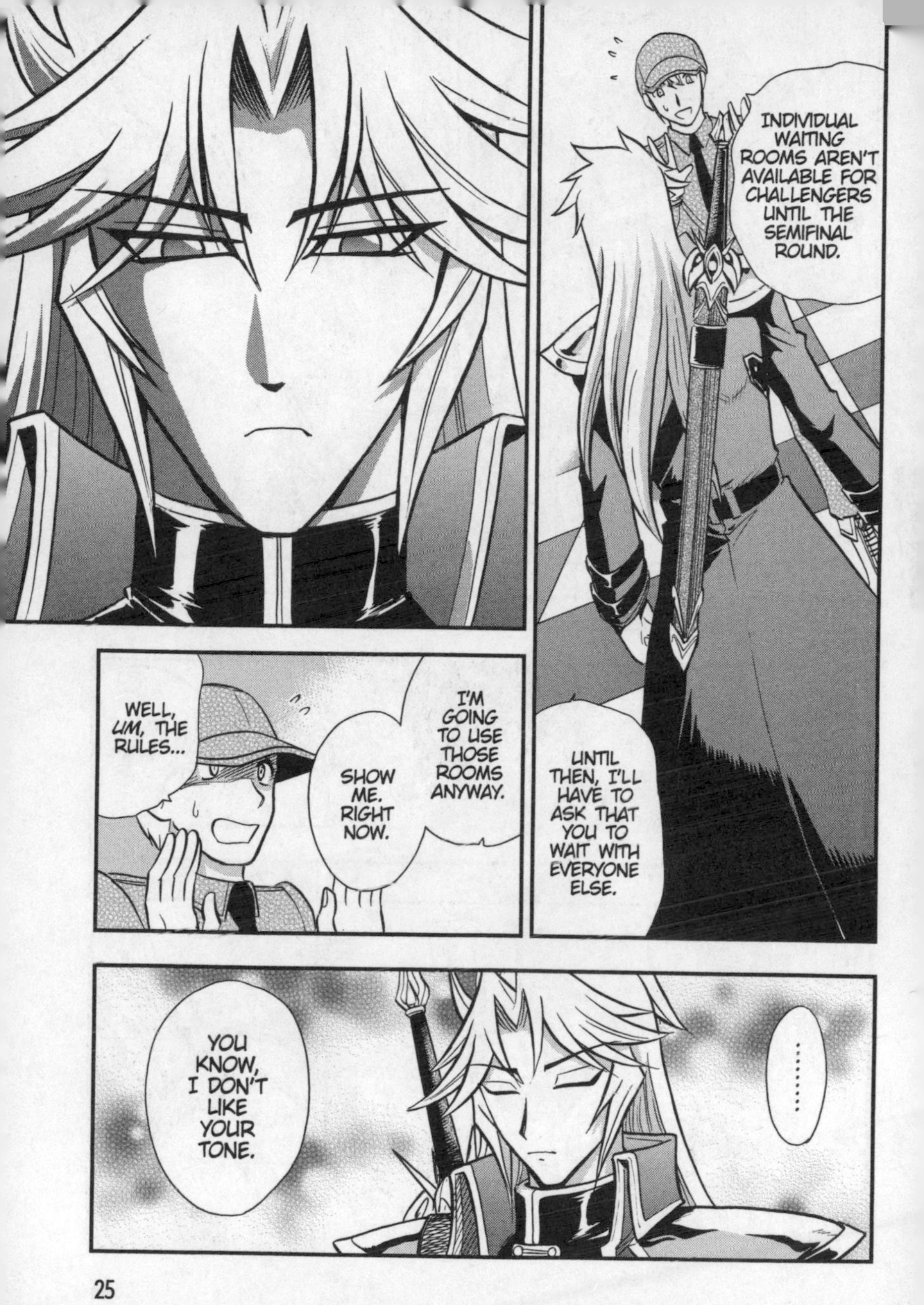

INDIVIDUAL WAITING ROOMS AREN'T AVAILABLE FOR CHALLENGERS UNTIL THE SEMIFINAL ROUND.
UNTIL THEN, I'LL HAVE TO ASK THAT YOU TO WAIT WITH EVERYONE ELSE.
I'M GOING TO USE THOSE ROOMS ANYWAY.
SHOW ME. RIGHT NOW.
WELL, UM, THE RULES...
......
YOU KNOW, I DON'T LIKE YOUR TONE.

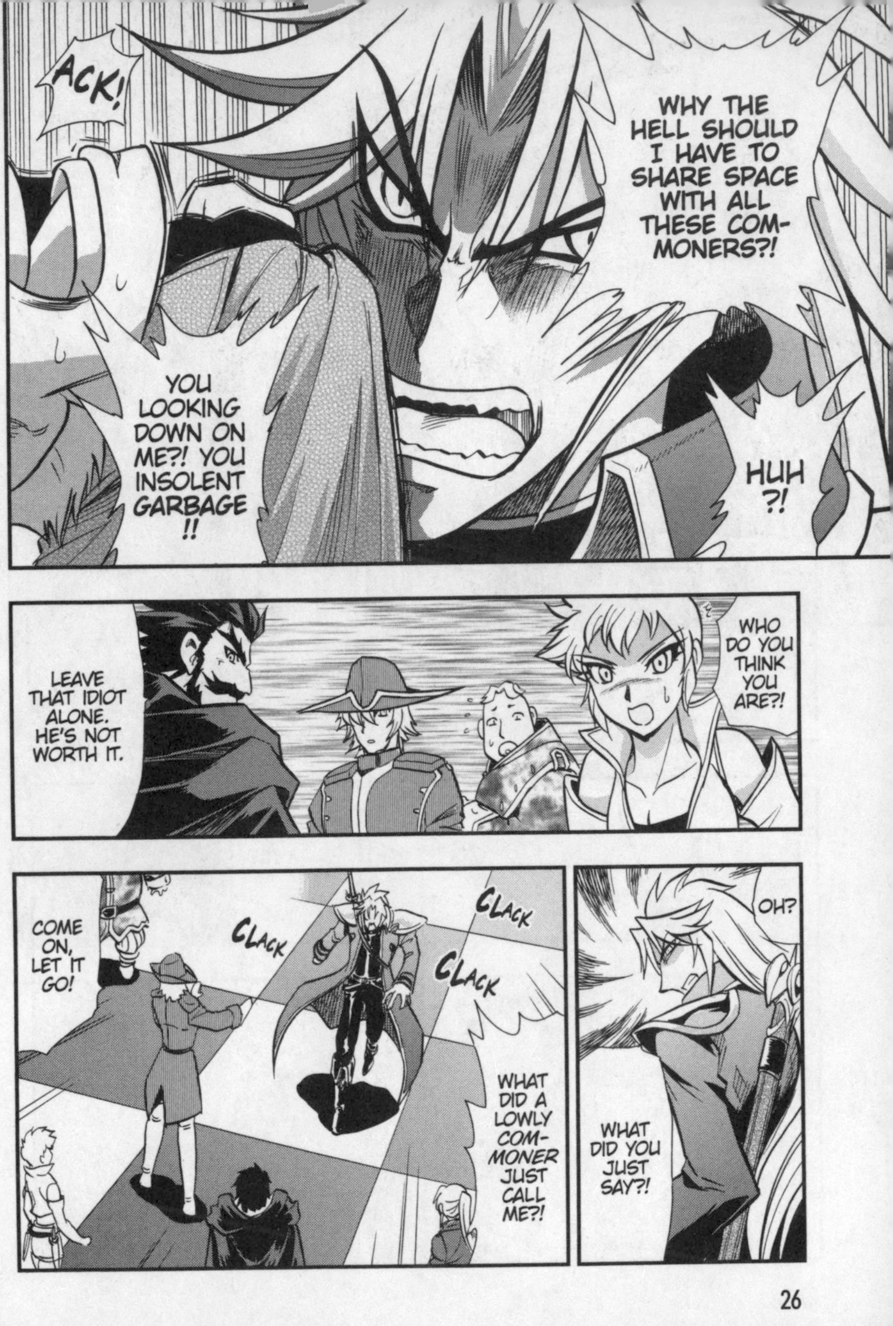
WHY THE HELL SHOULD I HAVE TO SHARE SPACE WITH ALL THESE COM-MONERS?!
HUH ?!
ACK!
YOU LOOKING DOWN ON ME?! YOU INSOLENT GARBAGE !!
WHO DO YOU THINK YOU ARE?!
LEAVE THAT IDIOT ALONE. HE'S NOT WORTH IT.
OH?
WHAT DID YOU JUST SAY?!
CLACK
CLACK
CLACK
WHAT DID A LOWLY COM-MONER JUST CALL ME?!
COME ON, LET IT GO!

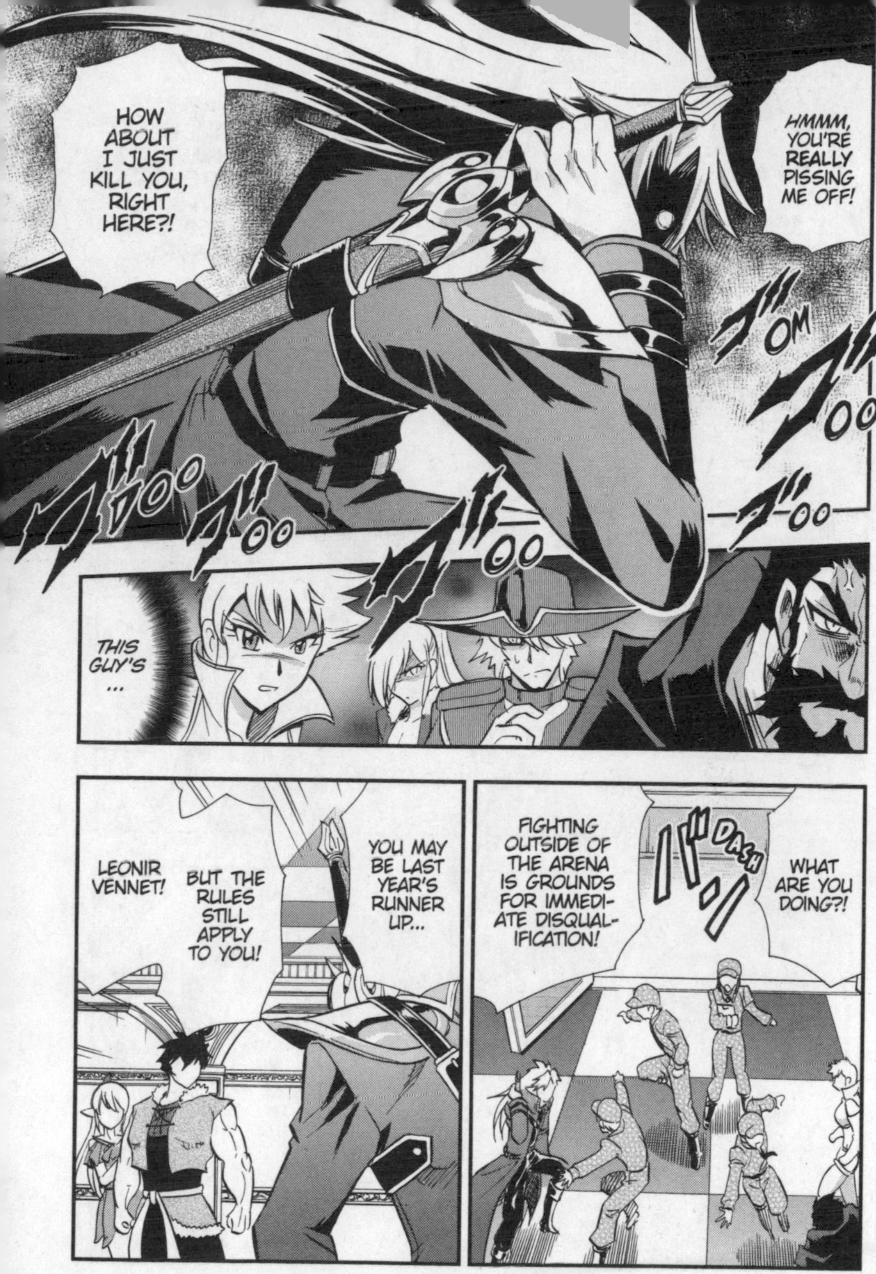
HMMM, YOU'RE REALLY PISSING ME OFF!
HOW ABOUT I JUST KILL YOU, RIGHT HERE?!
THIS GUY'S ...
WHAT ARE YOU DOING?!
DASH
FIGHTING OUTSIDE OF THE ARENA IS GROUNDS FOR IMMEDIATE DISQUALIFICATION!
YOU MAY BE LAST YEAR'S RUNNER UP...
BUT THE RULES STILL APPLY TO YOU!
LEONIR VENNET!

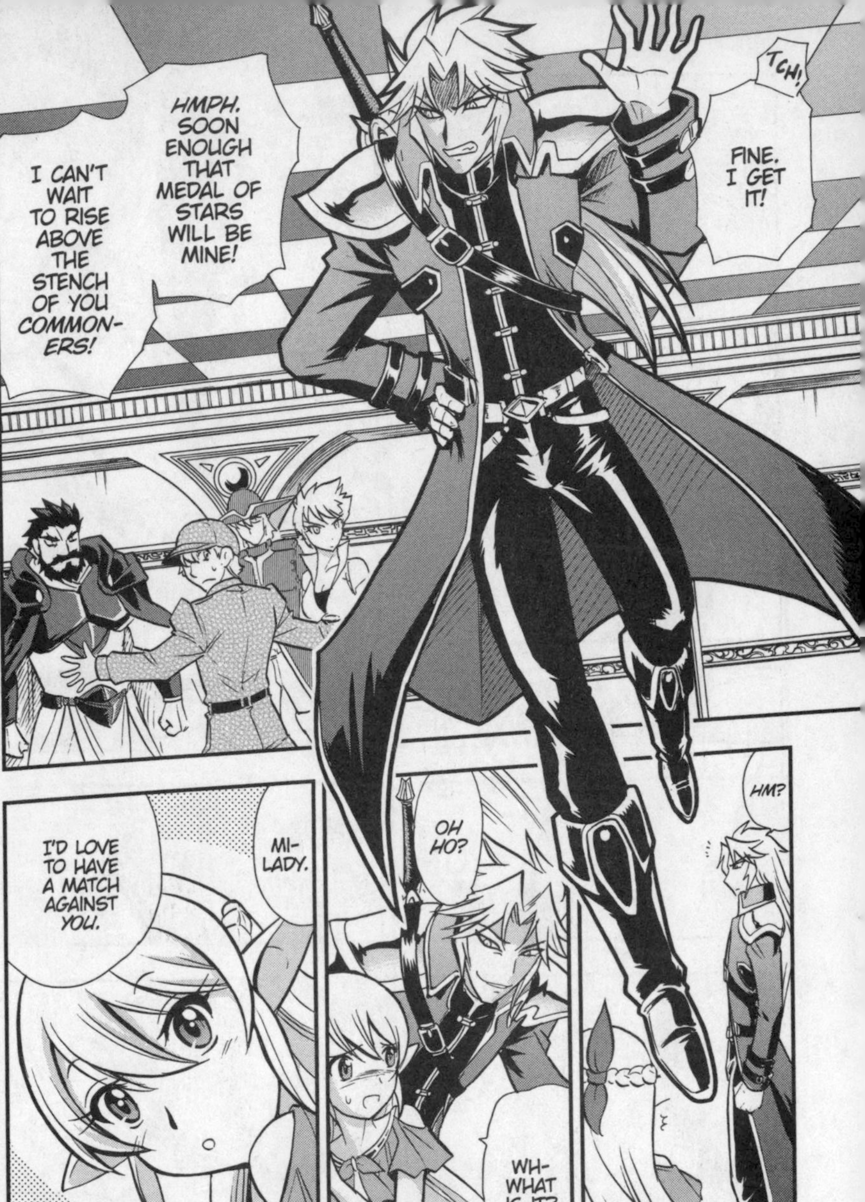
TCH!
FINE. I GET IT!
HMPH. SOON ENOUGH THAT MEDAL OF STARS WILL BE MINE!
I CAN'T WAIT TO RISE ABOVE THE STENCH OF YOU COMMON-ERS!
HM?
OH HO?
MI-LADY.
WH- WHAT IS IT?
I'D LOVE TO HAVE A MATCH AGAINST YOU.

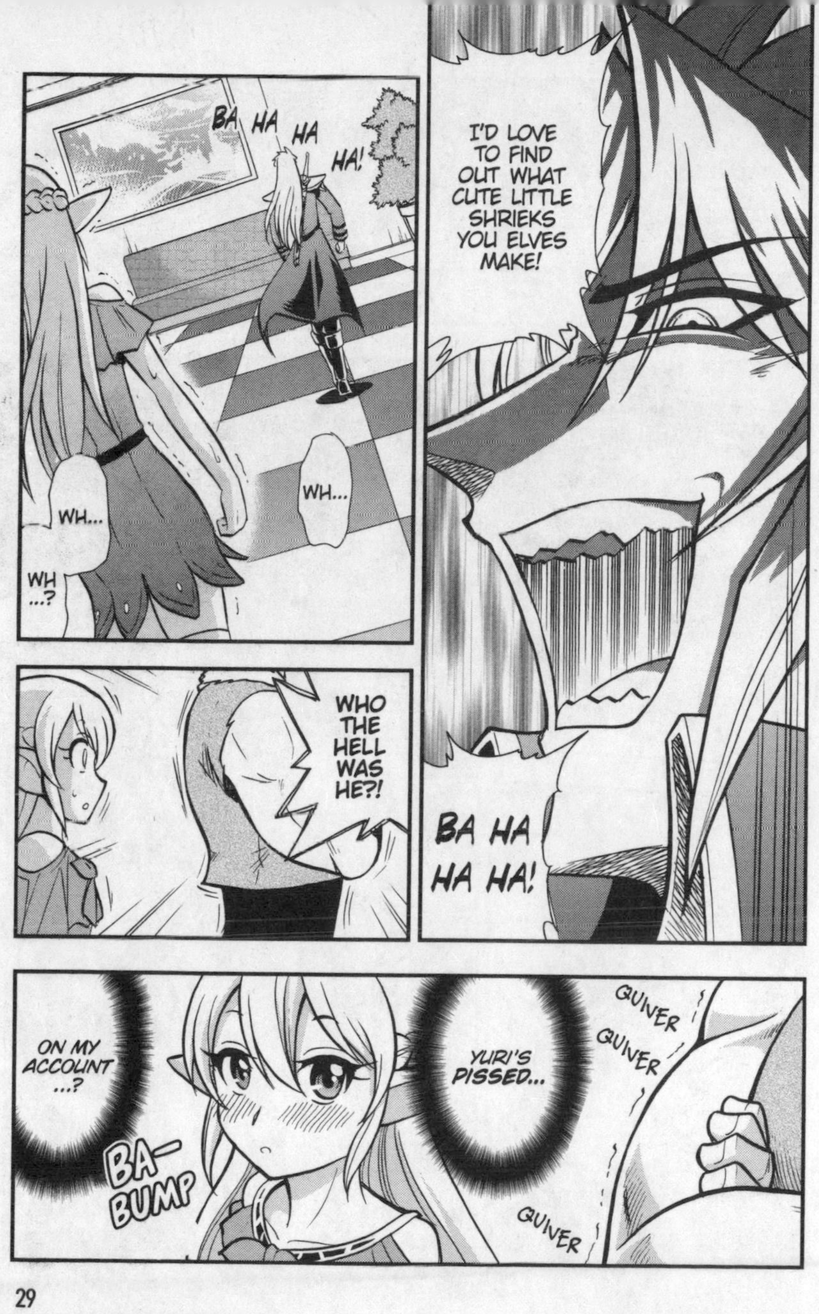
I'D LOVE TO FIND OUT WHAT CUTE LITTLE SHRIEKS YOU ELVES MAKE!
BA HA HA HA!
BA HA HA HA!
WH...
WH...
WH ...?
WHO THE HELL WAS HE?!
QUIVER
QUIVER
YURI'S PISSED...
ON MY ACCOUNT ...?
BA-BUMP
QUIVER

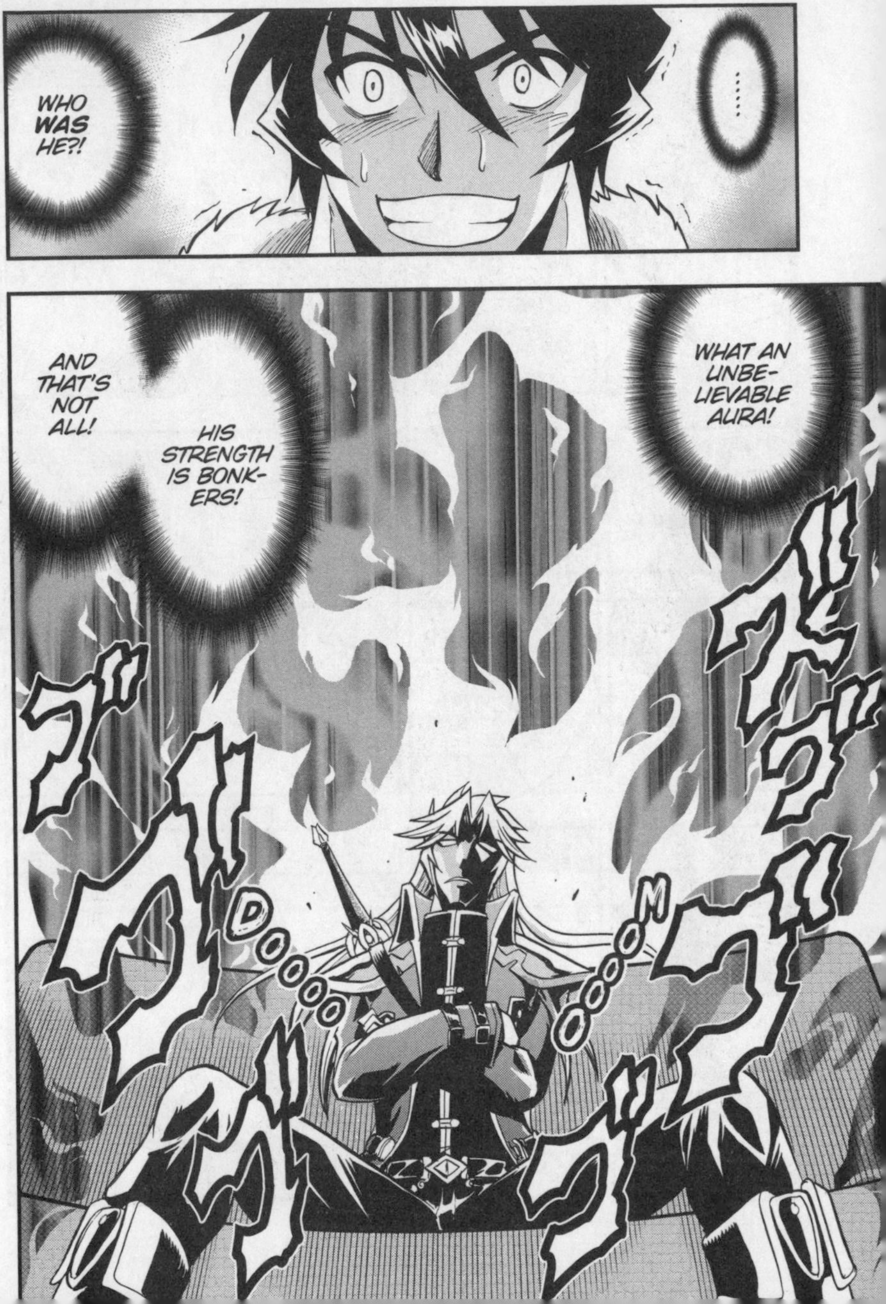
......
WHO WAS HE?!
WHAT AN UNBE-LIEVABLE AURA!
HIS STRENGTH IS BONKERS!
AND THAT'S NOT ALL!
DOOOOOOOOOM

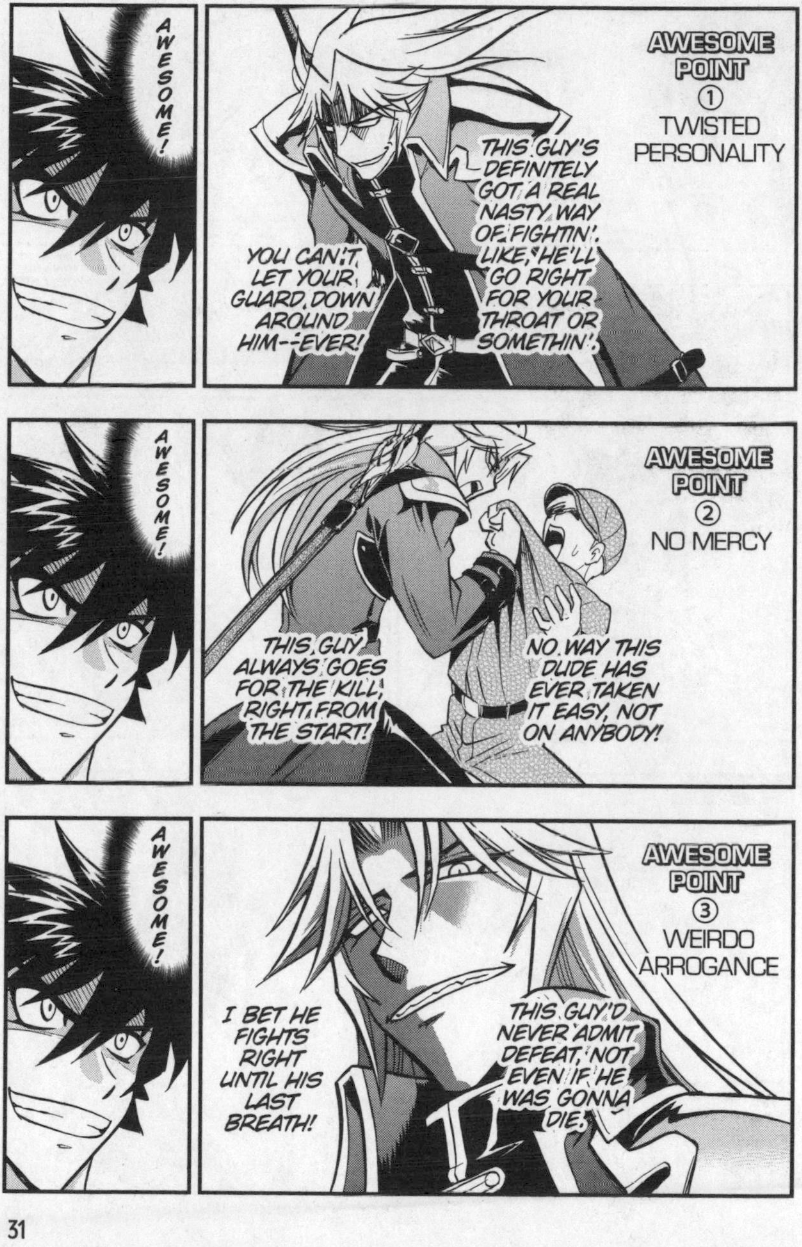
AWESOME POINT ① TWISTED PERSONALITY
THIS GUY'S DEFINITELY GOT A REAL NASTY WAY OF FIGHTIN'. LIKE, HE'LL GO RIGHT FOR YOUR THROAT OR SOMETHIN'.
YOU CAN'T LET YOUR GUARD DOWN AROUND HIM--EVER!
AWESOME!
AWESOME POINT ② NO MERCY
NO WAY THIS DUDE HAS EVER TAKEN IT EASY, NOT ON ANYBODY!
THIS GUY ALWAYS GOES FOR THE KILL, RIGHT FROM THE START!
AWESOME!
AWESOME POINT ③ WEIRDO ARROGANCE
THIS GUY'D NEVER ADMIT DEFEAT, NOT EVEN IF HE WAS GONNA DIE.
I BET HE FIGHTS RIGHT UNTIL HIS LAST BREATH!
AWESOME!

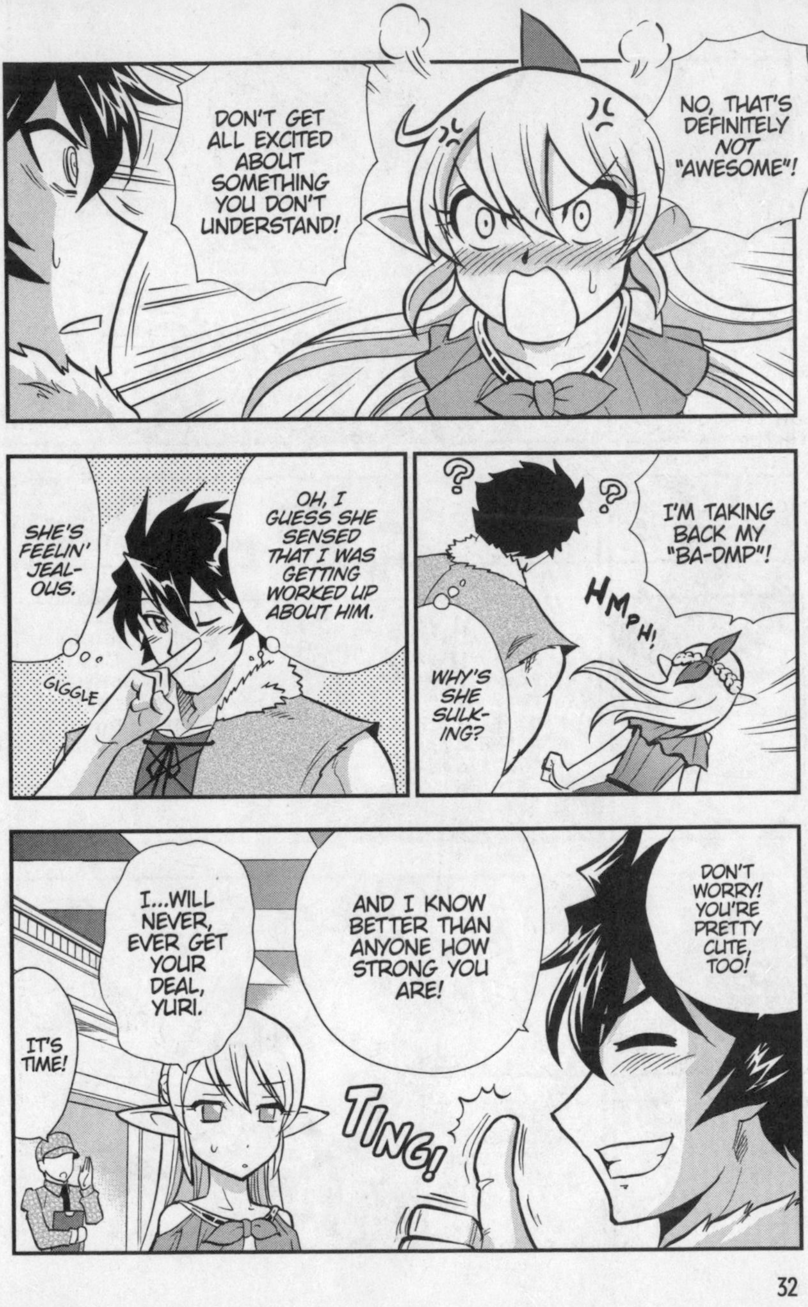
NO, THAT'S DEFINITELY *NOT* "AWESOME"!
DON'T GET ALL EXCITED ABOUT SOMETHING YOU DON'T UNDERSTAND!
I'M TAKING BACK MY "BA-DMP"!
HMPH!
WHY'S SHE SULKING?
OH, I GUESS SHE SENSED THAT I WAS GETTING WORKED UP ABOUT HIM.
SHE'S FEELIN' JEAL-OUS.
GIGGLE
DON'T WORRY! YOU'RE PRETTY CUTE, TOO!
AND I KNOW BETTER THAN ANYONE HOW STRONG YOU ARE!
TING!
I...WILL NEVER, EVER GET YOUR DEAL, YURI.
IT'S TIME!

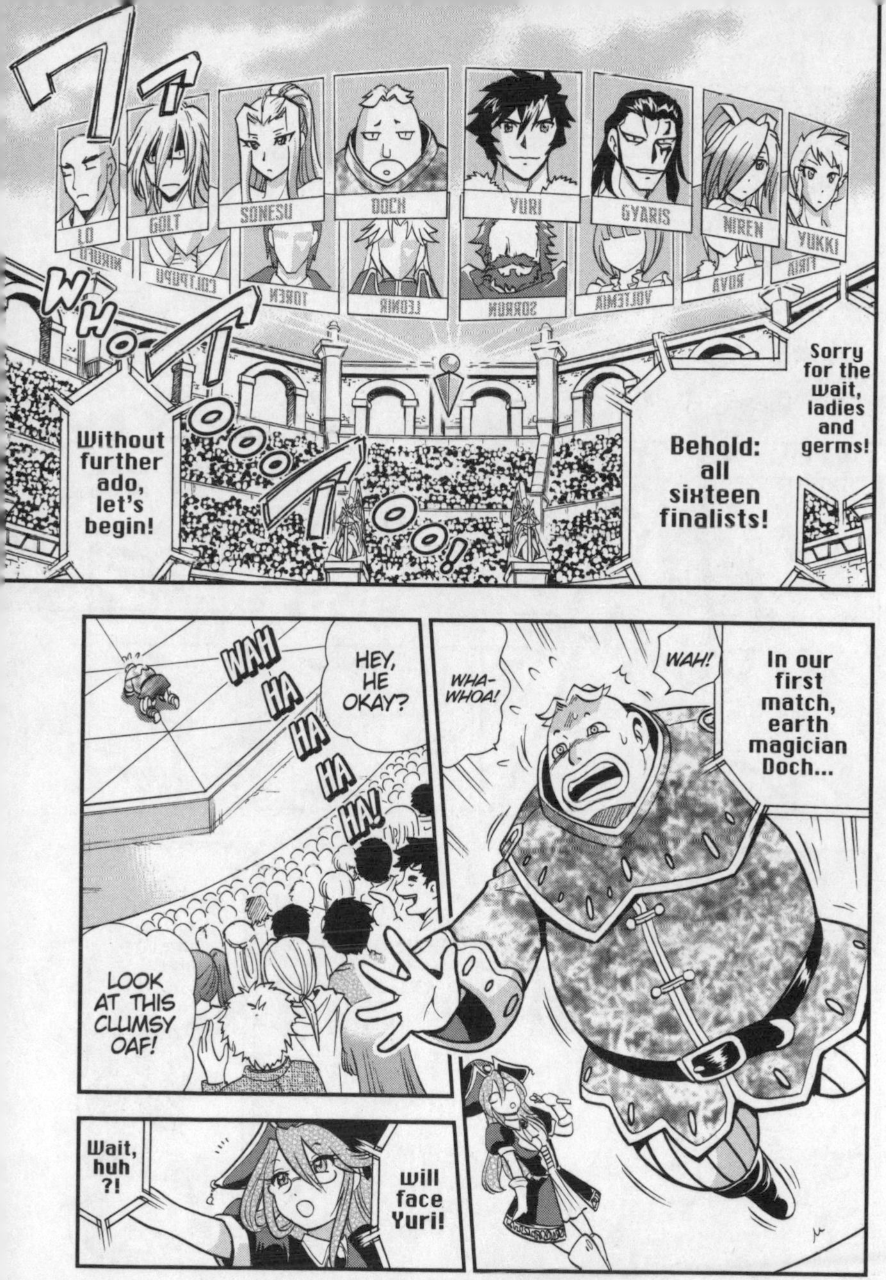
LO
GOLT
SONESU
DOCH
YURI
GYARIS
NIREN
YUKKI
Sorry for the wait, ladies and germs!
Behold: all sixteen finalists!
Without further ado, let's begin!
WHOOOOOOOO!
In our first match, earth magician Doch...
WAH!
WHA-WHOA!
HEY, HE OKAY?
WAH HA HA HA HA!
LOOK AT THIS CLUMSY OAF!
will face Yuri!
Wait, huh?!

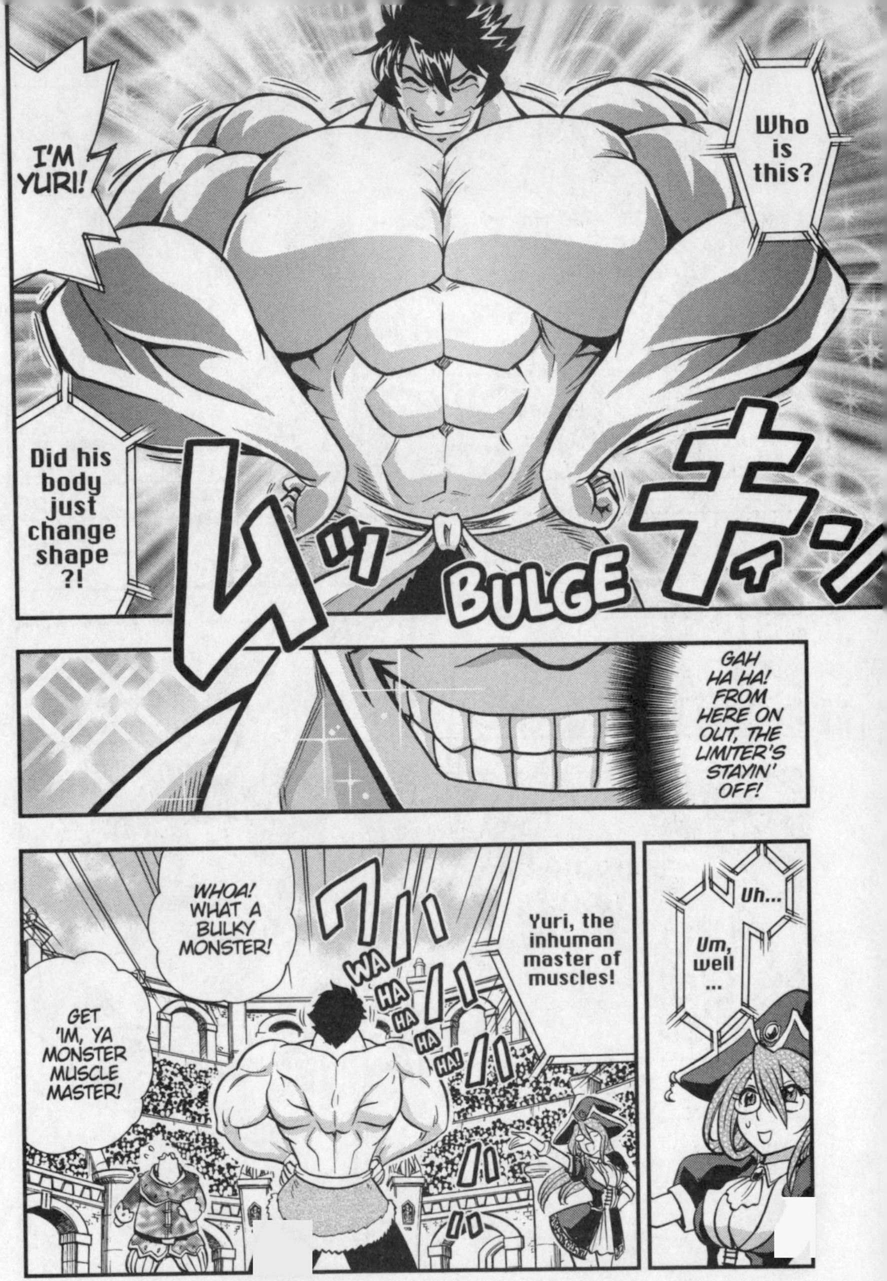
Who is this?
I'M YURI!
Did his body just change shape?!
ムッ
BULGE
キィーン
GAH HA HA! FROM HERE ON OUT, THE LIMITER'S STAYIN' OFF!
Uh...
Um, well ...
Yuri, the inhuman master of muscles!
WHOA! WHAT A BULKY MONSTER!
ワー
WA HA HA HA HA!
GET 'IM, YA MONSTER MUSCLE MASTER!

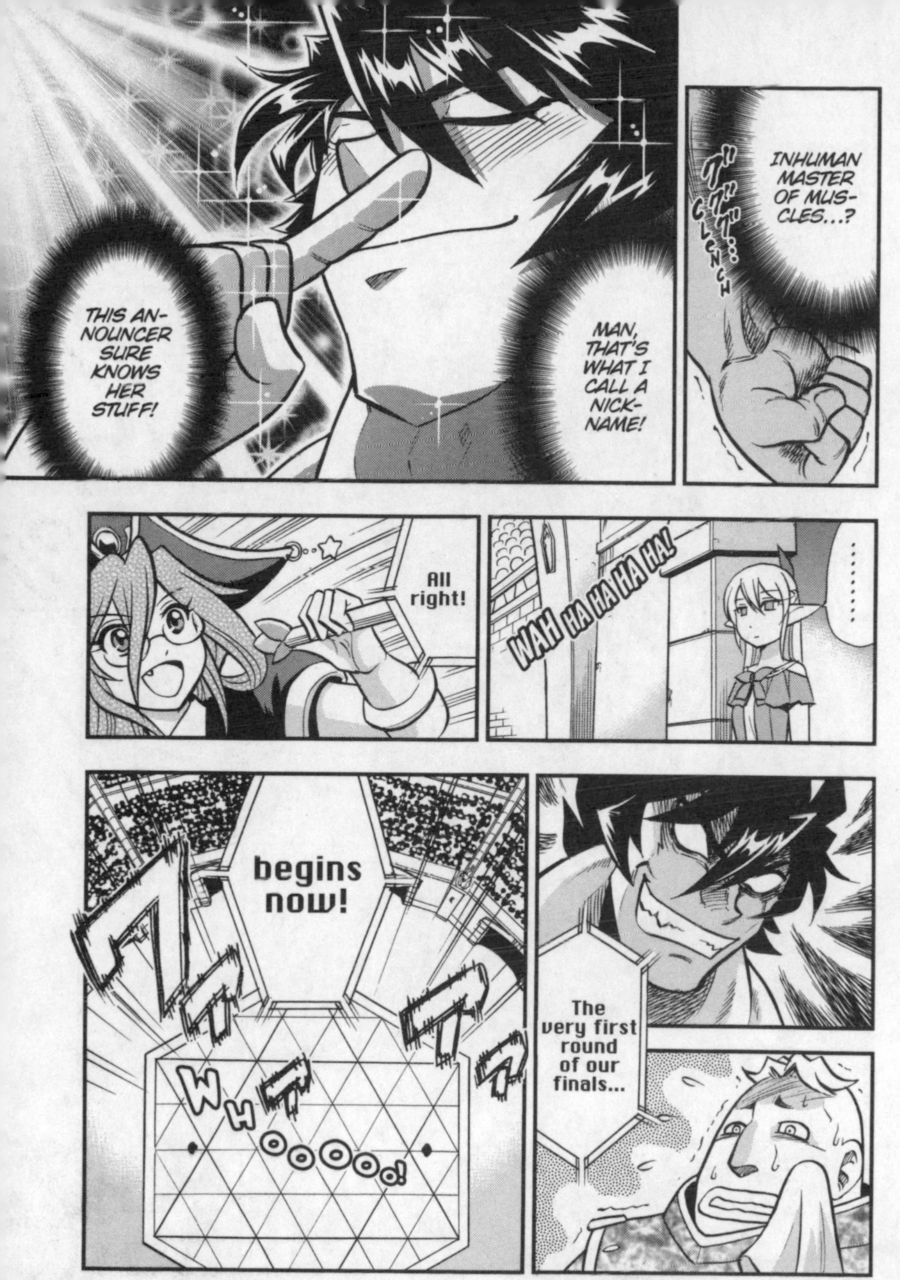
INHUMAN MASTER OF MUS-CLES...?
CLENCH
MAN, THAT'S WHAT I CALL A NICK-NAME!
THIS AN-NOUNCER SURE KNOWS HER STUFF!
....
WAH HA HA HA HA!
All right!
The very first round of our finals...
begins now!
WHOOOOOO!

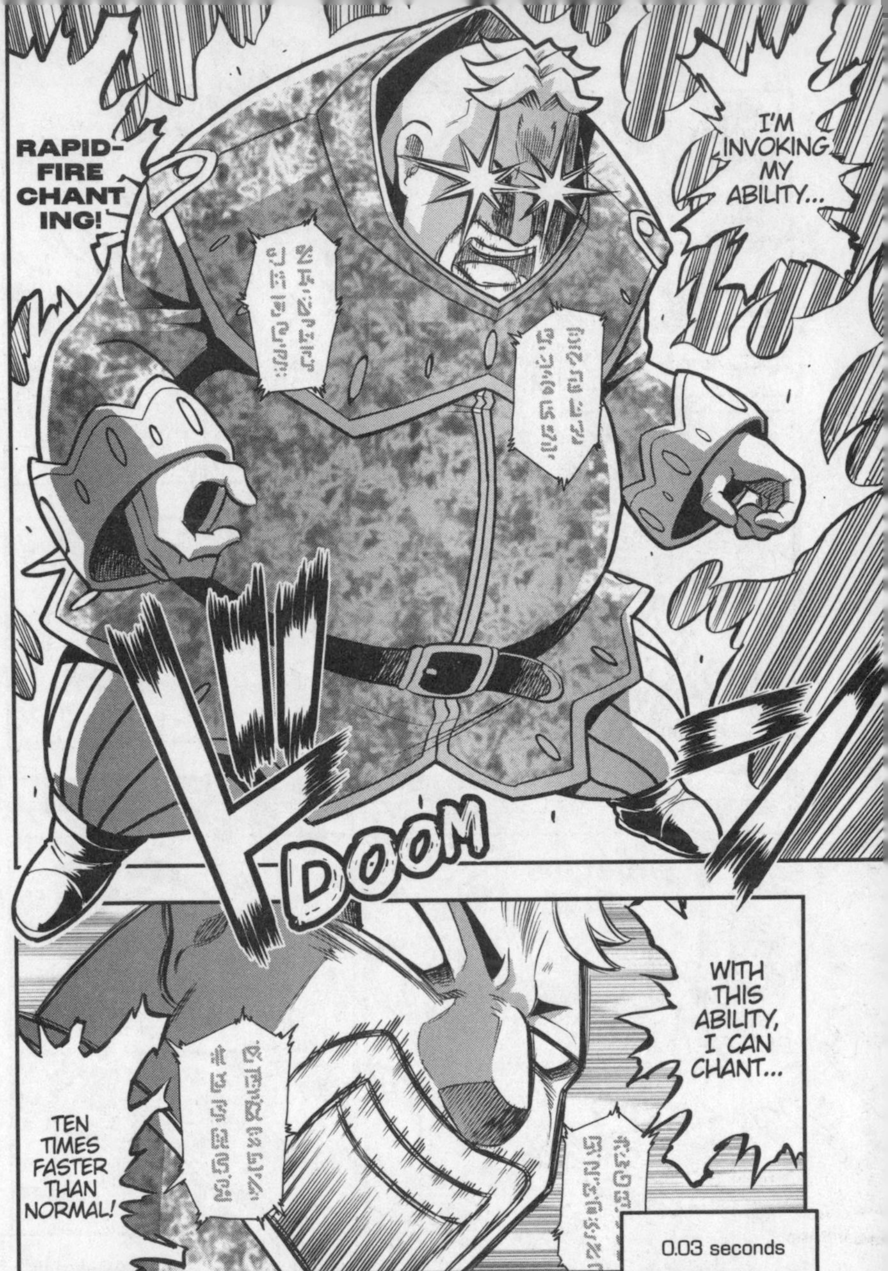
I'M INVOKING MY ABILITY...
RAPID-FIRE CHANTING!
DOOM
WITH THIS ABILITY, I CAN CHANT...
TEN TIMES FASTER THAN NORMAL!
0.03 seconds

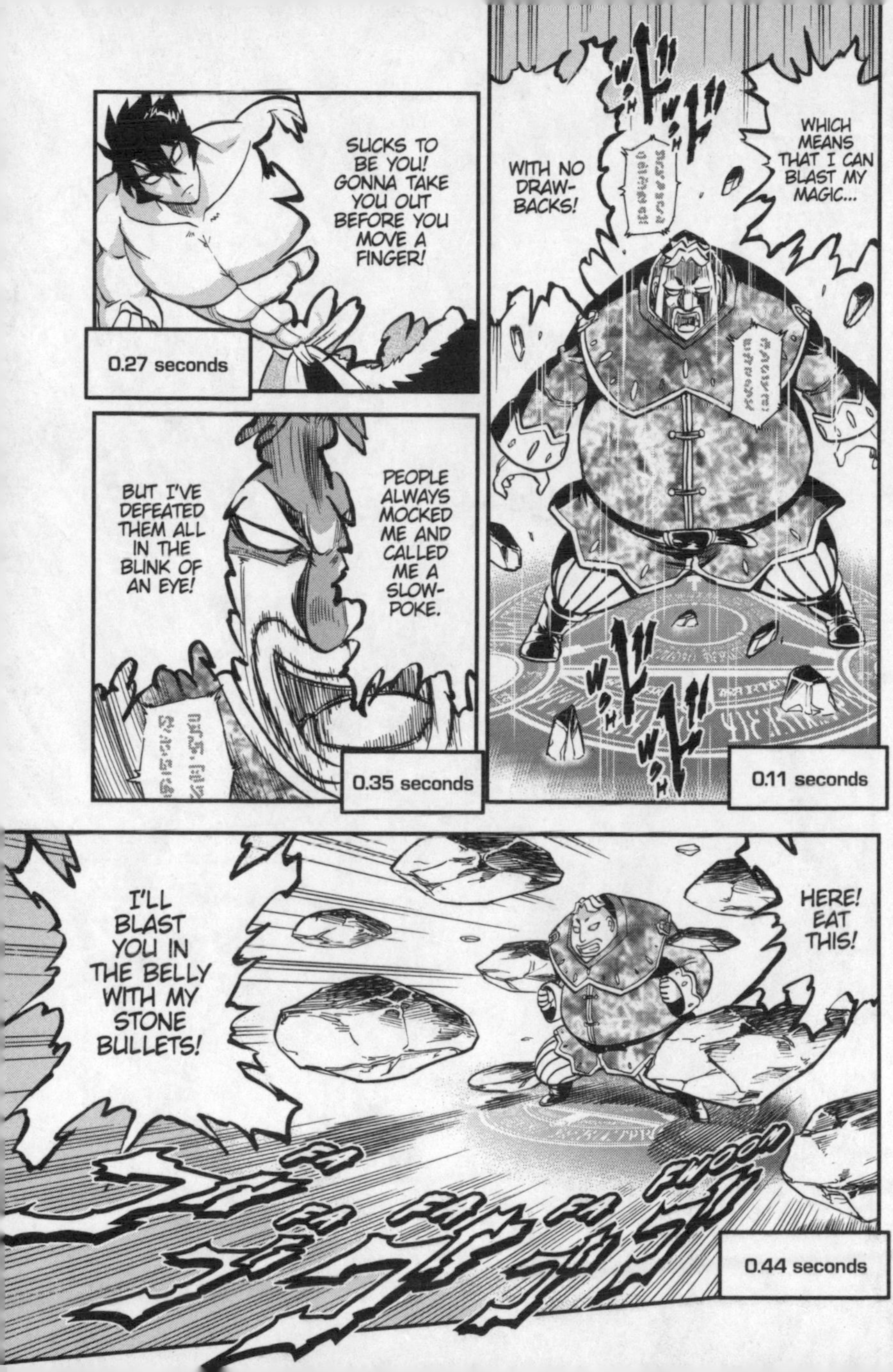
WHICH MEANS THAT I CAN BLAST MY MAGIC...
WITH NO DRAW-BACKS!
0.11 seconds
SUCKS TO BE YOU! GONNA TAKE YOU OUT BEFORE YOU MOVE A FINGER!
0.27 seconds
PEOPLE ALWAYS MOCKED ME AND CALLED ME A SLOW-POKE.
BUT I'VE DEFEATED THEM ALL IN THE BLINK OF AN EYE!
0.35 seconds
HERE! EAT THIS!
I'LL BLAST YOU IN THE BELLY WITH MY STONE BULLETS!
FWOOM
FA
FA
FA
0.44 seconds

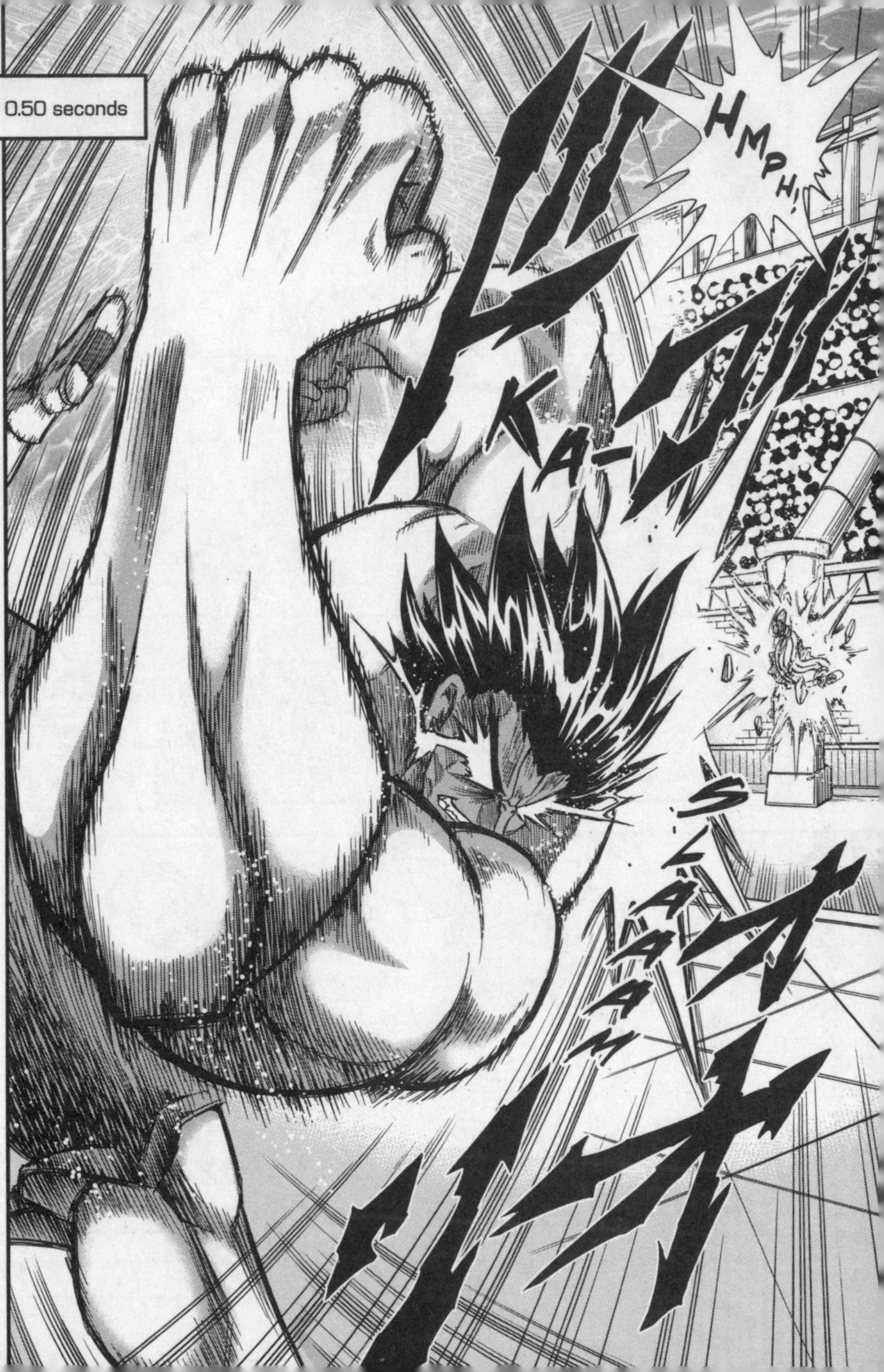

0.50 seconds
HMPH!
KA-
SLAAAM

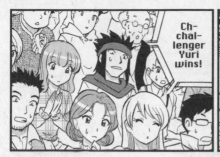

THUD
Ch-challenger Yuri wins!
Unfortunately, Challenger Doch wasn't even able to move a finger.
......
FLEX
THAT WASN'T INTEREST-IN' AT ALL!
USE MAGIC! MAGIC!!
BOO!
BOO!
BOO!
BOO!
BOO!
WE CAME HERE TO SEE A MAGIC BATTLE!
BOO!
BOO!
BOO!
HUH? THEY DON'T... UNDERSTAND THE SPLENDOR OF MUSCLES?!
I DON'T GET IT!
TMP
TMP

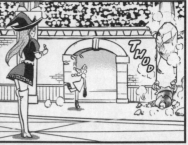

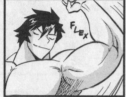

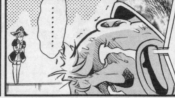

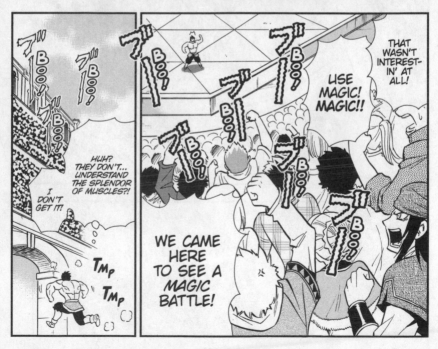

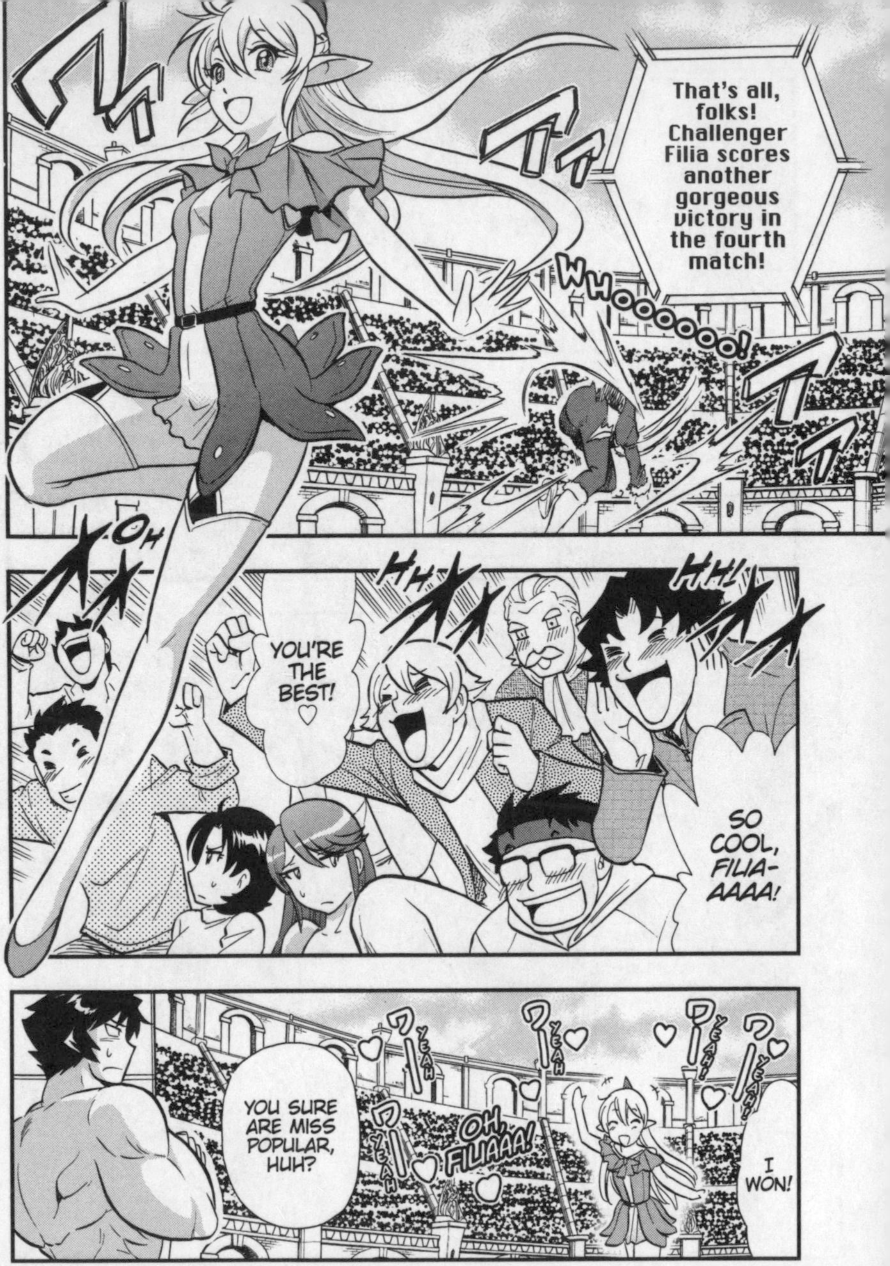
That's all, folks! Challenger Filia scores another gorgeous victory in the fourth match!
WHOOOOOOO!
SO COOL, FILIA-AAAA!
YOU'RE THE BEST! ♡
OH
I WON!
YEAH!
YEAH
OH, FILIAAA!
YOU SURE ARE MISS POPULAR, HUH?

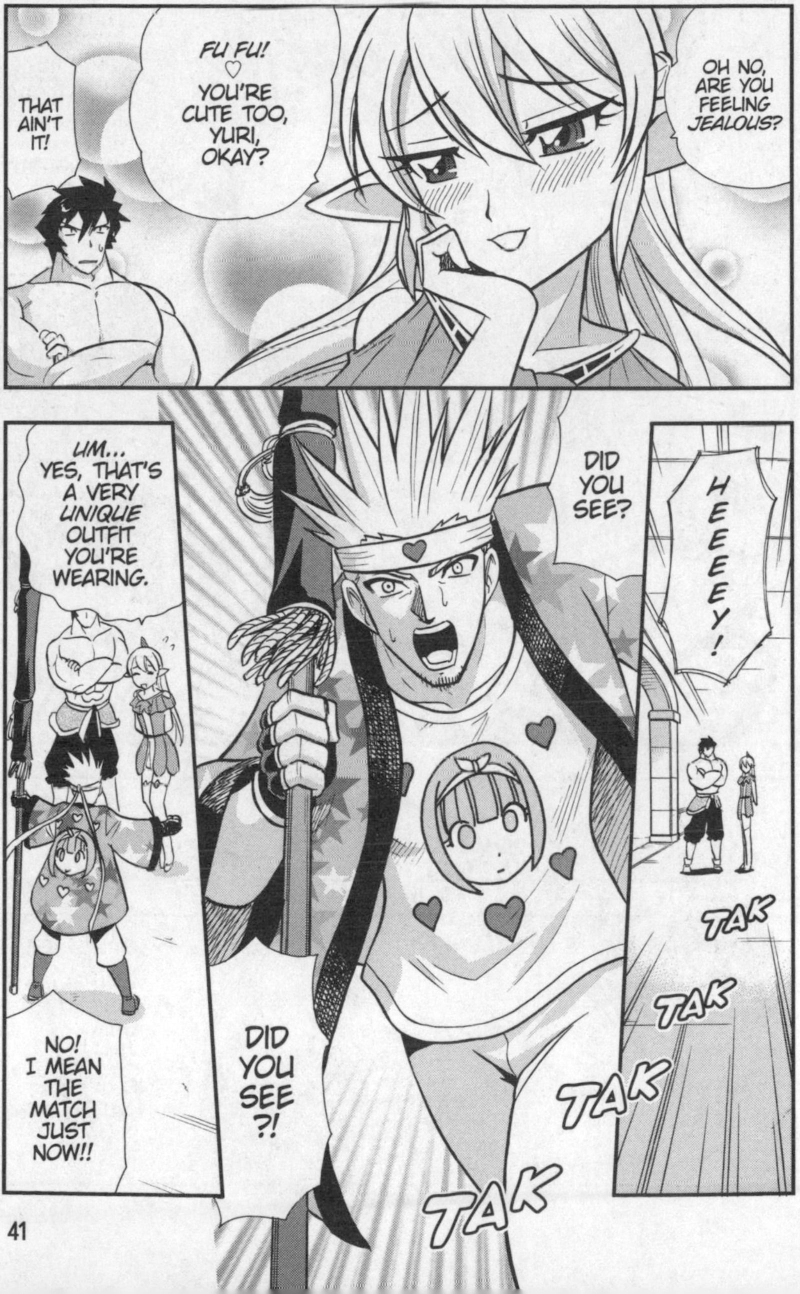
OH NO, ARE YOU FEELING JEALOUS?
FU FU! ♡ YOU'RE CUTE TOO, YURI, OKAY?
THAT AIN'T IT!
HEEEEEY!
TAK
TAK
TAK
TAK
DID YOU SEE?
DID YOU SEE?!
UM... YES, THAT'S A VERY UNIQUE OUTFIT YOU'RE WEARING.
NO! I MEAN THE MATCH JUST NOW!!

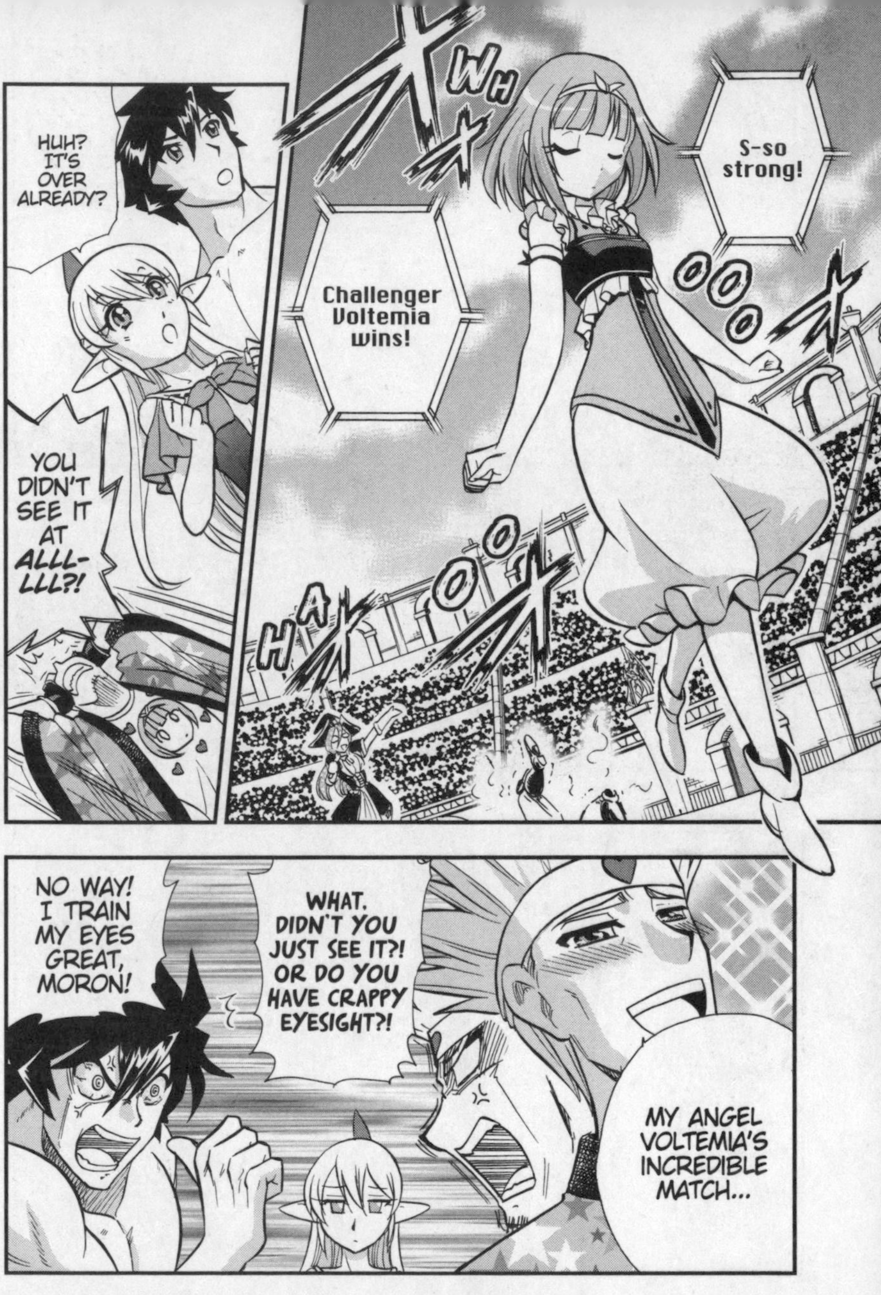
WHH
S-so strong!
Challenger Voltemia wins!
OOOO
HAOOO
HUH? IT'S OVER ALREADY?
YOU DIDN'T SEE IT AT ALLL-LLL?!
WHAT. DIDN'T YOU JUST SEE IT?! OR DO YOU HAVE CRAPPY EYESIGHT?!
MY ANGEL VOLTEMIA'S INCREDIBLE MATCH...
NO WAY! I TRAIN MY EYES GREAT, MORON!

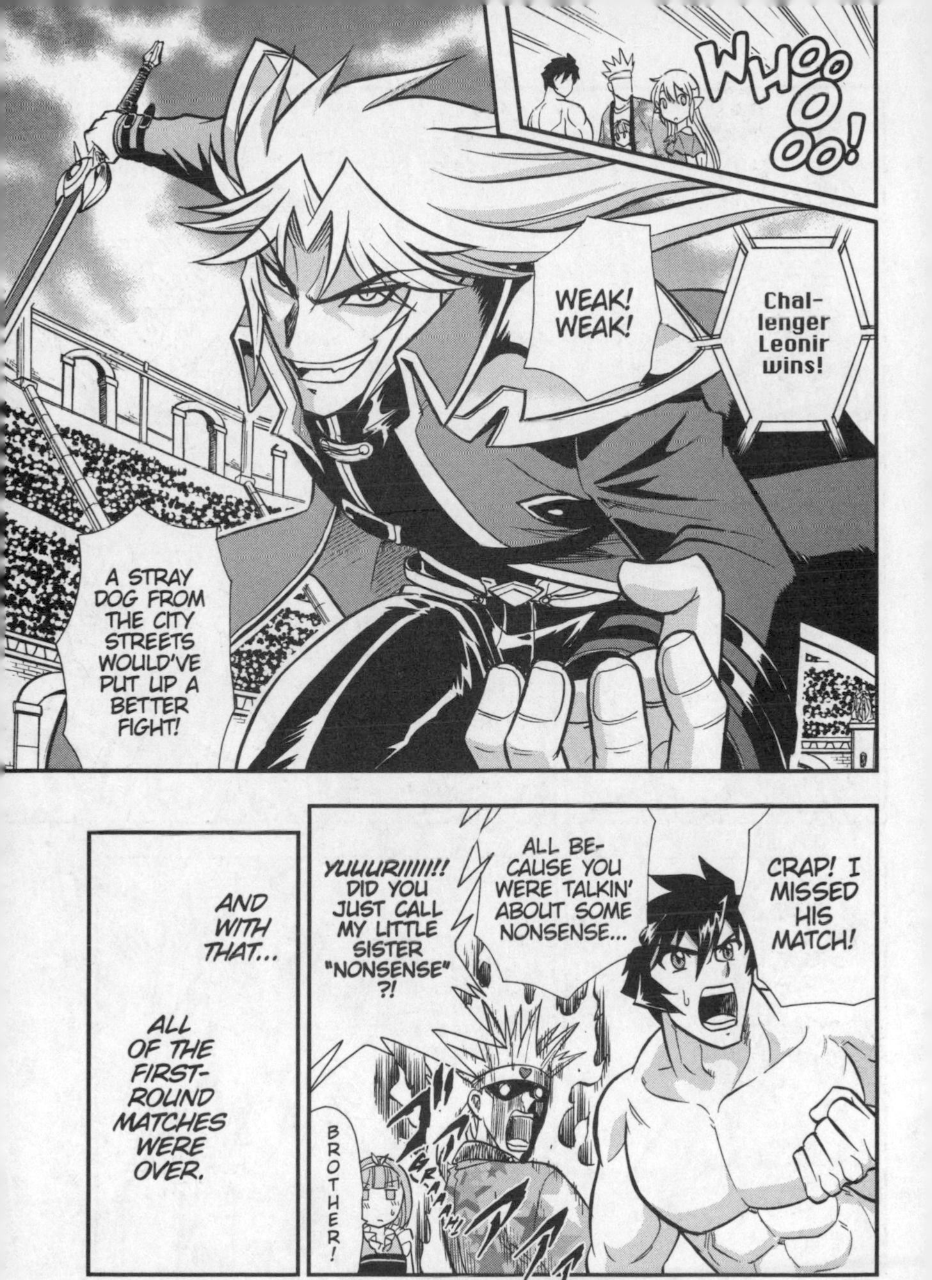

WHOOOOOO!
Challenger Leonir wins!
WEAK! WEAK!
A STRAY DOG FROM THE CITY STREETS WOULD'VE PUT UP A BETTER FIGHT!
CRAP! I MISSED HIS MATCH!
ALL BECAUSE YOU WERE TALKIN' ABOUT SOME NONSENSE...
YUUURIIIIII!! DID YOU JUST CALL MY LITTLE SISTER "NONSENSE"?!
BRAAAH!
BROTHER!
AND WITH THAT...
ALL OF THE FIRST-ROUND MATCHES WERE OVER.

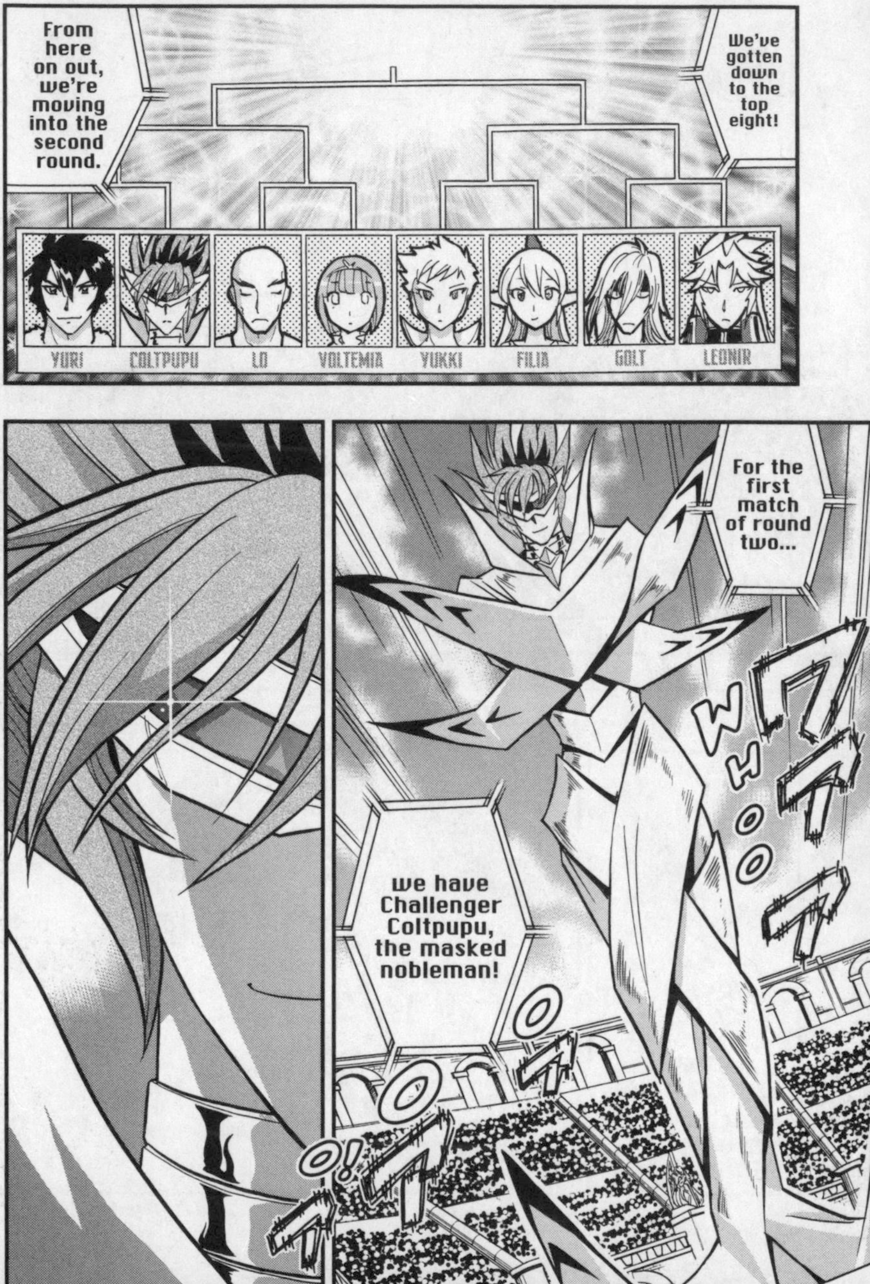
We've gotten down to the top eight!
From here on out, we're moving into the second round.
YURI
COLTPUPU
LO
VOLTEMIA
YUKKI
FILIA
GOLT
LEONIR
For the first match of round two...
WHOOO
we have Challenger Coltpupu, the masked nobleman!
O!

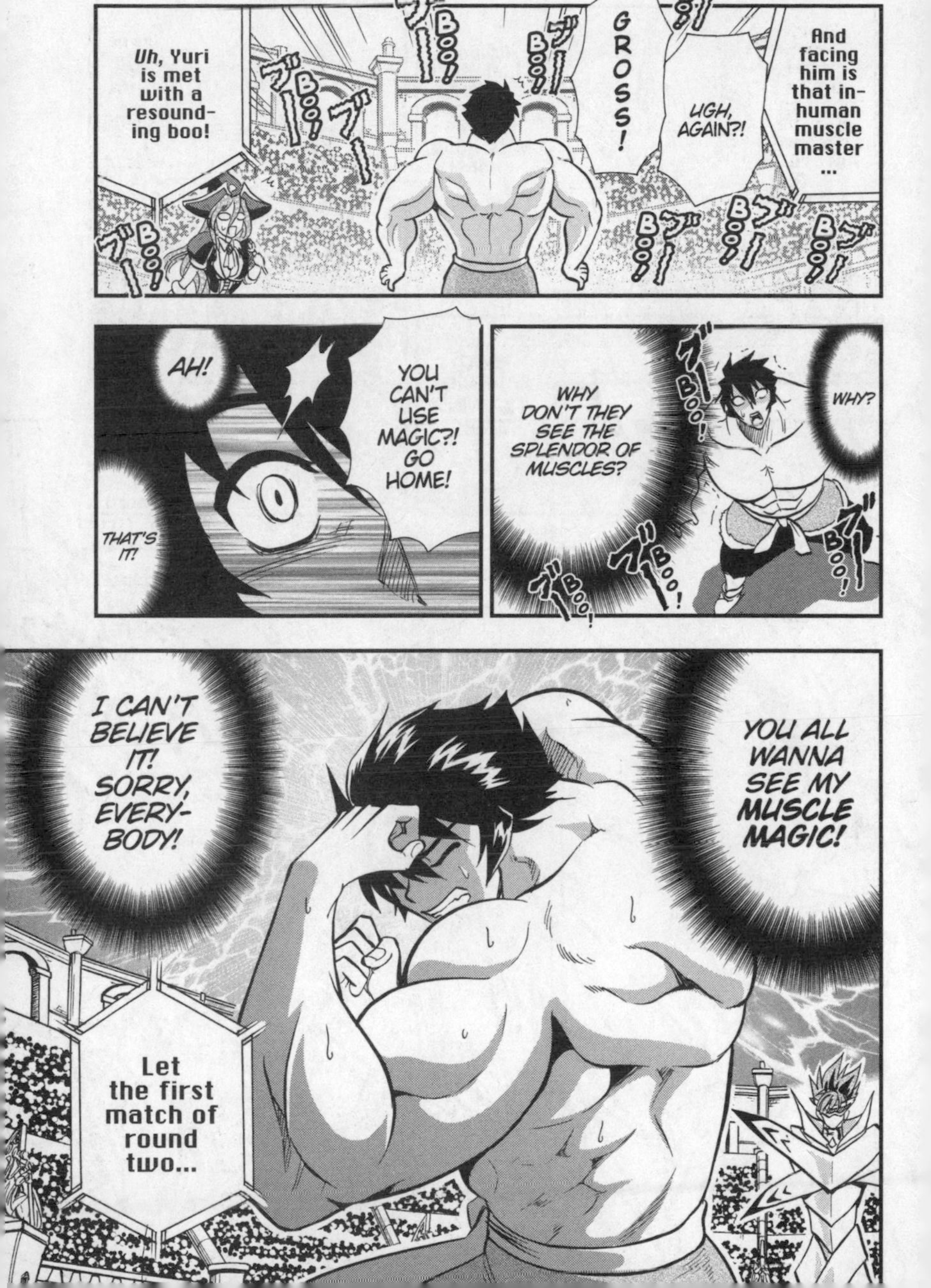
And facing him is that in-human muscle master ...
ブー BOO!
ブー BOO!
ブー BOO!
UGH, AGAIN?!
GROSS!
ブー BOO!
ブー BOO!
ブー BOO!
ブー BOO!
ブー BOO!
Uh, Yuri is met with a resounding boo!
WHY?
ブー BOO!
WHY DON'T THEY SEE THE SPLENDOR OF MUSCLES?
ブー BOO!
ブー BOO!
ブー BOO!
YOU CAN'T USE MAGIC?! GO HOME!
AH!
THAT'S IT!
YOU ALL WANNA SEE MY MUSCLE MAGIC!
I CAN'T BELIEVE IT! SORRY, EVERY-BODY!
Let the first match of round two...

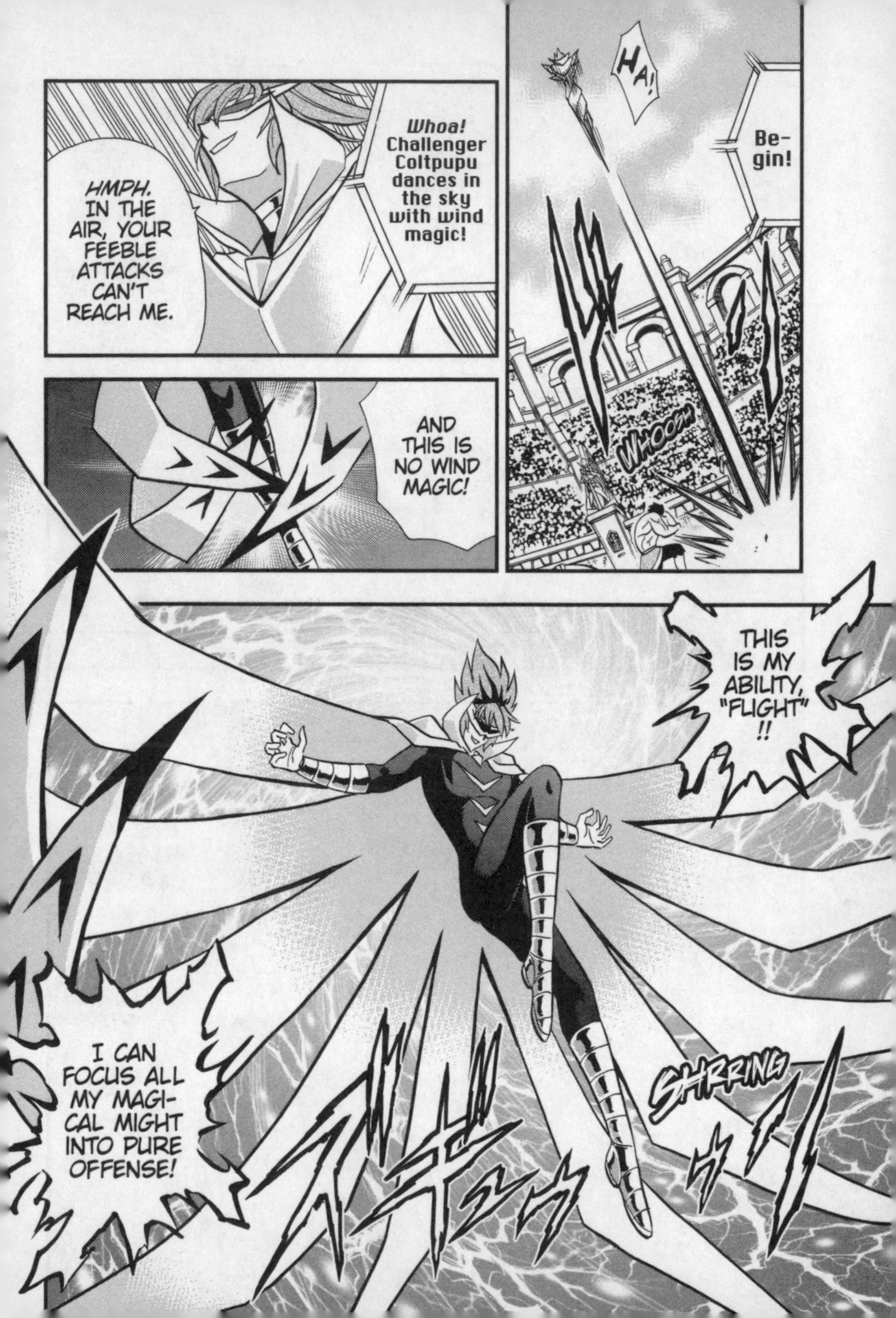
HA!
Be-gin!
WHOOSH
Whoa! Challenger Coltpupu dances in the sky with wind magic!
HMPH. IN THE AIR, YOUR FEEBLE ATTACKS CAN'T REACH ME.
AND THIS IS NO WIND MAGIC!
THIS IS MY ABILITY, "FLIGHT" !!
SHRRING
I CAN FOCUS ALL MY MAGI-CAL MIGHT INTO PURE OFFENSE!

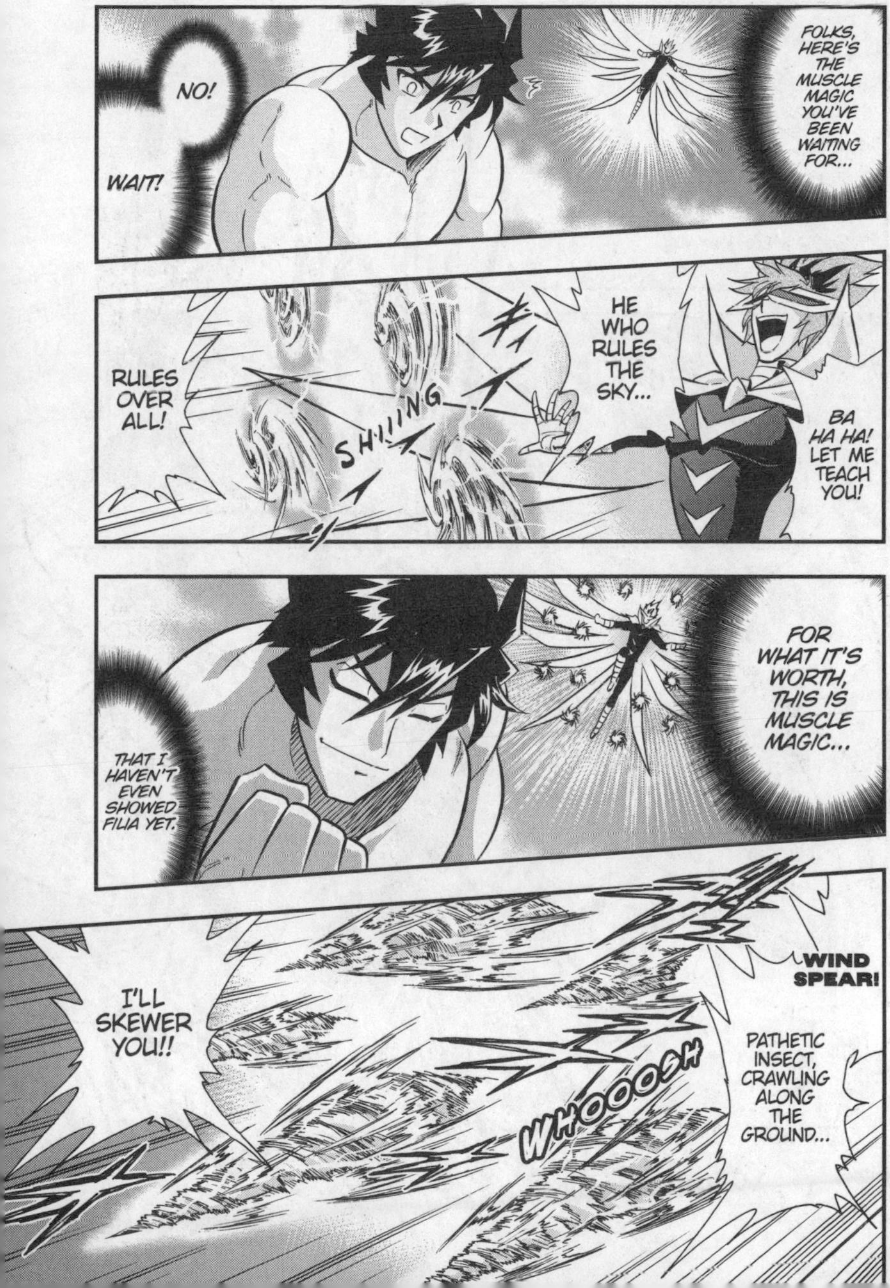
FOLKS, HERE'S THE MUSCLE MAGIC YOU'VE BEEN WAITING FOR...
NO!
WAIT!
BA HA HA! LET ME TEACH YOU!
HE WHO RULES THE SKY...
SHIIING
RULES OVER ALL!
FOR WHAT IT'S WORTH, THIS IS MUSCLE MAGIC...
THAT I HAVEN'T EVEN SHOWED FILIA YET.
WIND SPEAR!
PATHETIC INSECT, CRAWLING ALONG THE GROUND...
WHOOOOSH
I'LL SKEWER YOU!!

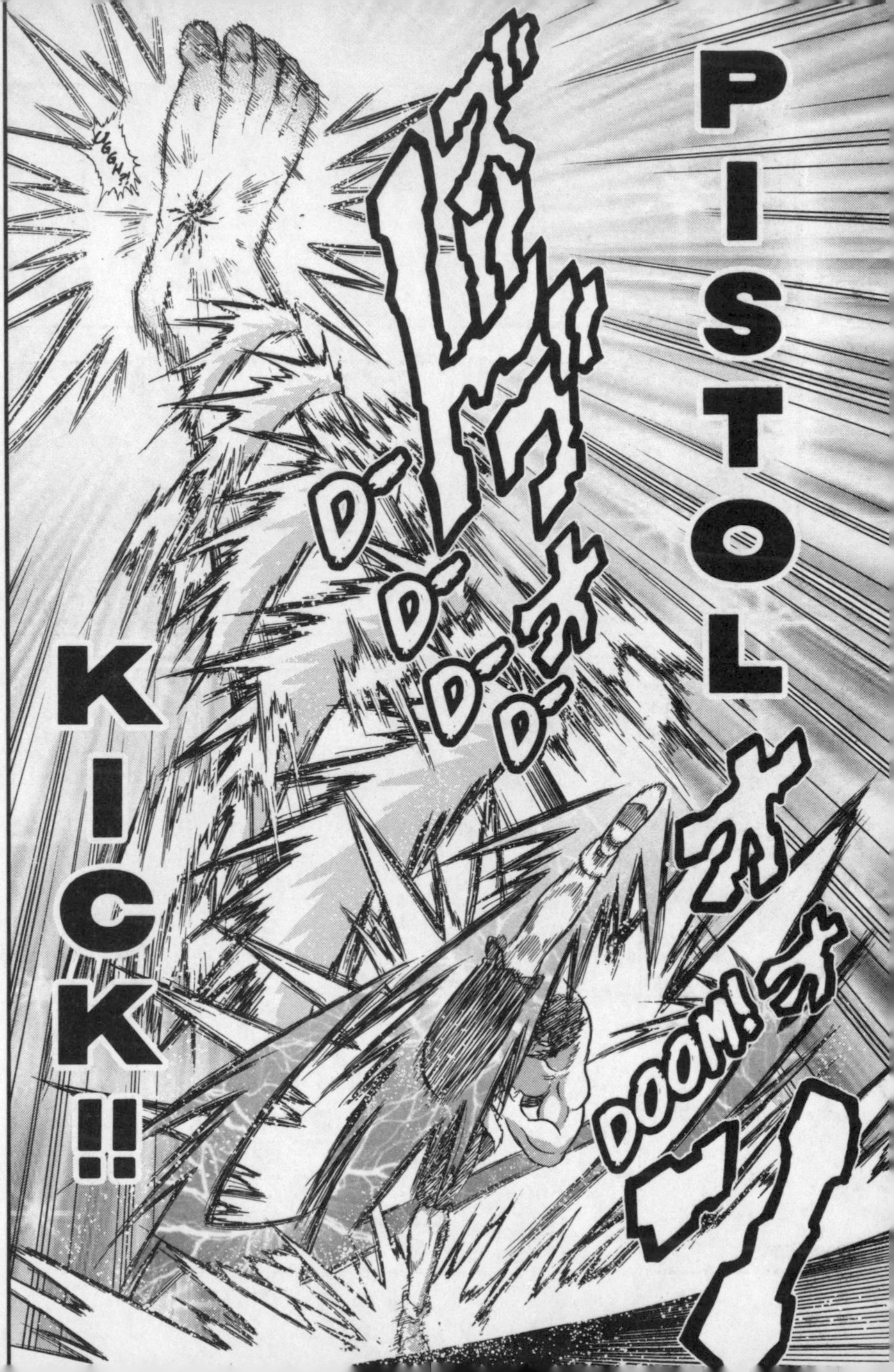
PISTOL
D-D-D-D-
UGGHA?!
KICK!!
DOOM!

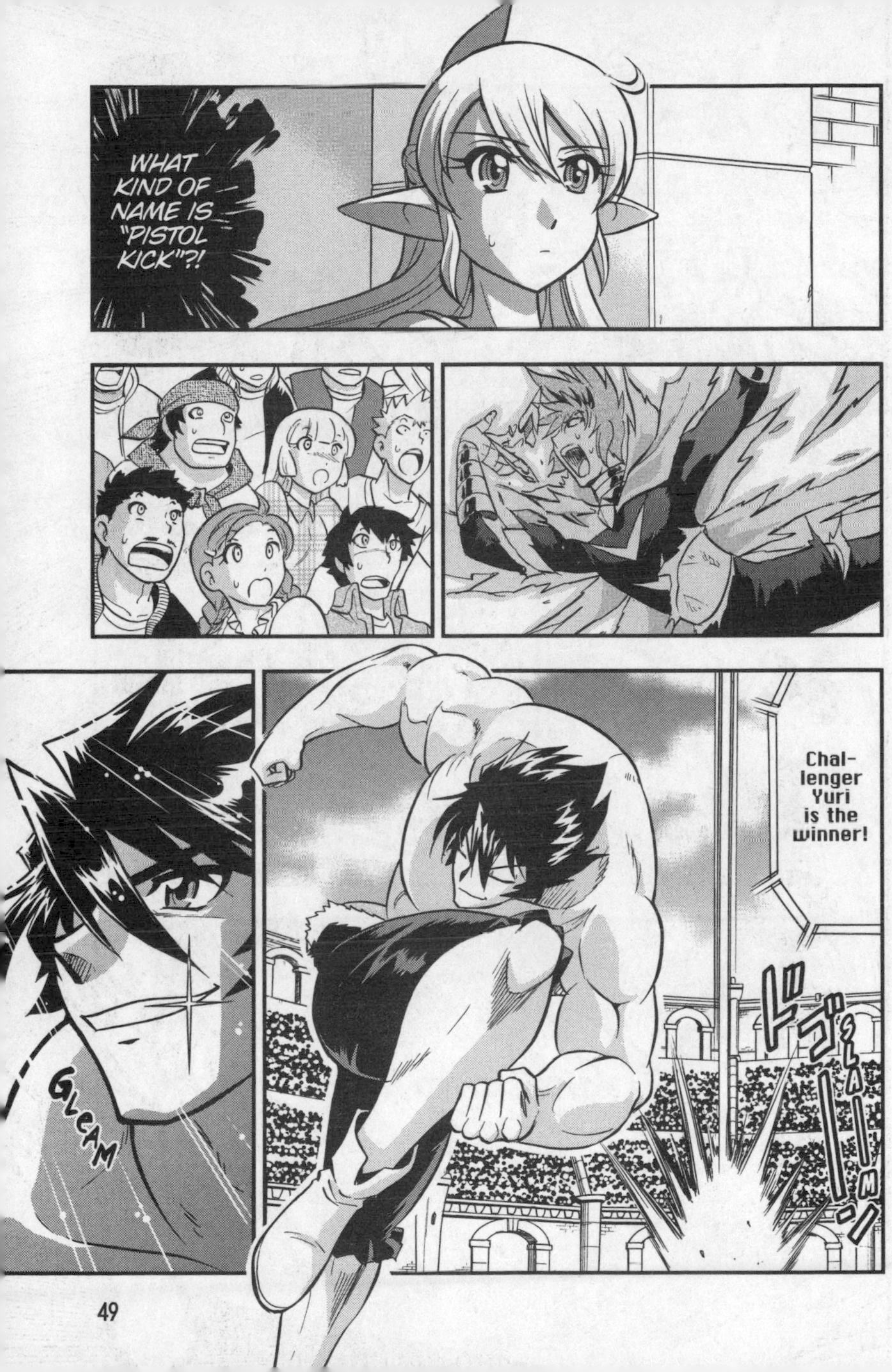
WHAT KIND OF NAME IS "PISTOL KICK"?!
Challenger Yuri is the winner!
SLAM!
GLEAM

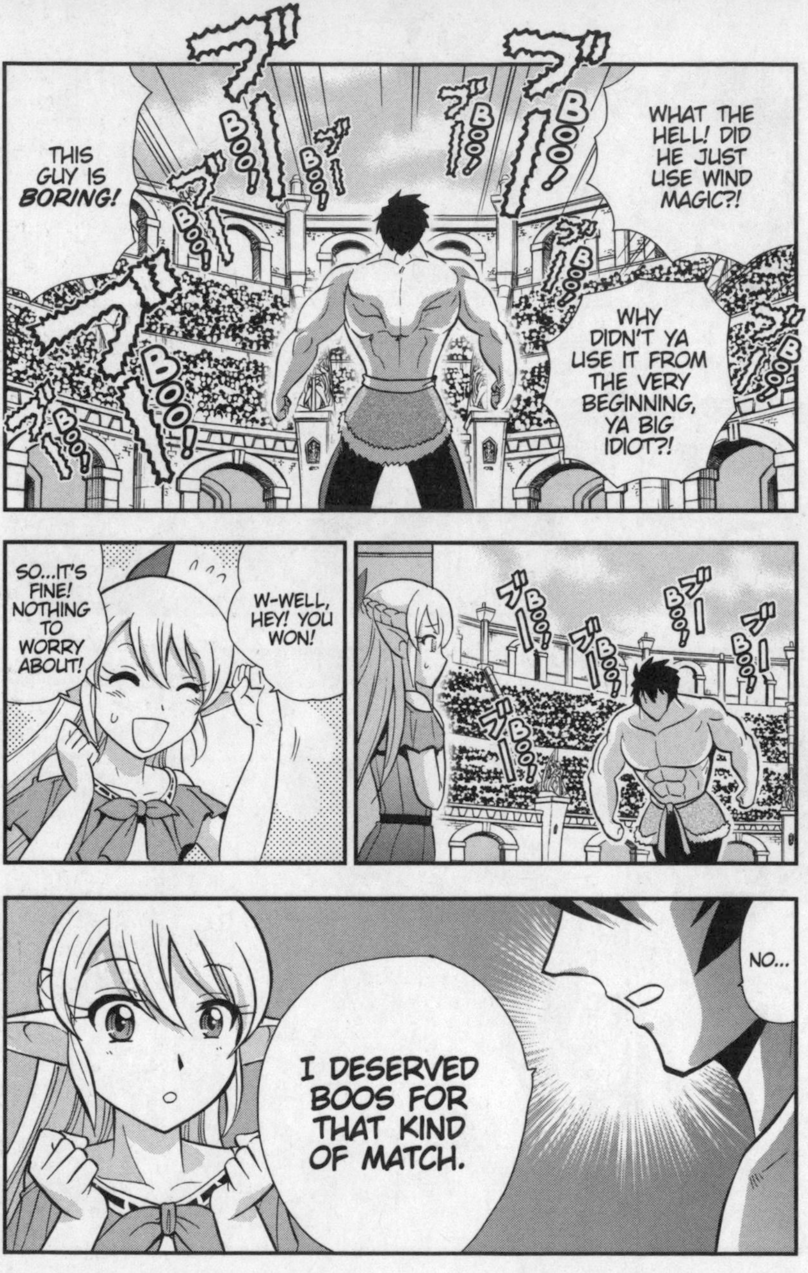
BOO!
WHAT THE HELL! DID HE JUST USE WIND MAGIC?!
BOO!
BOO!
BOO!
THIS GUY IS *BORING!*
BOO!
WHY DIDN'T YA USE IT FROM THE VERY BEGINNING, YA BIG IDIOT?!
BOO!
BOO!
BOO!
BOO!
BOO!
BOO!
BOO!
BOO!
W-WELL, HEY! YOU WON!
SO...IT'S FINE! NOTHING TO WORRY ABOUT!
NO...
I DESERVED BOOS FOR THAT KIND OF MATCH.

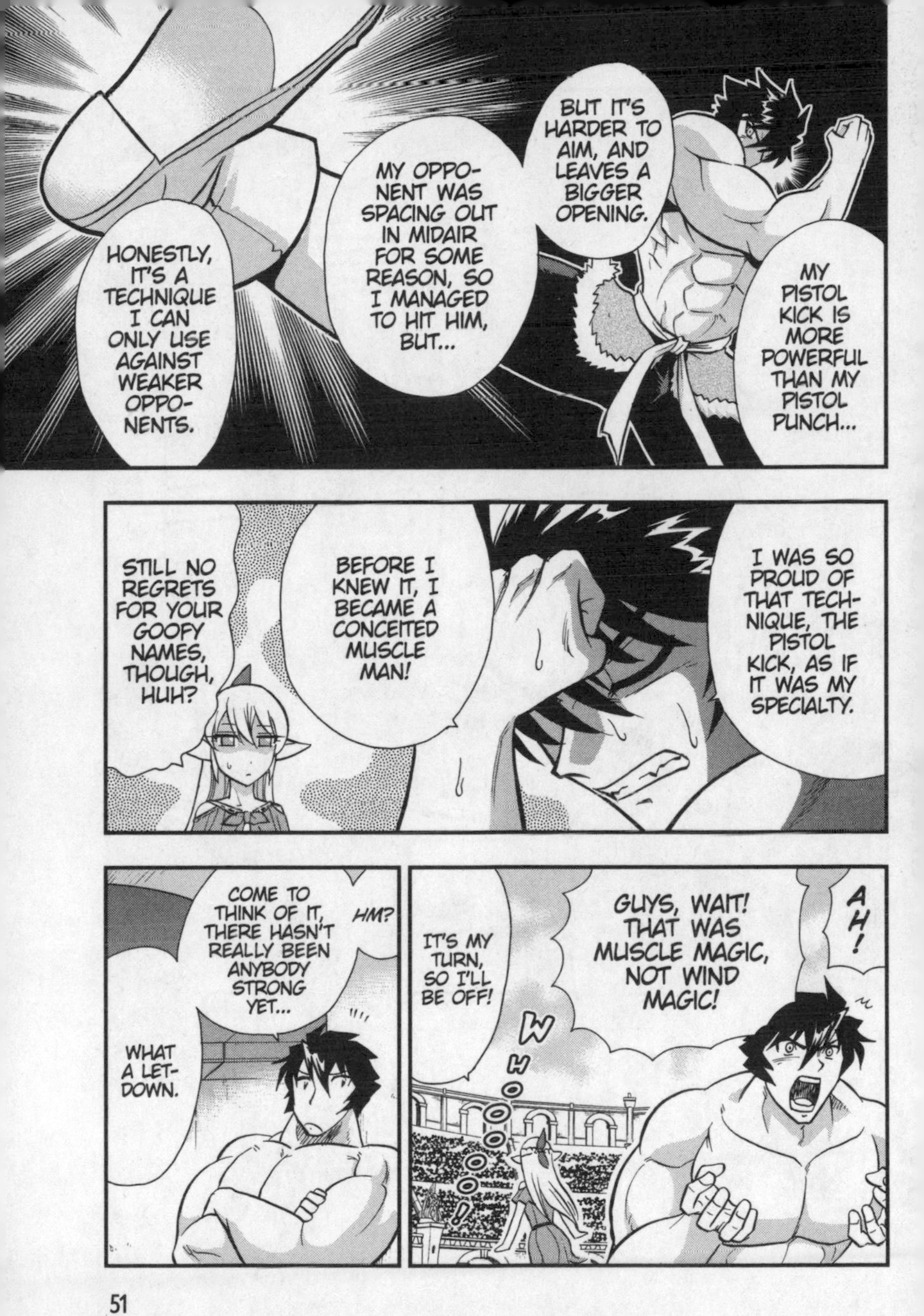
MY PISTOL KICK IS MORE POWERFUL THAN MY PISTOL PUNCH...
BUT IT'S HARDER TO AIM, AND LEAVES A BIGGER OPENING.
MY OPPONENT WAS SPACING OUT IN MIDAIR FOR SOME REASON, SO I MANAGED TO HIT HIM, BUT...
HONESTLY, IT'S A TECHNIQUE I CAN ONLY USE AGAINST WEAKER OPPONENTS.
I WAS SO PROUD OF THAT TECHNIQUE, THE PISTOL KICK, AS IF IT WAS MY SPECIALTY.
BEFORE I KNEW IT, I BECAME A CONCEITED MUSCLE MAN!
STILL NO REGRETS FOR YOUR GOOFY NAMES, THOUGH, HUH?
AH!
GUYS, WAIT! THAT WAS MUSCLE MAGIC, NOT WIND MAGIC!
IT'S MY TURN, SO I'LL BE OFF!
WHOOOOOOOO!
HM?
COME TO THINK OF IT, THERE HASN'T REALLY BEEN ANYBODY STRONG YET...
WHAT A LETDOWN.

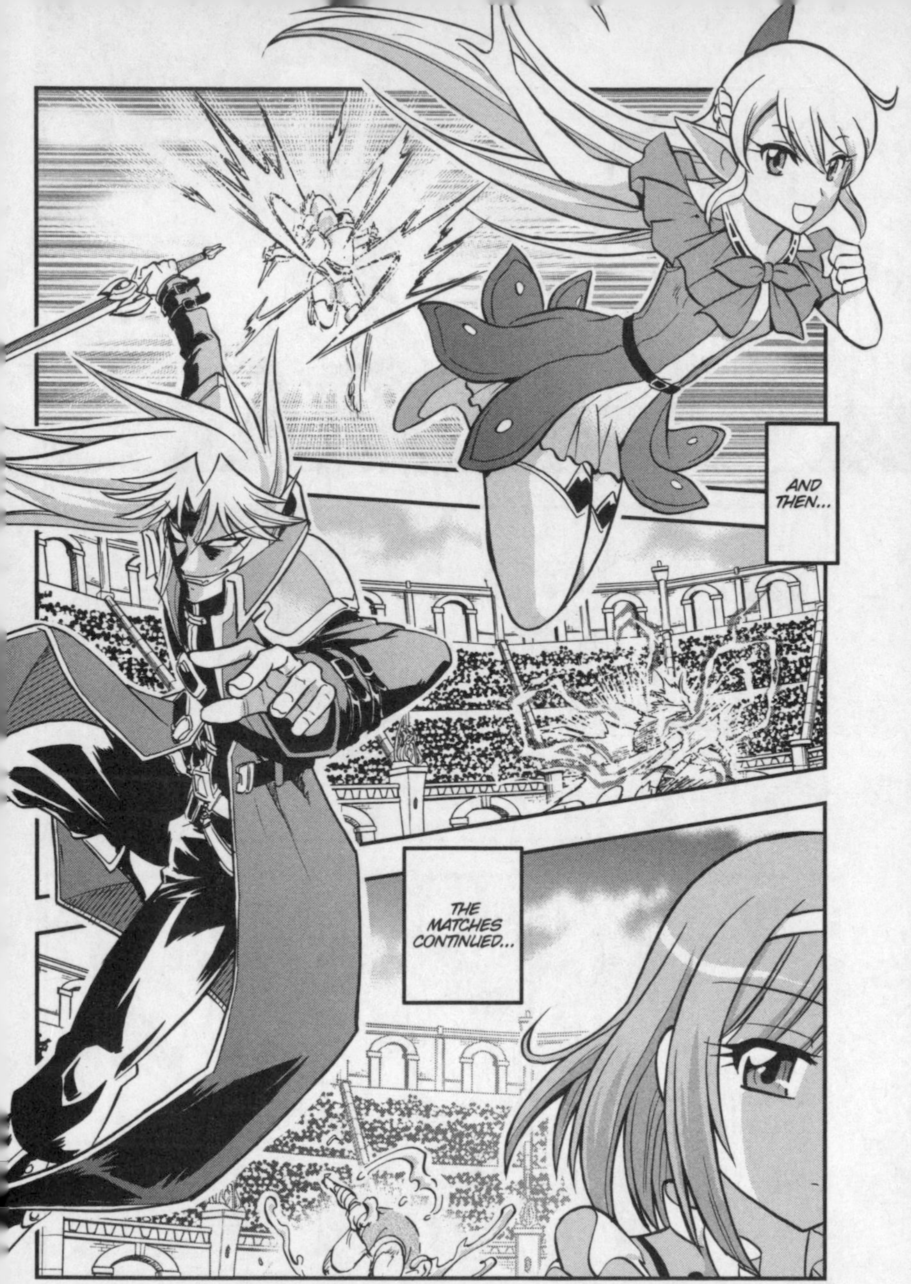
AND THEN...
THE MATCHES CONTINUED...

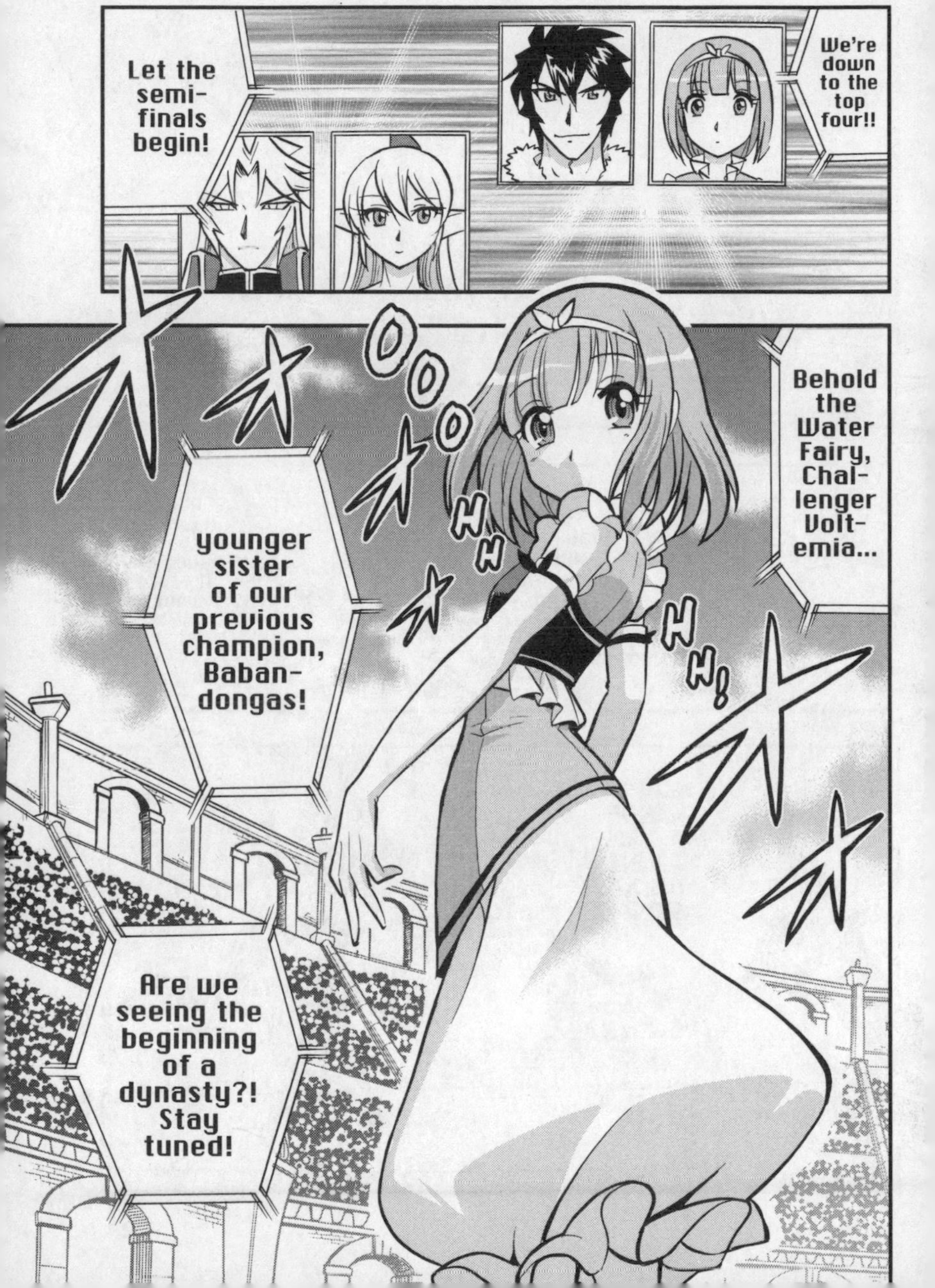
We're down to the top four!!
Let the semi-finals begin!
Behold the Water Fairy, Challenger Voltemia...
OOOOHHHHH!
younger sister of our previous champion, Babandongas!
Are we seeing the beginning of a dynasty?! Stay tuned!

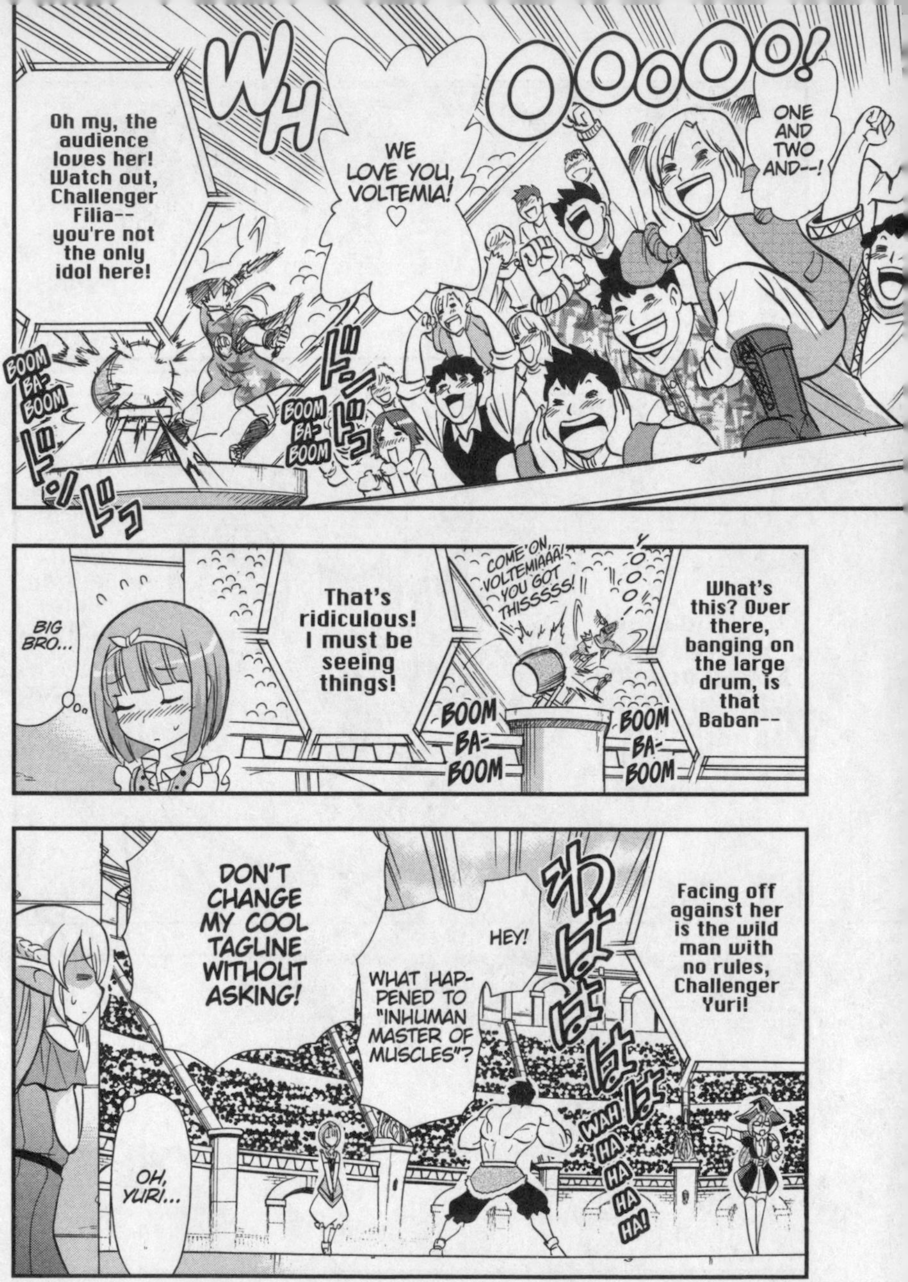
ONE AND TWO AND--!
WHOOOoOO!
WE LOVE YOU, VOLTEMIA! ♡
Oh my, the audience loves her! Watch out, Challenger Filia-- you're not the only idol here!
BOOM BA BOOM
BOOM BA BOOM
What's this? Over there, banging on the large drum, is that Baban--
YOOOO!
COME ON, VOLTEMIAAA! YOU GOT THISSSSS!
BOOM BA BOOM
BOOM BA BOOM
That's ridiculous! I must be seeing things!
BIG BRO...
Facing off against her is the wild man with no rules, Challenger Yuri!
わははは
WAH HA HA HA HA HA!
HEY!
WHAT HAPPENED TO "INHUMAN MASTER OF MUSCLES"?
DON'T CHANGE MY COOL TAGLINE WITHOUT ASKING!
OH, YURI...

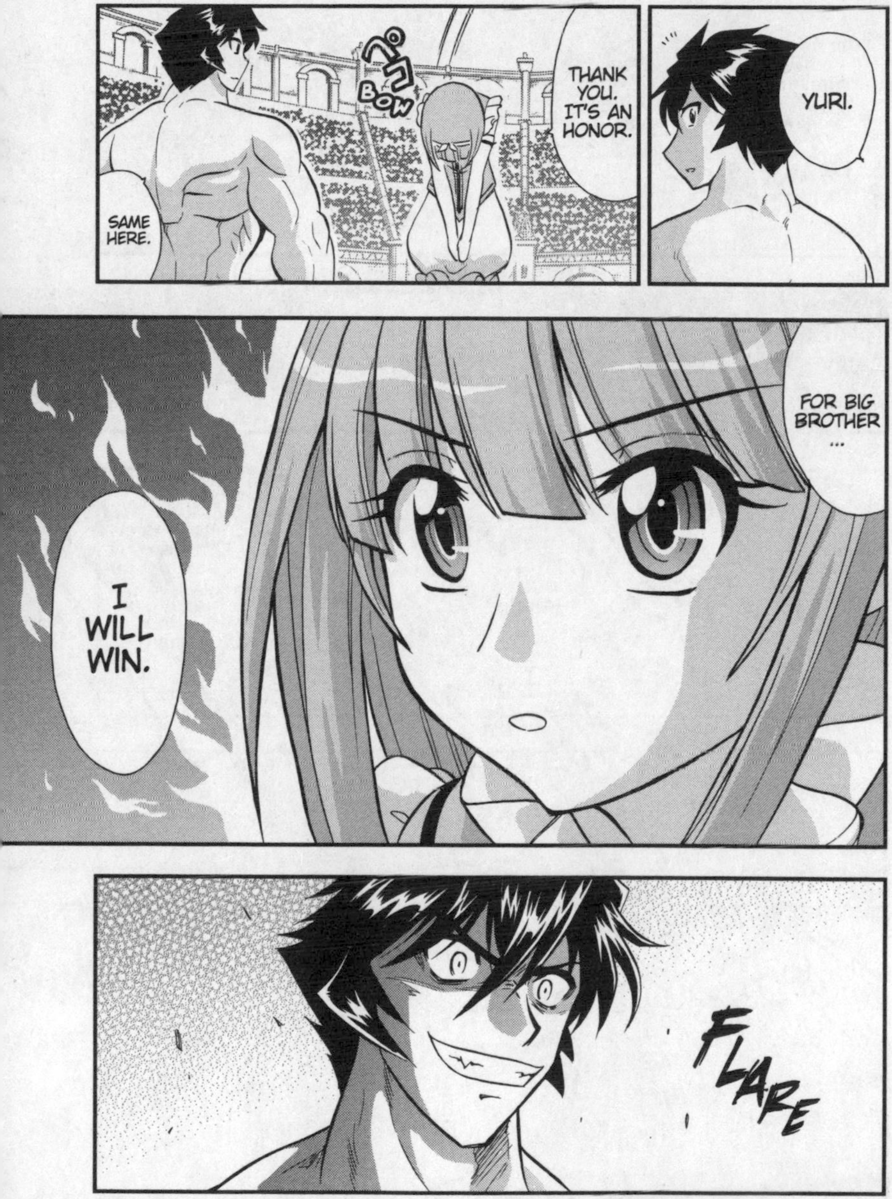
YURI.
THANK YOU. IT'S AN HONOR.
BOW
SAME HERE.
FOR BIG BROTHER...
I WILL WIN.
FLARE

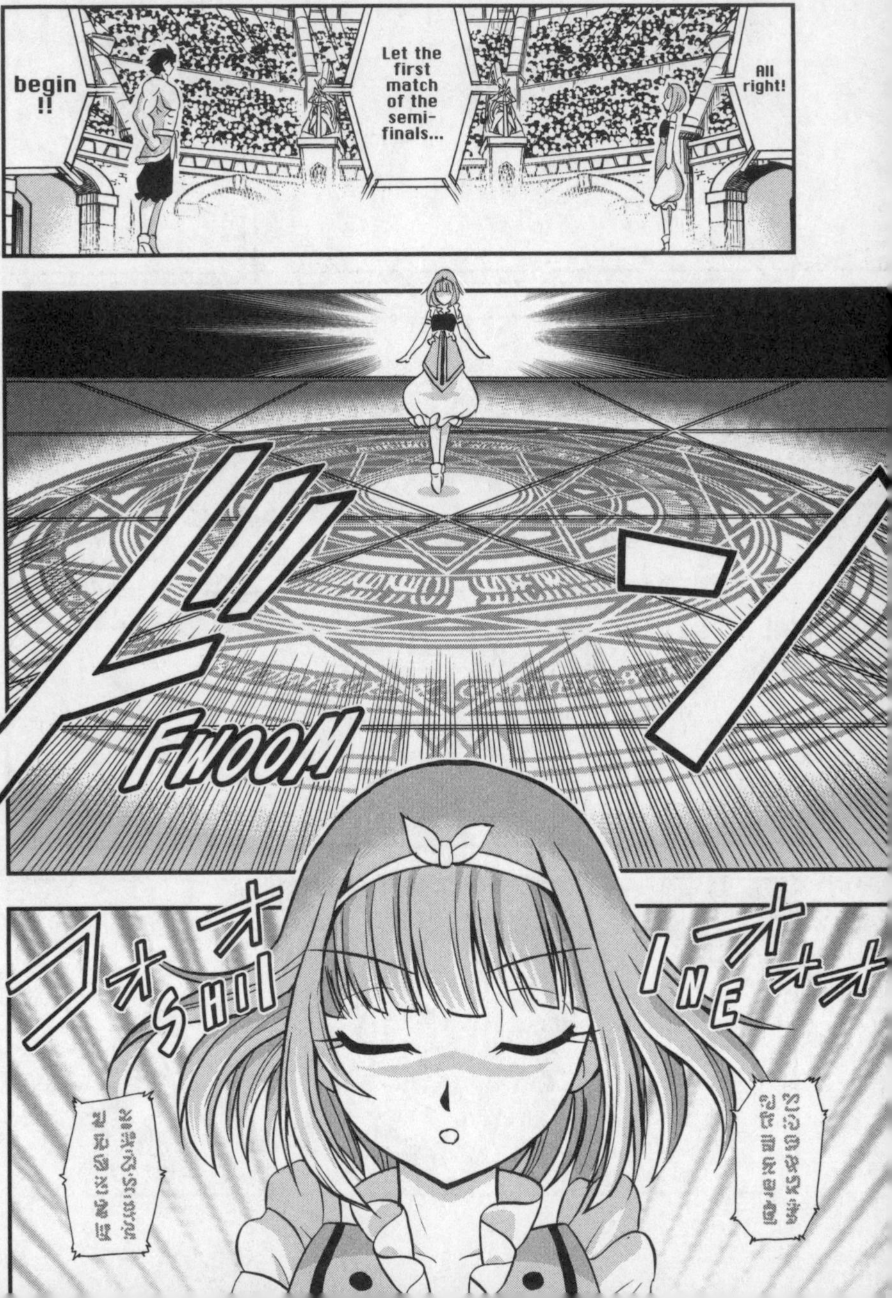
All right!
Let the first match of the semi-finals...
begin!!
FWOOM
SHIINE

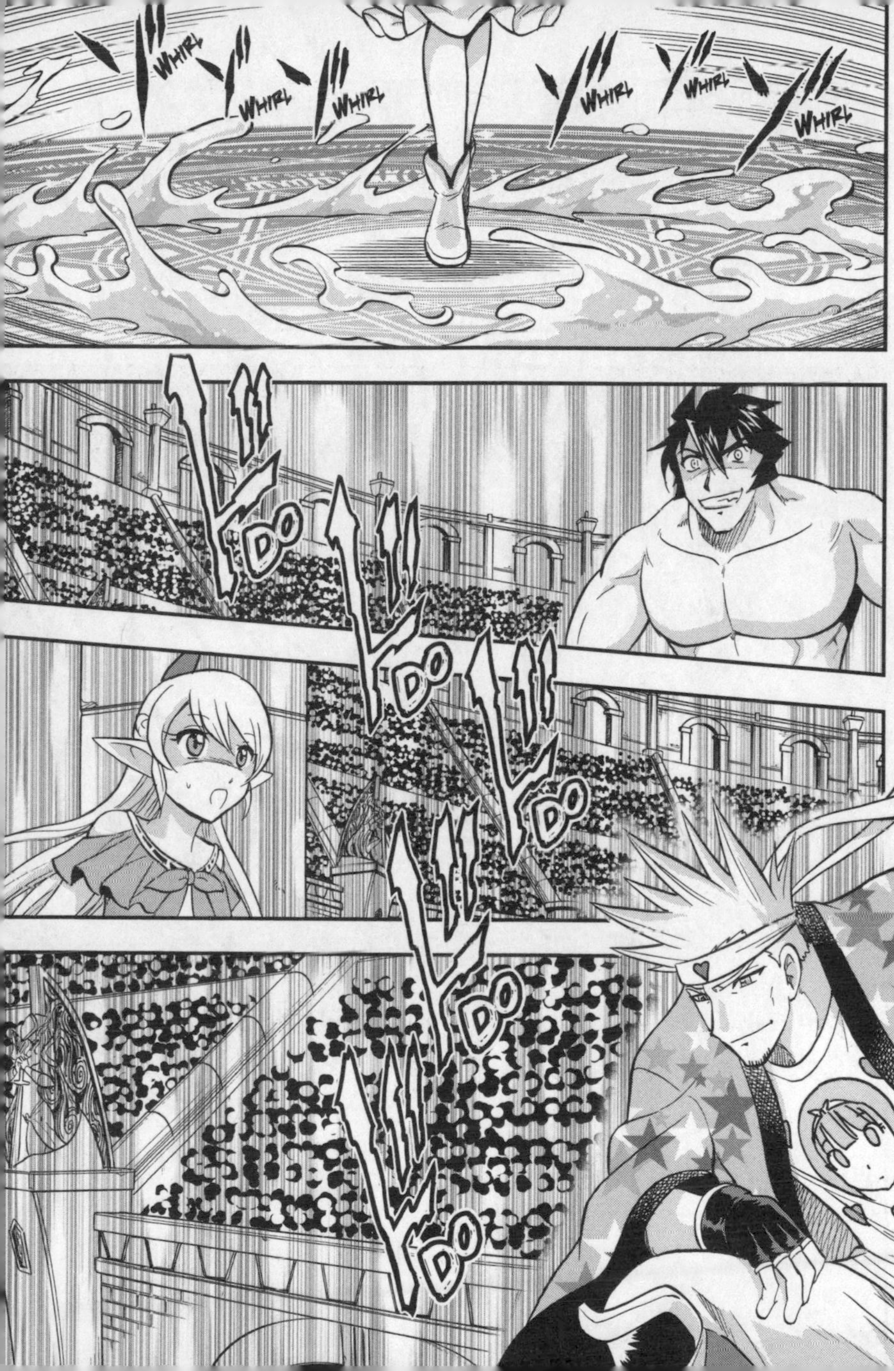
WHIRL
WHIRL
WHIRL
WHIRL
WHIRL
WHIRL
WHIRL
DO
DO
DO
DO
DO
DO

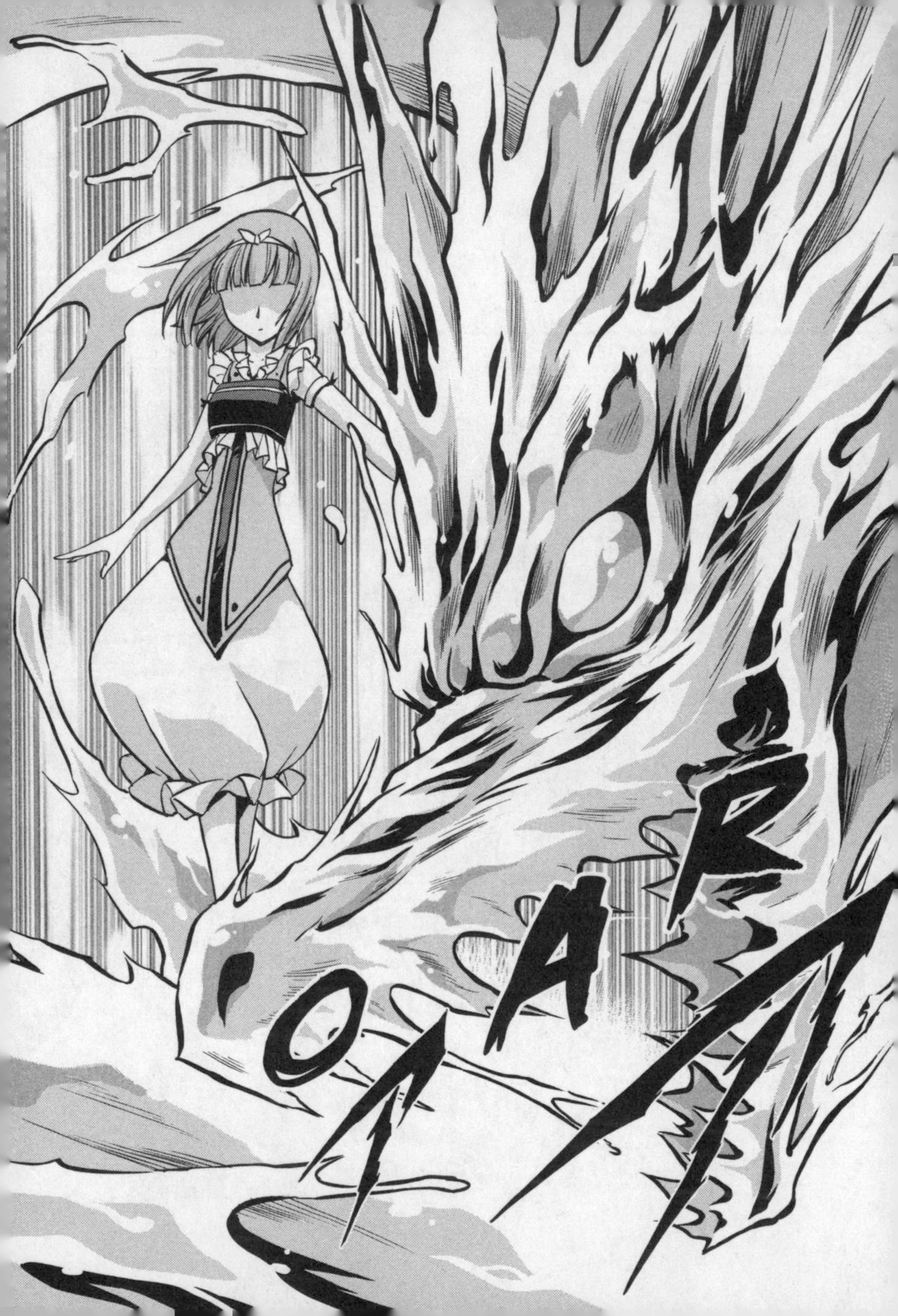
OAR

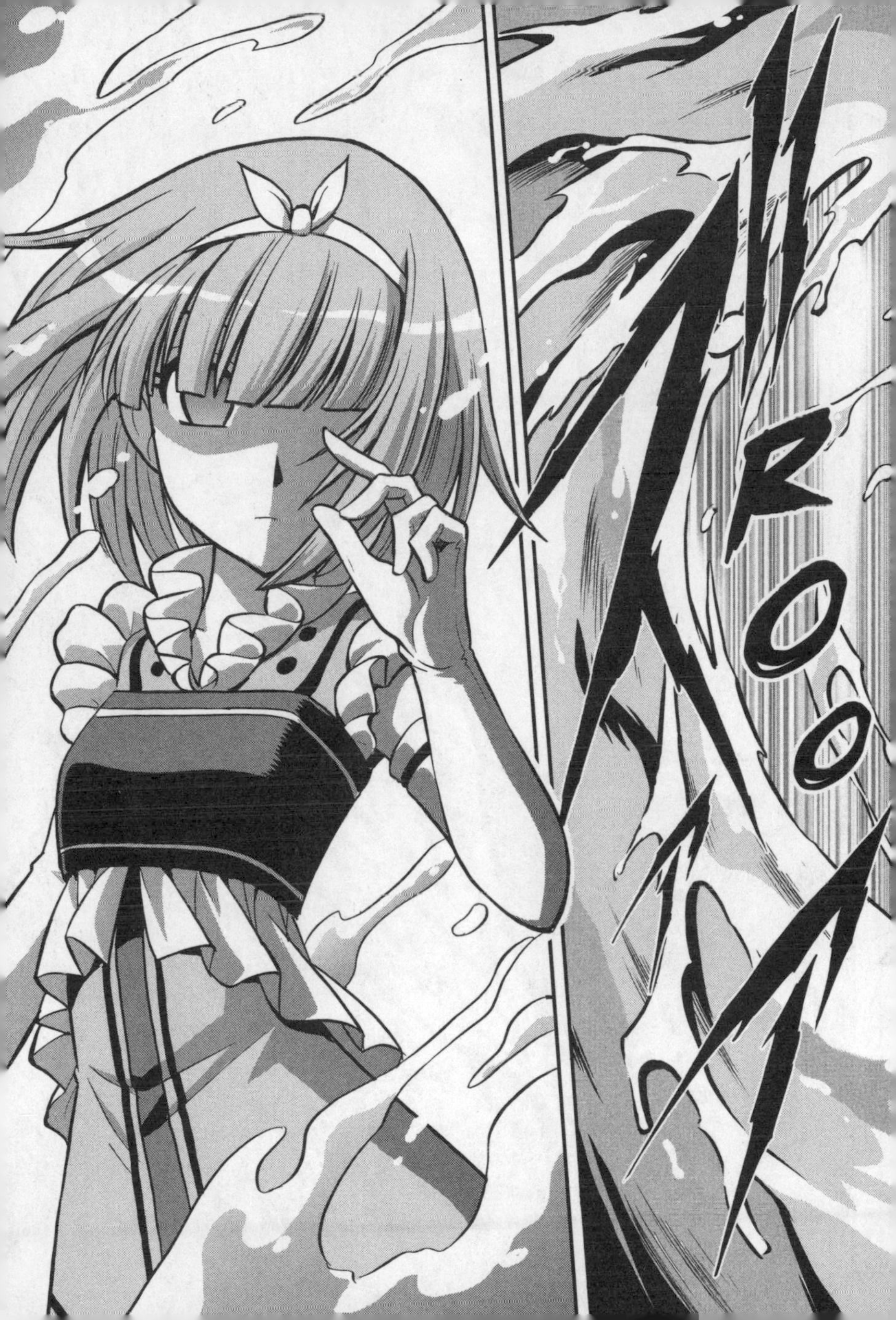

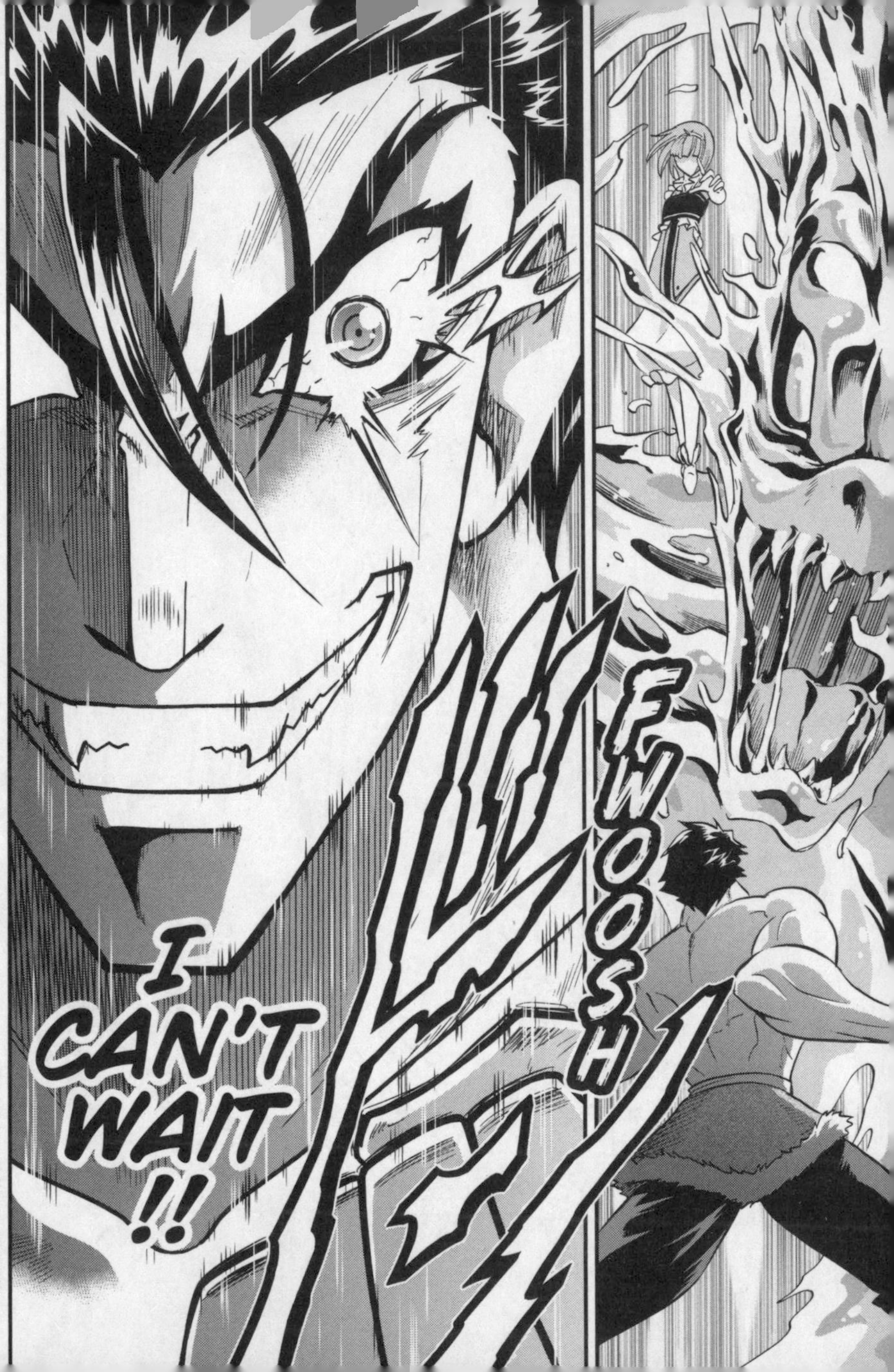
FWOOSH
I CAN'T WAIT!!

CHAPTER 12 END

A mysterious friendship has blossomed!

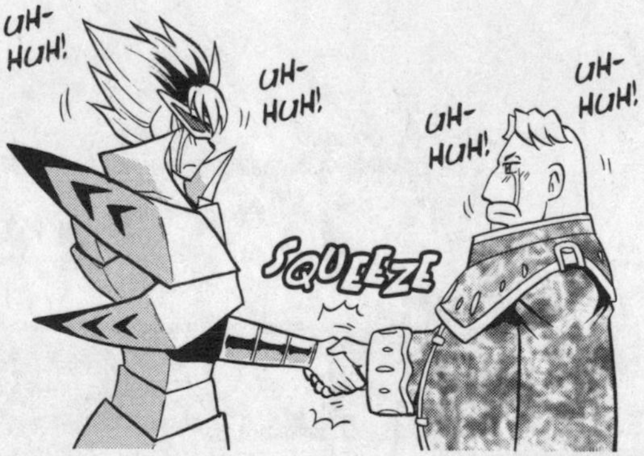
UH-HUH!
UH-HUH!
UH-HUH!
UH-HUH!
SQUEEZE

MUSCLES ARE BETTER THAN MAGIC!

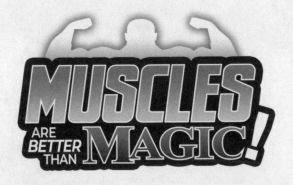

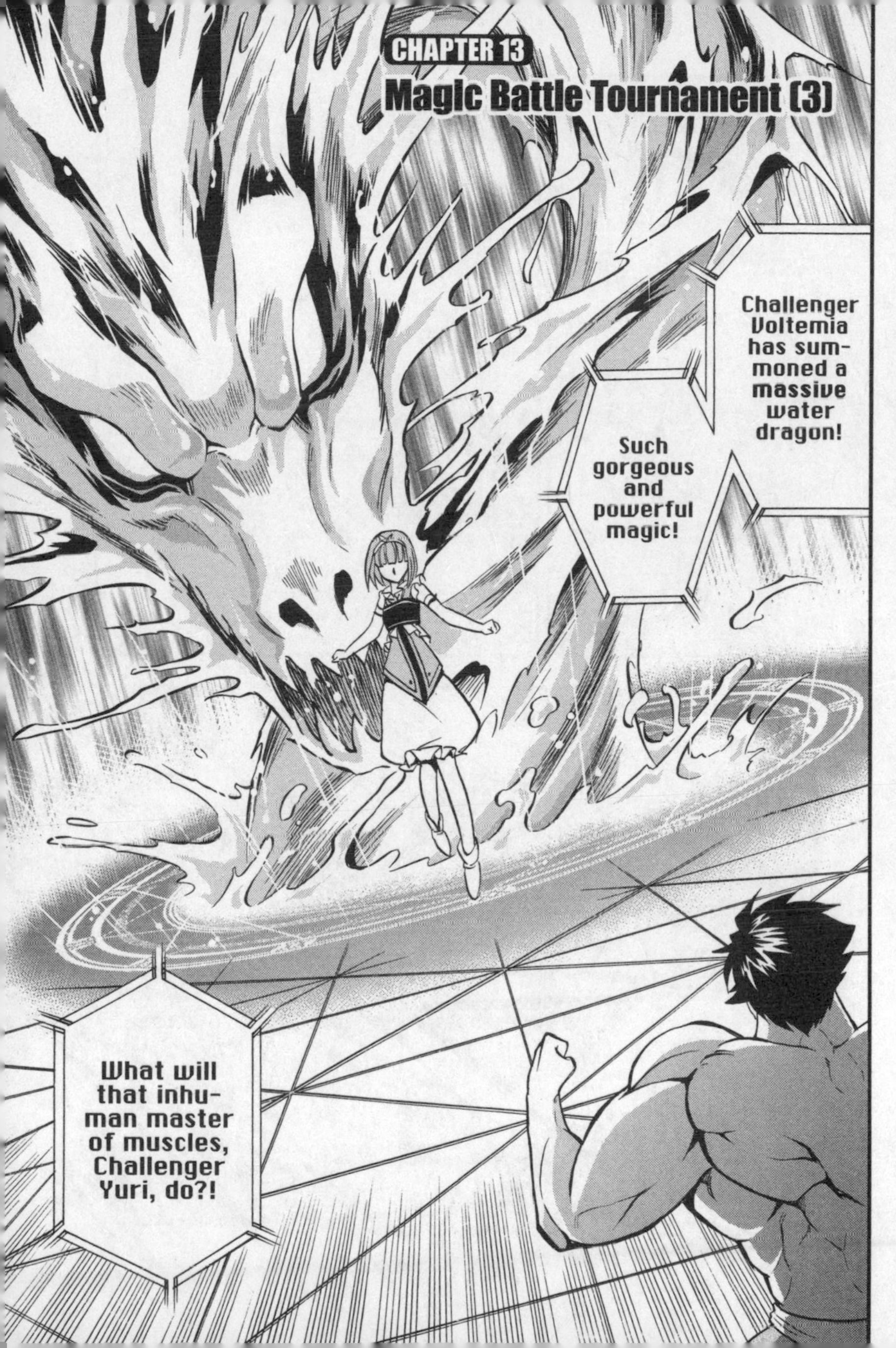
CHAPTER 13
Magic Battle Tournament (3)
Challenger Voltemia has summoned a massive water dragon!
Such gorgeous and powerful magic!
What will that inhuman master of muscles, Challenger Yuri, do?!

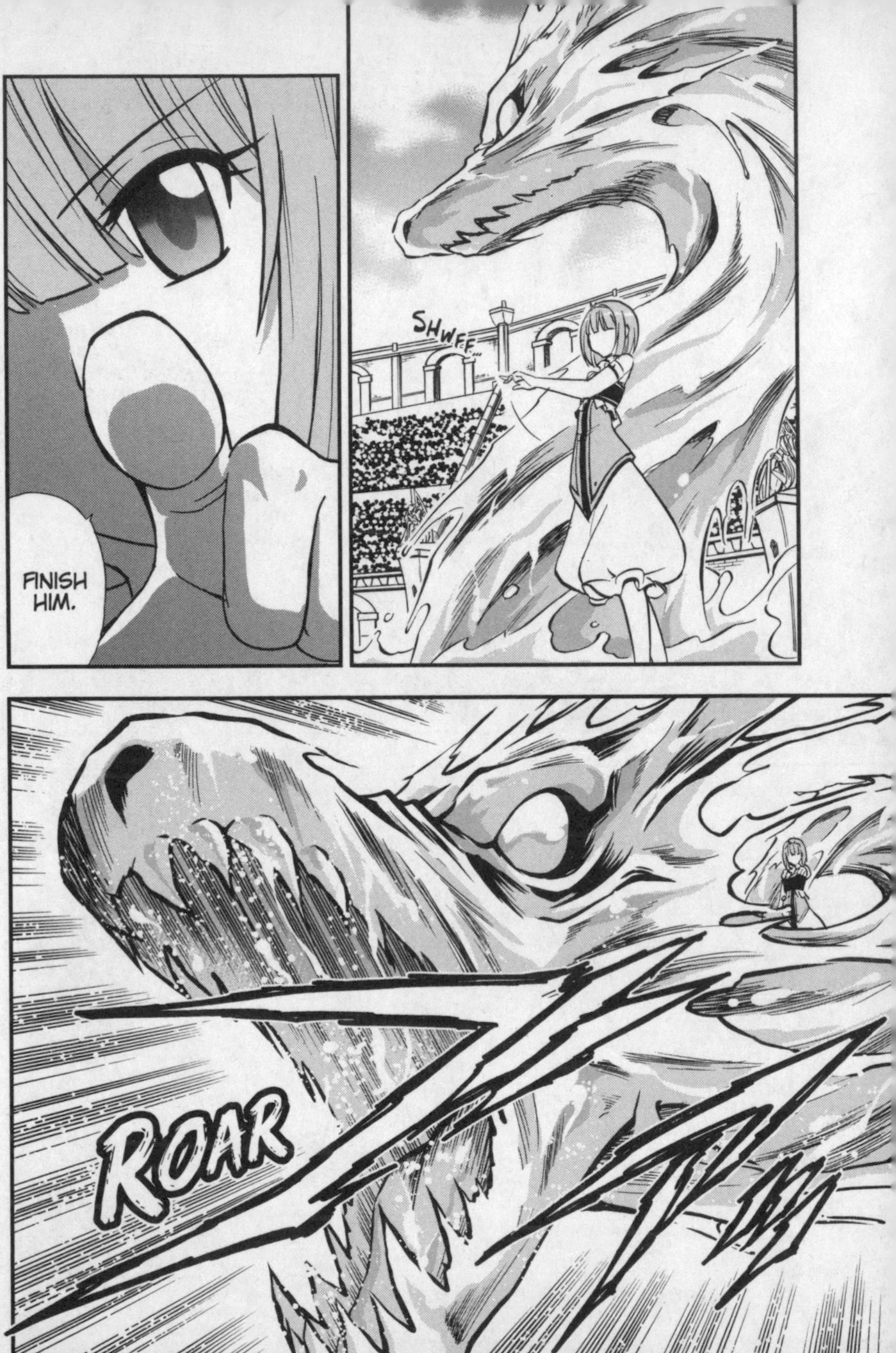
SHWFF...
FINISH HIM.
ROAR

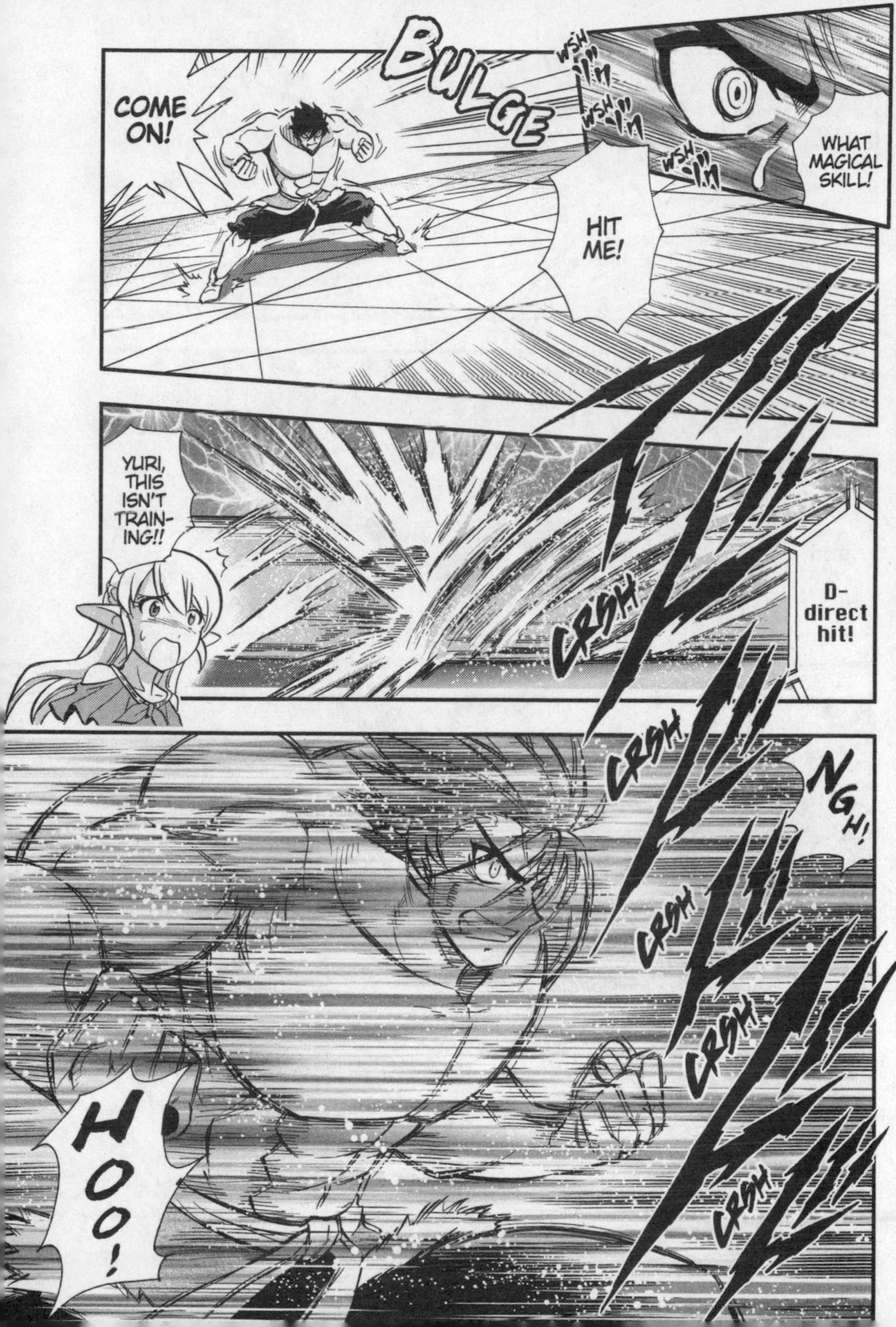
WSH
WSH
WSH
WHAT MAGICAL SKILL!
BULGE
HIT ME!
COME ON!
D-direct hit!
CRSH
YURI, THIS ISN'T TRAIN-ING!!
NGH!
CRSH
CRSH
CRSH
CRSH
CRSH
HOO!

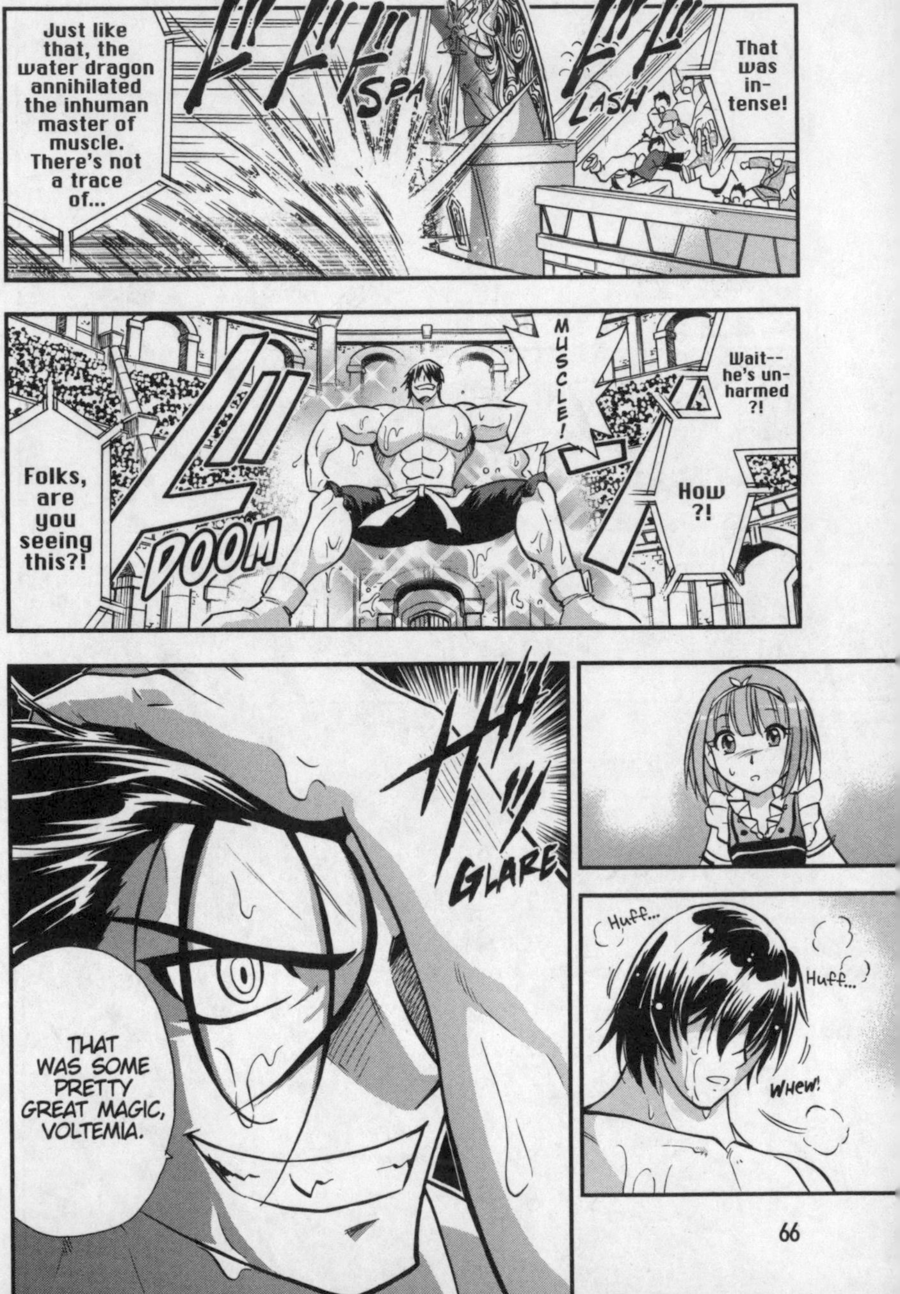
That was in-tense!
SPA
LASH
Just like that, the water dragon annihilated the inhuman master of muscle. There's not a trace of...
Wait-- he's un-harmed?!
MUSCLE!
How?!
Folks, are you seeing this?!
DOOM
Huff...
Huff...
Whew!
GLARE
THAT WAS SOME PRETTY GREAT MAGIC, VOLTEMIA.

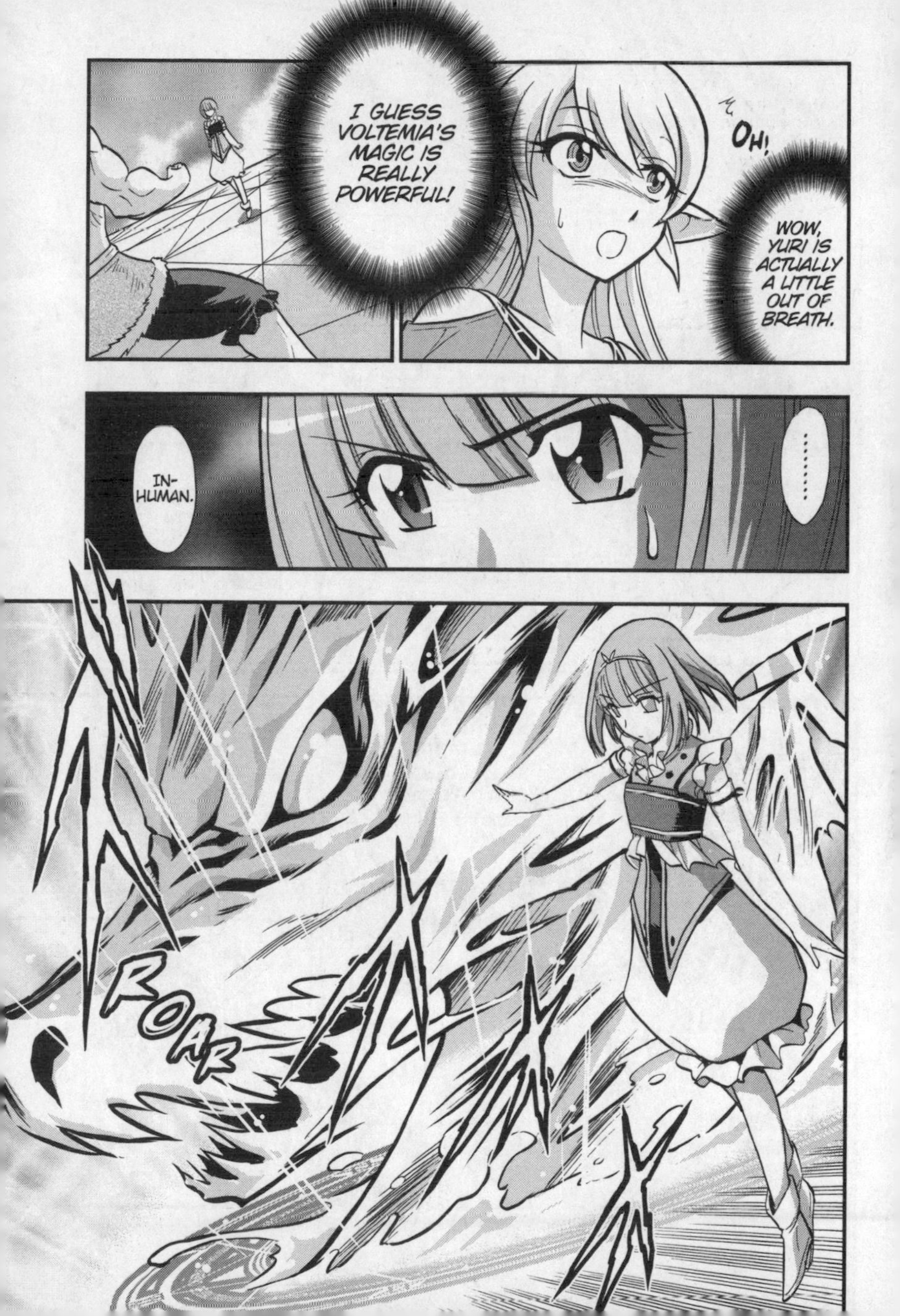
OH!
WOW, YURI IS ACTUALLY A LITTLE OUT OF BREATH.
I GUESS VOLTEMIA'S MAGIC IS REALLY POWERFUL!
......
IN-HUMAN.
ROAR

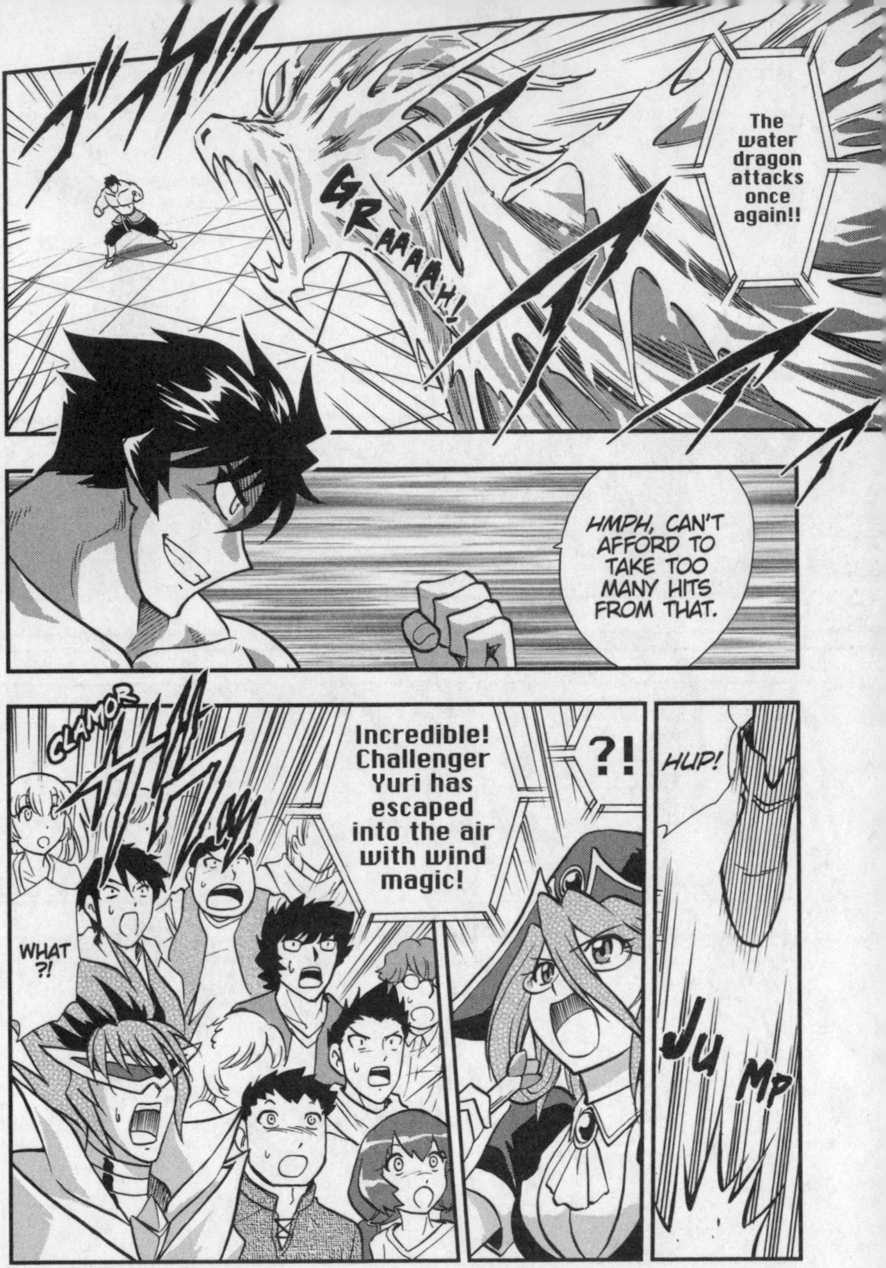
The water dragon attacks once again!!
GRAAAAAH!
HMPH, CAN'T AFFORD TO TAKE TOO MANY HITS FROM THAT.
HUP!
JUMP
?!
Incredible! Challenger Yuri has escaped into the air with wind magic!
CLAMOR
WHAT ?!

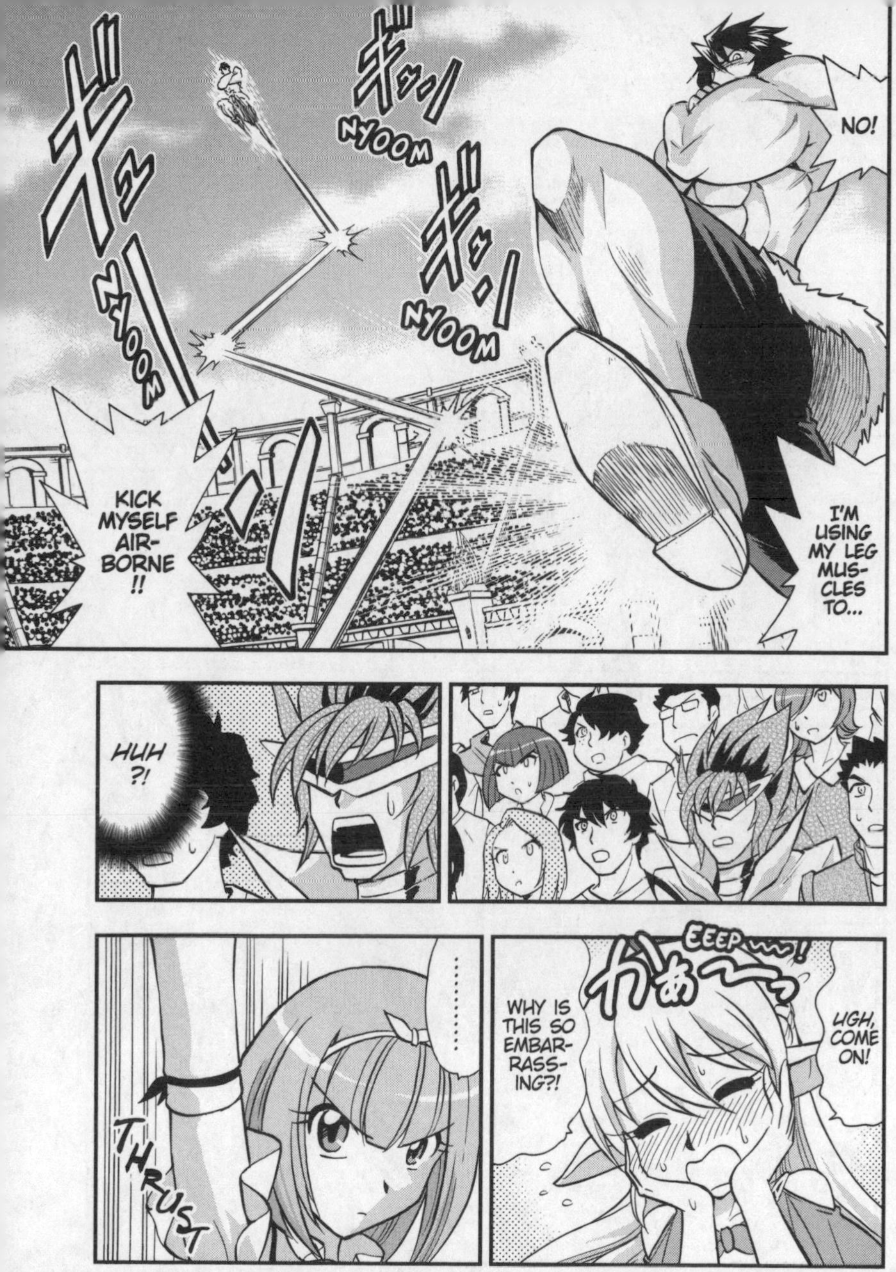
NO!
I'M USING MY LEG MUS-CLES TO...
NYOOM
NYOOM
ZAOOM
KICK MYSELF AIR-BORNE!!
HUH ?!
EEEP~!
わぁ～っ
UGH, COME ON!
WHY IS THIS SO EMBAR-RASS-ING?!
......
THRUST

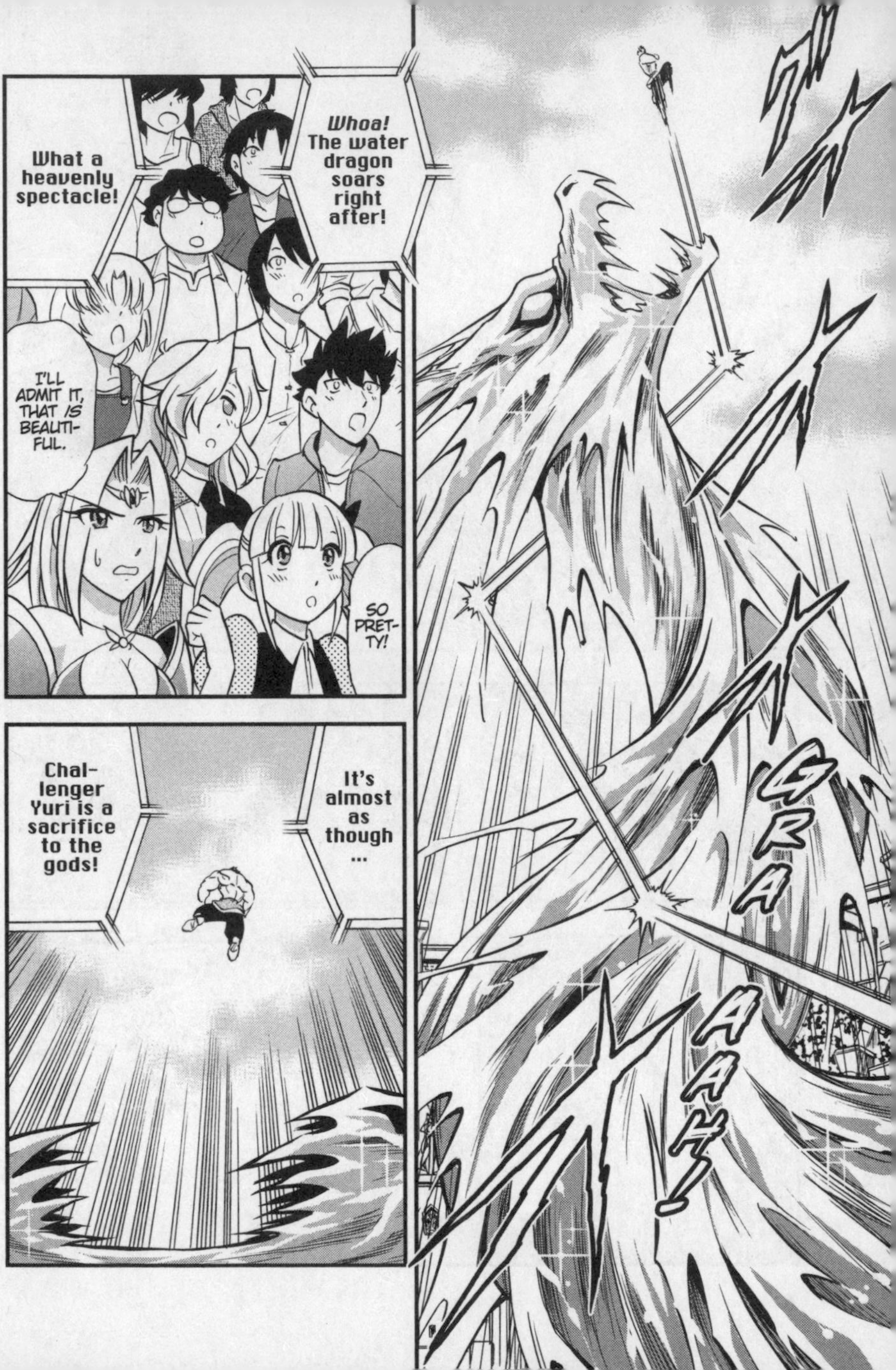
GRAAAAAH!
Whoa! The water dragon soars right after!
What a heavenly spectacle!
I'LL ADMIT IT, THAT IS BEAUTIFUL.
SO PRETTY!
It's almost as though...
Challenger Yuri is a sacrifice to the gods!

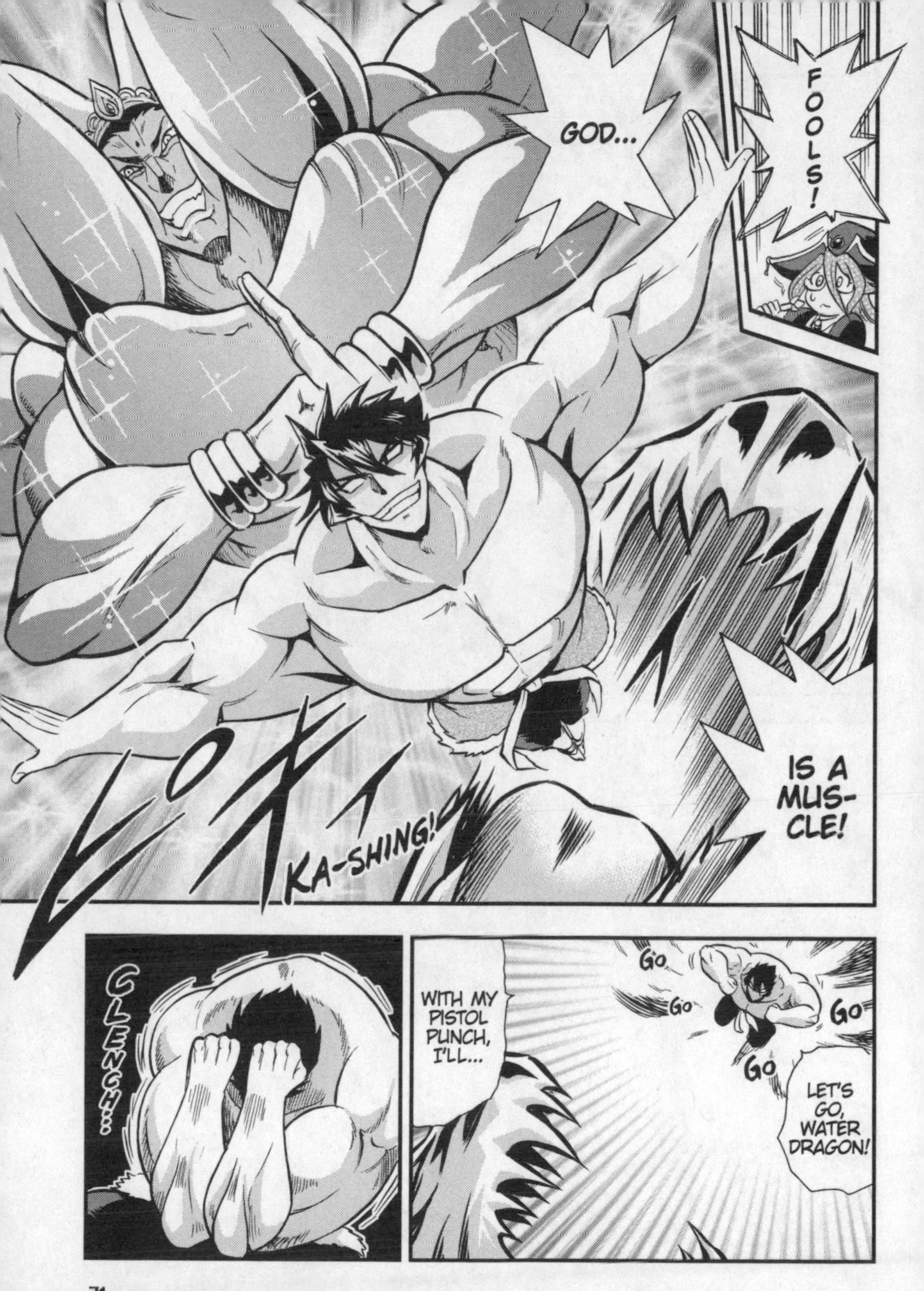
FOOLS!
GOD...
IS A MUS-CLE!
KA-SHING!
GO
GO
GO
GO
LET'S GO, WATER DRAGON!
WITH MY PISTOL PUNCH, I'LL...
CLENCH...

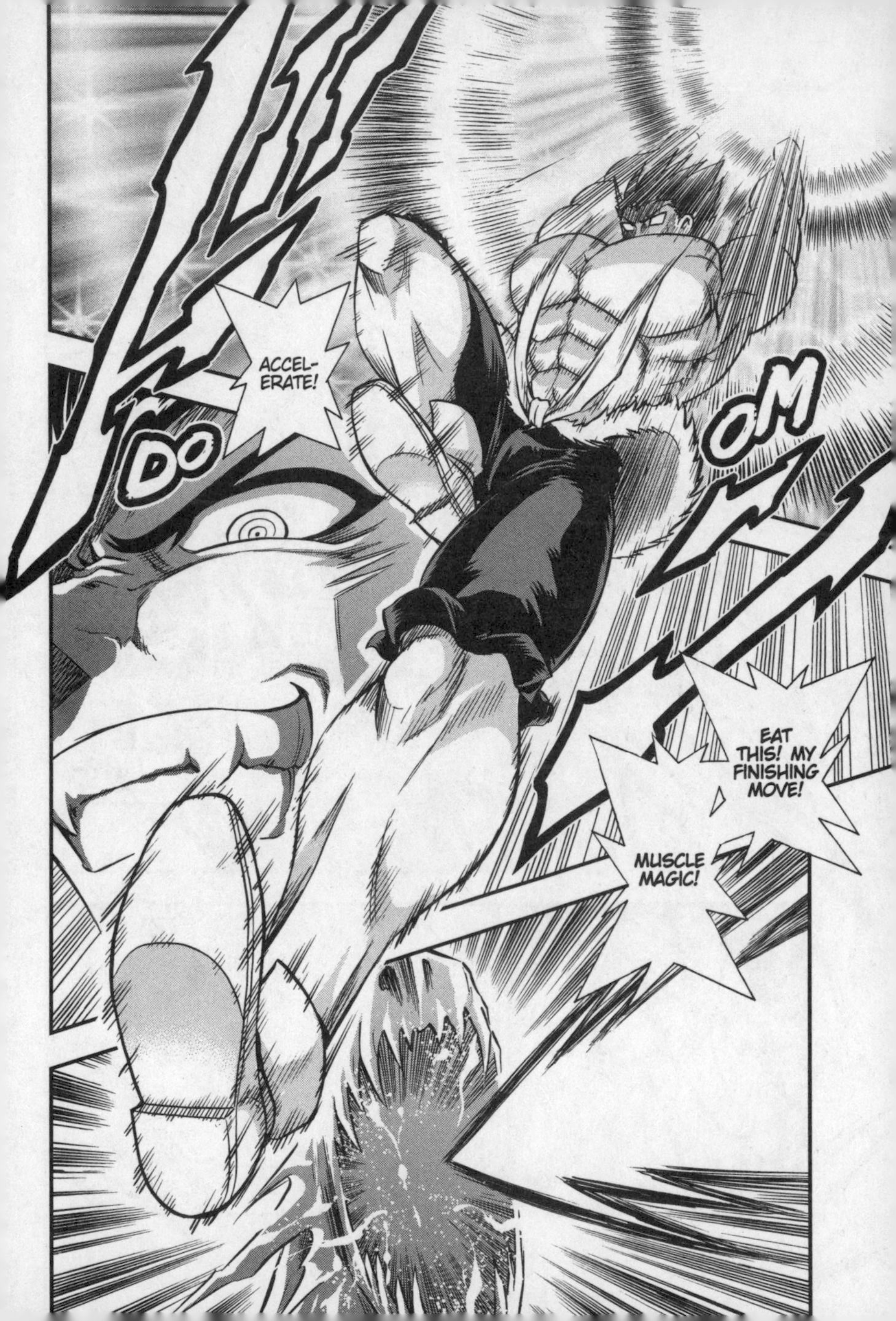
ACCEL-ERATE!
DO
OM
EAT THIS! MY FINISHING MOVE!
MUSCLE MAGIC!

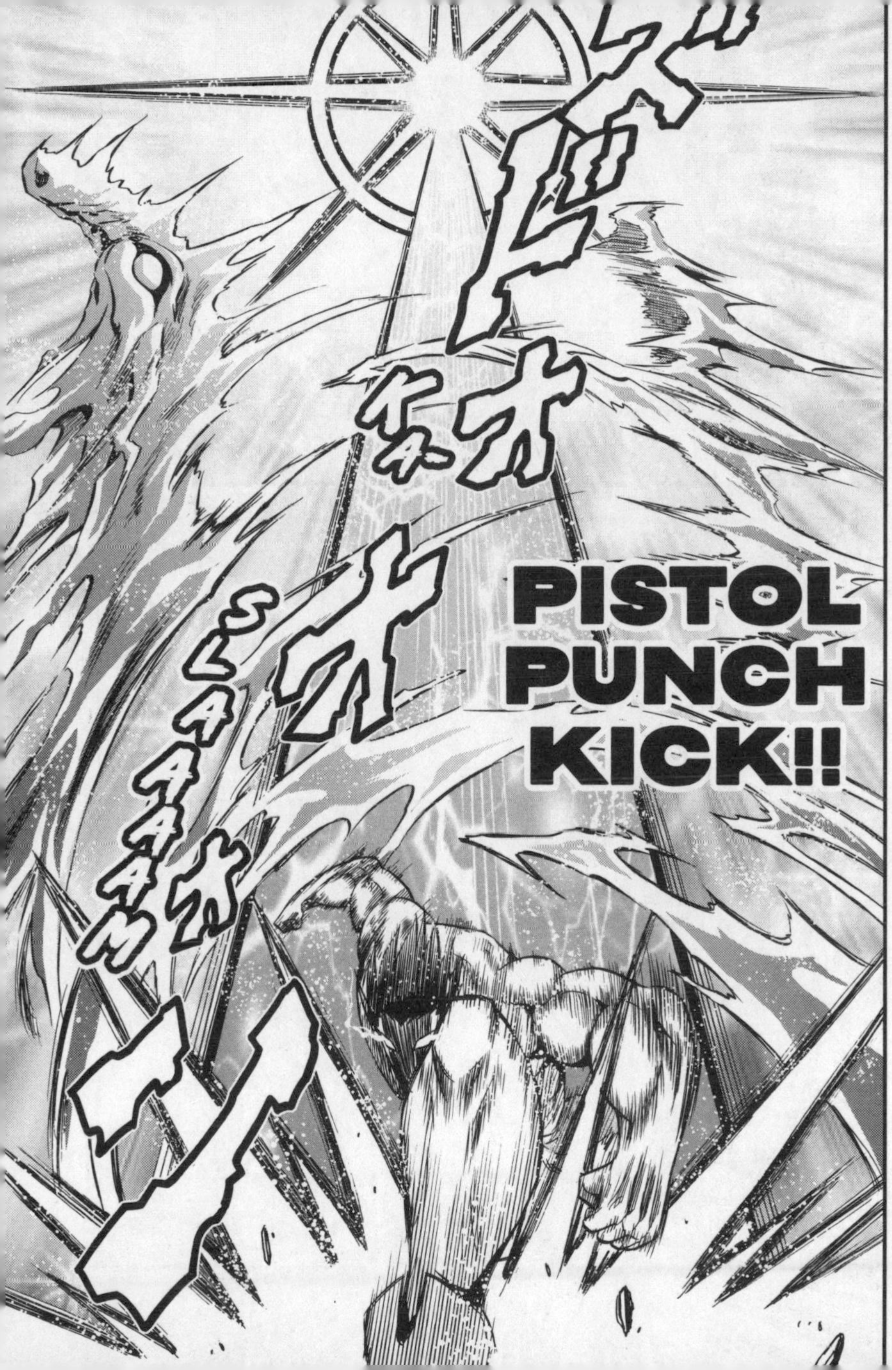
PISTOL PUNCH KICK!!
SLAAAAAM

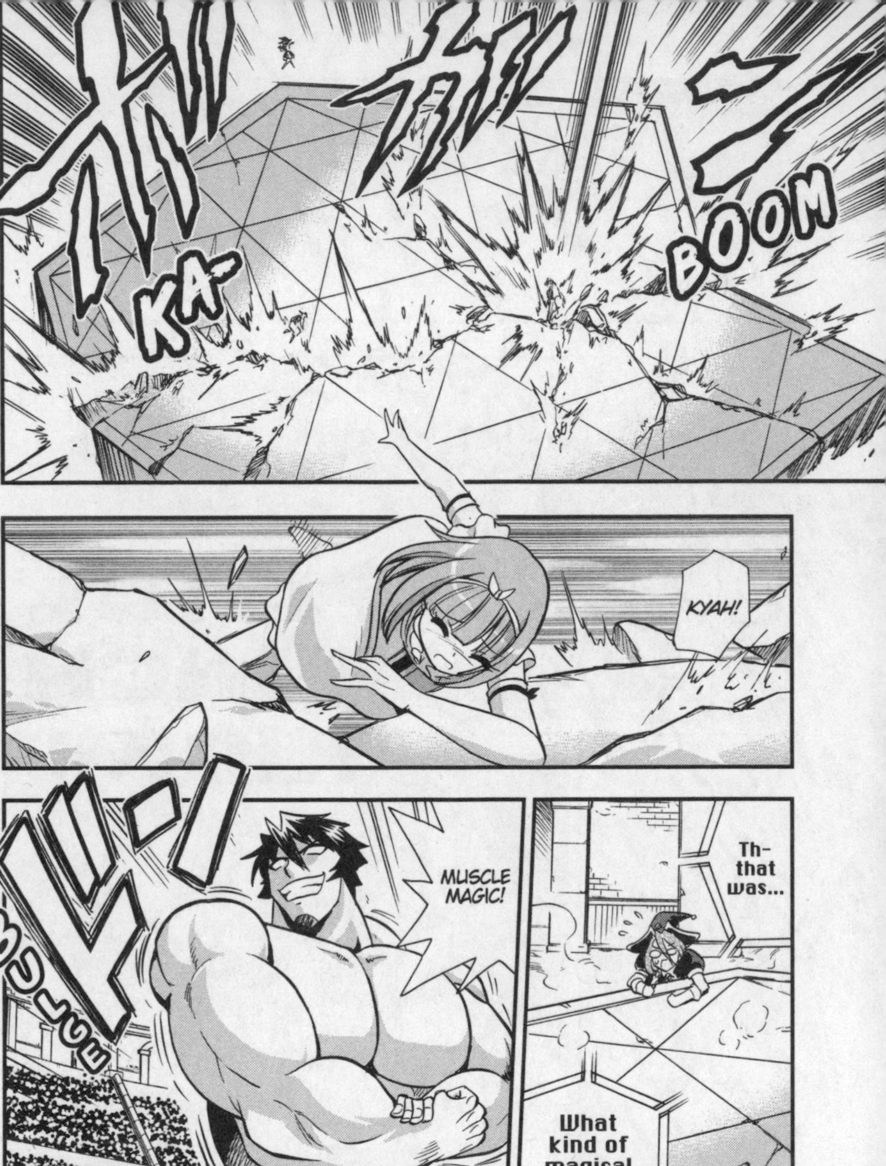
KA-BOOM
KYAH!
Th- that was...
What kind of magical power was that?!
MUSCLE MAGIC!
BULGE

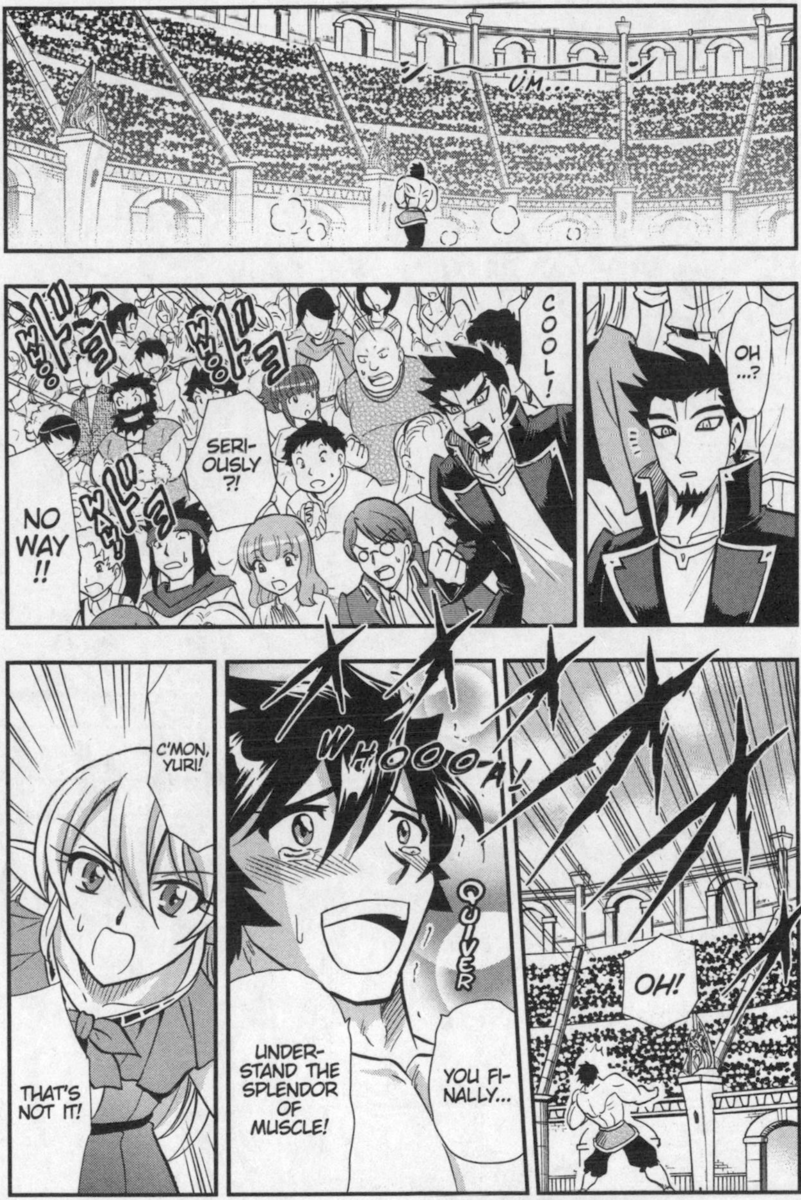
UM...
OH...?
COOL!
SERI-OUSLY?!
NO WAY!!
OH!
WHOOOO-A!
QUIVER
YOU FI-NALLY...
UNDER-STAND THE SPLENDOR OF MUSCLE!
C'MON, YURI!
THAT'S NOT IT!

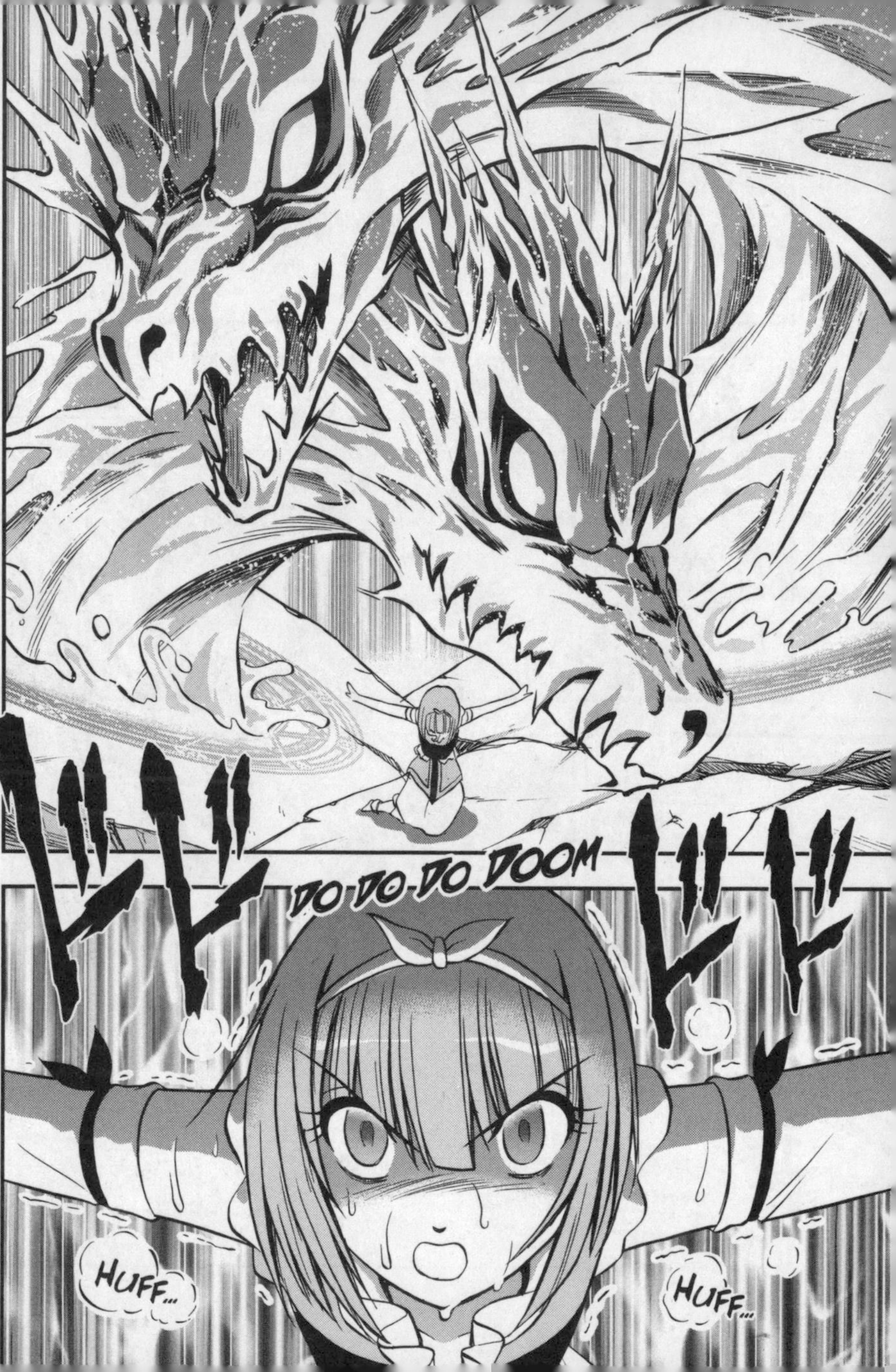
DO DO DO DOOM
HUFF...
HUFF...

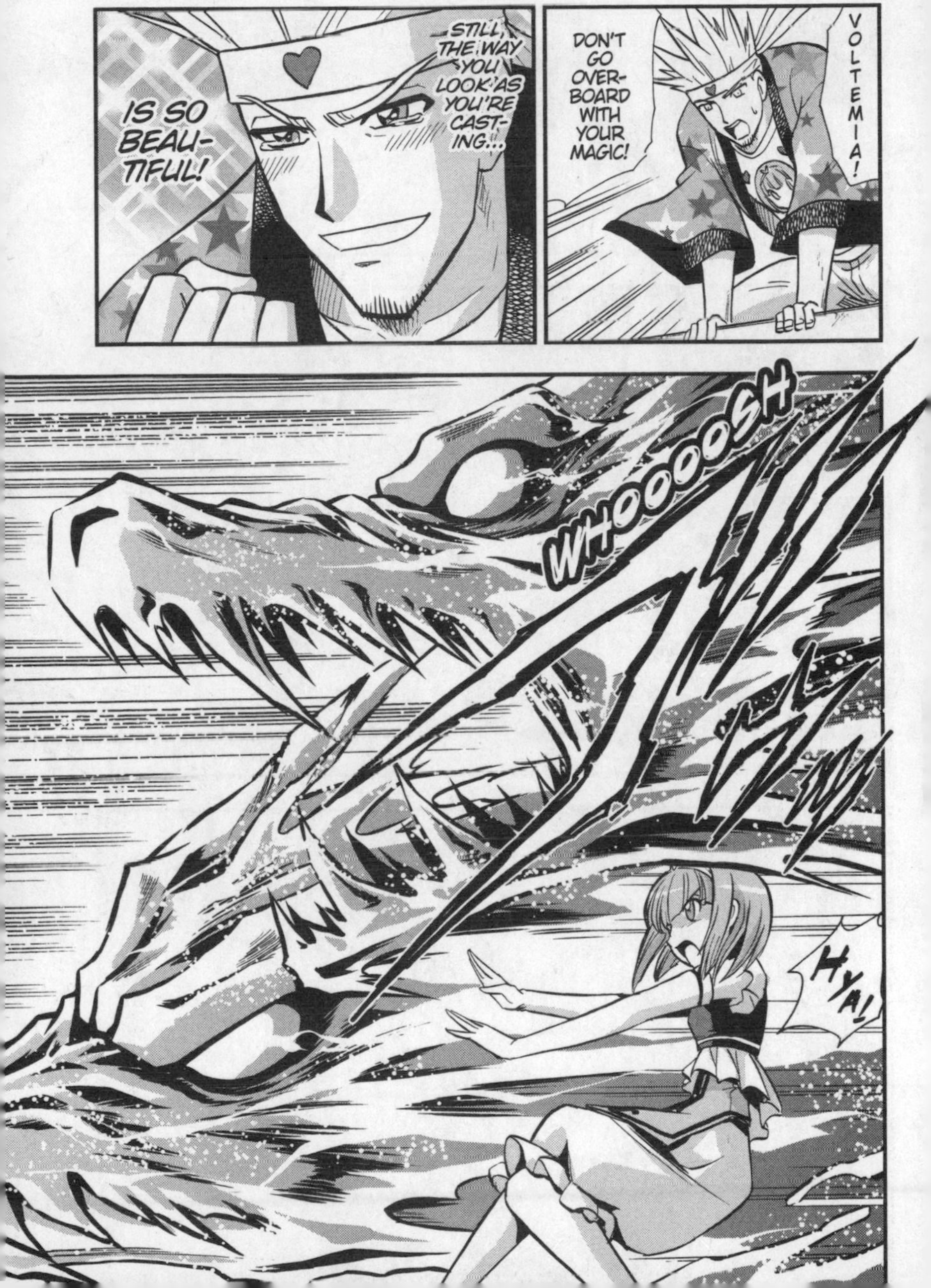
VOLTEMIA!
DON'T GO OVER-BOARD WITH YOUR MAGIC!
STILL, THE WAY YOU LOOK AS YOU'RE CAST-ING...
IS SO BEAU-TIFUL!
WHOOOOOSH
HYA!

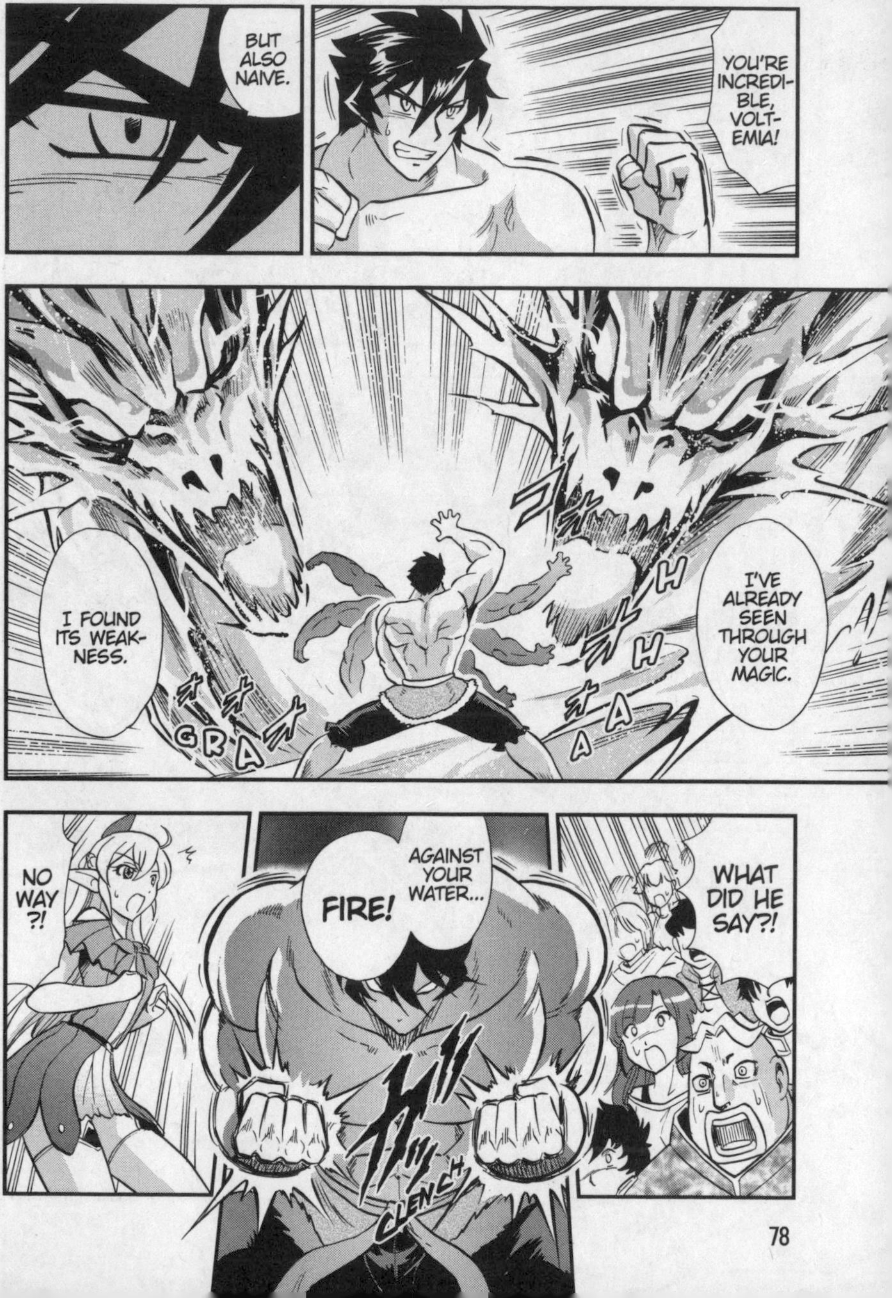
YOU'RE INCREDIBLE, VOLTEMIA!
BUT ALSO NAIVE.
I'VE ALREADY SEEN THROUGH YOUR MAGIC.
HAAAH
I FOUND ITS WEAKNESS.
GRAA
WHAT DID HE SAY?!
AGAINST YOUR WATER...
FIRE!
CLENCH
NO WAY?!

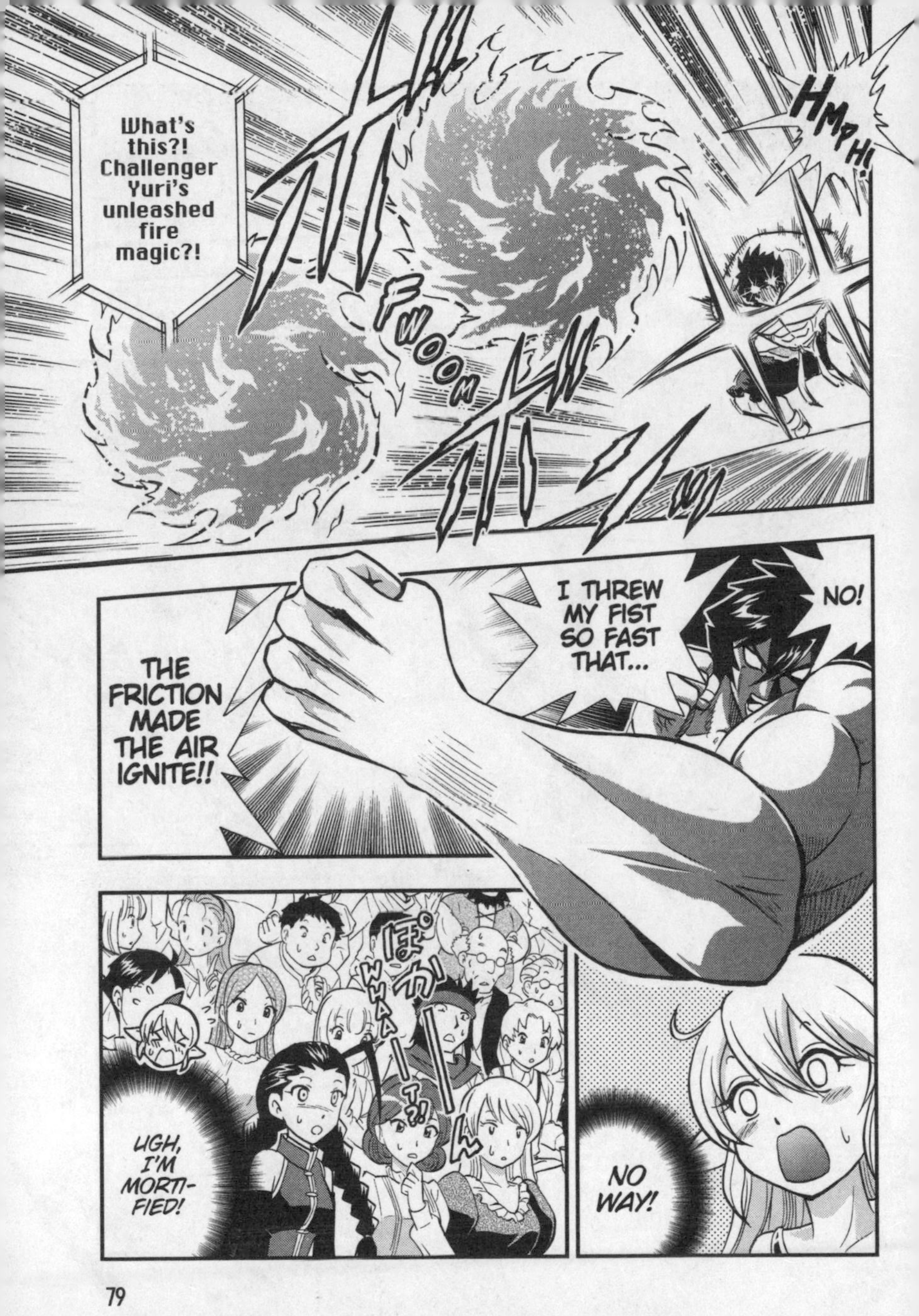
HMPH!
What's this?! Challenger Yuri's unleashed fire magic?!
FWOOOM
NO!
I THREW MY FIST SO FAST THAT...
THE FRICTION MADE THE AIR IGNITE!!
NO WAY!
ぽかーん
WHAA—T?!
UGH, I'M MORTI-FIED!

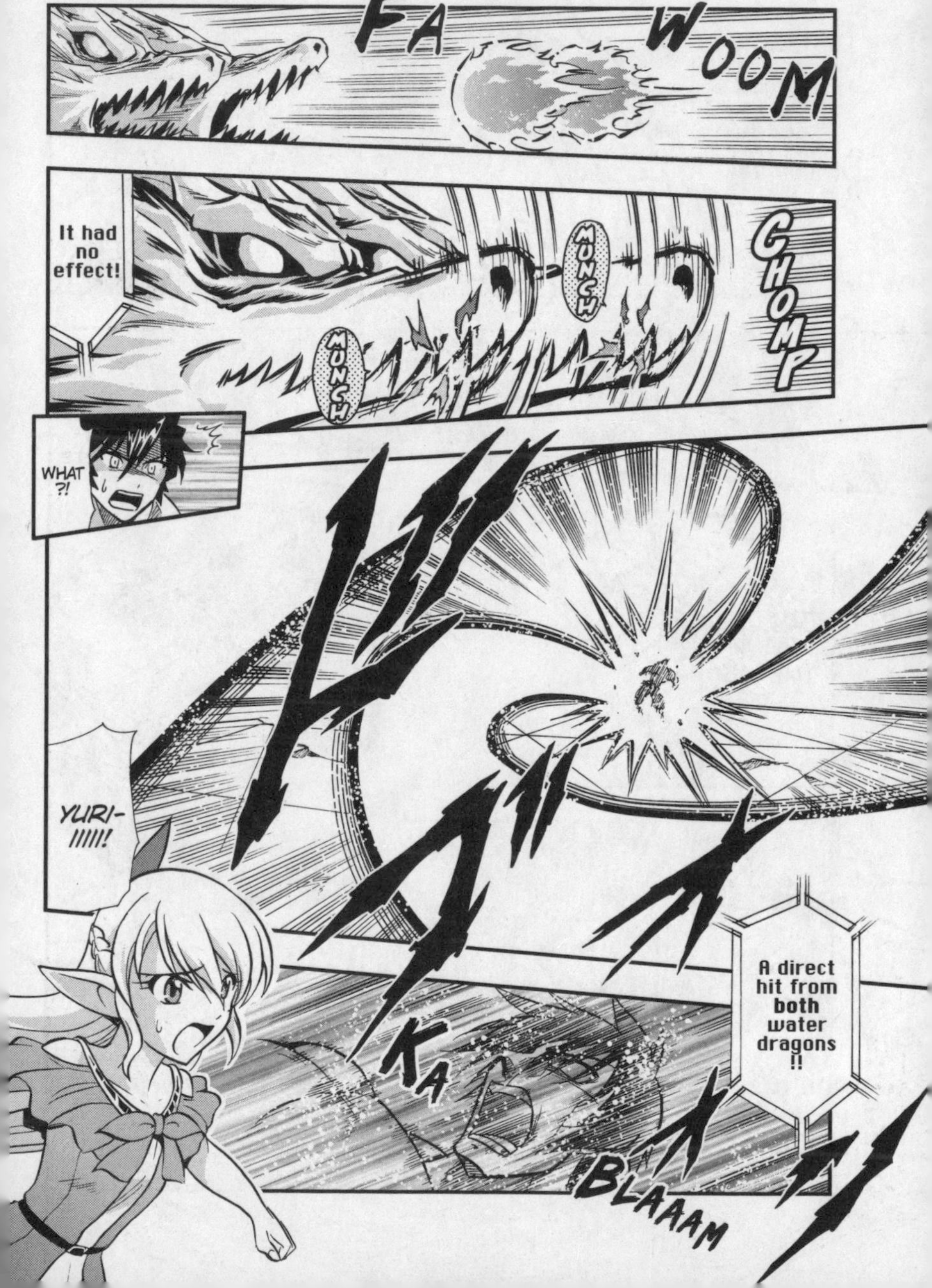
FA WOOM
CHOMP
MUNCH
MUNCH
It had no effect!
WHAT?!
A direct hit from both water dragons!!
KA
BLAAAM
YURI-IIIIII!

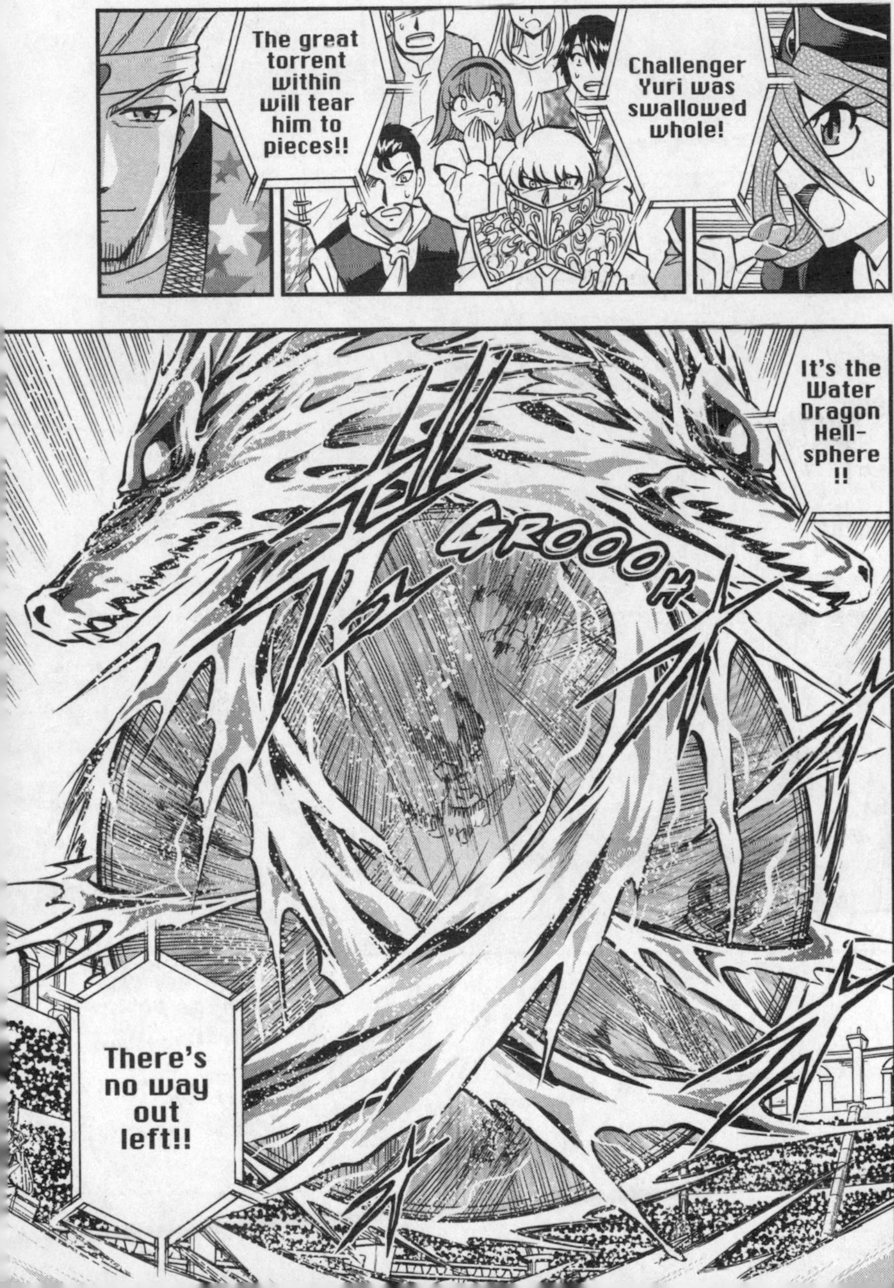
Challenger Yuri was swallowed whole!
The great torrent within will tear him to pieces!!
It's the Water Dragon Hell-sphere!!
GROOOOH
There's no way out left!!

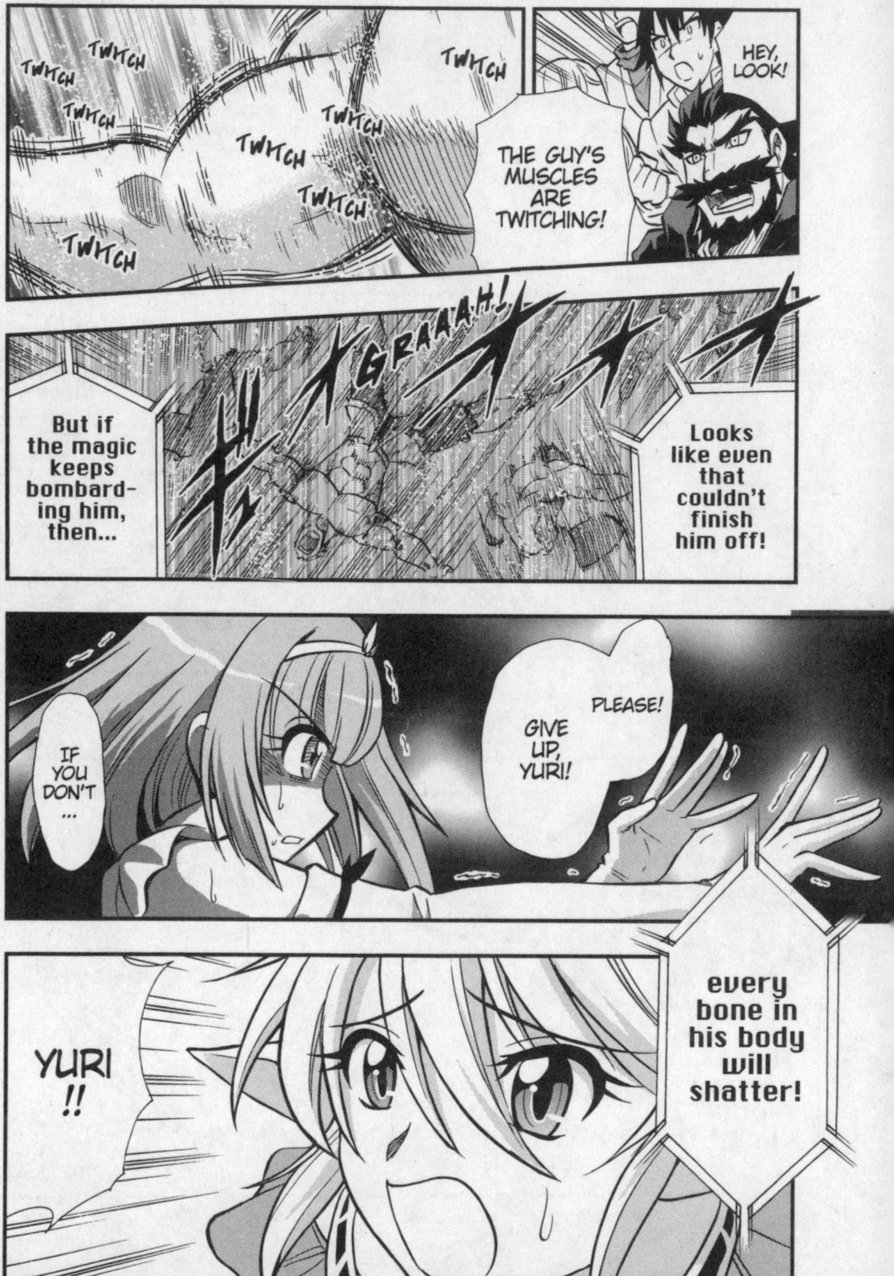
HEY, LOOK!
THE GUY'S MUSCLES ARE TWITCHING!
TWITCH
TWITCH
TWITCH
TWITCH
TWITCH
TWITCH
TWITCH
Looks like even that couldn't finish him off!
GRAAAAH!
But if the magic keeps bombard-ing him, then...
PLEASE!
GIVE UP, YURI!
IF YOU DON'T ...
every bone in his body will shatter!
YURI !!

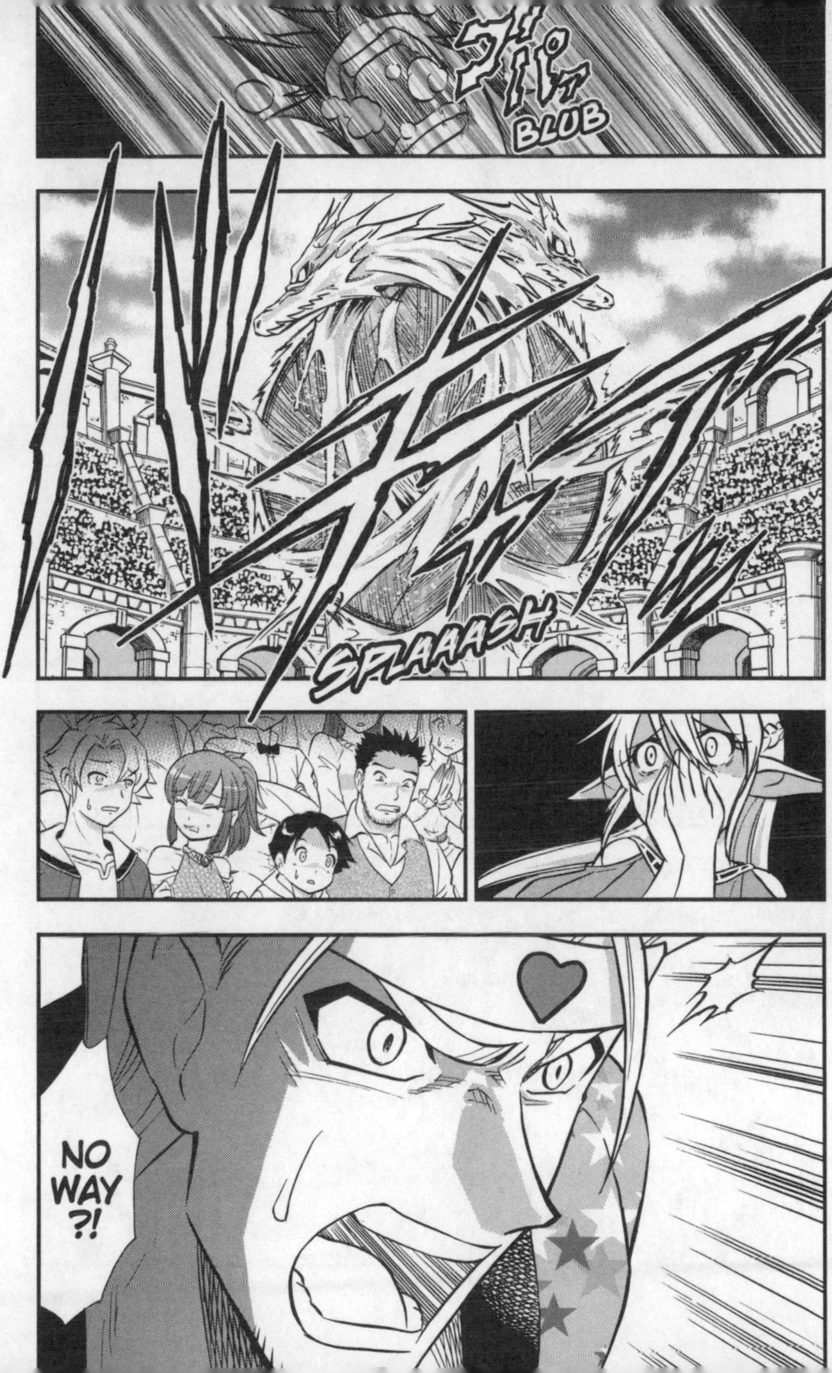

ゴパァ
BLUB
ズバシャァァッ
SPLAAASH
NO WAY?!

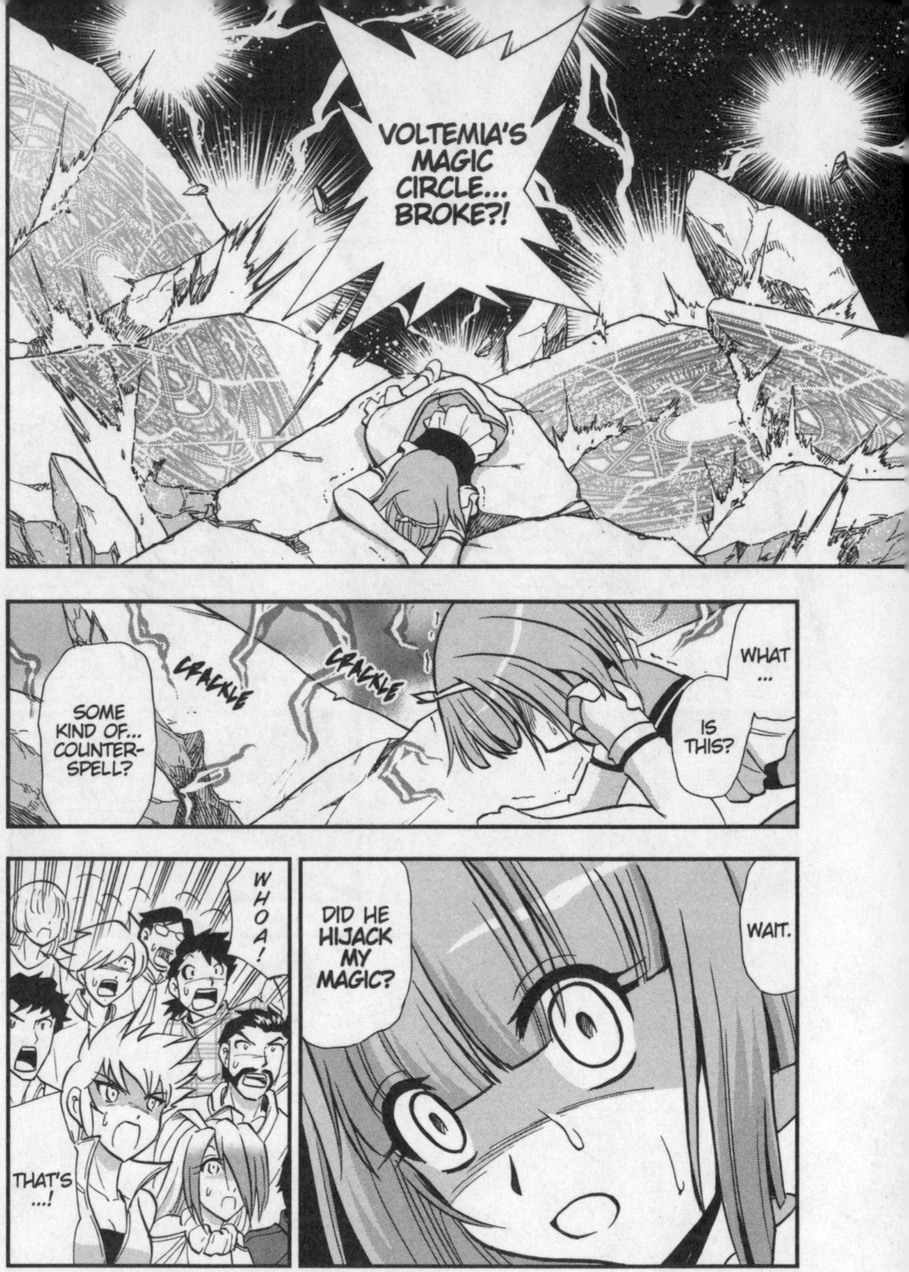
VOLTEMIA'S MAGIC CIRCLE... BROKE?!
WHAT ... IS THIS?
CRACKLE
CRACKLE
SOME KIND OF... COUNTER-SPELL?
WAIT.
DID HE HIJACK MY MAGIC?
WHOA!
THAT'S ...!

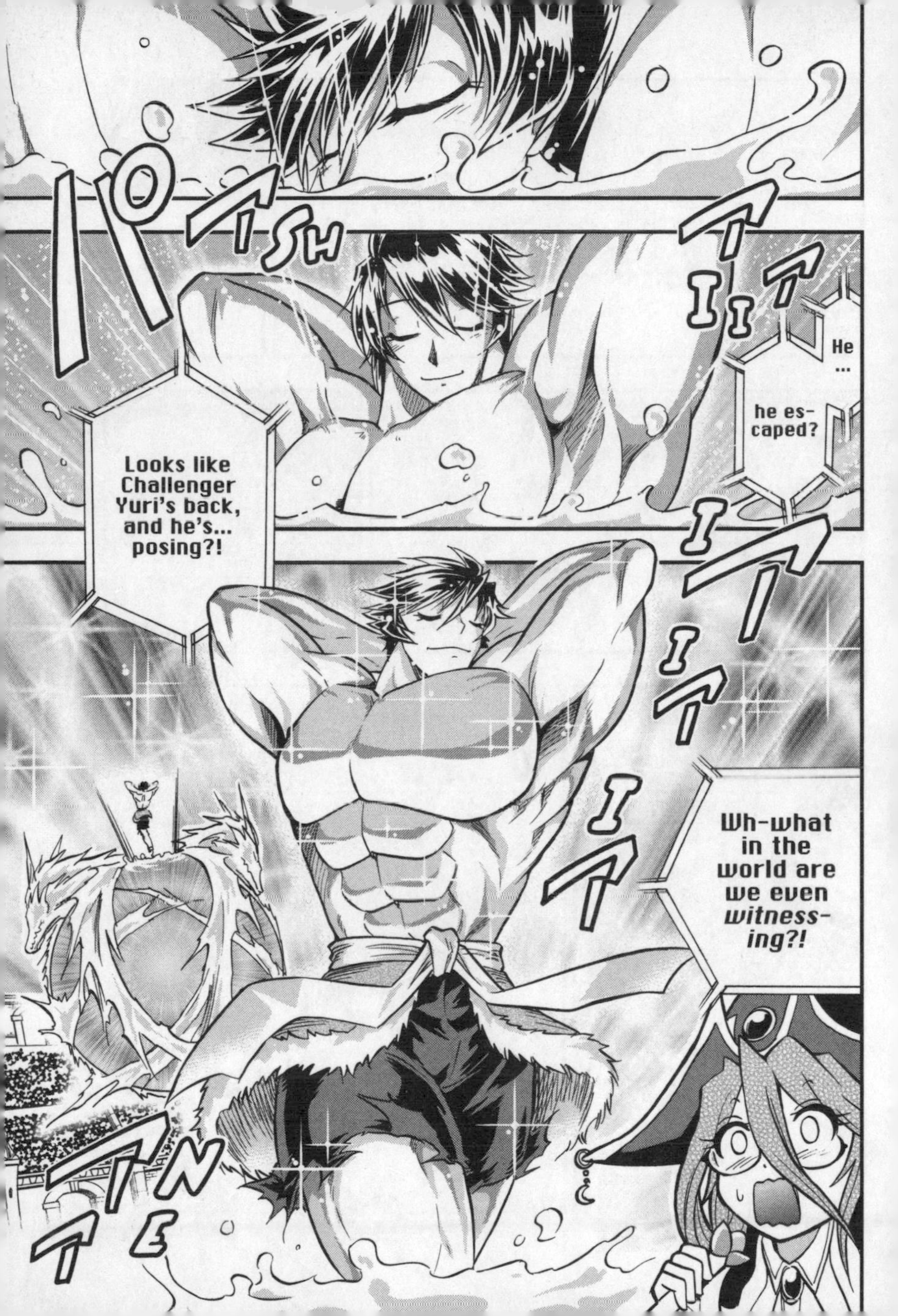
He... he escaped?
Looks like Challenger Yuri's back, and he's... posing?!
Wh-what in the world are we even *witnessing*?!

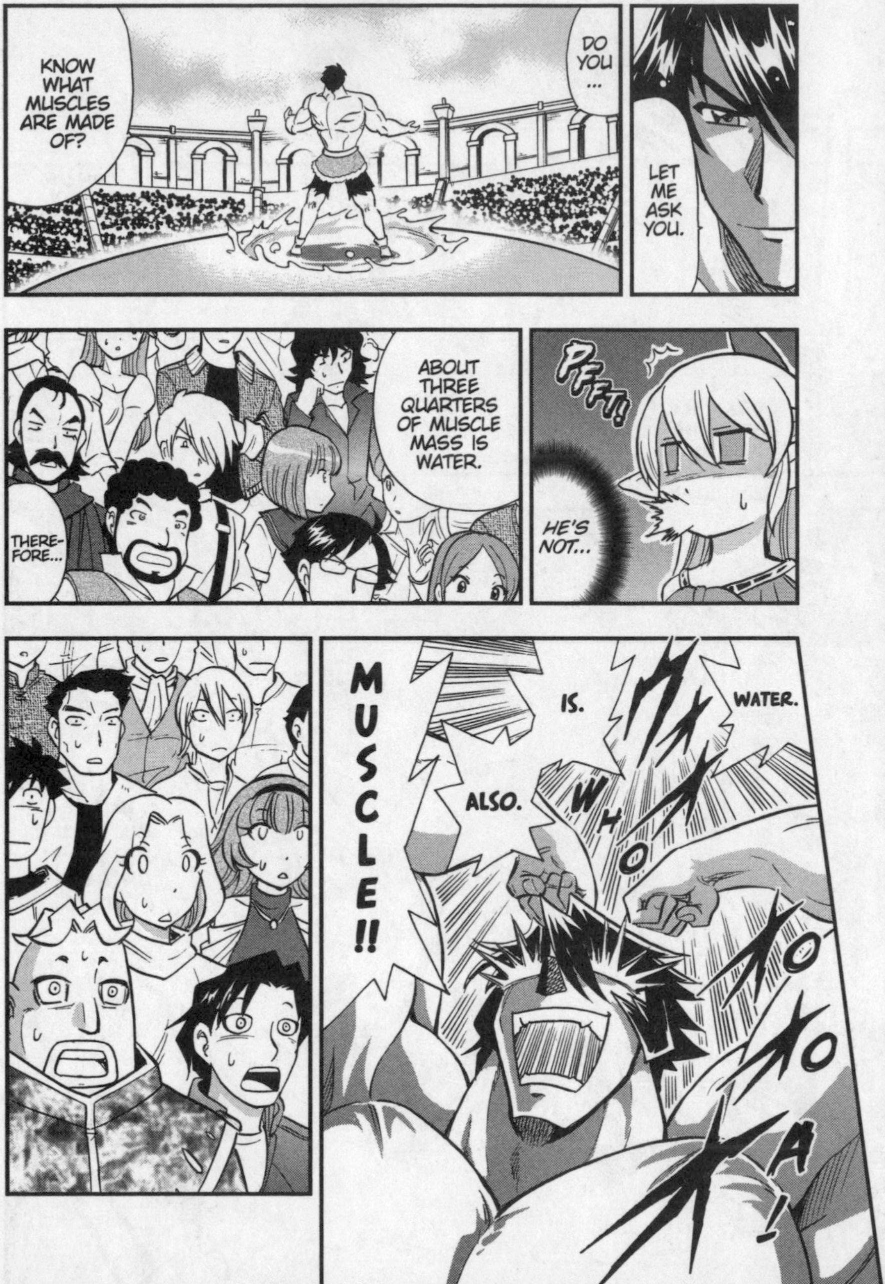
LET ME ASK YOU.
DO YOU ...
KNOW WHAT MUSCLES ARE MADE OF?
PFFT!!
HE'S NOT...
ABOUT THREE QUARTERS OF MUSCLE MASS IS WATER.
THEREFORE...
WATER.
IS.
WHOOOA!
ALSO.
MUSCLE!!

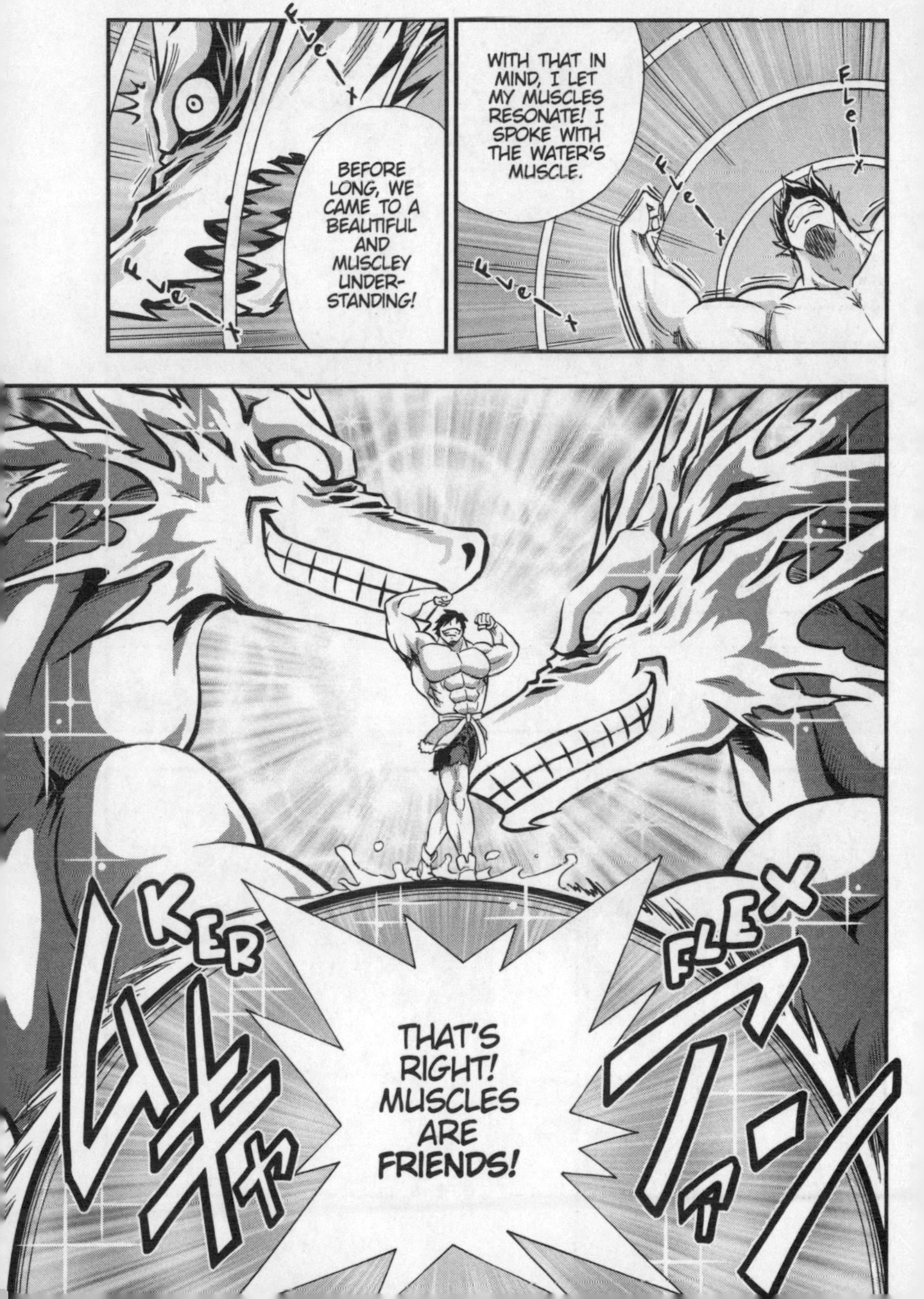
Flex
Flex
Flex
WITH THAT IN MIND, I LET MY MUSCLES RESONATE! I SPOKE WITH THE WATER'S MUSCLE.
Flex
Flex
BEFORE LONG, WE CAME TO A BEAUTIFUL AND MUSCLEY UNDER-STANDING!
KER
FLEX
THAT'S RIGHT! MUSCLES ARE FRIENDS!

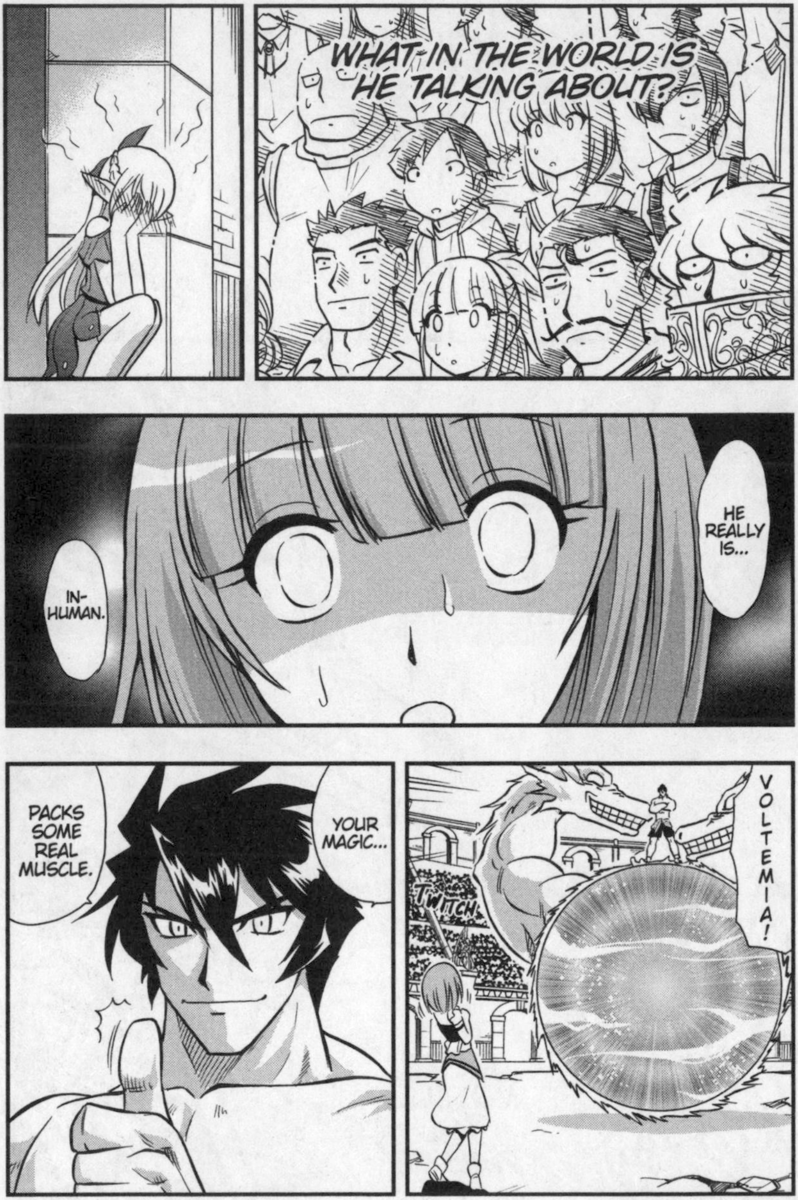

WHAT IN THE WORLD IS HE TALKING ABOUT?
HE REALLY IS...
IN-HUMAN.
VOLTEMIA!
TWITCH
YOUR MAGIC...
PACKS SOME REAL MUSCLE.

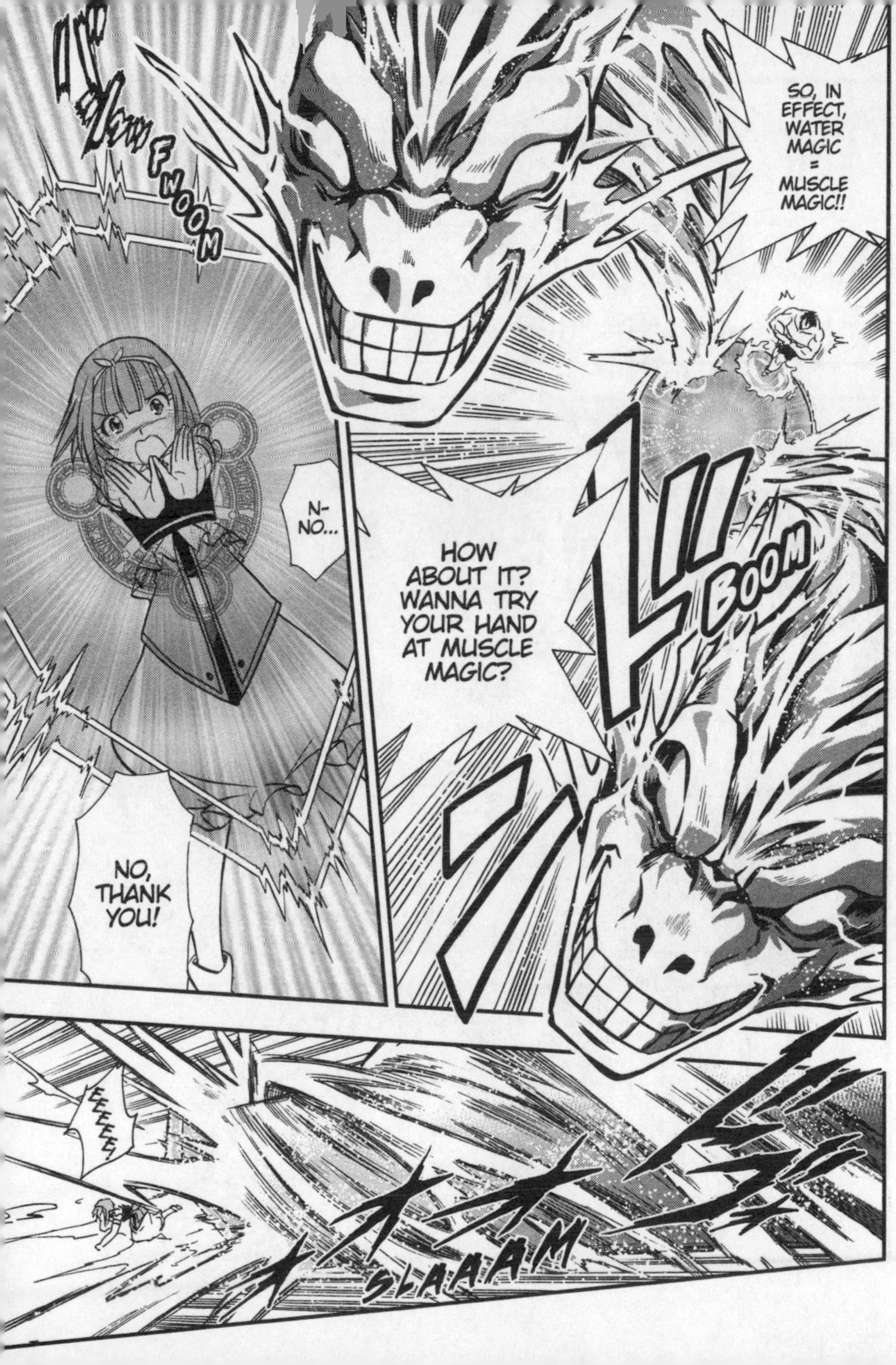
SO, IN EFFECT, WATER MAGIC = MUSCLE MAGIC!!
HOW ABOUT IT? WANNA TRY YOUR HAND AT MUSCLE MAGIC?
BOOM
FWOOM
N-NO...
NO, THANK YOU!
EEEEEE!
SLAAAM

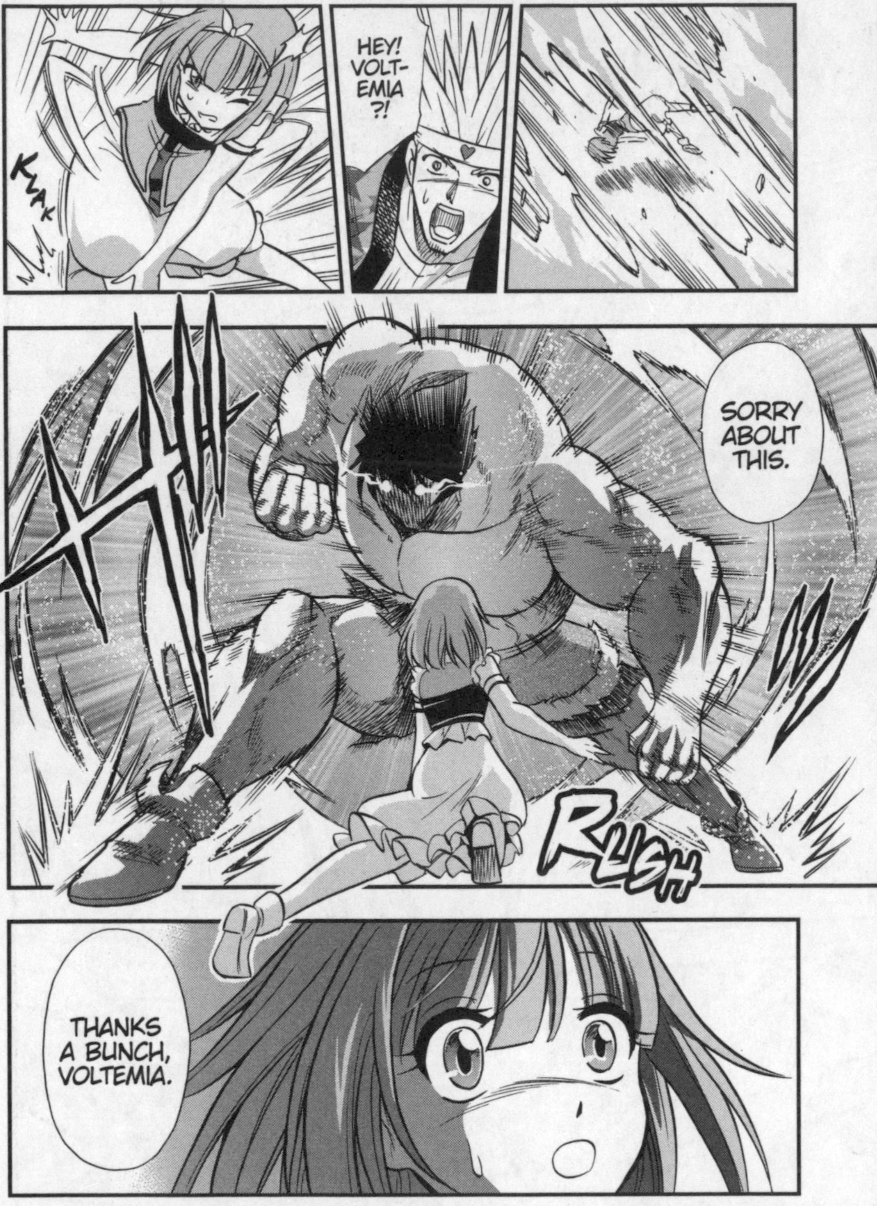
HEY! VOLT-EMIA ?!
KLAK
SORRY ABOUT THIS.
RUSH
THANKS A BUNCH, VOLTEMIA.

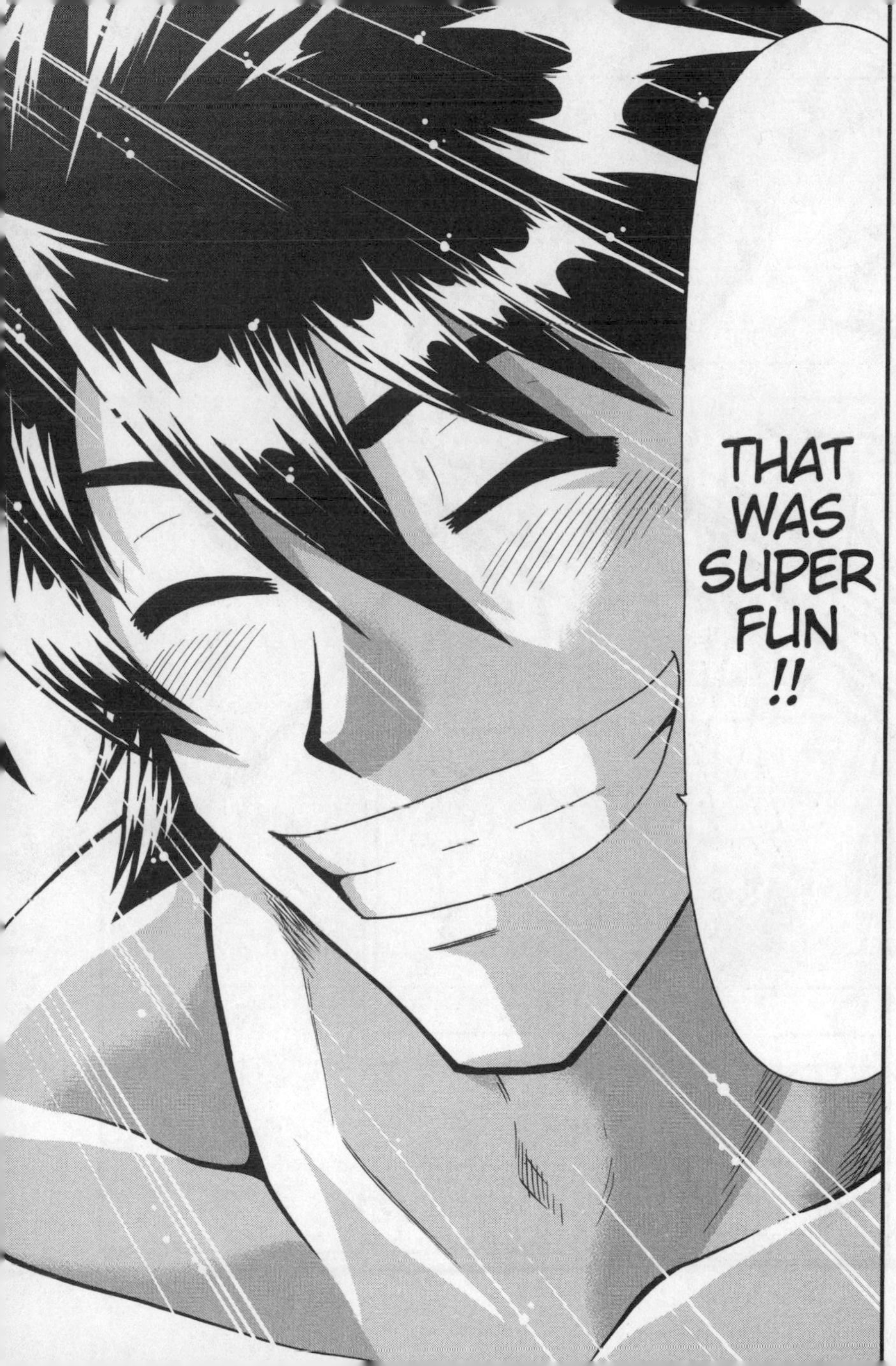
THAT WAS SUPER FUN !!

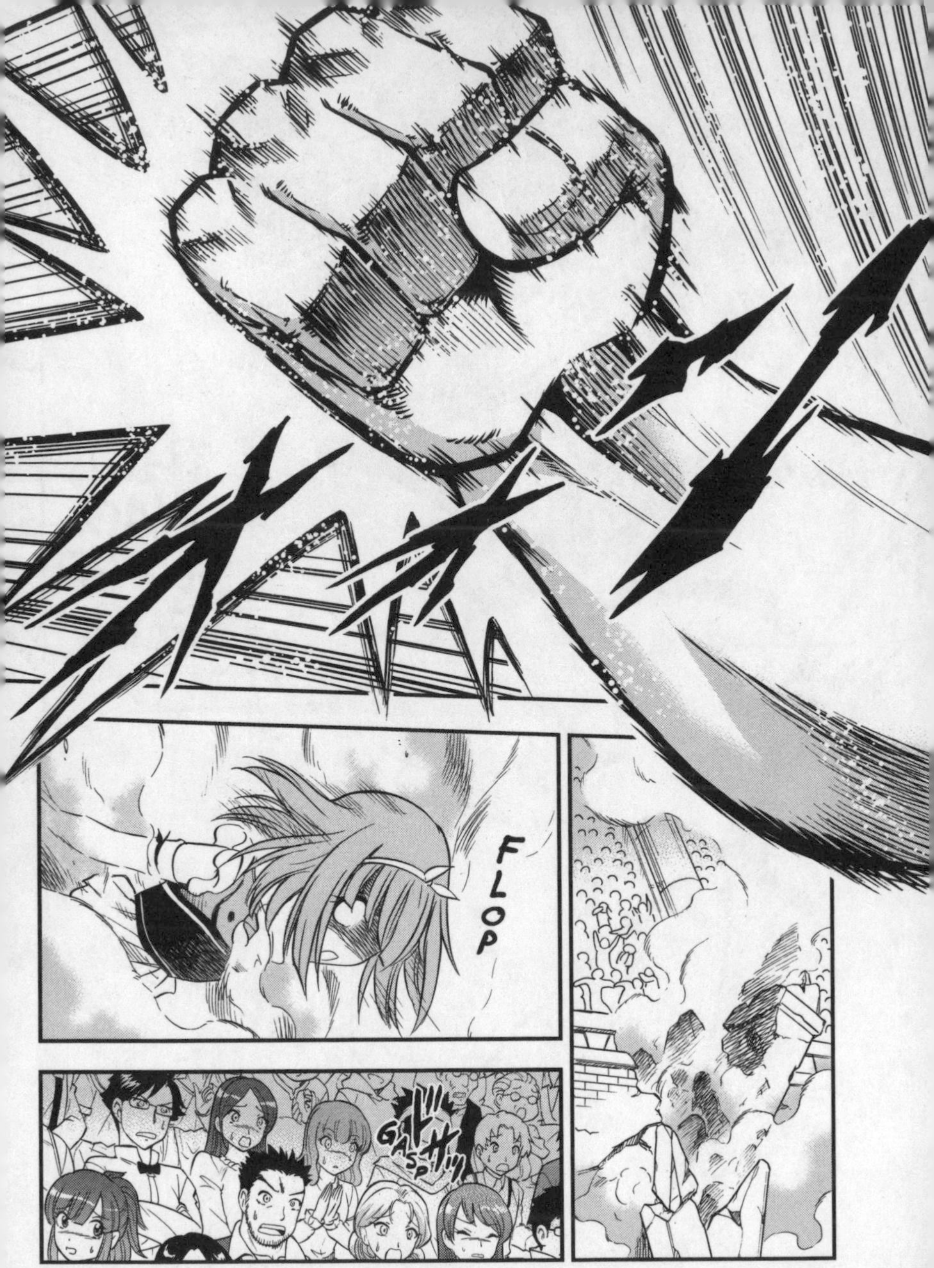
FLOP
GASP!!

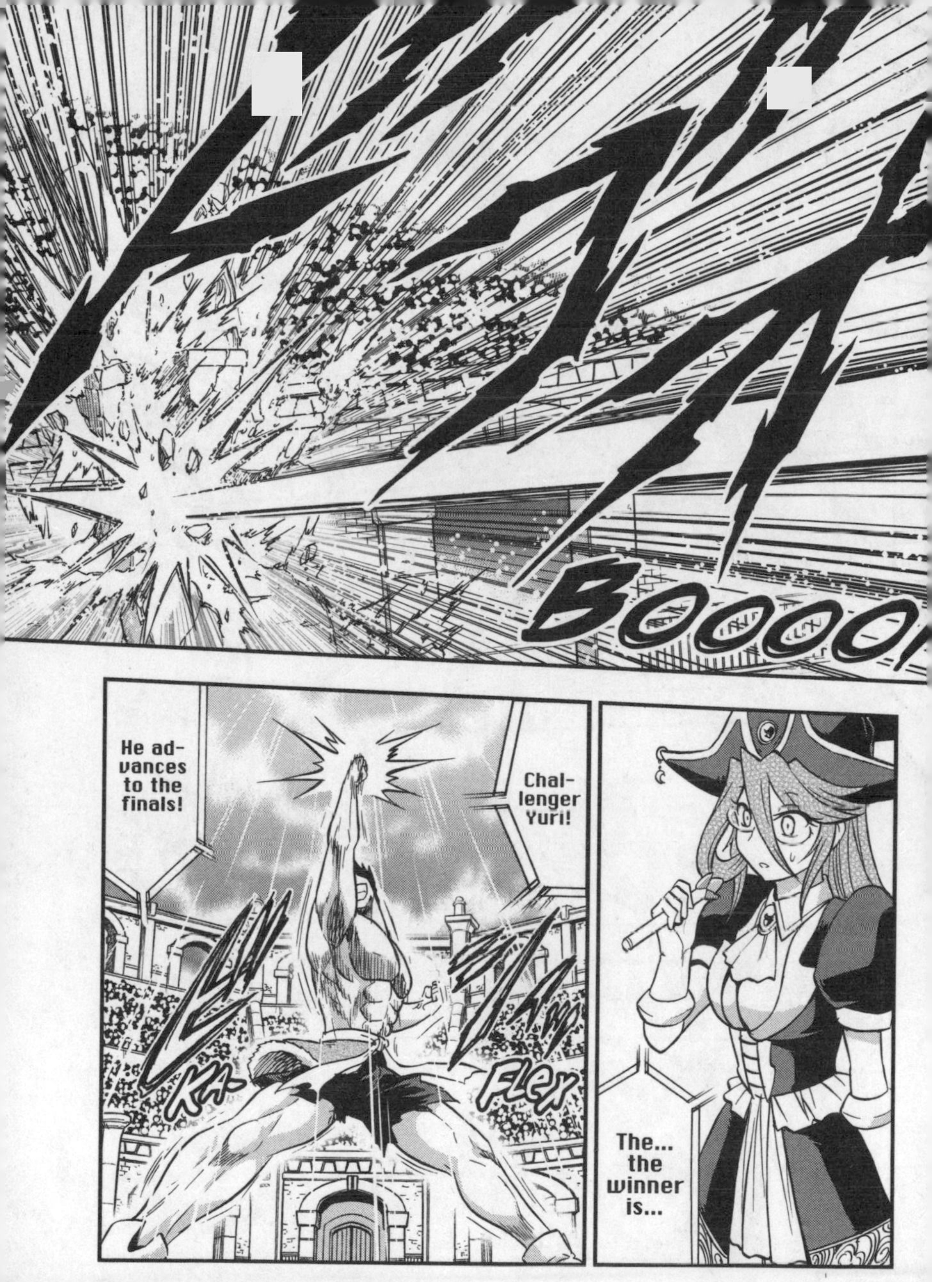
BOOOO
The... the winner is...
Chal-lenger Yuri!
He ad-vances to the finals!
Flex
KA

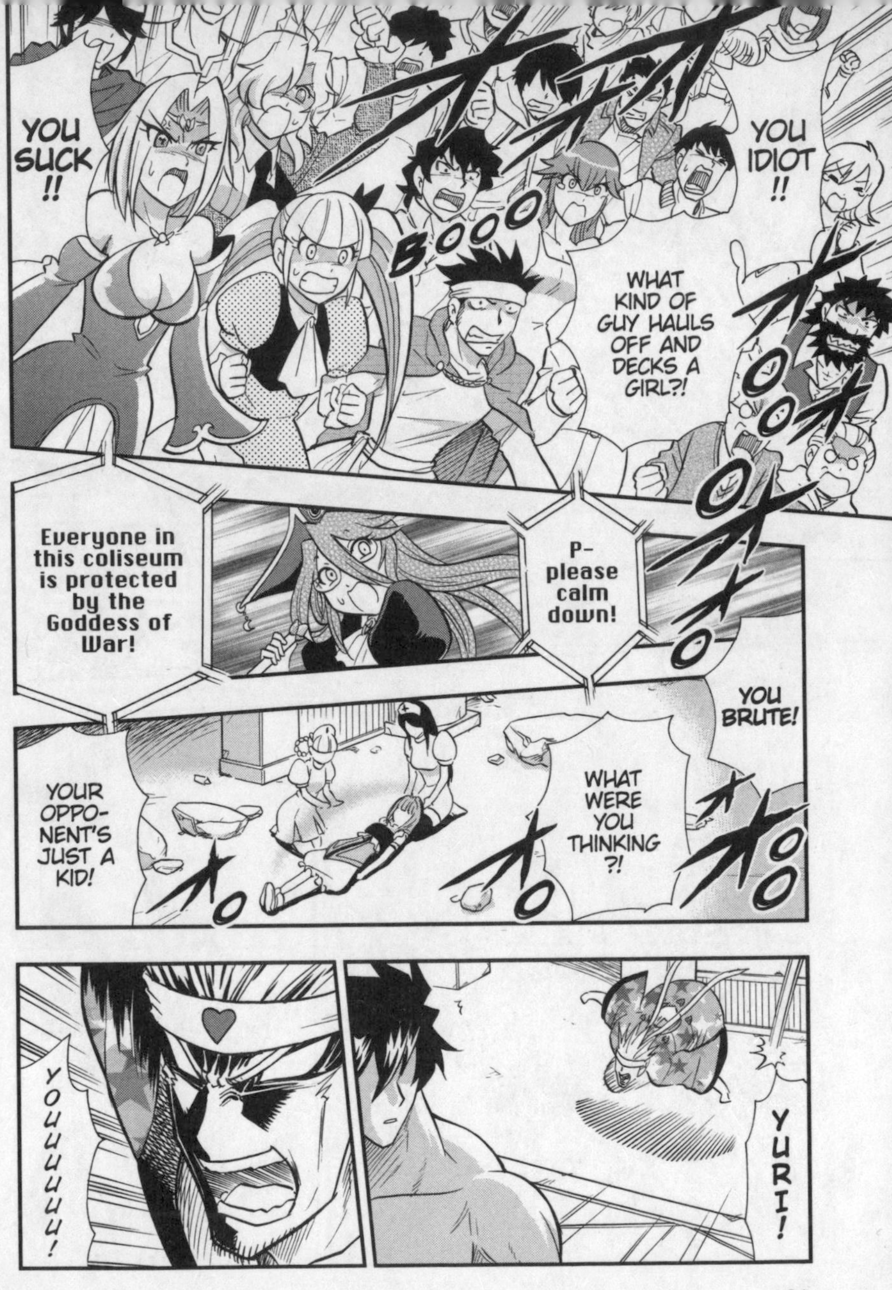
YOU IDIOT!!
WHAT KIND OF GUY HAULS OFF AND DECKS A GIRL?!
BOOO
YOU SUCK!!
P-please calm down!
Everyone in this coliseum is protected by the Goddess of War!
YOU BRUTE!
WHAT WERE YOU THINKING?!
YOUR OPPONENT'S JUST A KID!
YURI!
YOUUUUUUU!

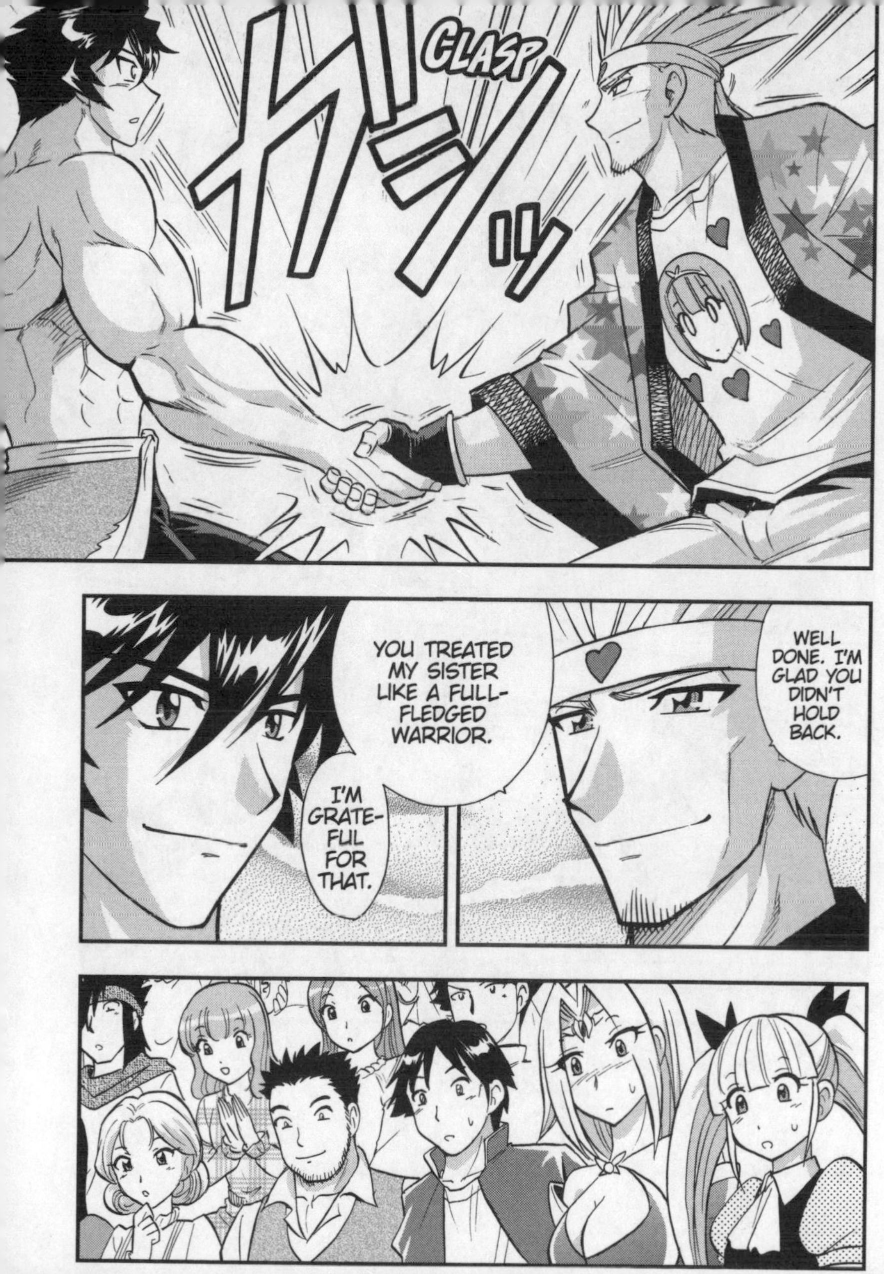
CLASP
WELL DONE. I'M GLAD YOU DIDN'T HOLD BACK.
YOU TREATED MY SISTER LIKE A FULL-FLEDGED WARRIOR.
I'M GRATE-FUL FOR THAT.

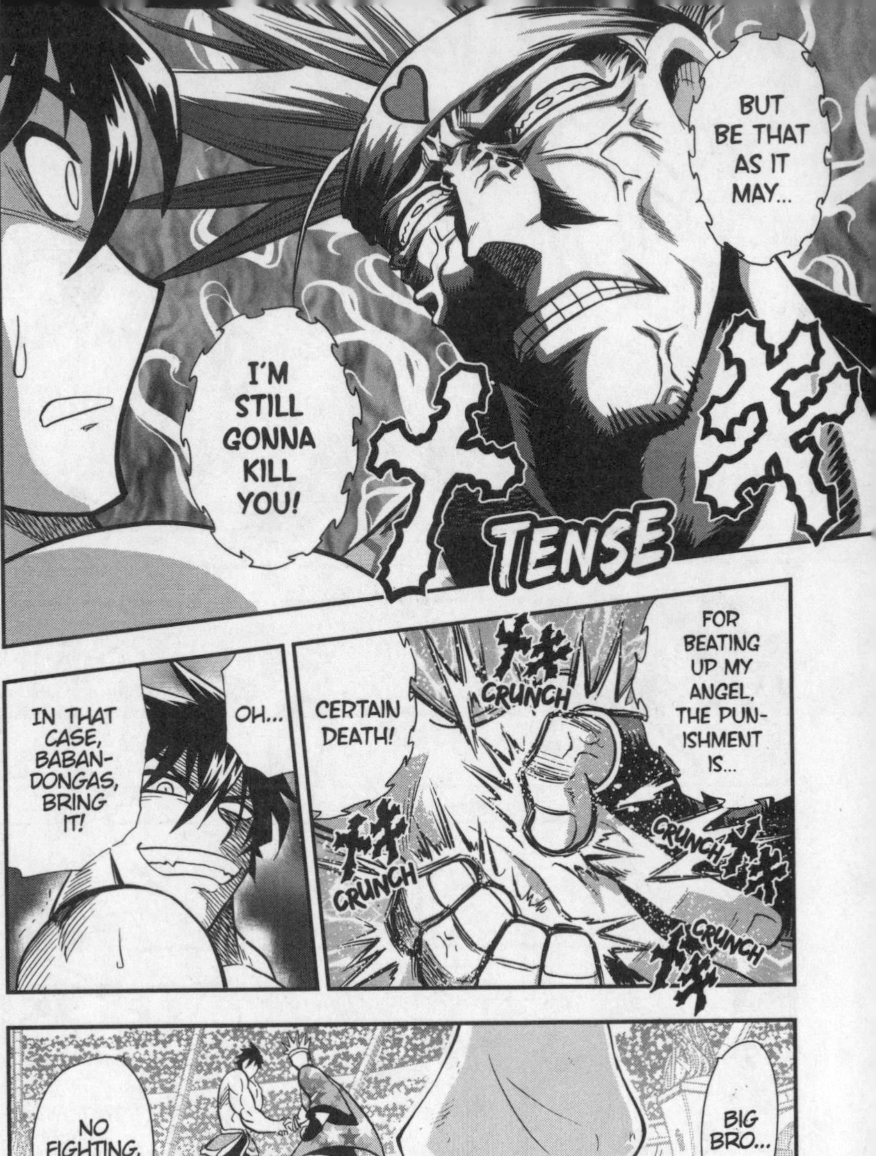
BUT BE THAT AS IT MAY...
I'M STILL GONNA KILL YOU!
TENSE
FOR BEATING UP MY ANGEL, THE PUNISHMENT IS...
CRUNCH
CRUNCH
CRUNCH
CRUNCH
CERTAIN DEATH!
OH...
IN THAT CASE, BABANDONGAS, BRING IT!
BIG BRO...
NO FIGHTING, OKAY?

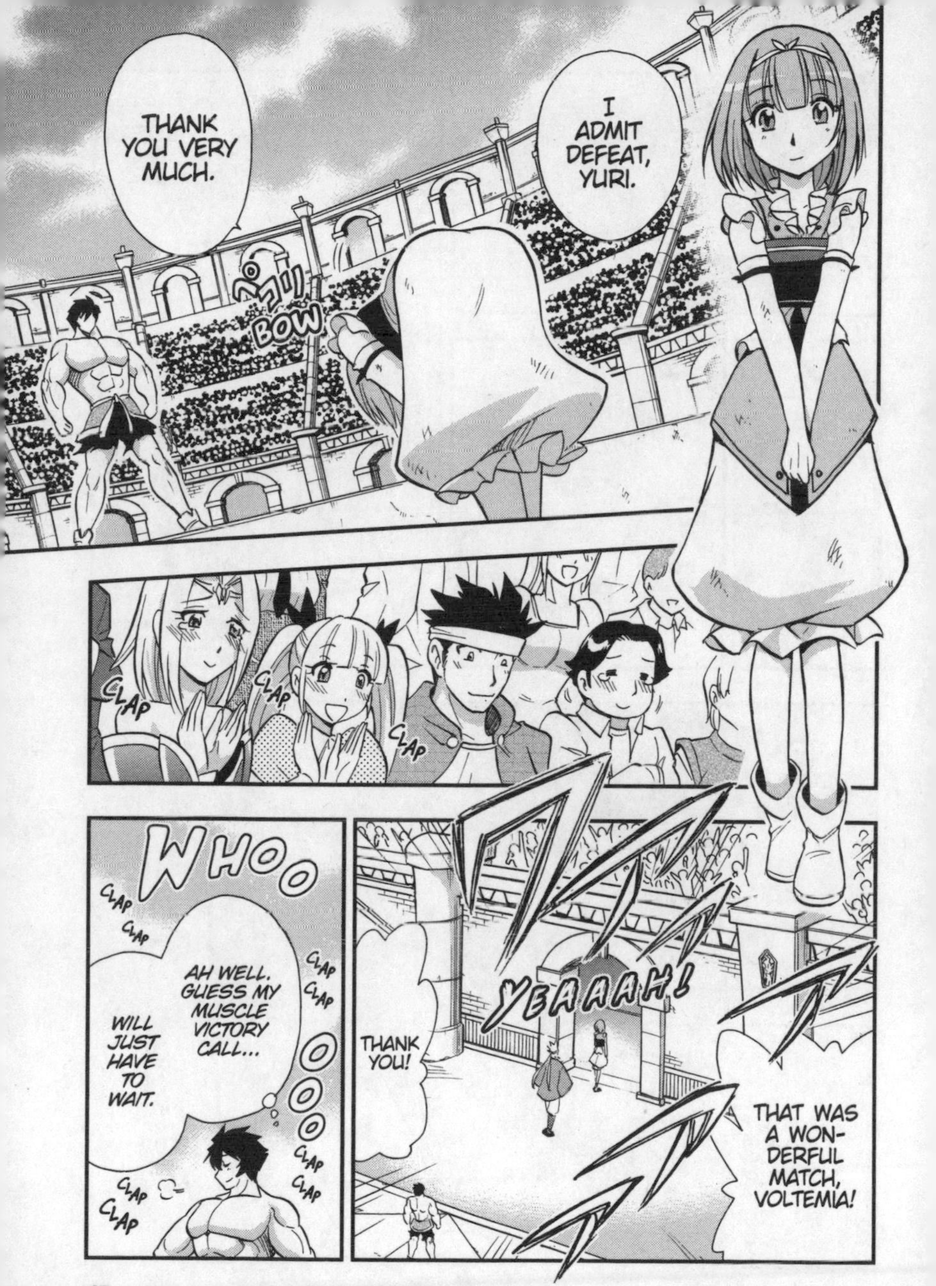
I ADMIT DEFEAT, YURI.
THANK YOU VERY MUCH.
BOW
CLAP
CLAP
CLAP
WHOOOOOOO
CLAP CLAP
CLAP CLAP
AH WELL. GUESS MY MUSCLE VICTORY CALL...
WILL JUST HAVE TO WAIT.
CLAP CLAP
CLAP CLAP
YEAAAAH!
THANK YOU!
THAT WAS A WON-DERFUL MATCH, VOLTEMIA!

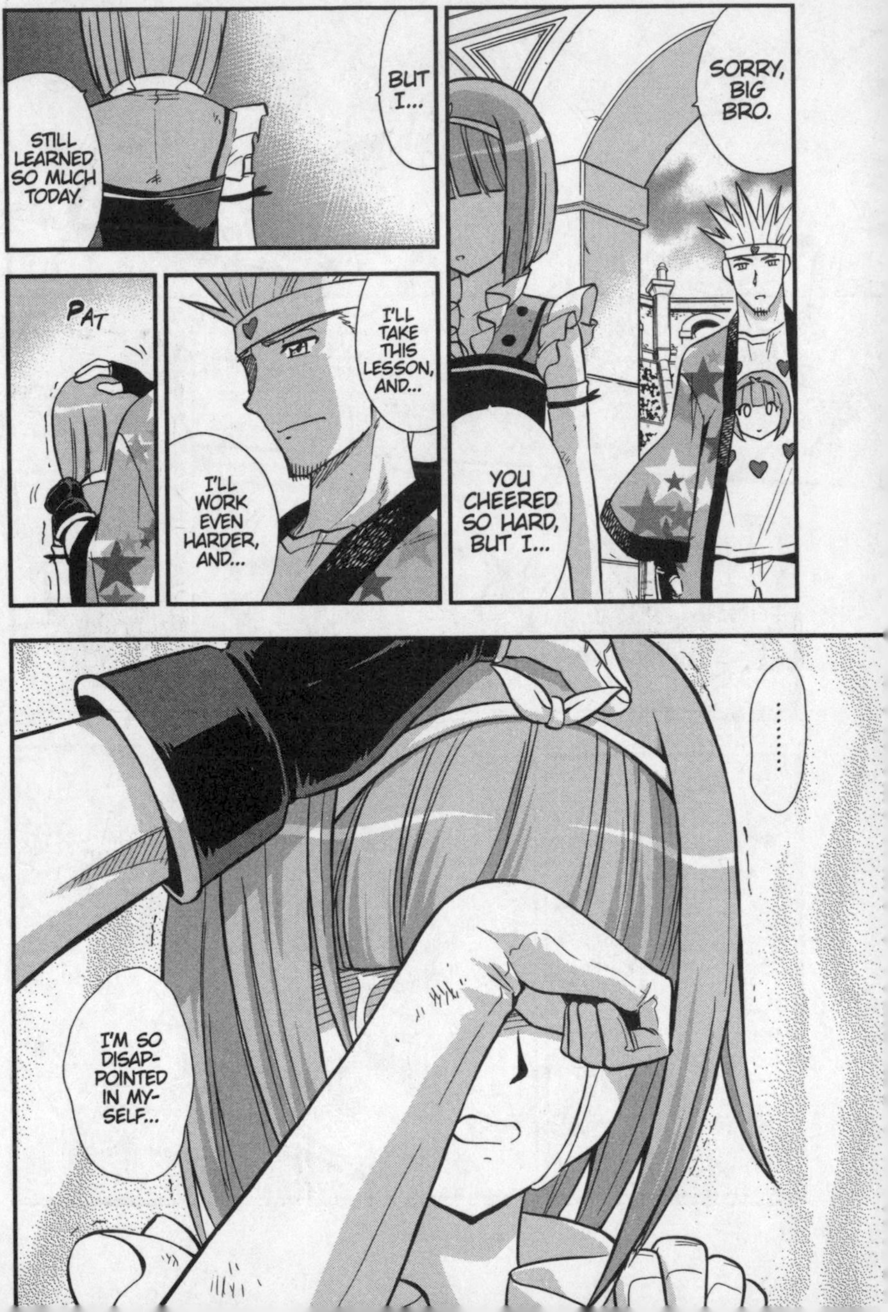
SORRY, BIG BRO.
YOU CHEERED SO HARD, BUT I...
BUT I...
STILL LEARNED SO MUCH TODAY.
I'LL TAKE THIS LESSON, AND...
I'LL WORK EVEN HARDER, AND...
PAT
......
I'M SO DISAP-POINTED IN MY-SELF...

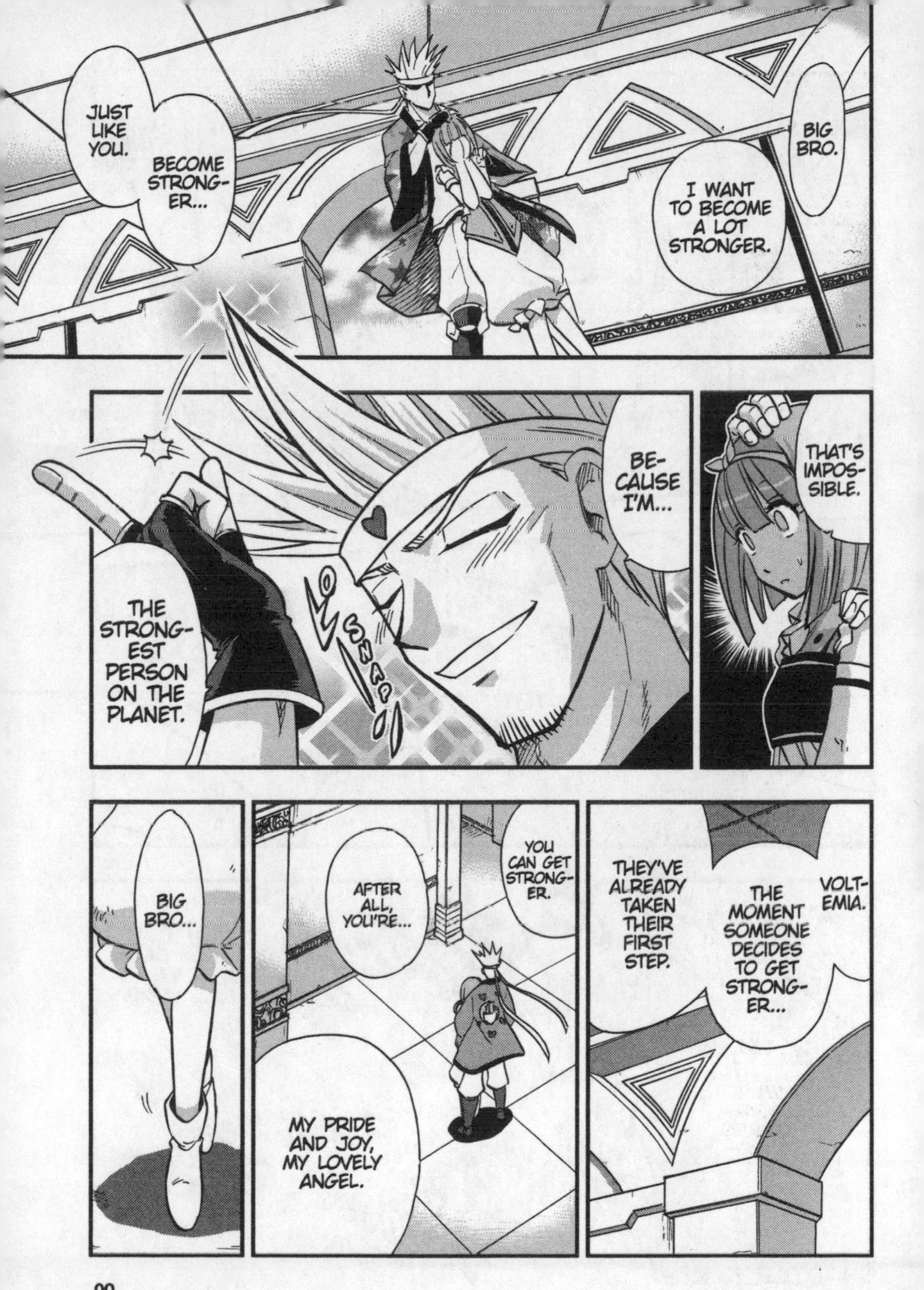
BIG BRO.
I WANT TO BECOME A LOT STRONGER.
BECOME STRONGER...
JUST LIKE YOU.
THAT'S IMPOSSIBLE.
BECAUSE I'M...
SNAP
THE STRONGEST PERSON ON THE PLANET.
VOLTEMIA.
THE MOMENT SOMEONE DECIDES TO GET STRONGER...
THEY'VE ALREADY TAKEN THEIR FIRST STEP.
YOU CAN GET STRONGER.
AFTER ALL, YOU'RE...
MY PRIDE AND JOY, MY LOVELY ANGEL.
BIG BRO...

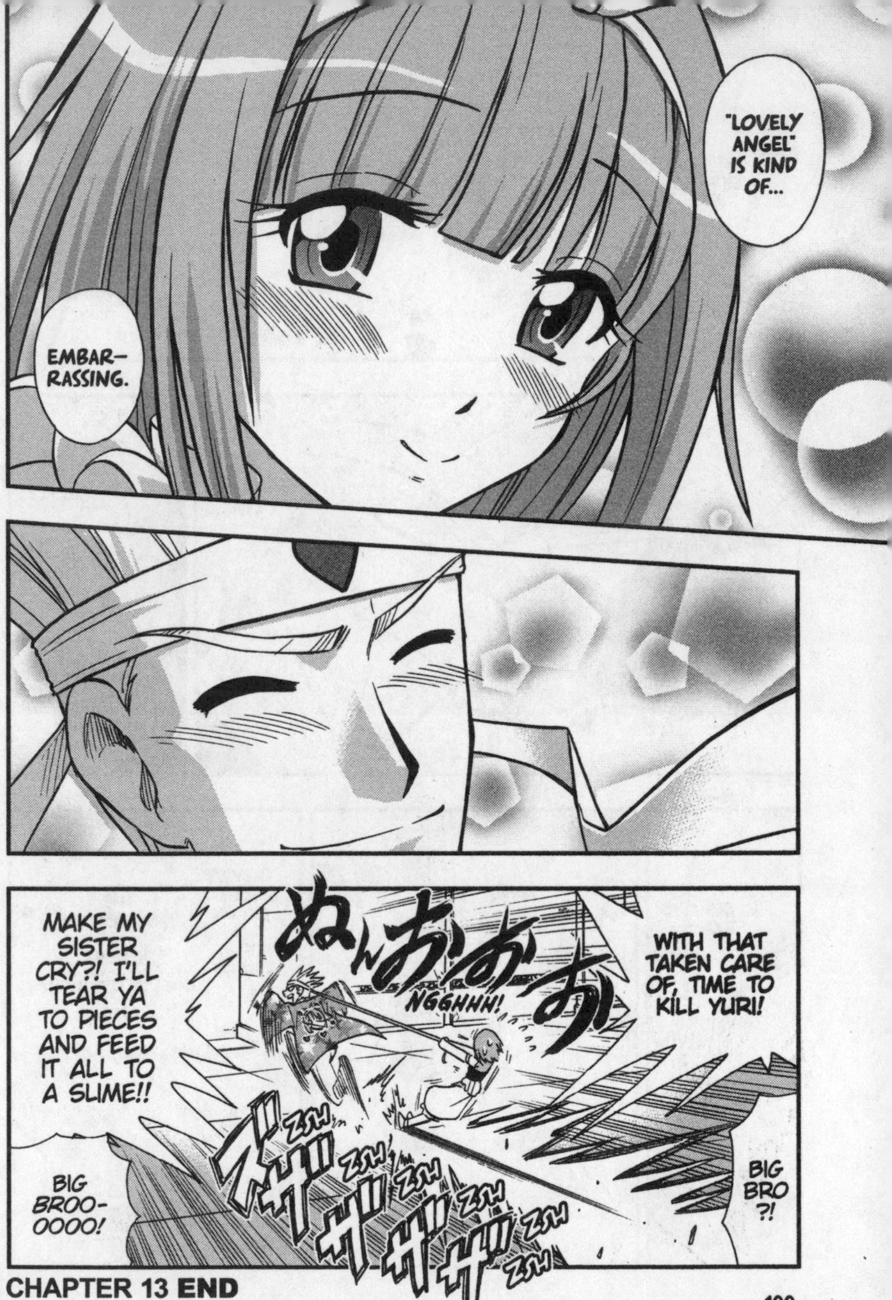
"LOVELY ANGEL" IS KIND OF...
EMBAR-RASSING.
WITH THAT TAKEN CARE OF, TIME TO KILL YURI!
NGGHHN!
MAKE MY SISTER CRY?! I'LL TEAR YA TO PIECES AND FEED IT ALL TO A SLIME!!
BIG BRO?!
ZAH ZAH ZAH ZAH ZAH ZAH
BIG BROO-OOOO!

CHAPTER 13 END

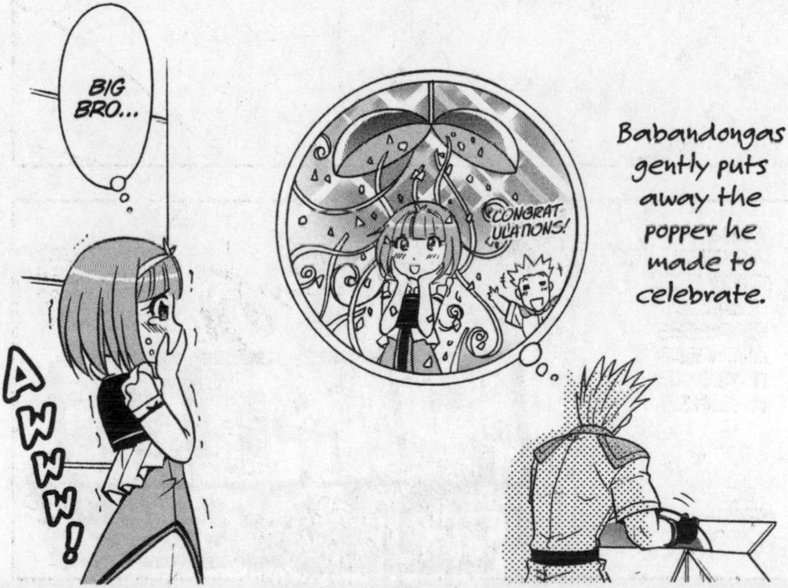
Babandongas gently puts away the popper he made to celebrate.
CONGRATULATIONS!
BIG BRO...
AWWWW!

MUSCLES ARE BETTER THAN MAGIC!

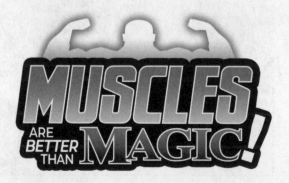

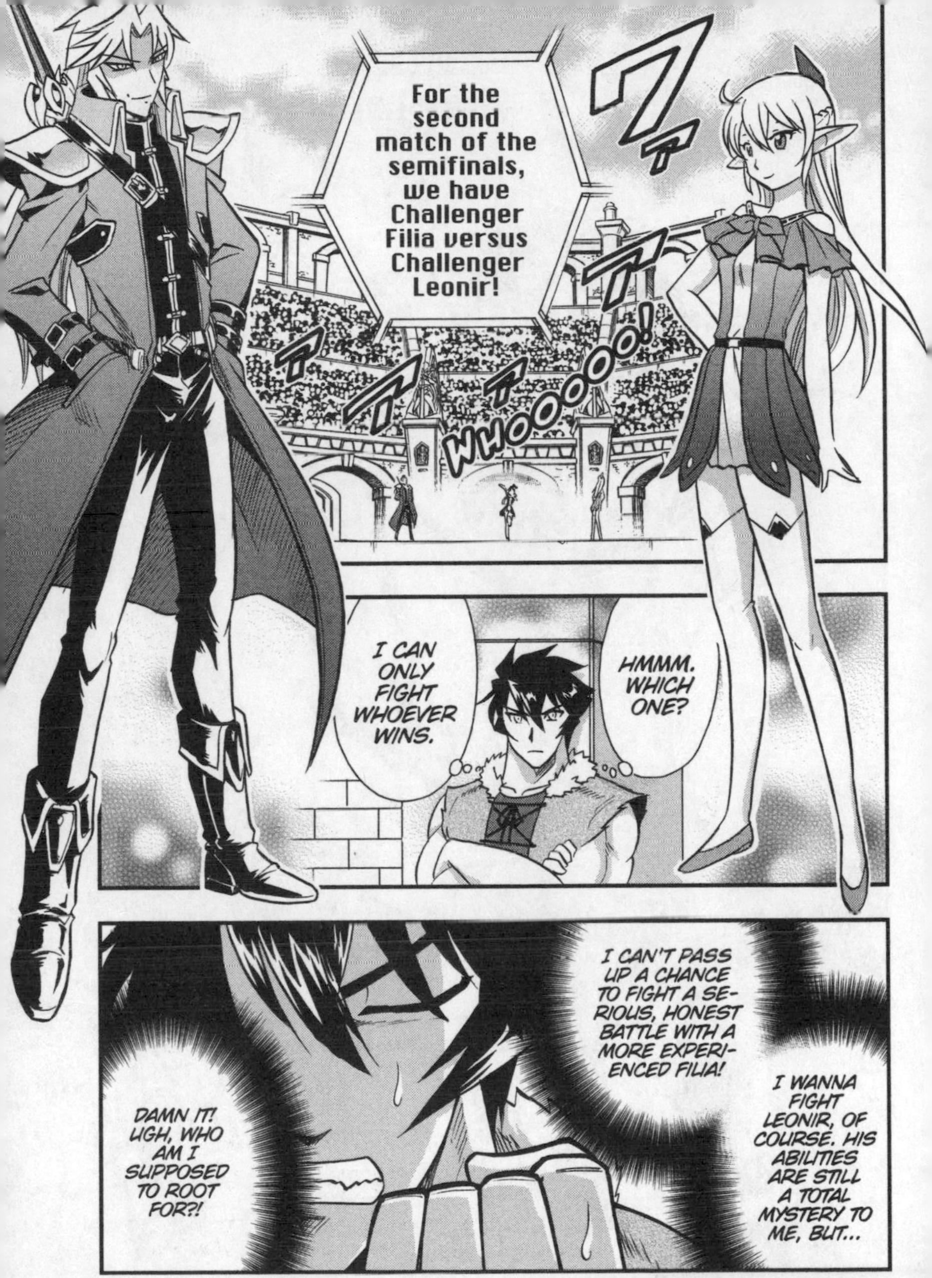
For the second match of the semifinals, we have Challenger Filia versus Challenger Leonir!
WHOOOOOO!
HMMM. WHICH ONE?
I CAN ONLY FIGHT WHOEVER WINS.
I WANNA FIGHT LEONIR, OF COURSE. HIS ABILITIES ARE STILL A TOTAL MYSTERY TO ME, BUT...
I CAN'T PASS UP A CHANCE TO FIGHT A SE-RIOUS, HONEST BATTLE WITH A MORE EXPERI-ENCED FILIA!
DAMN IT! UGH, WHO AM I SUPPOSED TO ROOT FOR?!

CHAPTER 14
Magic Battle Tournament (4)

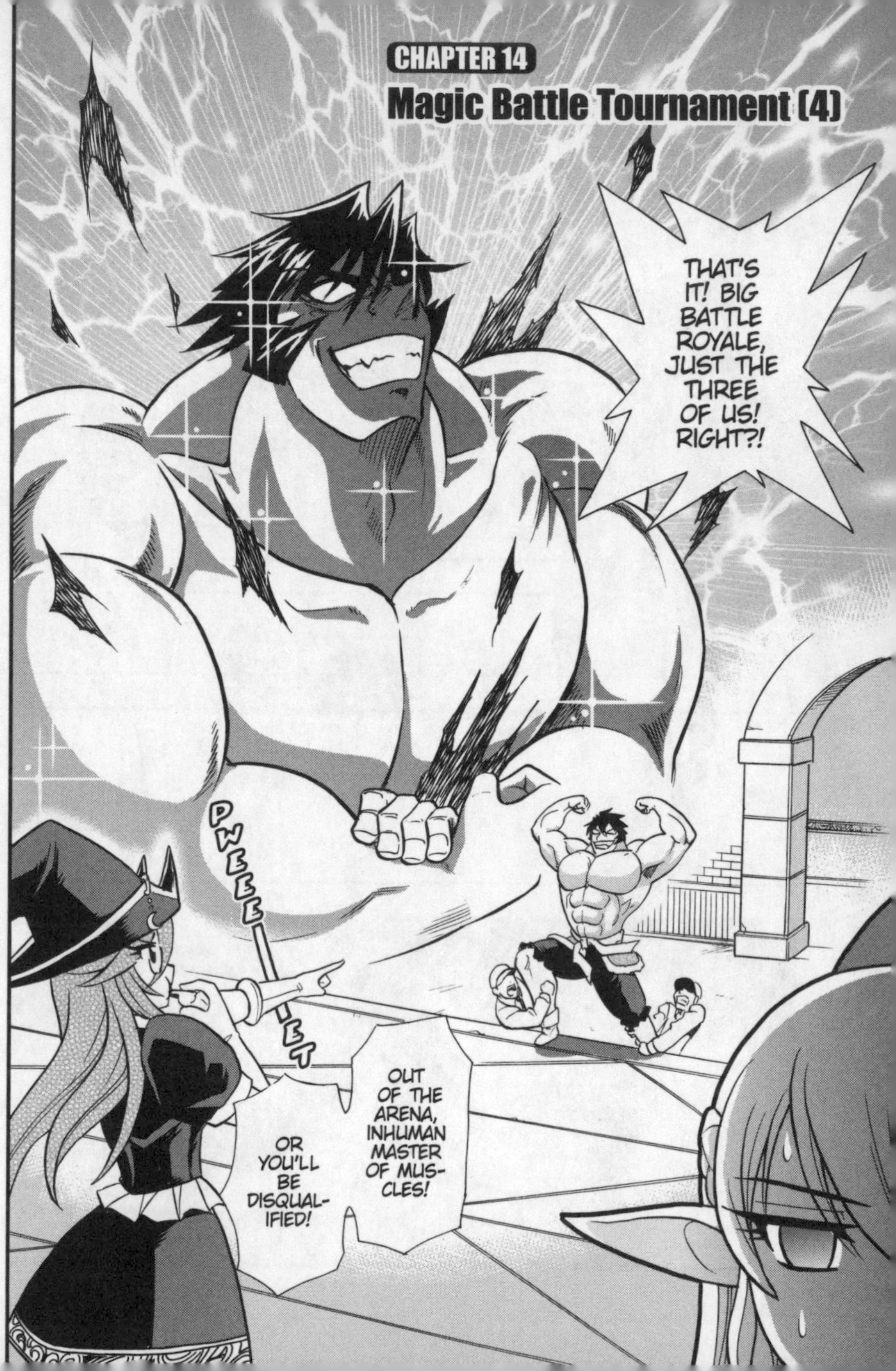

THAT'S IT! BIG BATTLE ROYALE, JUST THE THREE OF US! RIGHT?!
PWEEEEET
OUT OF THE ARENA, INHUMAN MASTER OF MUS-CLES!
OR YOU'LL BE DISQUAL-IFIED!

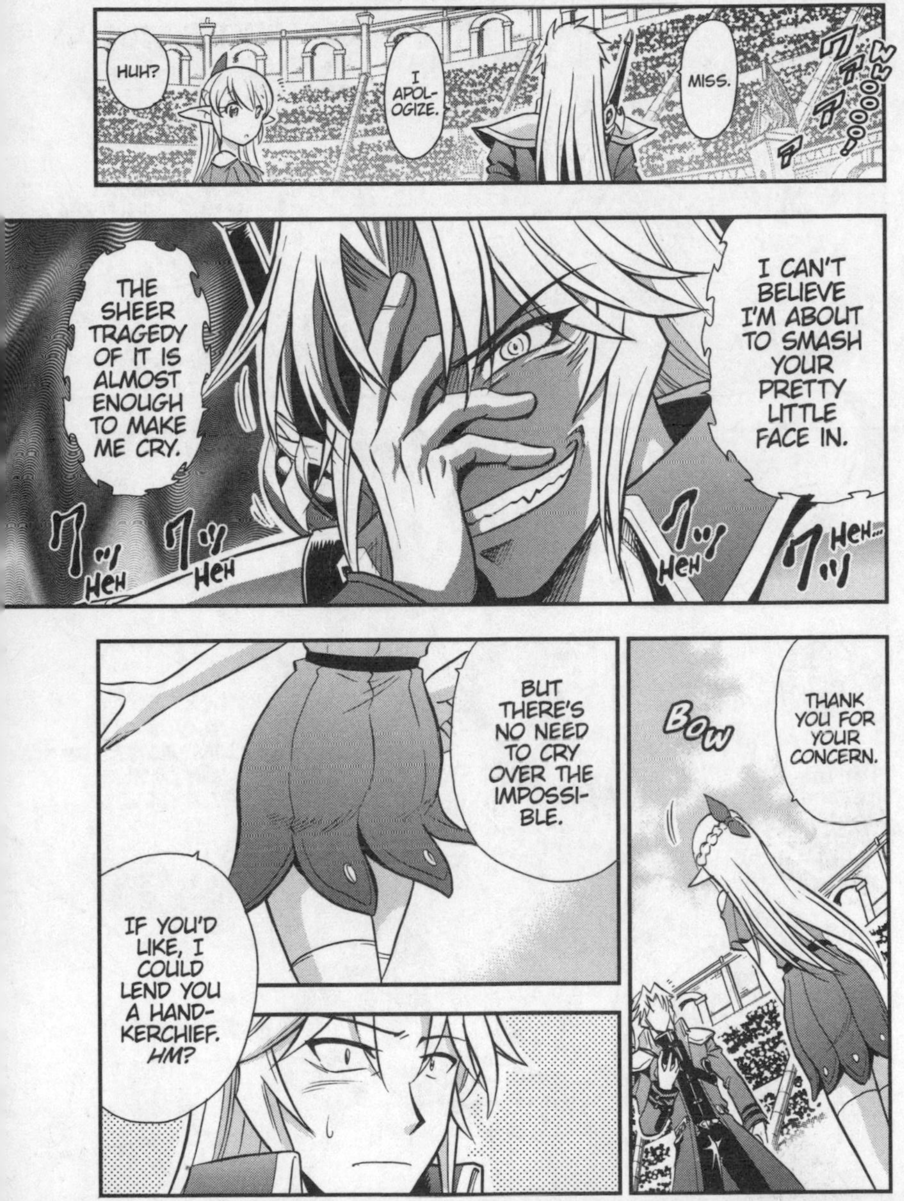
WHOOOO!
MISS.
I APOLOGIZE.
HUH?
I CAN'T BELIEVE I'M ABOUT TO SMASH YOUR PRETTY LITTLE FACE IN.
THE SHEER TRAGEDY OF IT IS ALMOST ENOUGH TO MAKE ME CRY.
HEH...
HEH
HEH
HEH
THANK YOU FOR YOUR CONCERN.
BOW
BUT THERE'S NO NEED TO CRY OVER THE IMPOSSIBLE.
IF YOU'D LIKE, I COULD LEND YOU A HANDKERCHIEF. HM?

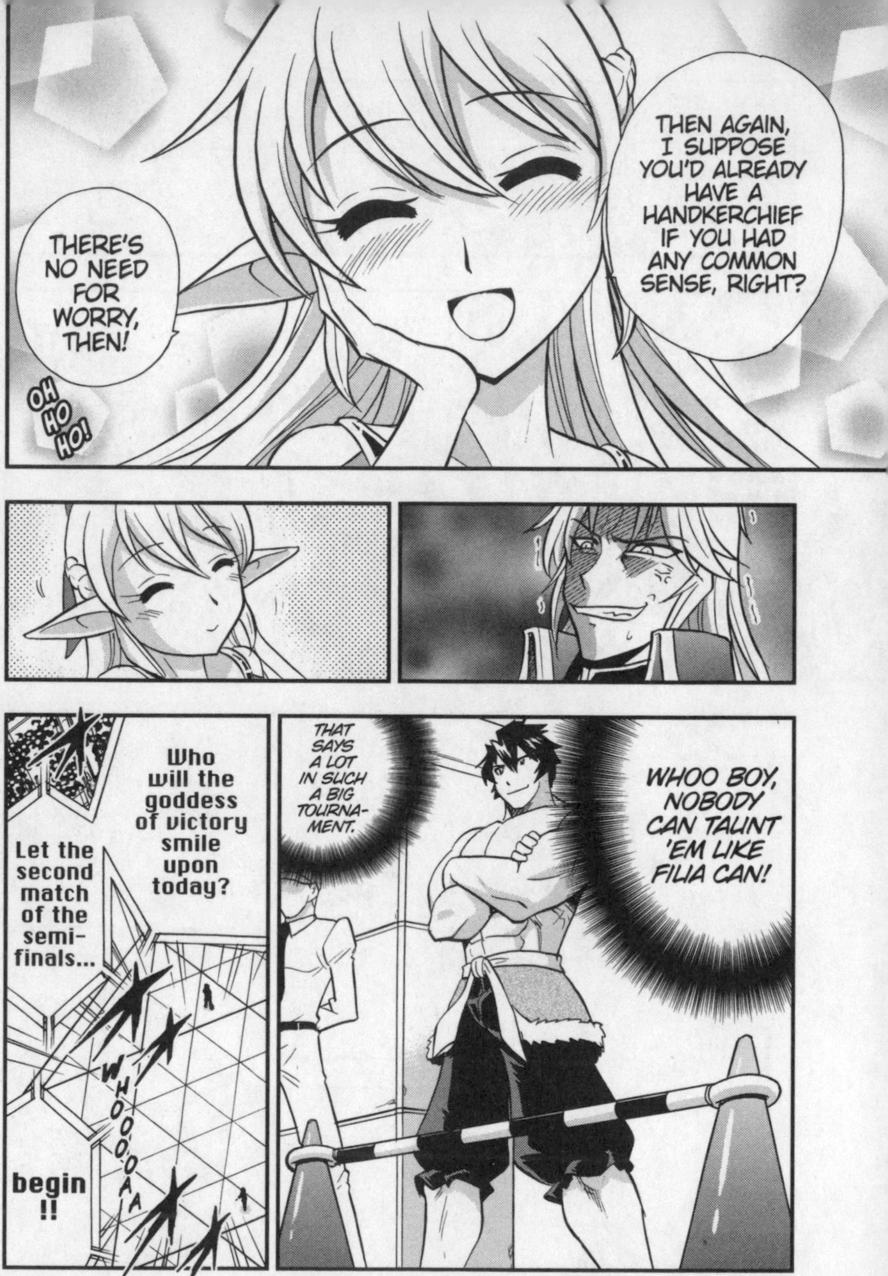
THEN AGAIN, I SUPPOSE YOU'D ALREADY HAVE A HANDKERCHIEF IF YOU HAD ANY COMMON SENSE, RIGHT?
THERE'S NO NEED FOR WORRY, THEN!
OH HO HO!
WHOO BOY, NOBODY CAN TAUNT 'EM LIKE FILIA CAN!
THAT SAYS A LOT IN SUCH A BIG TOURNAMENT.
Who will the goddess of victory smile upon today?
Let the second match of the semi-finals...
begin!!
WHOOOOOAA

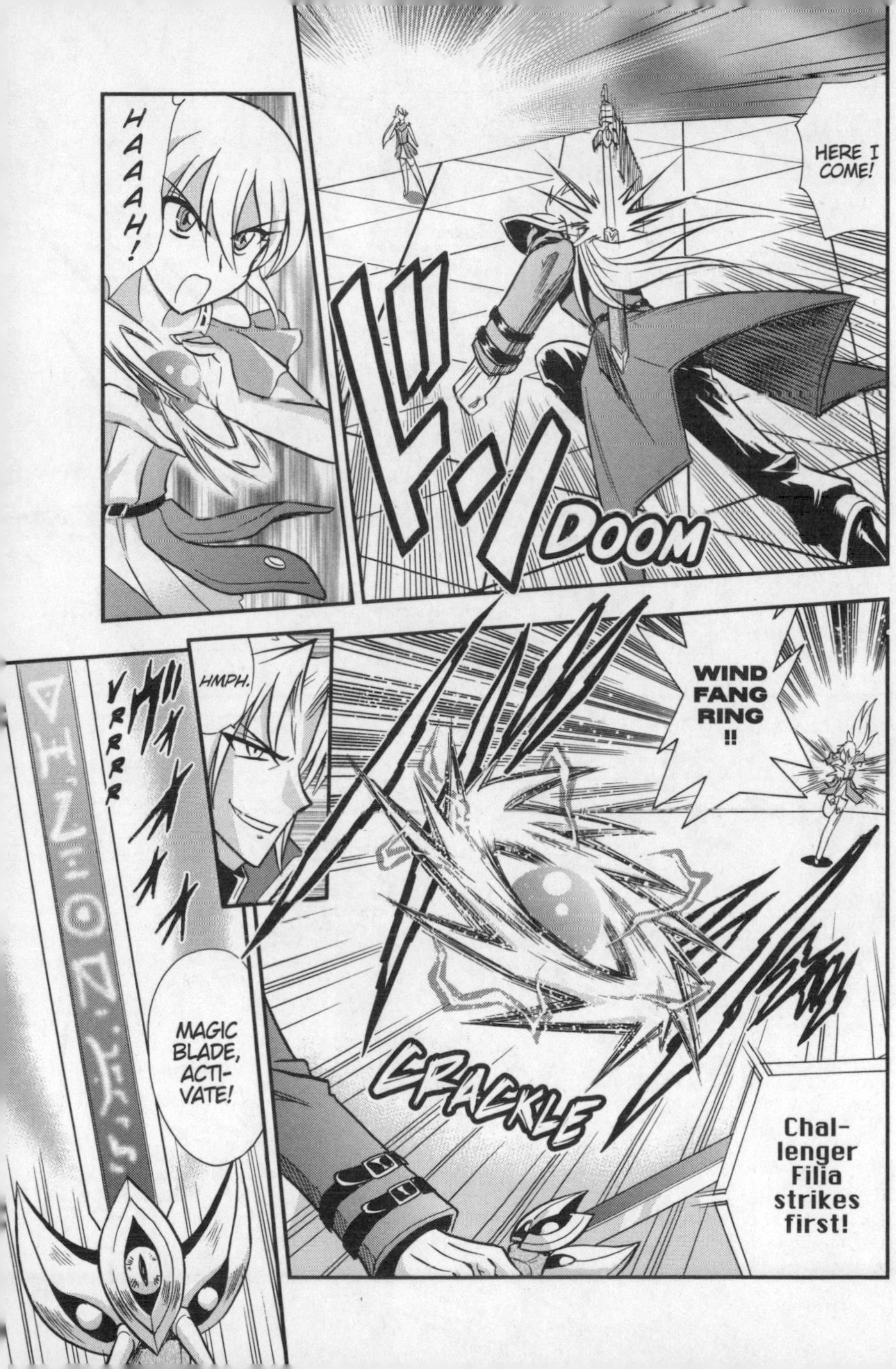
HERE I COME!
DOOM
HAAAAH!
WIND FANG RING!!
CRACKLE
Challenger Filia strikes first!
HMPH.
VRRRR
MAGIC BLADE, ACTIVATE!

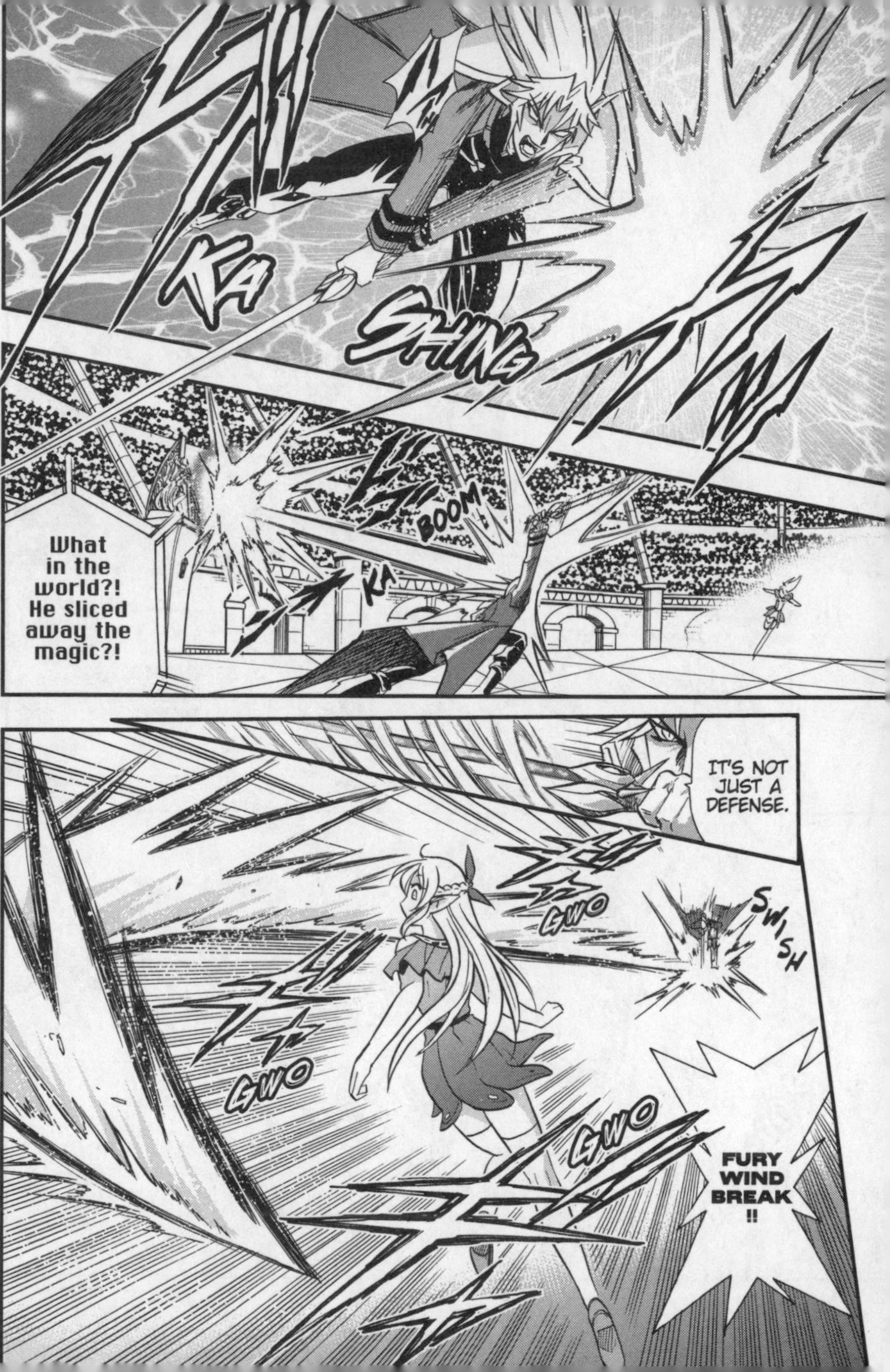
KA
SHING
BOOM
KA
What in the world?! He sliced away the magic?!
IT'S NOT JUST A DEFENSE.
SWISH
GWO
GWO
GWO
FURY WIND BREAK !!

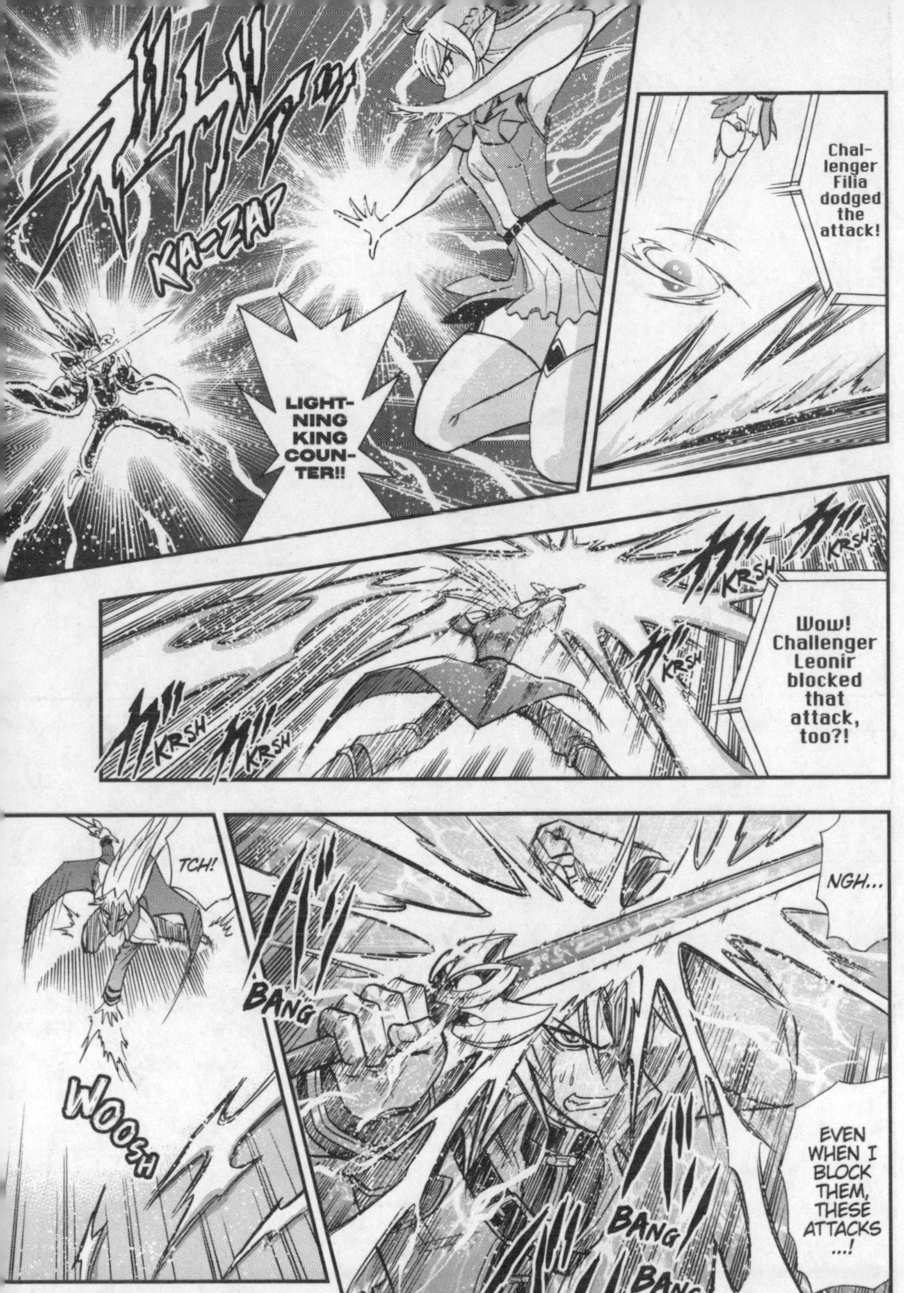
Chal-
lenger
Filia
dodged
the
attack!
KA-ZAP
LIGHT-
NING
KING
COUN-
TER!!
KRSH
KRSH
KRSH
Wow!
Challenger
Leonir
blocked
that
attack,
too?!
KRSH
KRSH
NGH...
BANG
EVEN
WHEN I
BLOCK
THEM,
THESE
ATTACKS
...!
BANG
BANG
BANG
TCH!
WOOSH

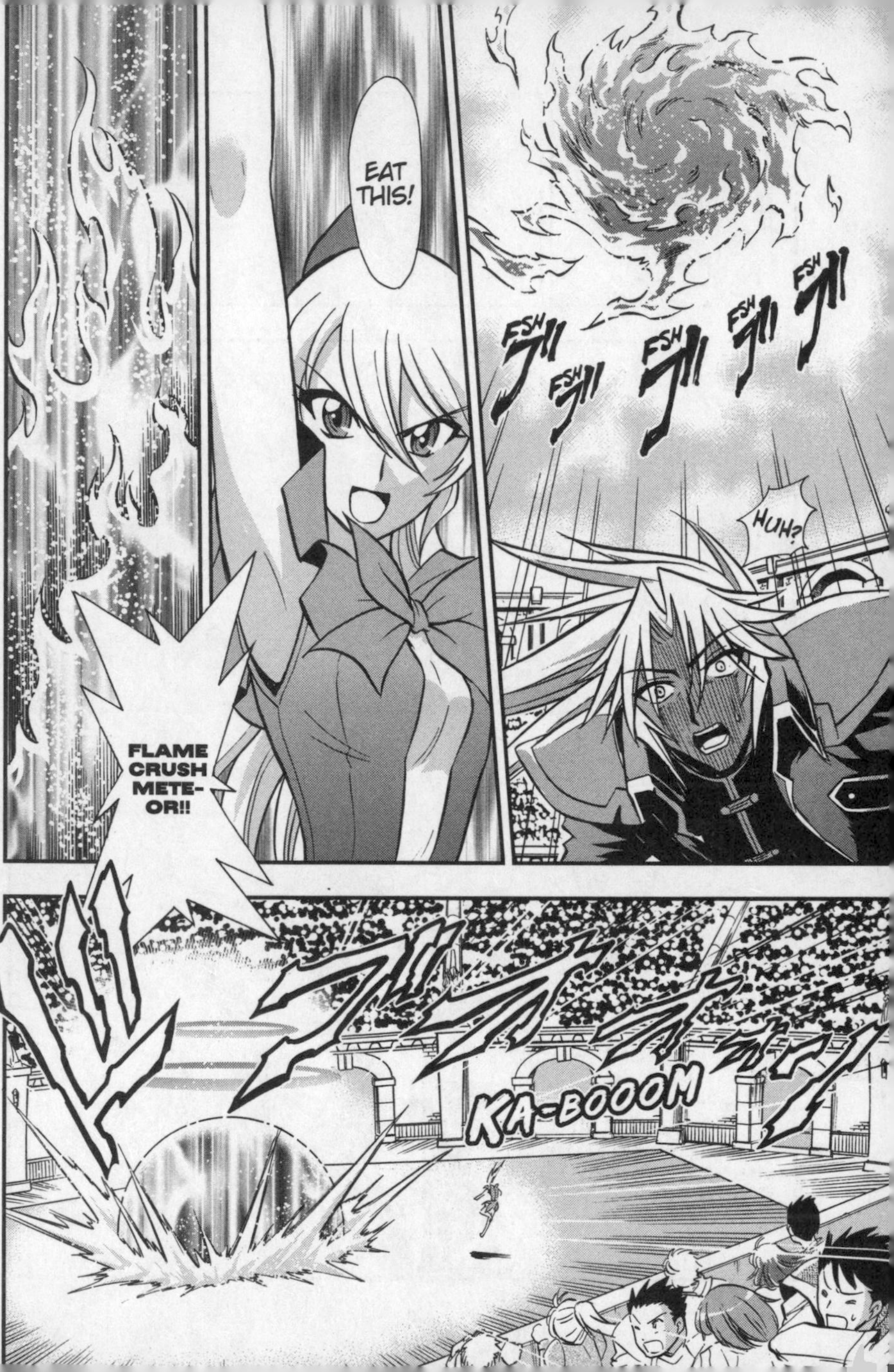
FSH
FSH
FSH
FSH
FSH
HUH?
EAT THIS!
FLAME CRUSH METE-OR!!
KA-BOOOM

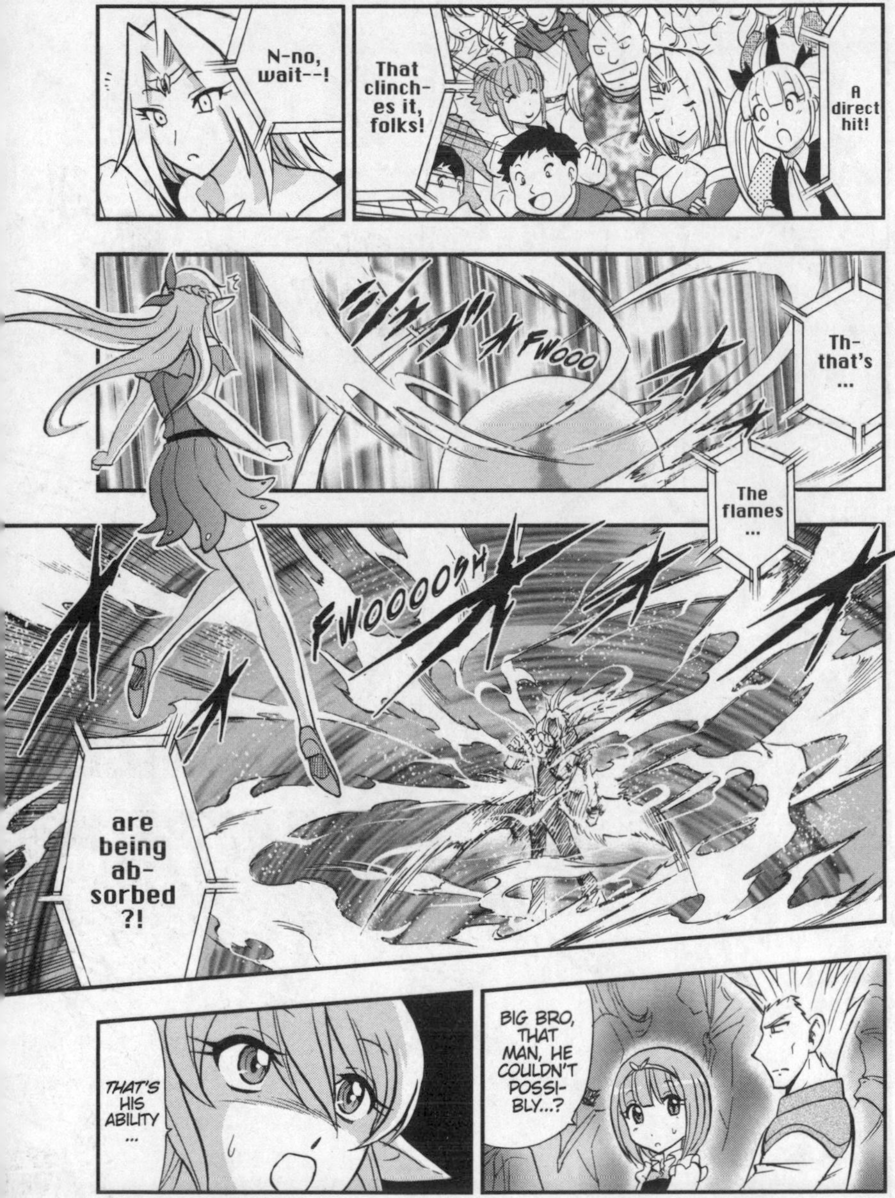

A direct hit!
That clinches it, folks!
N-no, wait--!
Th-that's ...
FWOOO
The flames ...
FWOOOOSH
are being ab-sorbed ?!
BIG BRO, THAT MAN, HE COULDN'T POSSI-BLY...?
THAT'S HIS ABILITY ...

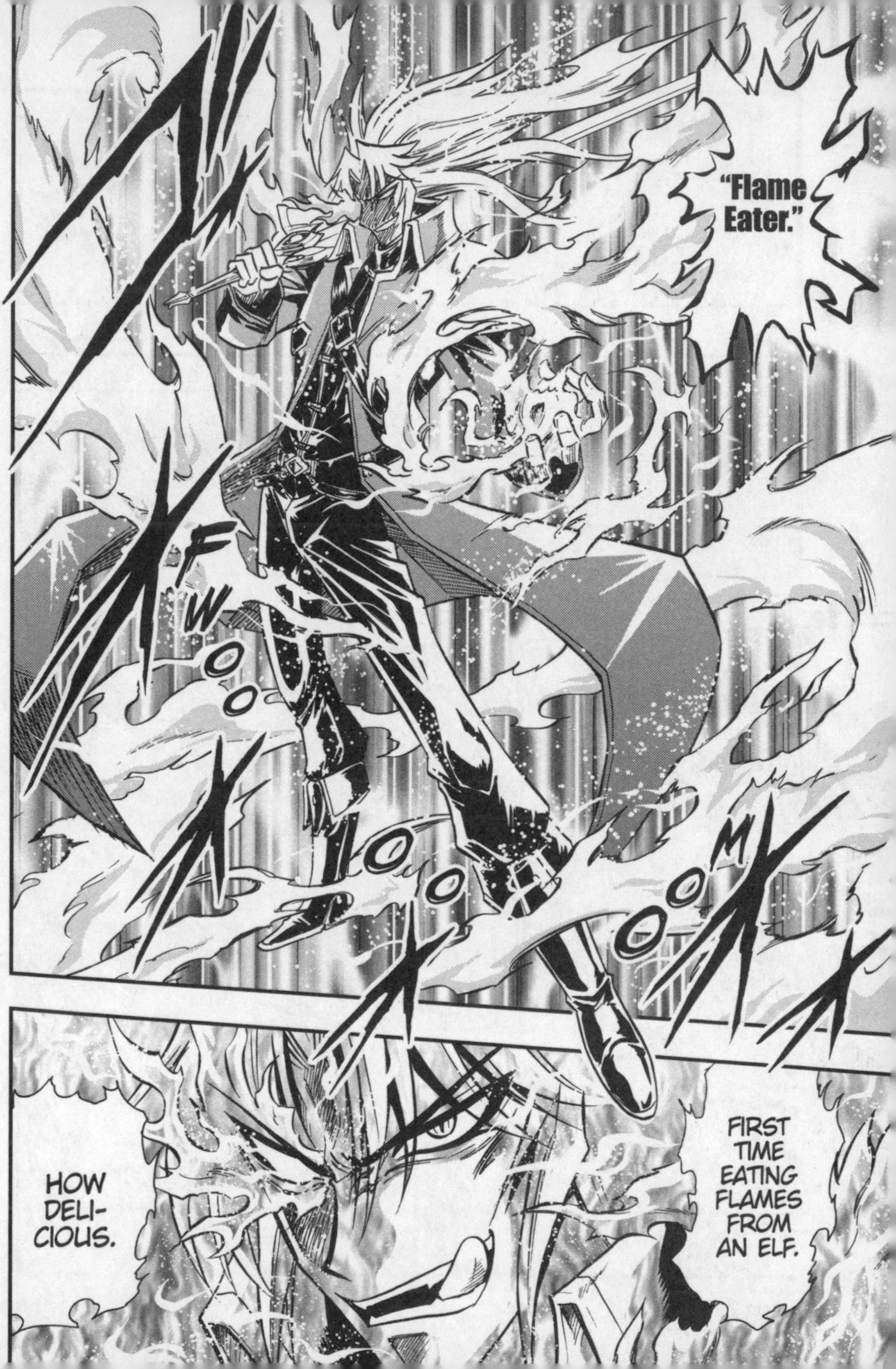
"Flame Eater."
FWOOOOOOOOOM
FIRST TIME EATING FLAMES FROM AN ELF.
HOW DELI-CIOUS.

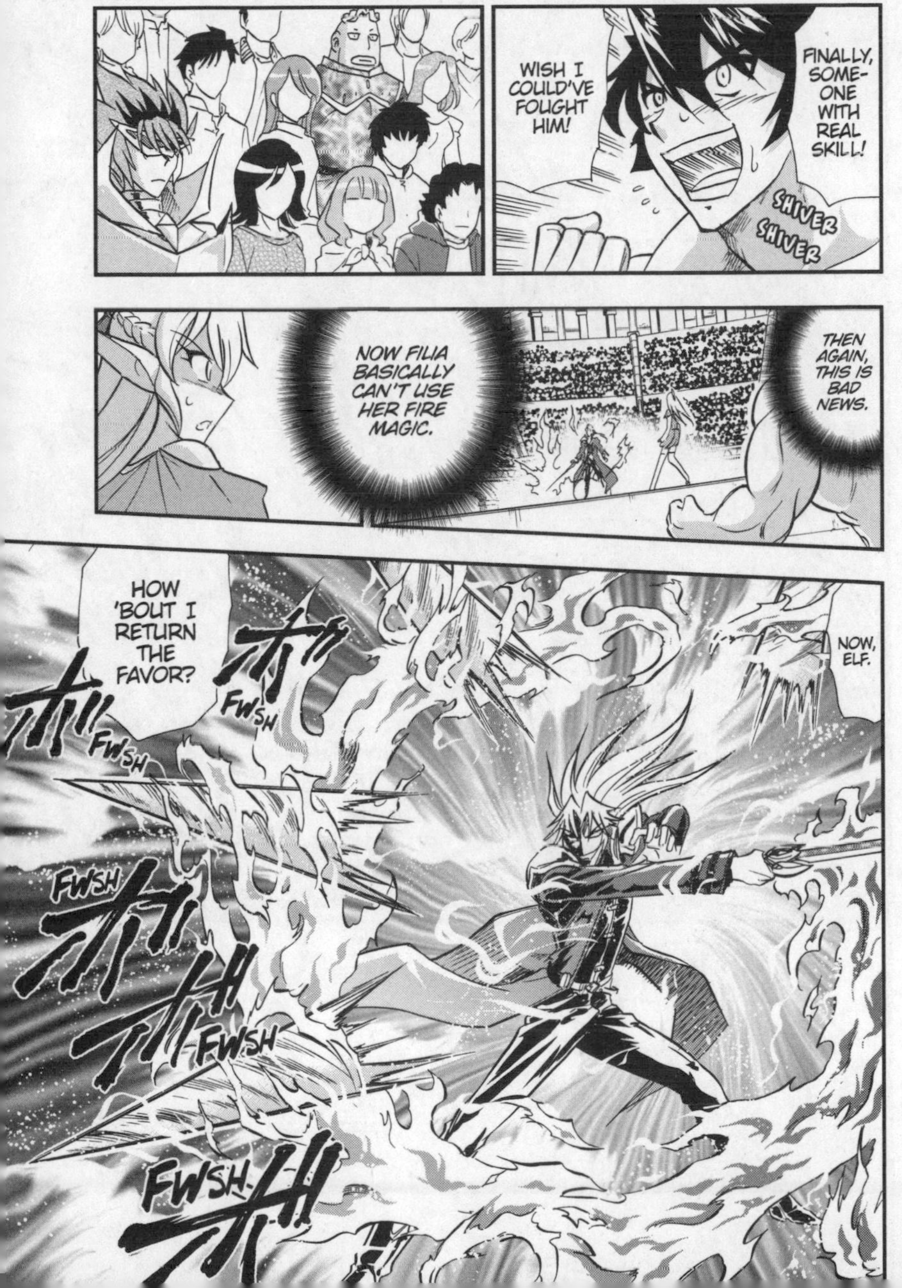
FINALLY, SOME-ONE WITH REAL SKILL!
WISH I COULD'VE FOUGHT HIM!
SHIVER SHIVER
THEN AGAIN, THIS IS BAD NEWS.
NOW FILIA BASICALLY CAN'T USE HER FIRE MAGIC.
NOW, ELF.
HOW 'BOUT I RETURN THE FAVOR?
FWSH
FWSH
FWSH
FWSH
FWSH-

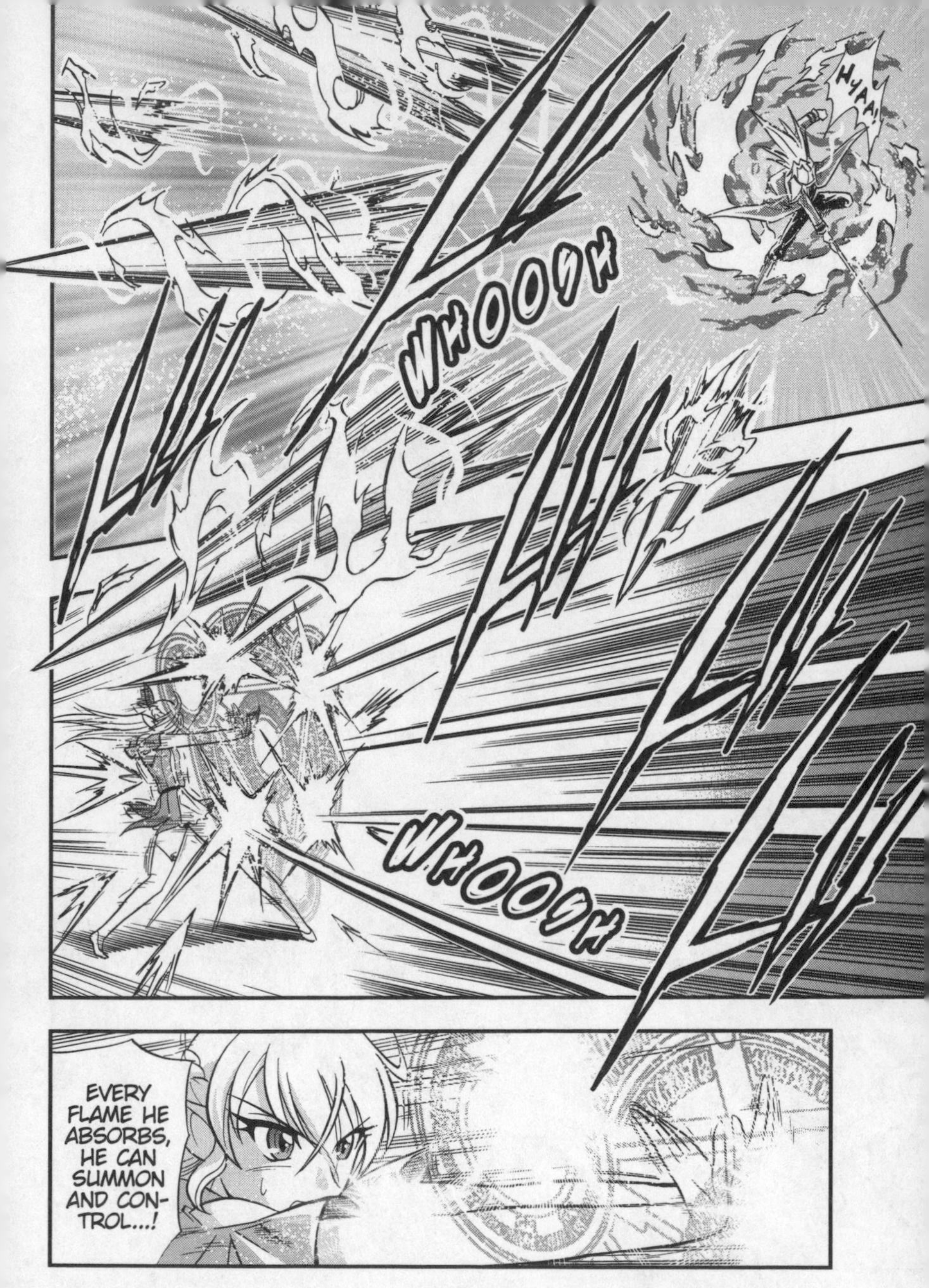
HYAA!
WHOOSH
WHOOSH
EVERY FLAME HE ABSORBS, HE CAN SUMMON AND CONTROL...!

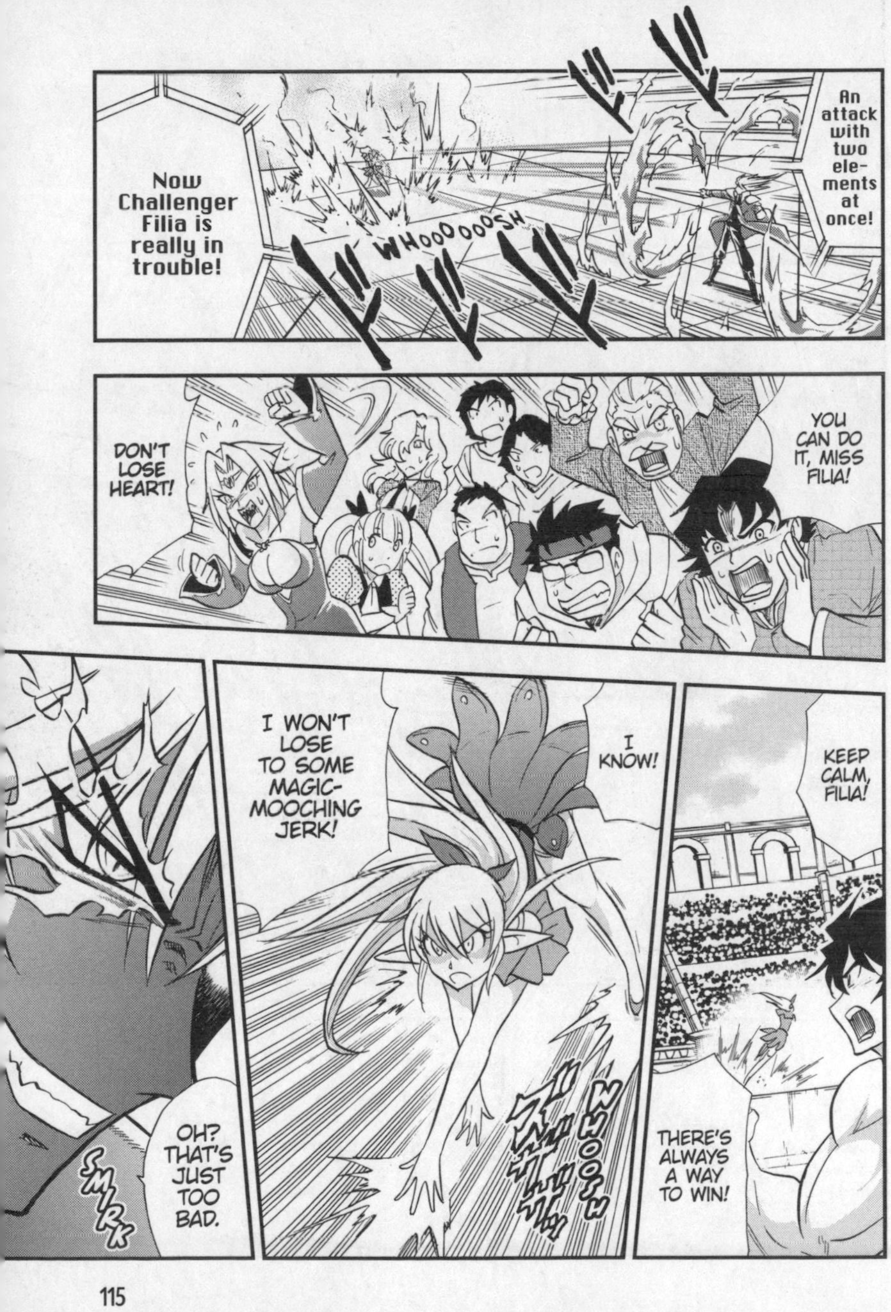
An attack with two elements at once!
Now Challenger Filia is really in trouble!
WHOOOOOOSH
YOU CAN DO IT, MISS FILIA!
DON'T LOSE HEART!
KEEP CALM, FILIA!
THERE'S ALWAYS A WAY TO WIN!
I KNOW!
I WON'T LOSE TO SOME MAGIC-MOOCHING JERK!
WHOOOSH
OH? THAT'S JUST TOO BAD.
SMIRK

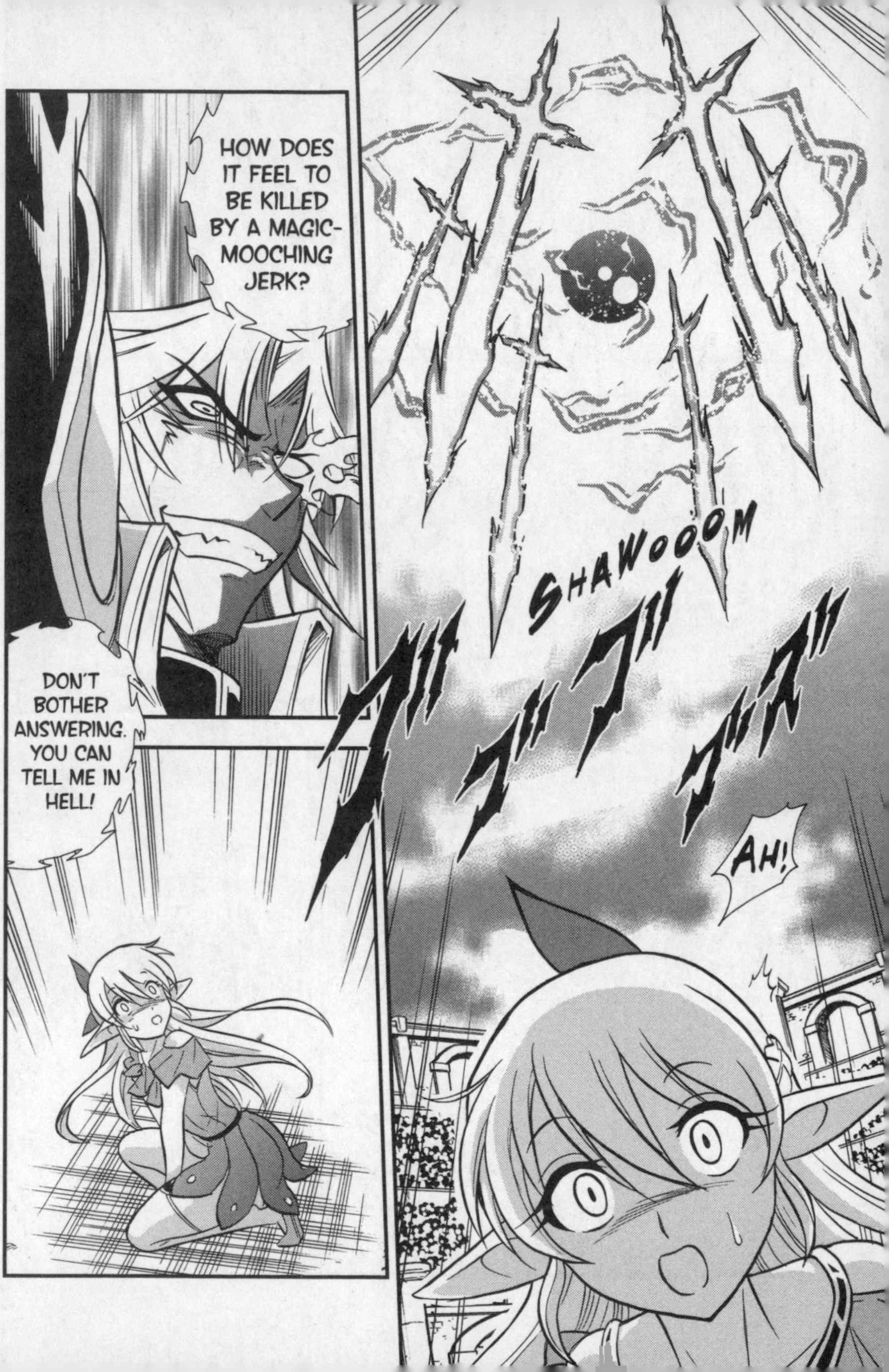
SHAWOOOM
AH!
HOW DOES IT FEEL TO BE KILLED BY A MAGIC-MOOCHING JERK?
DON'T BOTHER ANSWERING. YOU CAN TELL ME IN HELL!

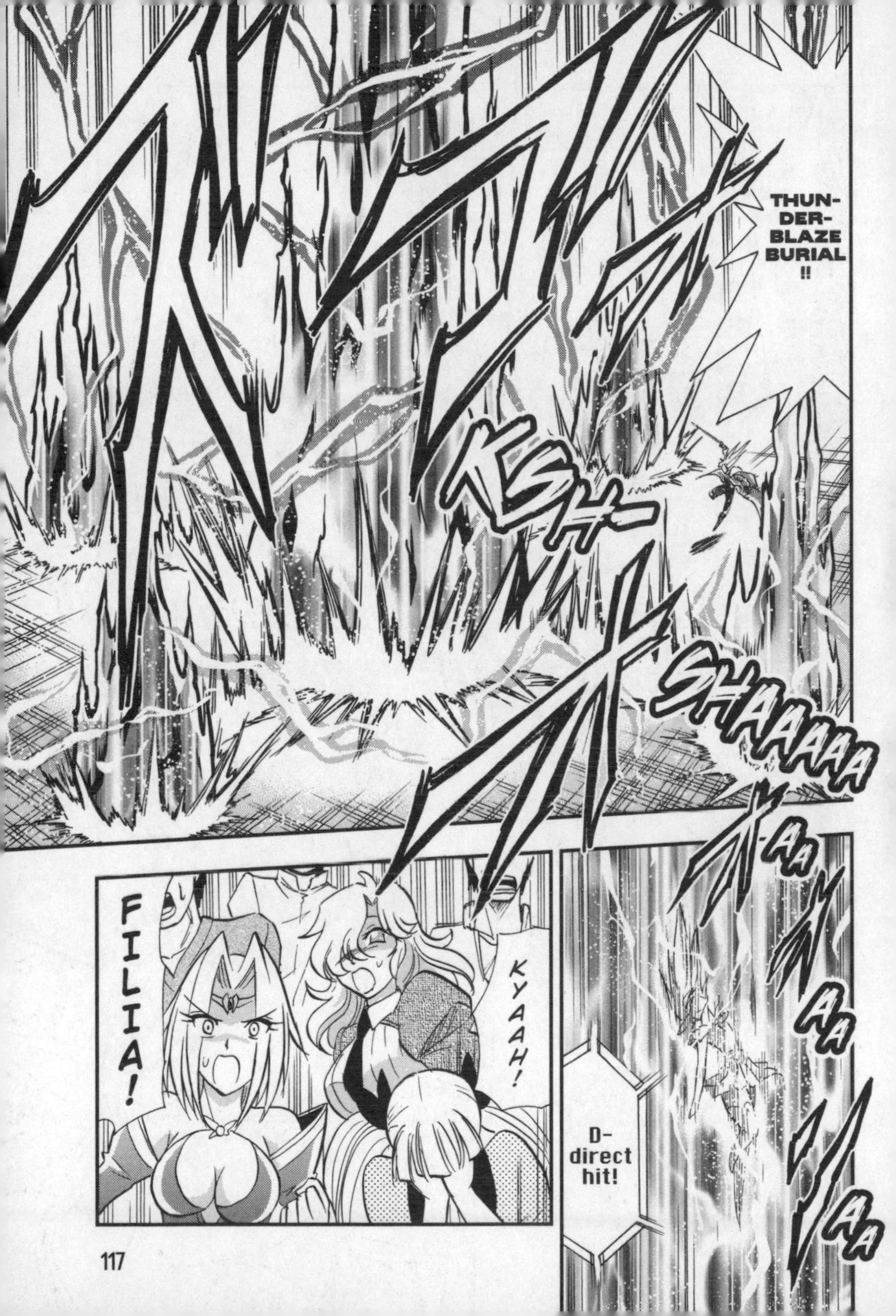
THUNDER-BLAZE BURIAL!!
KSHH-
SHAAAAAAAAAAAAAAA
D-direct hit!
KYAAAH!
FILIA!

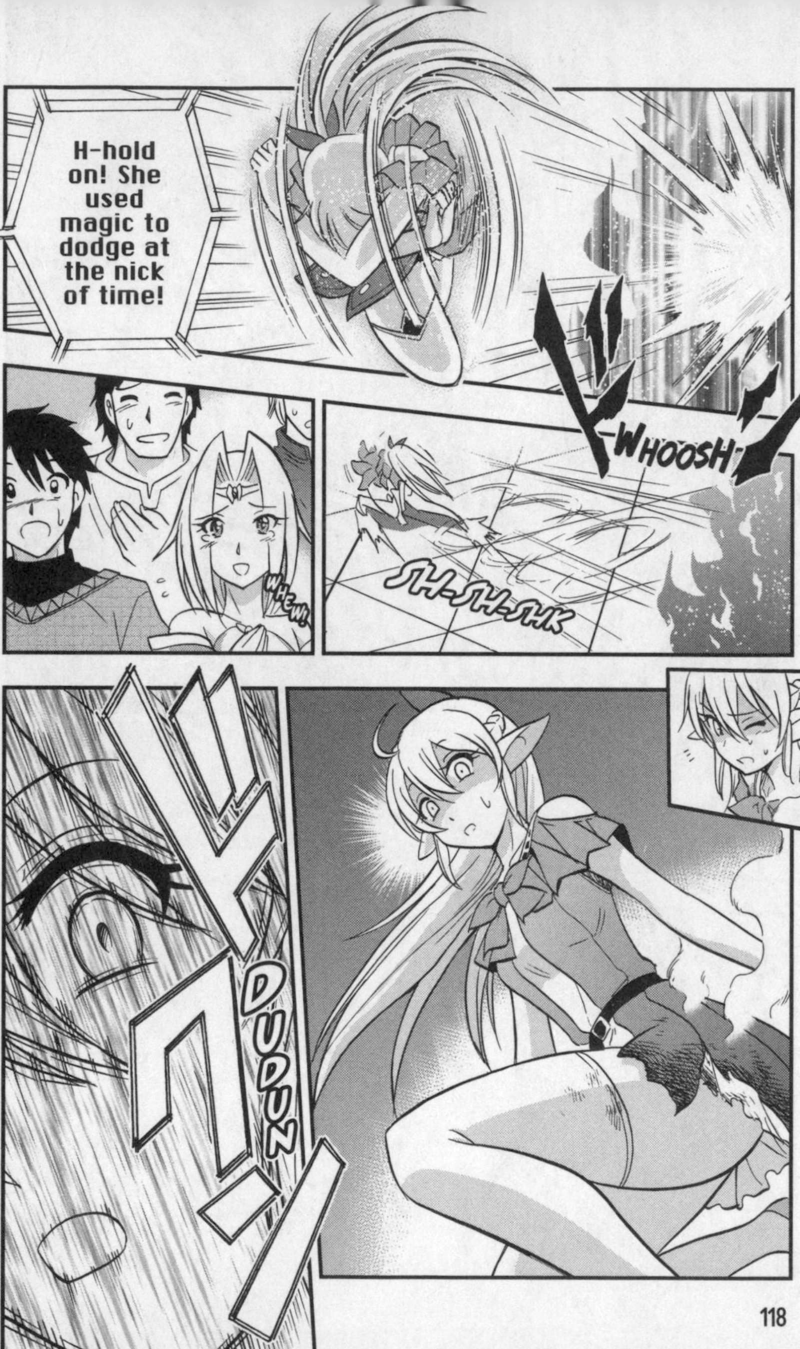
H-hold on! She used magic to dodge at the nick of time!
WHOOSH
SH-SH-SHK
WHEW!
DUDUN

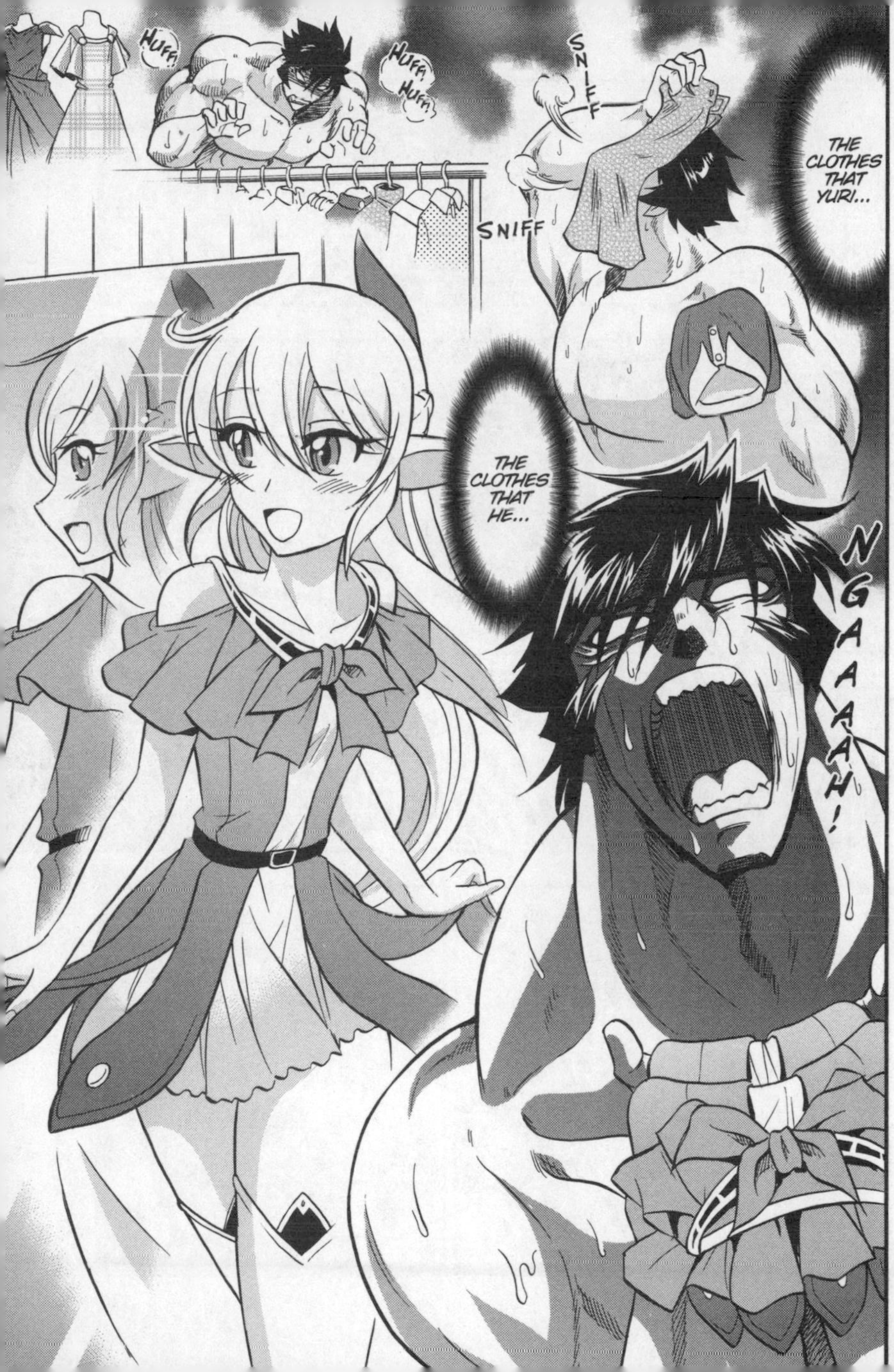
THE CLOTHES THAT YURI...
SNIFF
SNIFF
HUFF! HUFF!
HUFF!
NGAAAAAH!
THE CLOTHES THAT HE...

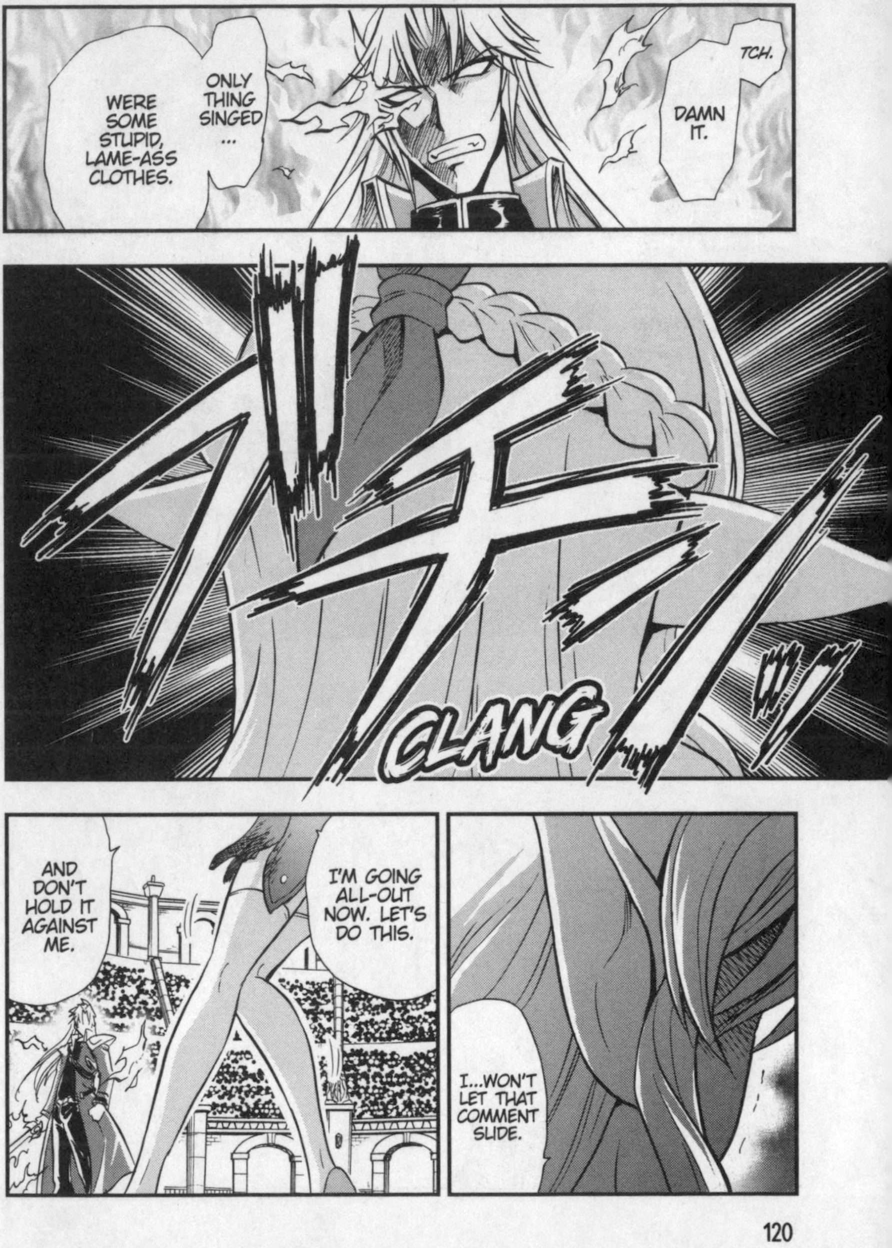
TCH.
DAMN IT.
ONLY THING SINGED ...
WERE SOME STUPID, LAME-ASS CLOTHES.
CLANG
I...WON'T LET THAT COMMENT SLIDE.
I'M GOING ALL-OUT NOW. LET'S DO THIS.
AND DON'T HOLD IT AGAINST ME.

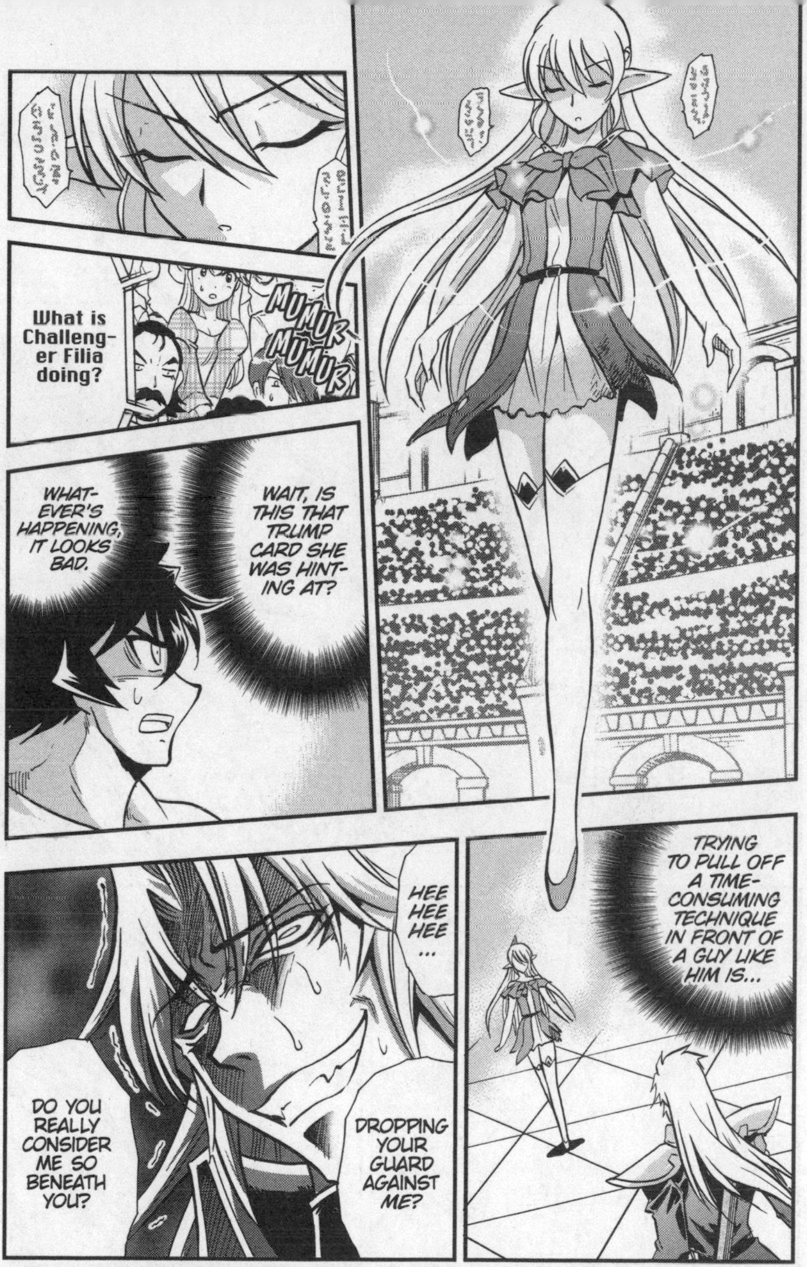
MUMUR MUMUR
What is Challenger Filia doing?
WAIT, IS THIS THAT TRUMP CARD SHE WAS HINTING AT?
WHATEVER'S HAPPENING, IT LOOKS BAD.
TRYING TO PULL OFF A TIME-CONSUMING TECHNIQUE IN FRONT OF A GUY LIKE HIM IS...
HEE HEE HEE...
DROPPING YOUR GUARD AGAINST ME?
DO YOU REALLY CONSIDER ME SO BENEATH YOU?

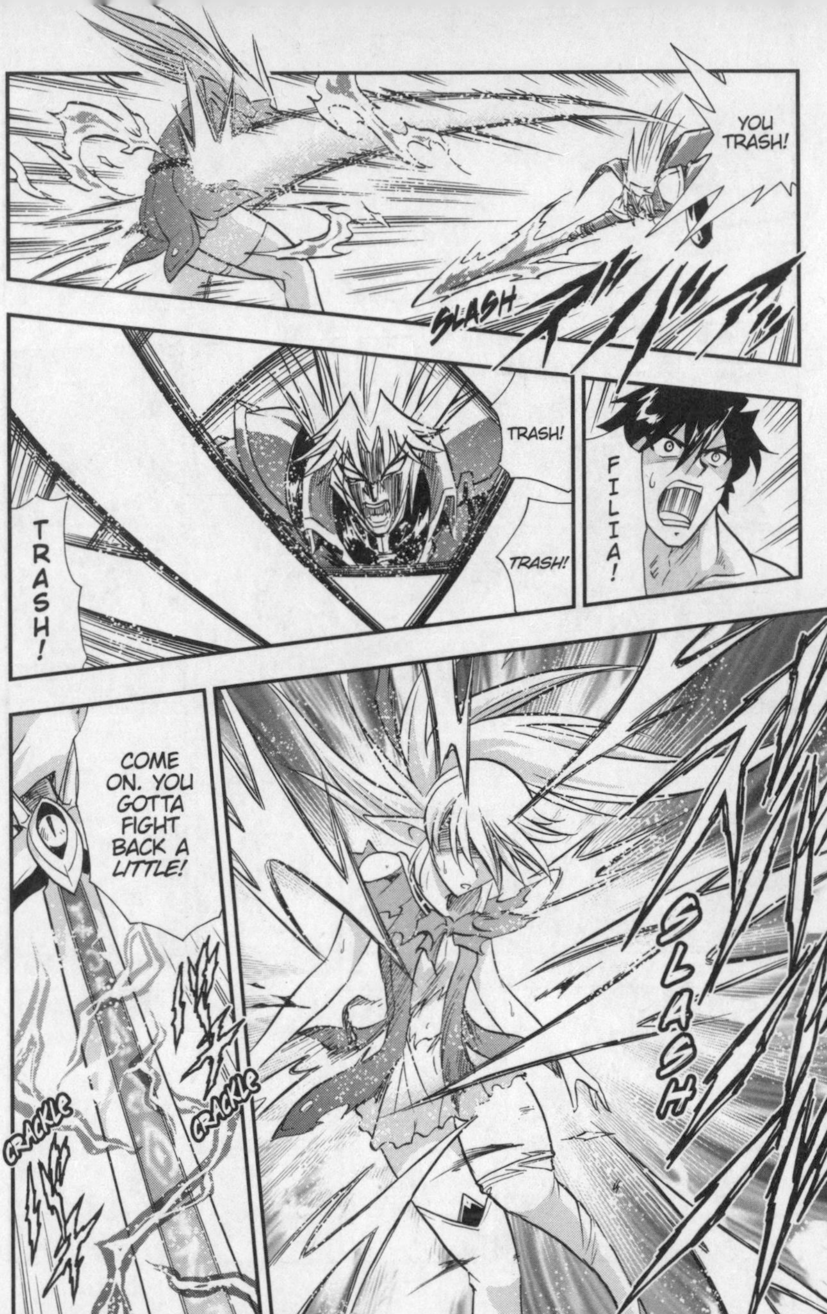

YOU TRASH!
SLASH
FILIA!
TRASH!
TRASH!
TRASH!
SLASH
COME ON. YOU GOTTA FIGHT BACK A LITTLE!
CRACKLE
CRACKLE

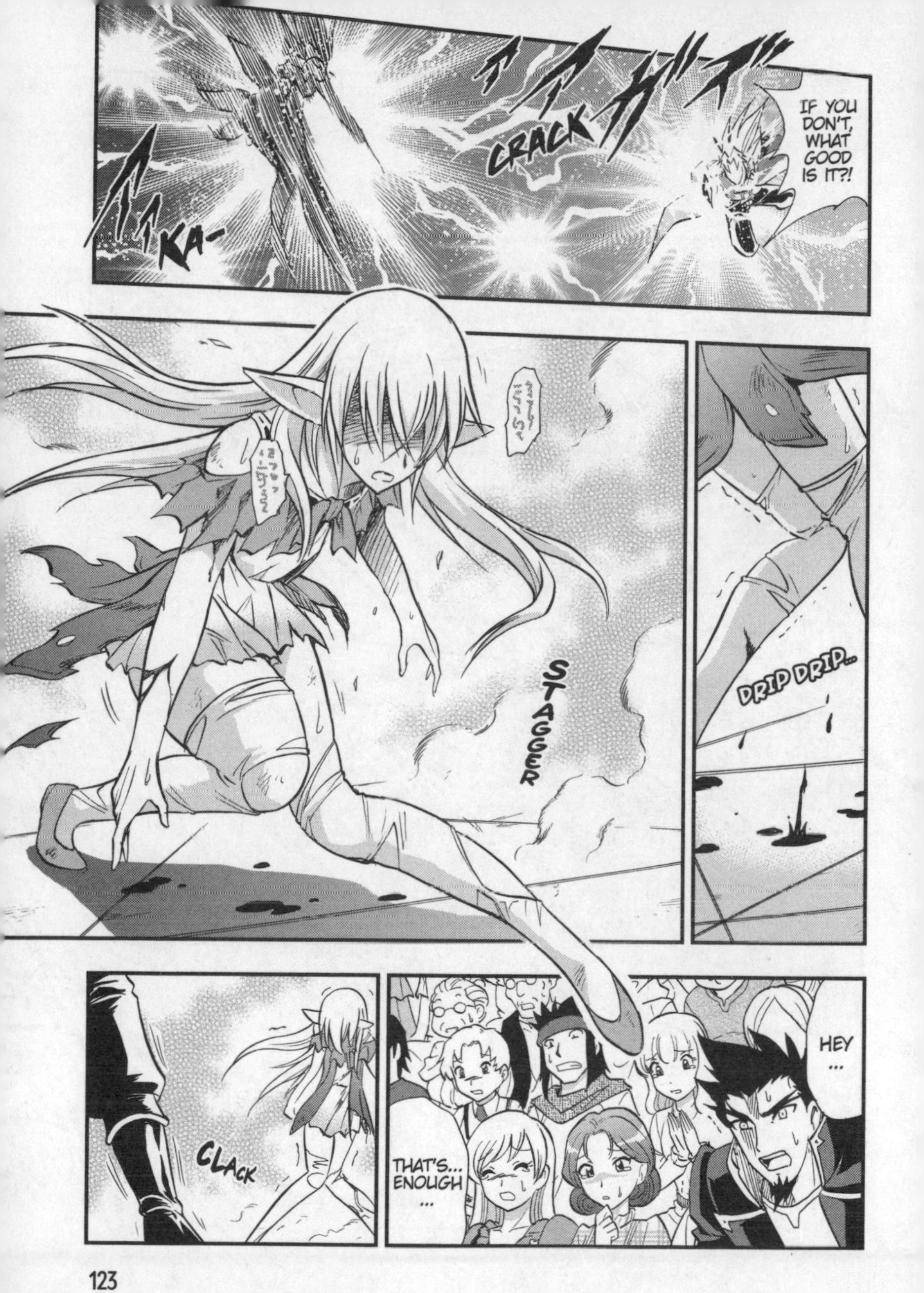
IF YOU DON'T, WHAT GOOD IS IT?!
CRACK
KA-
DRIP DRIP...
STAGGER
HEY...
THAT'S... ENOUGH...
CLACK

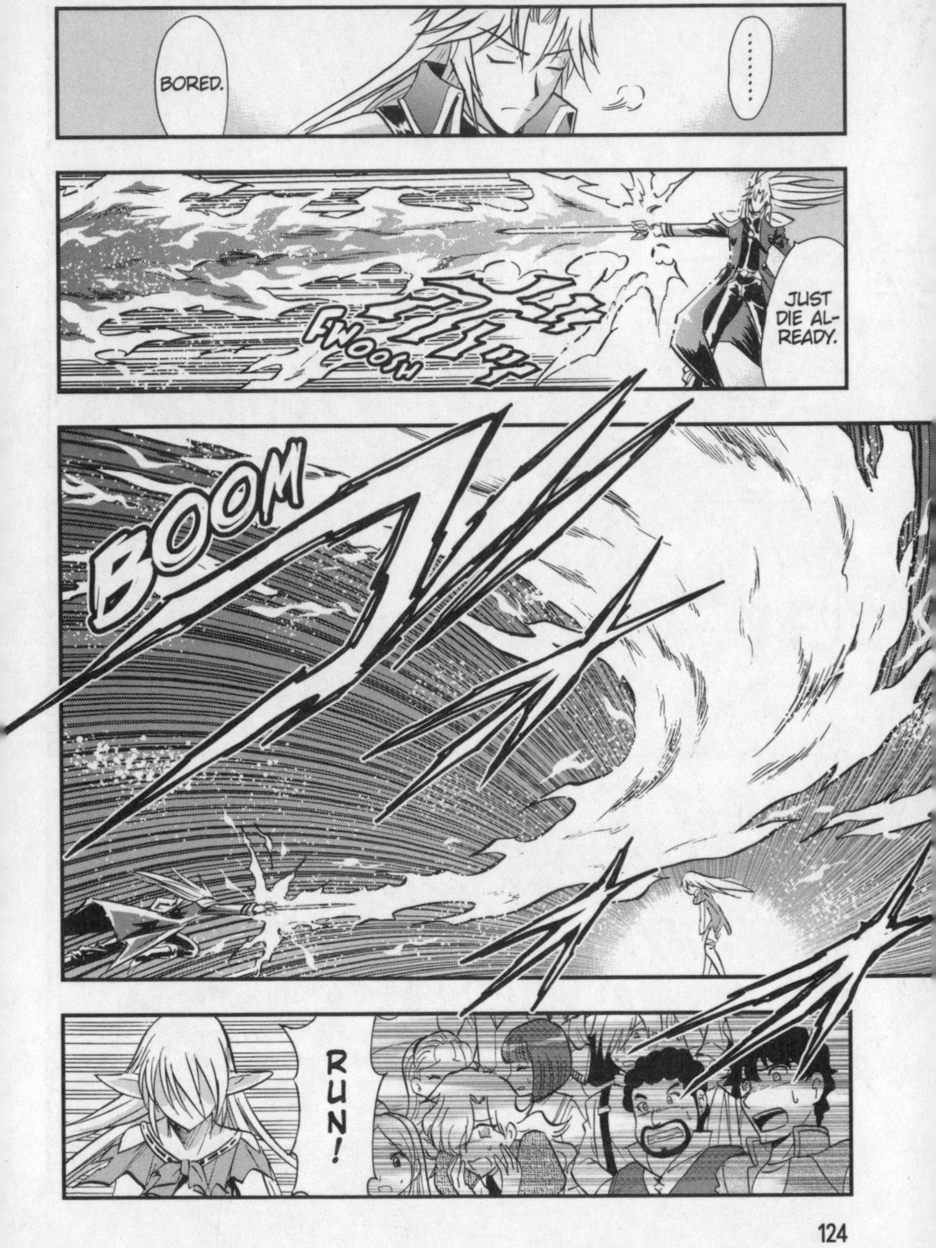
......
BORED.
JUST DIE AL-READY.
FWOOSH
BOOM
RUN!

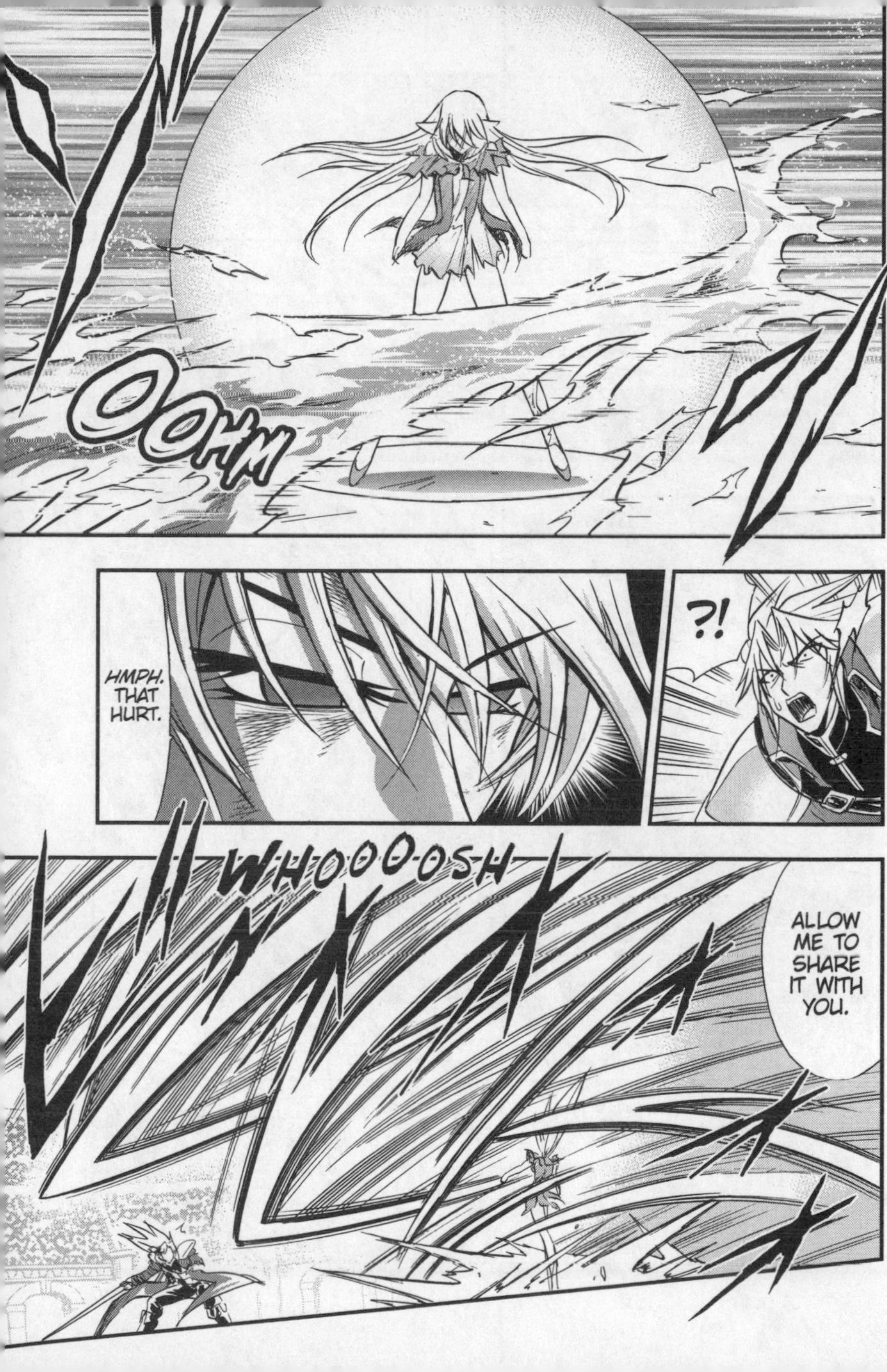
VOOOHM
?!
HMPH. THAT HURT.
ALLOW ME TO SHARE IT WITH YOU.
WHOOO-OSH

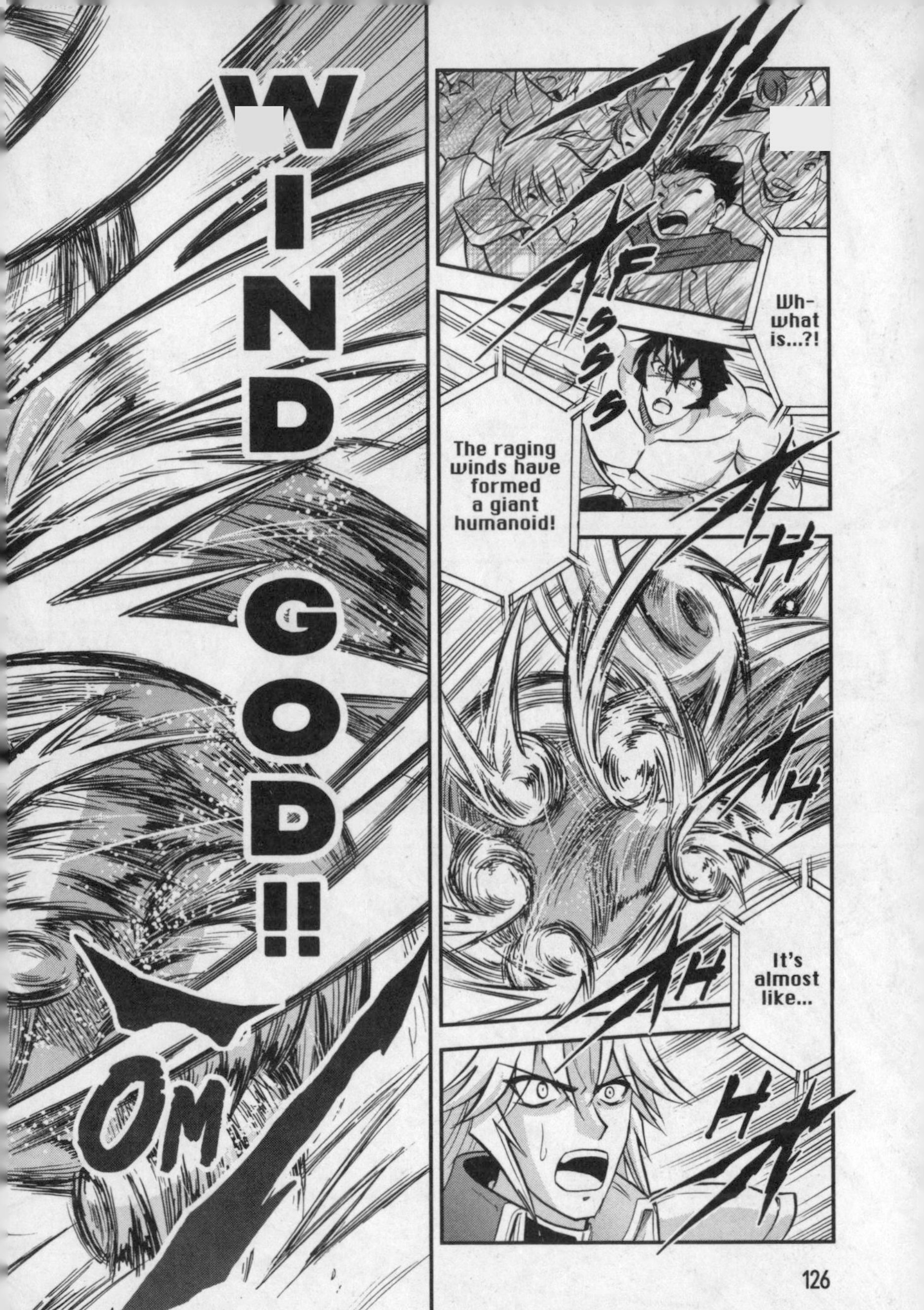
FSSS
Wh-
what
is...?!
The raging
winds have
formed
a giant
humanoid!
HHHHH
It's
almost
like...
WIND GOD!!
OM

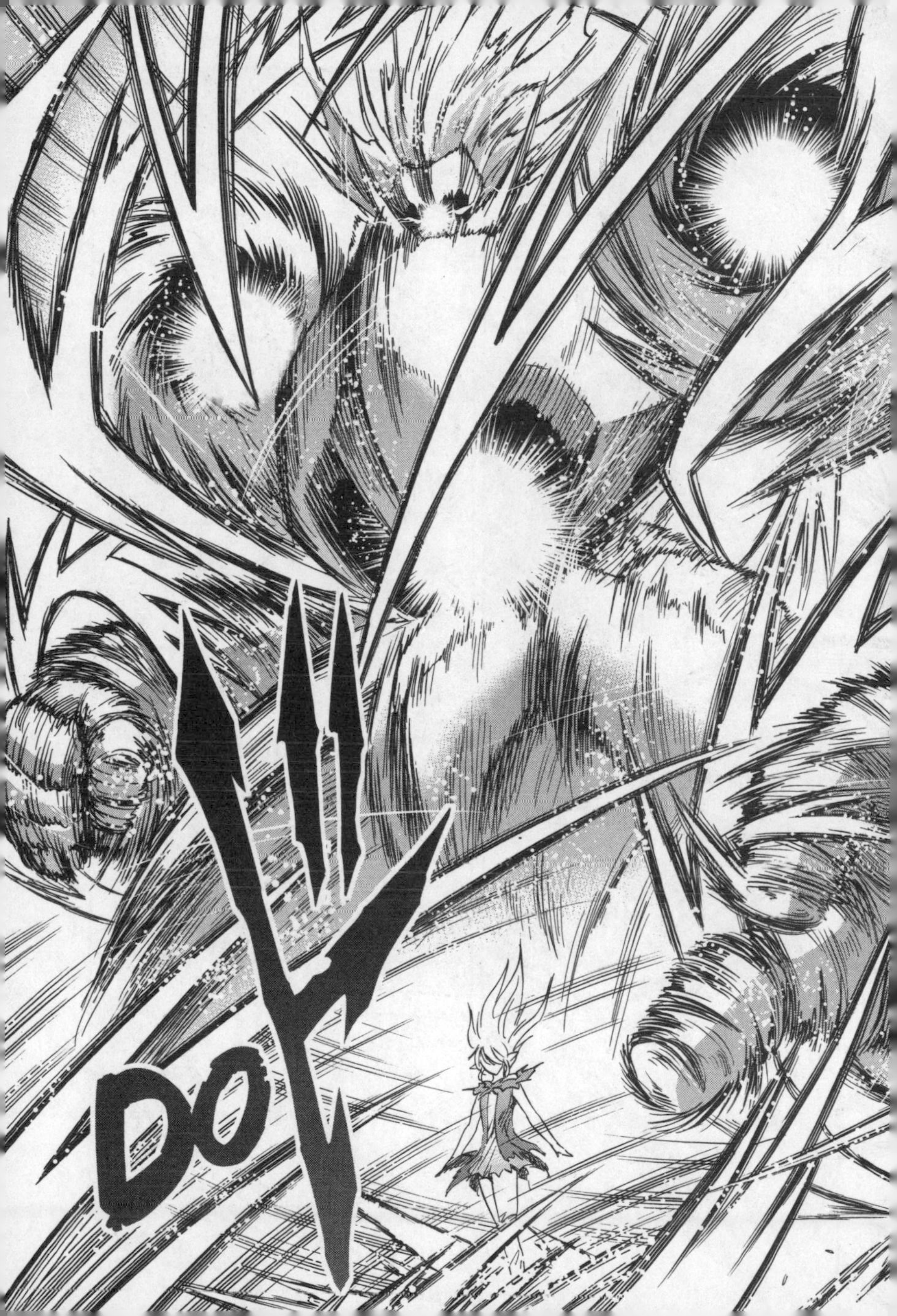
DON

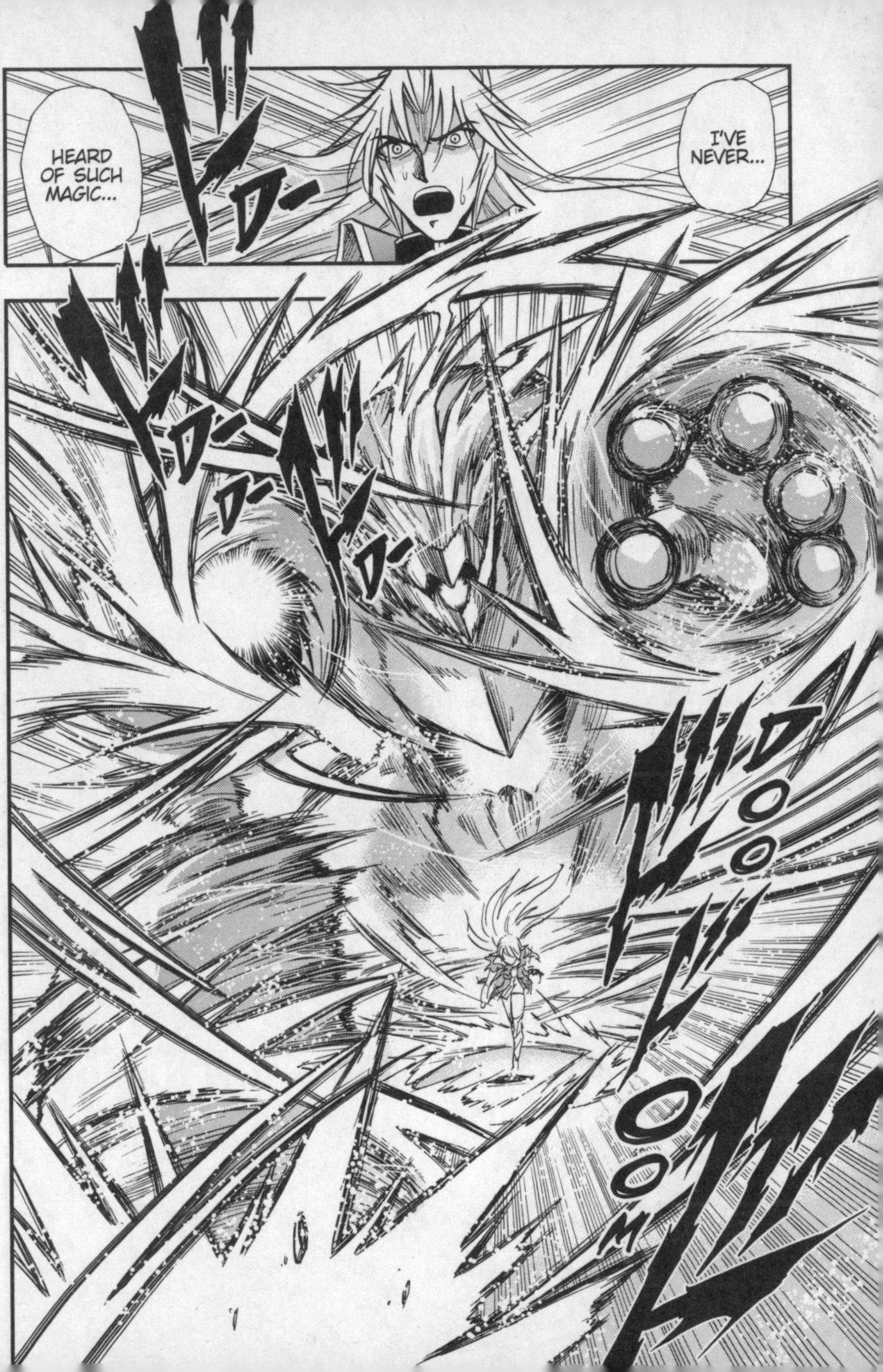
I'VE NEVER...
HEARD OF SUCH MAGIC...
DOOOOOOM

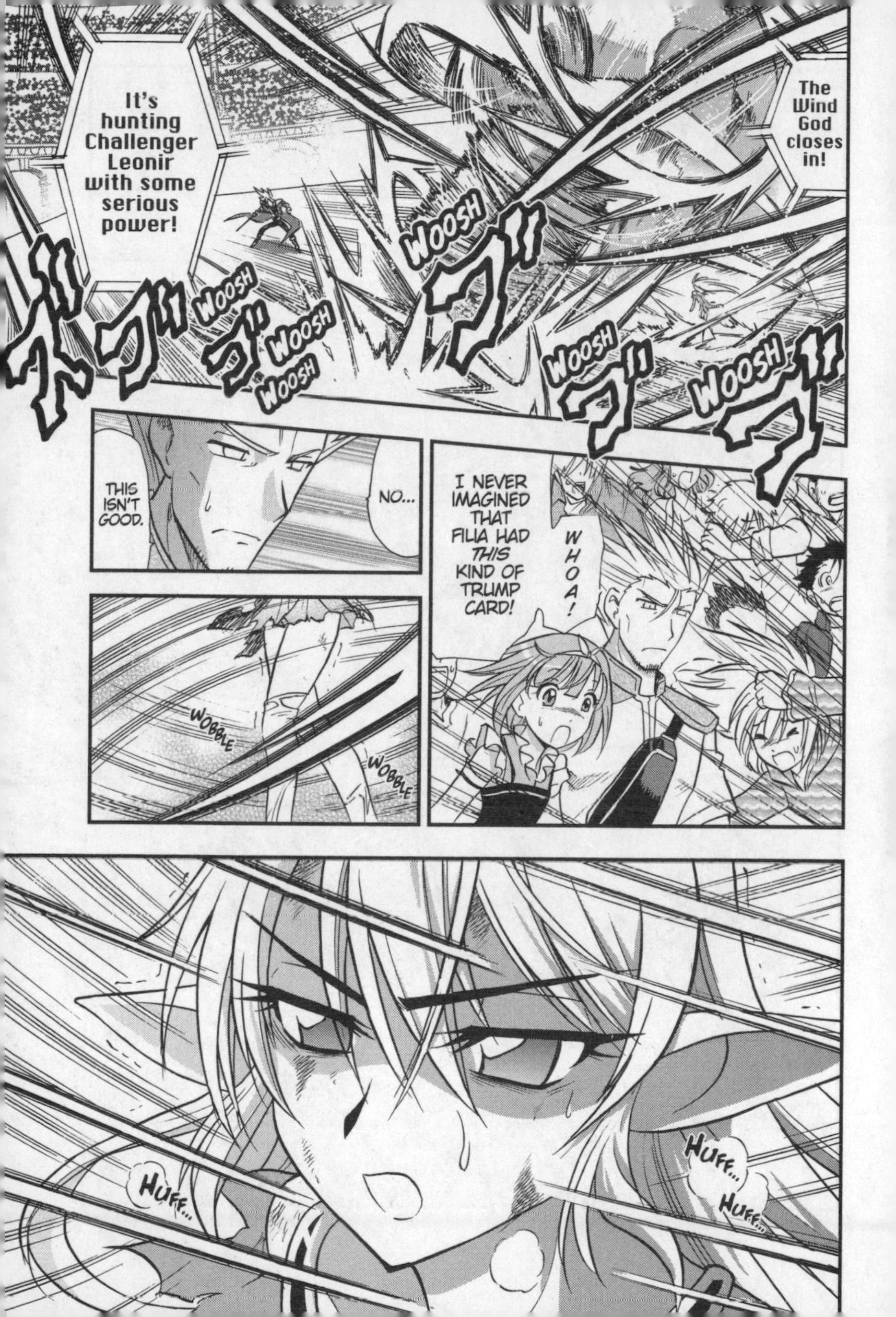
The Wind God closes in!
It's hunting Challenger Leonir with some serious power!
WOOSH
WOOSH
WOOSH
WOOSH
WOOSH
WOOSH
WOOSH
I NEVER IMAGINED THAT FILIA HAD *THIS* KIND OF TRUMP CARD!
WHOA!
NO...
THIS ISN'T GOOD.
WOBBLE
WOBBLE
HUFF...
HUFF...
HUFF...

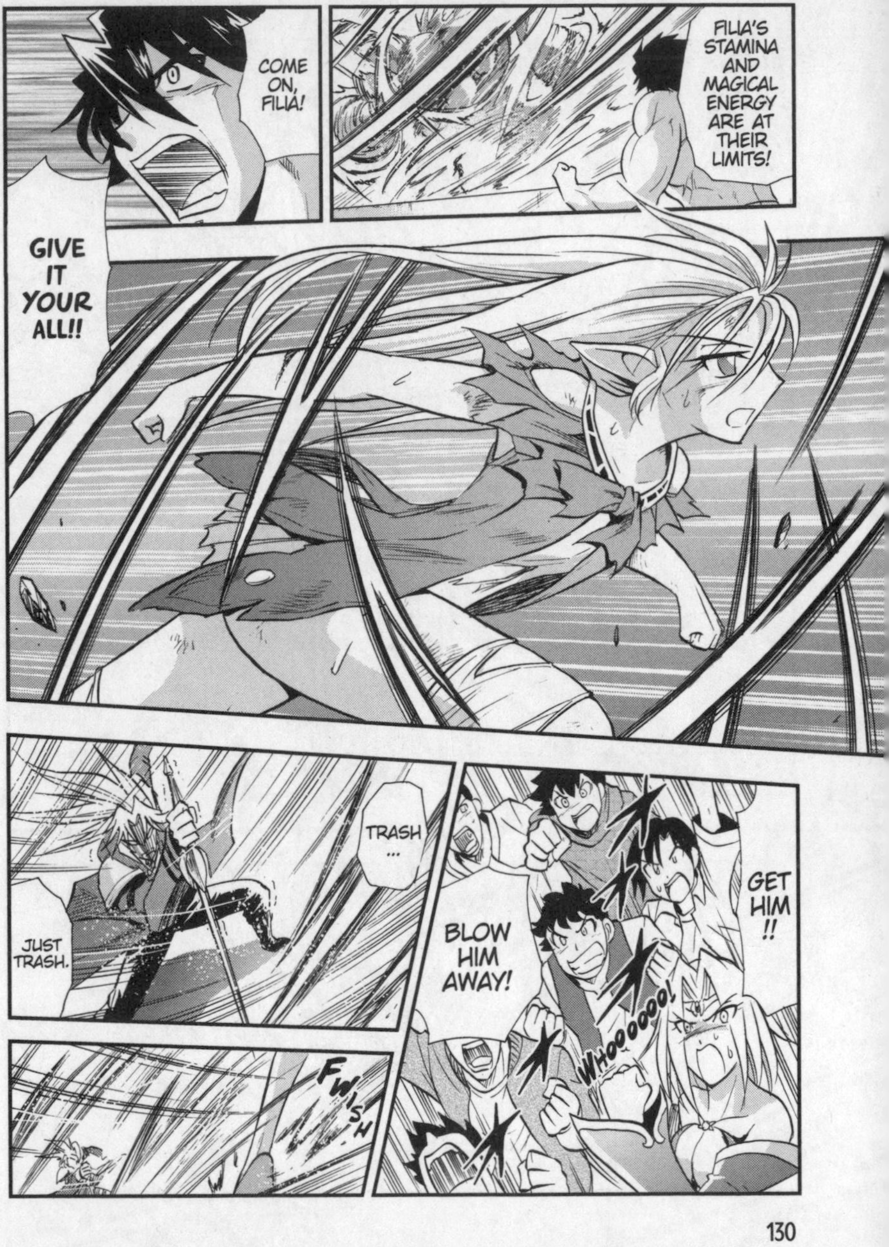
FILIA'S STAMINA AND MAGICAL ENERGY ARE AT THEIR LIMITS!
COME ON, FILIA!
GIVE IT YOUR ALL!!
GET HIM!!
WHOOOOOO!
BLOW HIM AWAY!
TRASH...
JUST TRASH.
FWISH

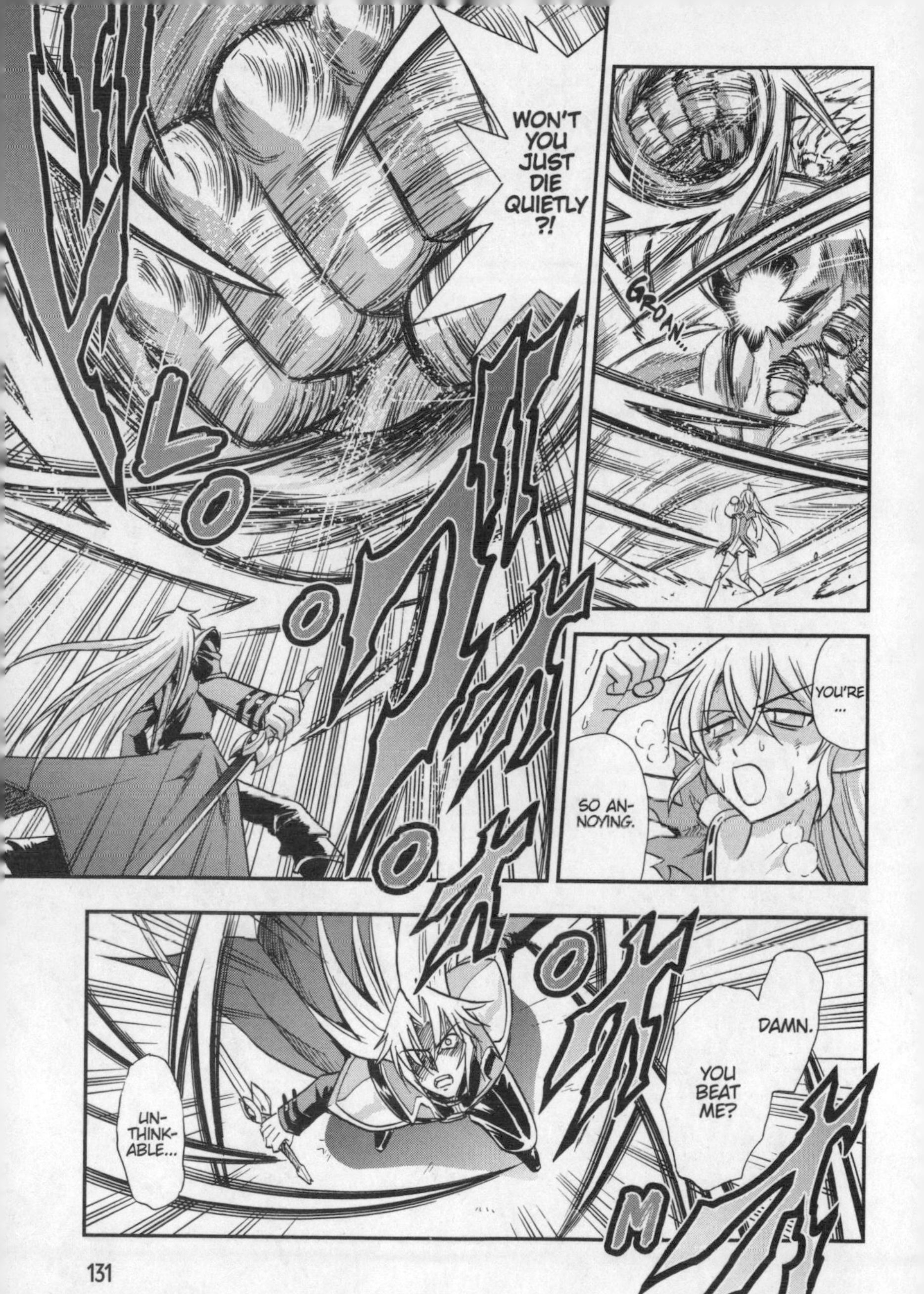
GROAN...
YOU'RE...
SO ANNOYING.
WON'T YOU JUST DIE QUIETLY?!
DAMN.
YOU BEAT ME?
UNTHINKABLE...

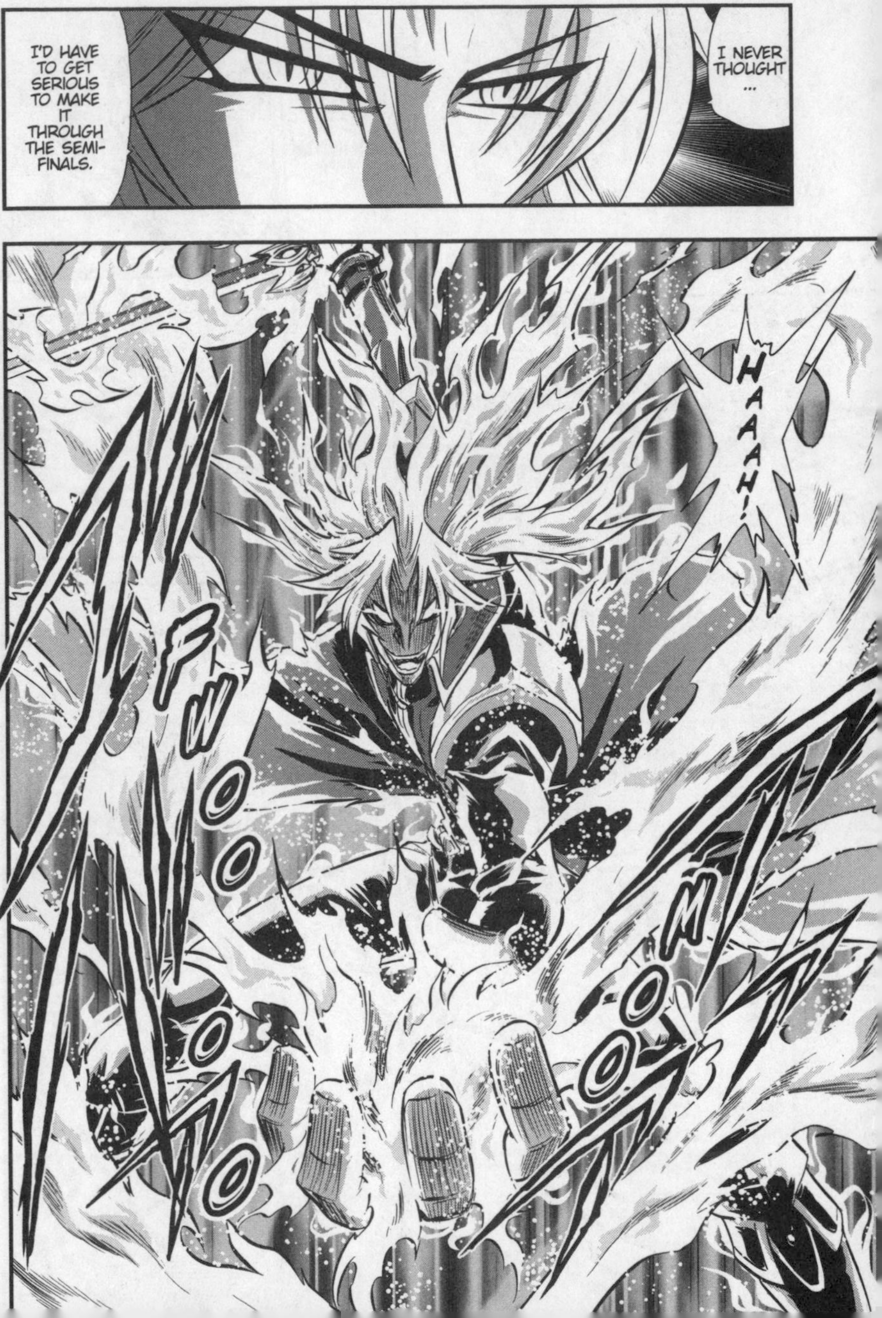
I NEVER THOUGHT ...
I'D HAVE TO GET SERIOUS TO MAKE IT THROUGH THE SEMI-FINALS.
HAAAH!
FWOOOOOOOM

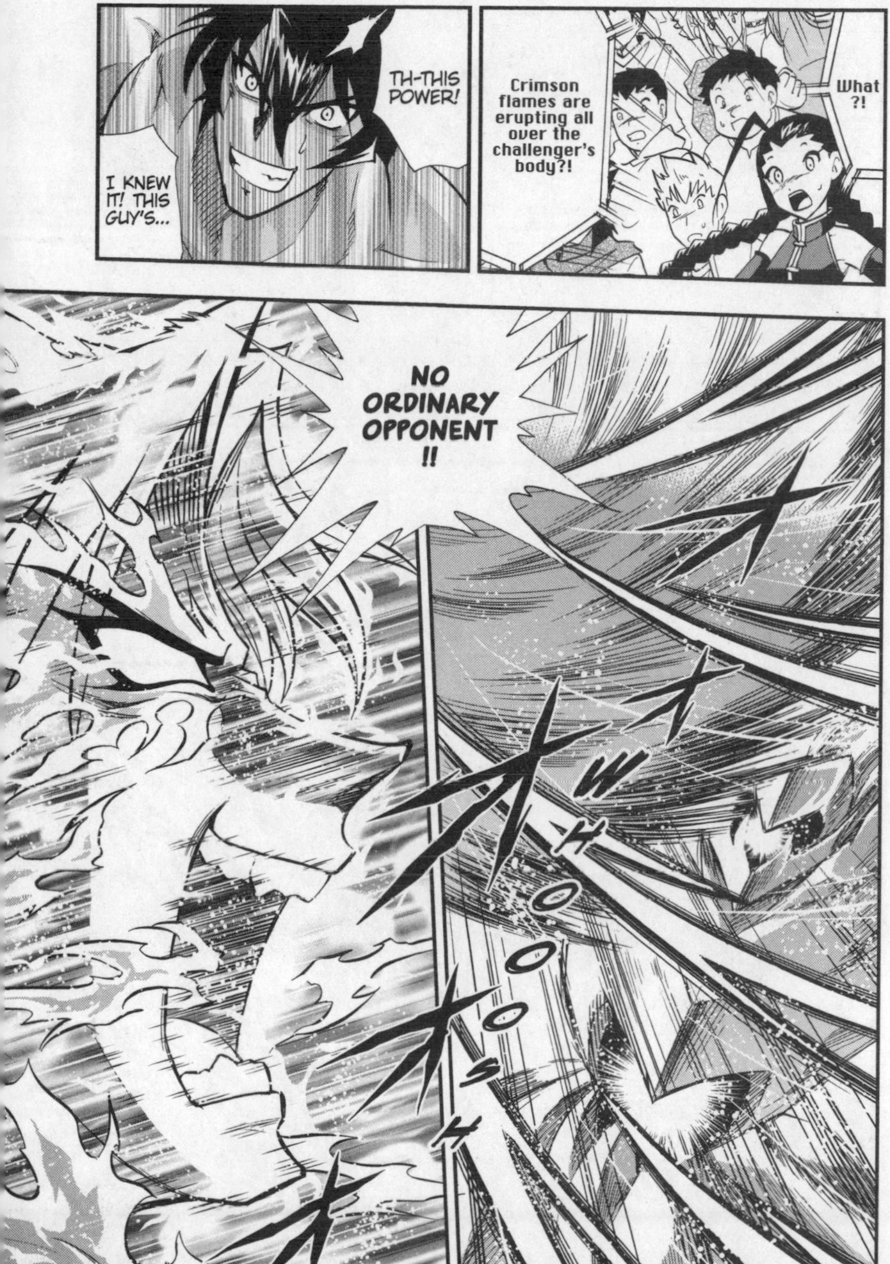
What?!
Crimson flames are erupting all over the challenger's body?!
TH-THIS POWER!
I KNEW IT! THIS GUY'S...
NO ORDINARY OPPONENT!!
WHOOOSH

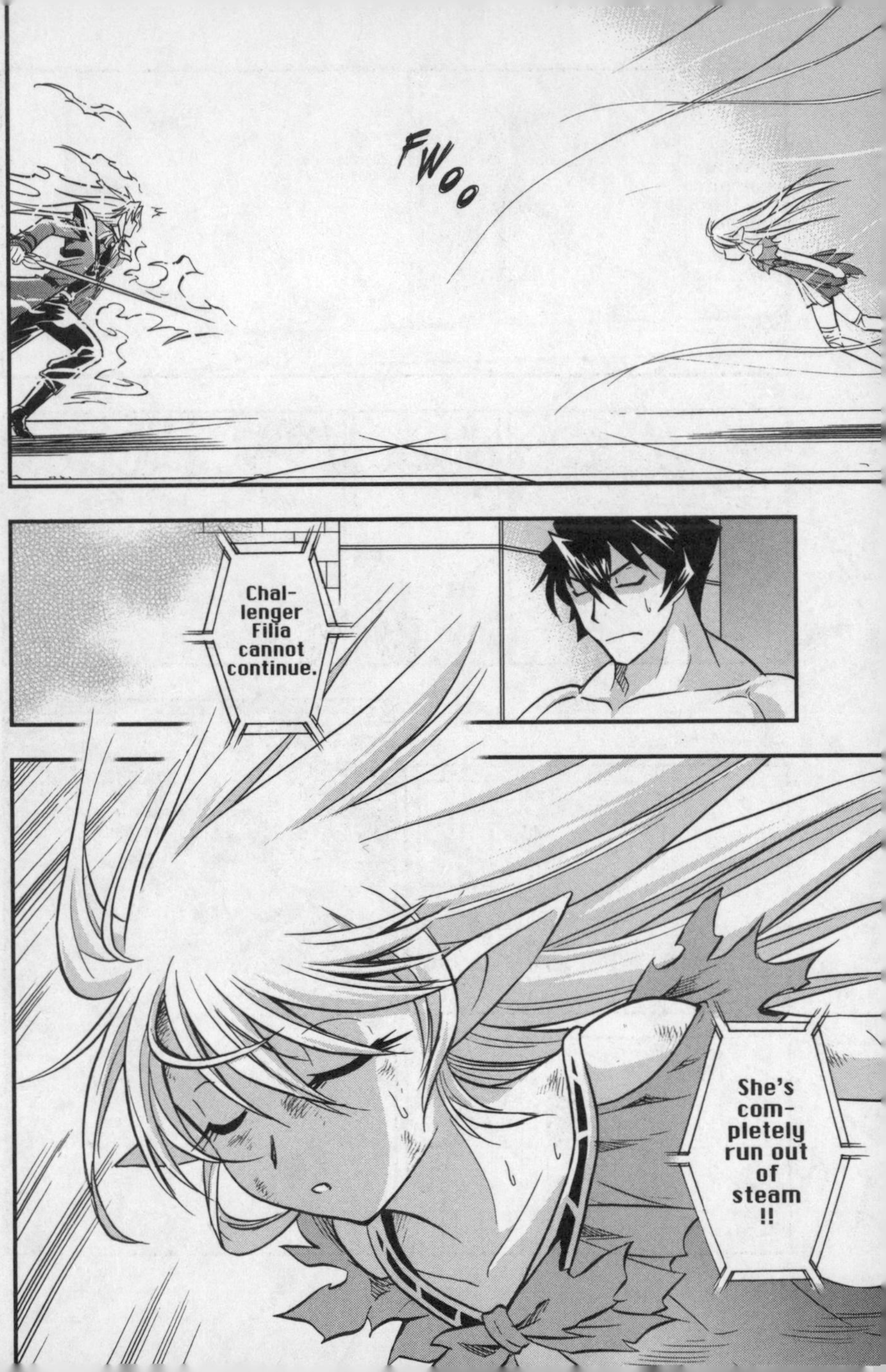
FWOO
Challenger Filia cannot continue.
She's completely run out of steam!!

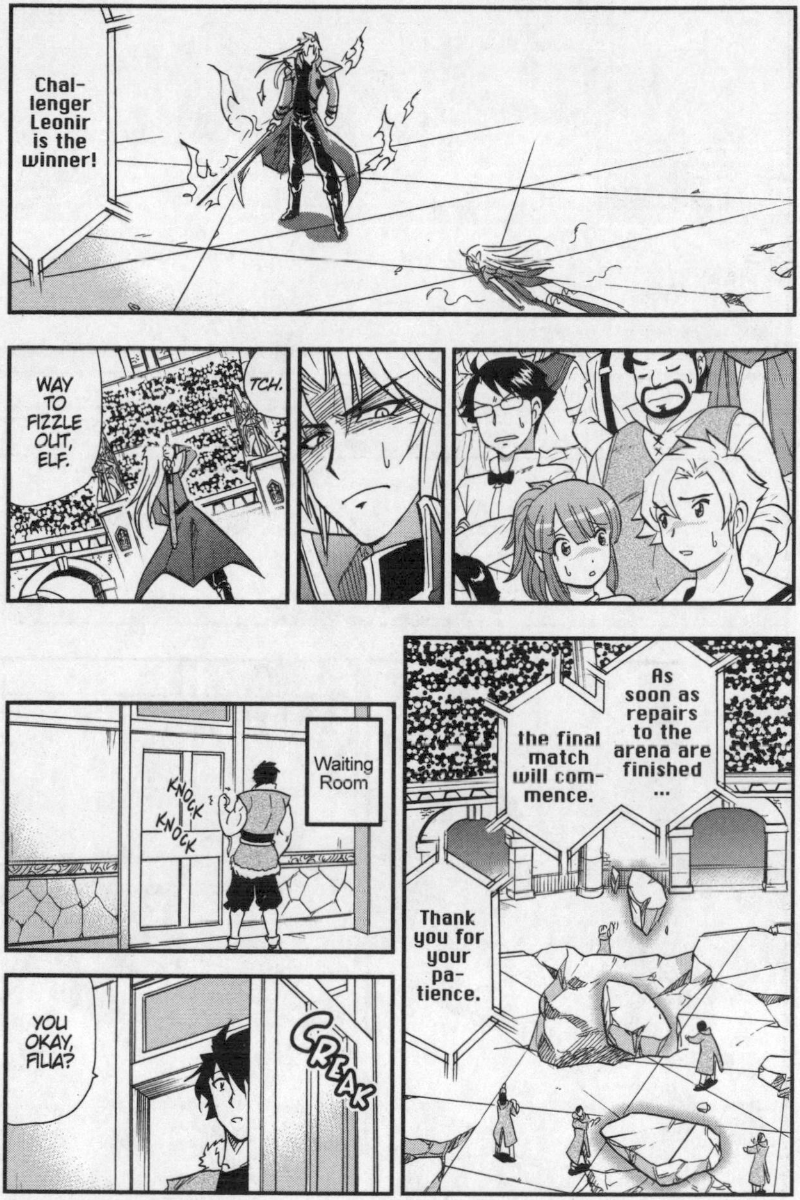
Challenger Leonir is the winner!
WAY TO FIZZLE OUT, ELF.
TCH.
As soon as repairs to the arena are finished...
the final match will commence.
Thank you for your patience.
Waiting Room
KNOCK KNOCK
CREAK
YOU OKAY, FILIA?

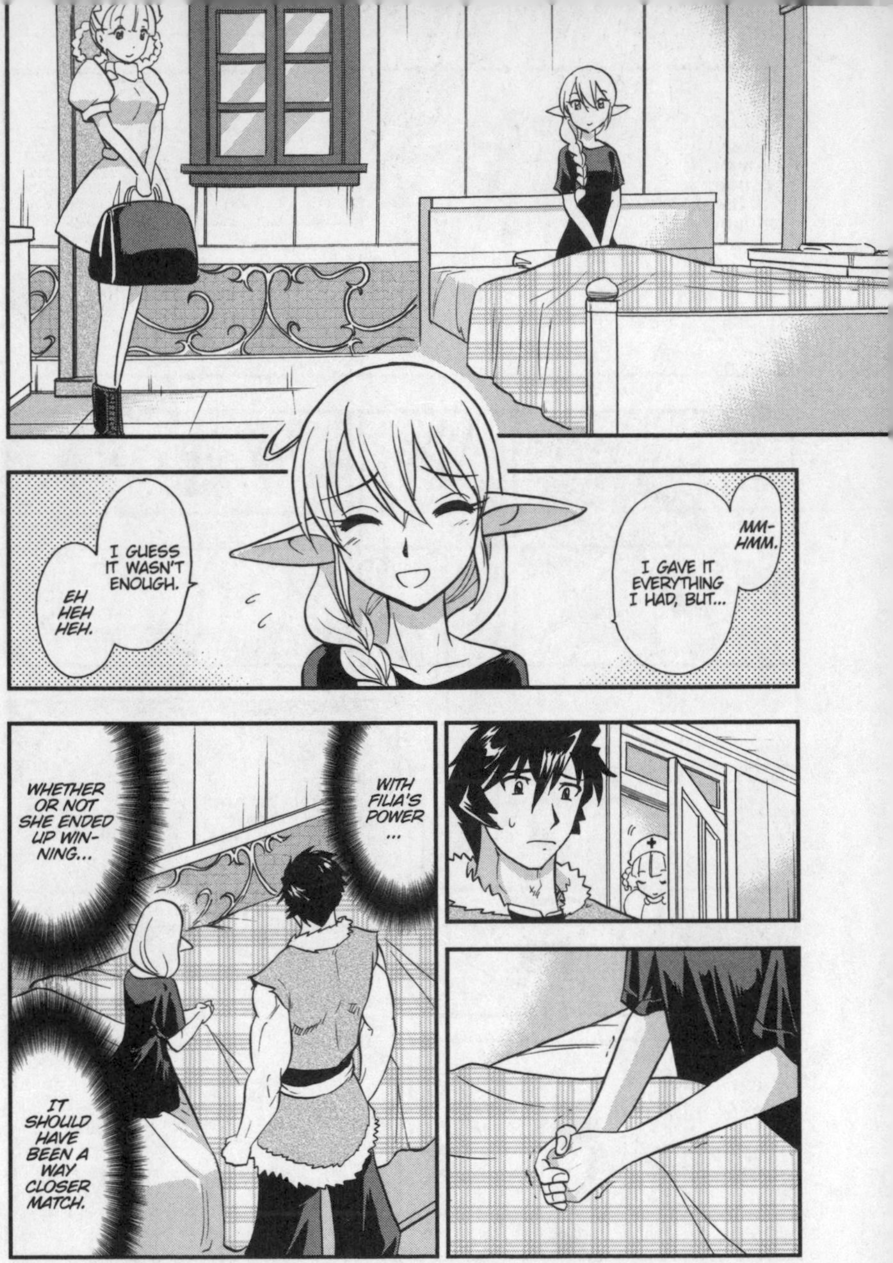
MM-HMM.
I GAVE IT EVERYTHING I HAD, BUT...
I GUESS IT WASN'T ENOUGH.
EH HEH HEH.
WITH FILIA'S POWER...
WHETHER OR NOT SHE ENDED UP WIN-NING...
IT SHOULD HAVE BEEN A WAY CLOSER MATCH.

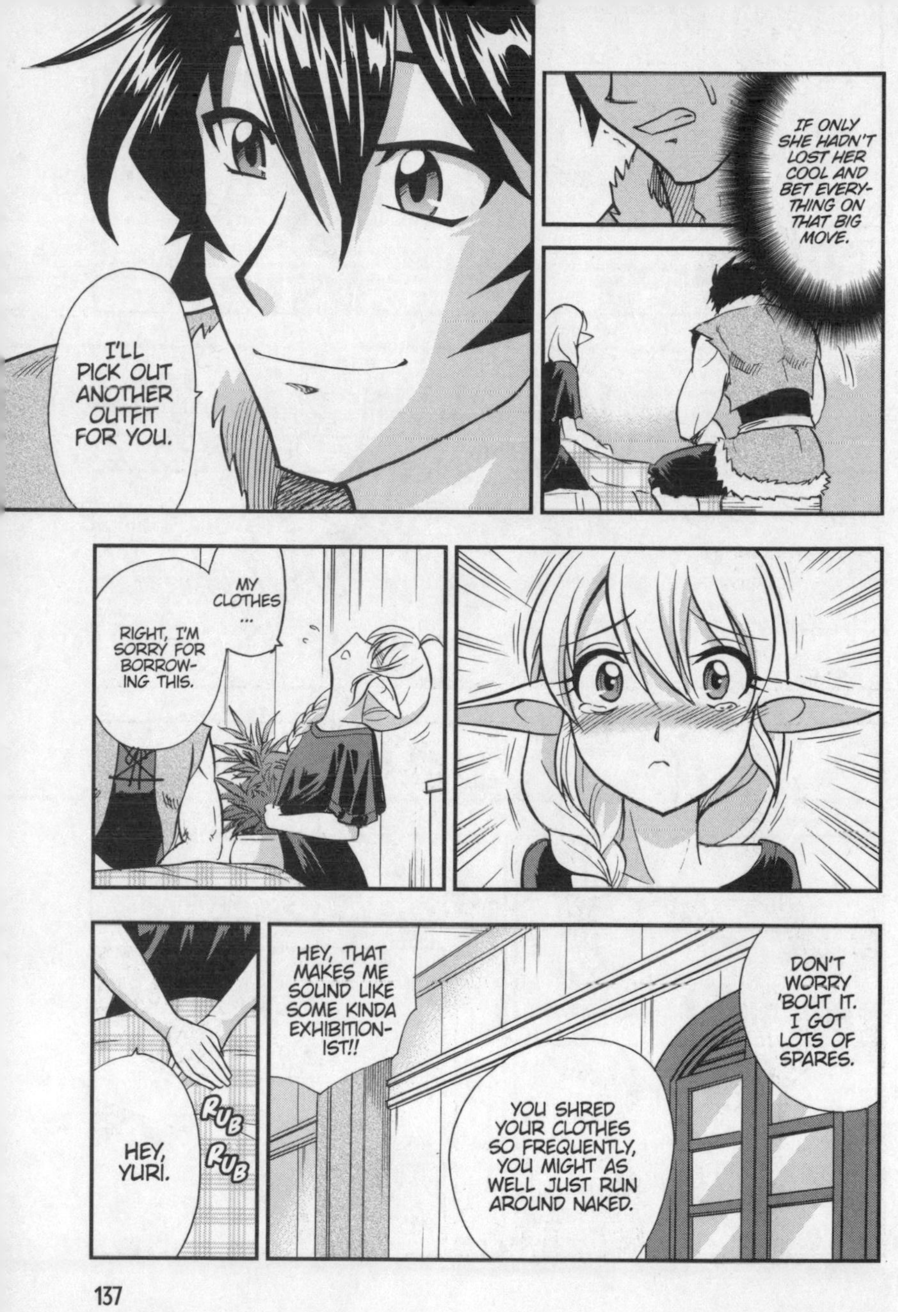
IF ONLY SHE HADN'T LOST HER COOL AND BET EVERY-THING ON THAT BIG MOVE.
I'LL PICK OUT ANOTHER OUTFIT FOR YOU.
MY CLOTHES ...
RIGHT, I'M SORRY FOR BORROW-ING THIS.
DON'T WORRY 'BOUT IT. I GOT LOTS OF SPARES.
YOU SHRED YOUR CLOTHES SO FREQUENTLY, YOU MIGHT AS WELL JUST RUN AROUND NAKED.
HEY, THAT MAKES ME SOUND LIKE SOME KINDA EXHIBITION-IST!!
RUB
RUB
HEY, YURI.

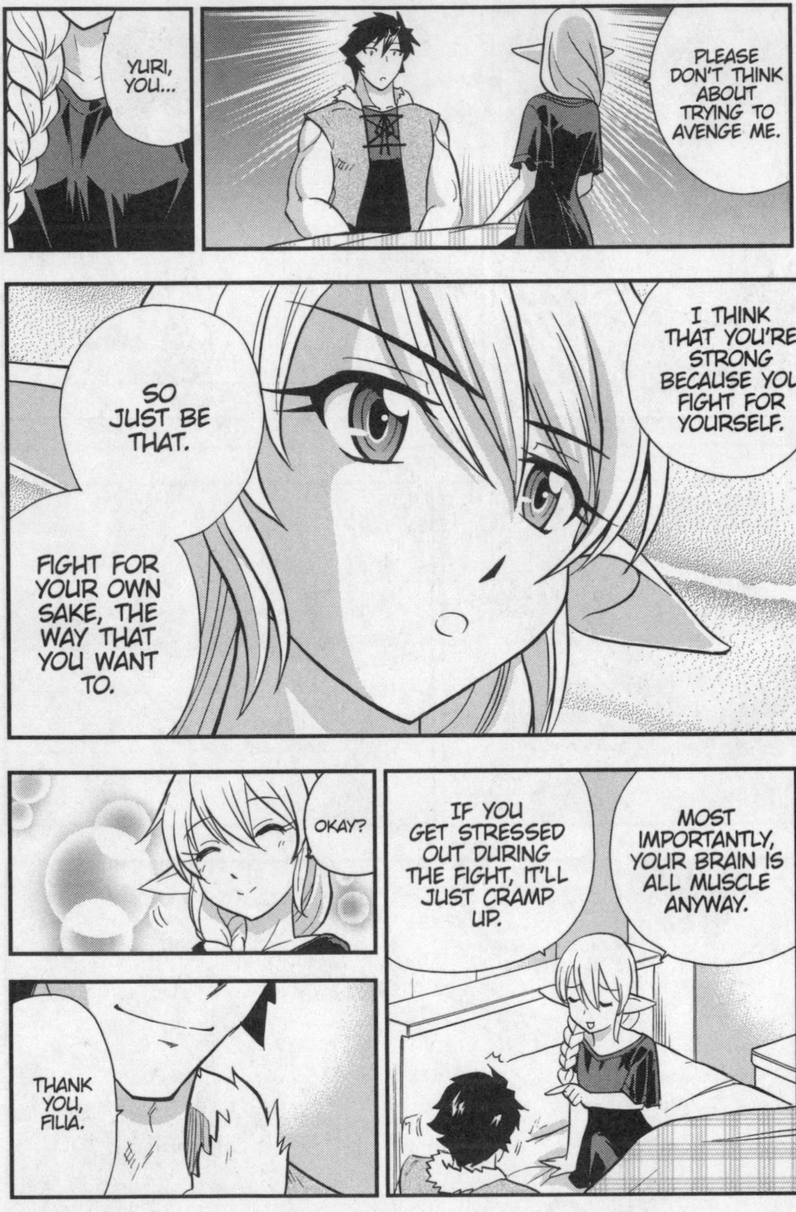
PLEASE DON'T THINK ABOUT TRYING TO AVENGE ME.
YURI, YOU...
I THINK THAT YOU'RE STRONG BECAUSE YOU FIGHT FOR YOURSELF.
SO JUST BE THAT.
FIGHT FOR YOUR OWN SAKE, THE WAY THAT YOU WANT TO.
MOST IMPORTANTLY, YOUR BRAIN IS ALL MUSCLE ANYWAY.
IF YOU GET STRESSED OUT DURING THE FIGHT, IT'LL JUST CRAMP UP.
OKAY?
THANK YOU, FILIA.

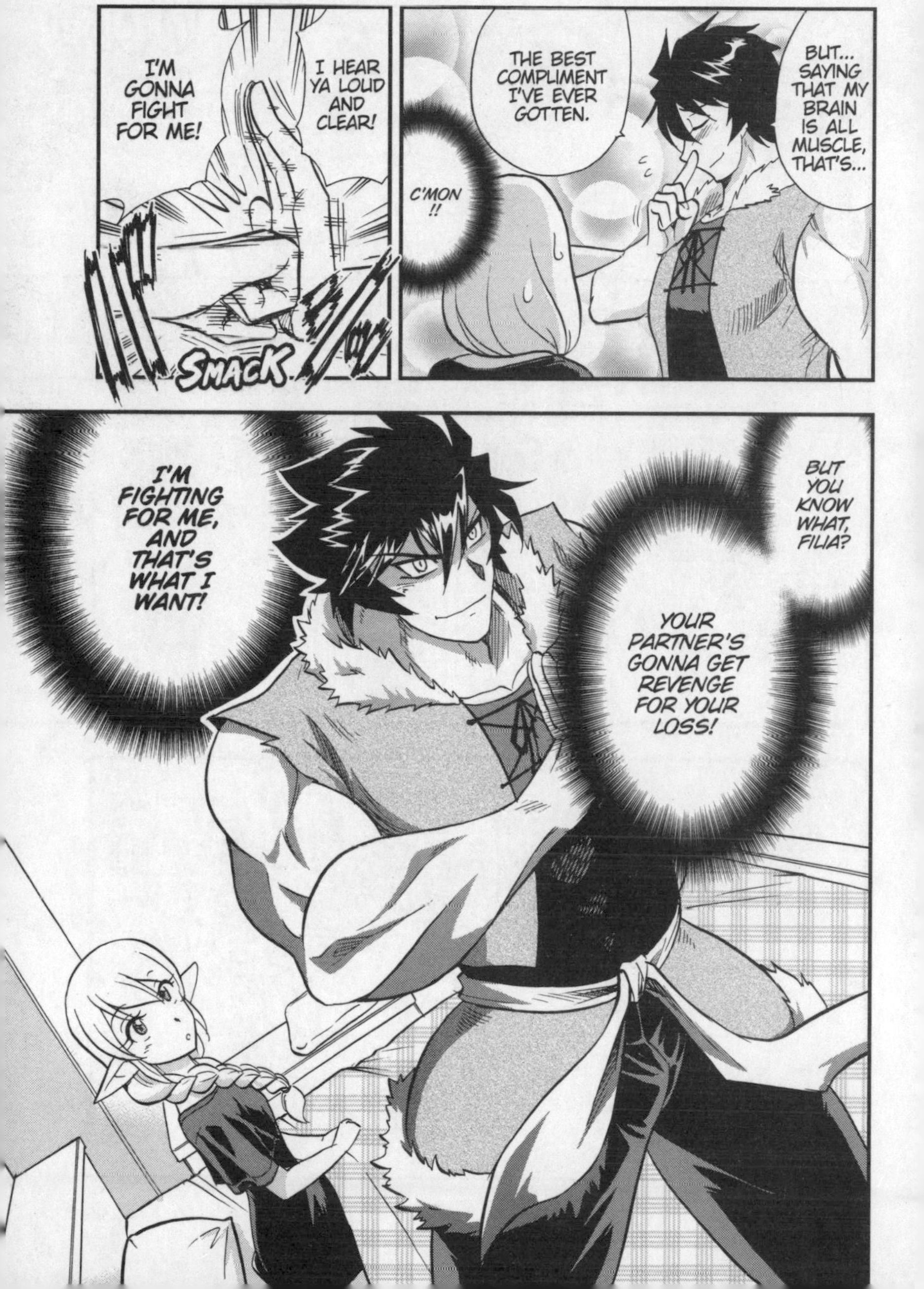
BUT... SAYING THAT MY BRAIN IS ALL MUSCLE, THAT'S...
THE BEST COMPLIMENT I'VE EVER GOTTEN.
C'MON!!
I HEAR YA LOUD AND CLEAR!
I'M GONNA FIGHT FOR ME!
SMACK
BUT YOU KNOW WHAT, FILIA?
YOUR PARTNER'S GONNA GET REVENGE FOR YOUR LOSS!
I'M FIGHTING FOR ME, AND THAT'S WHAT I WANT!

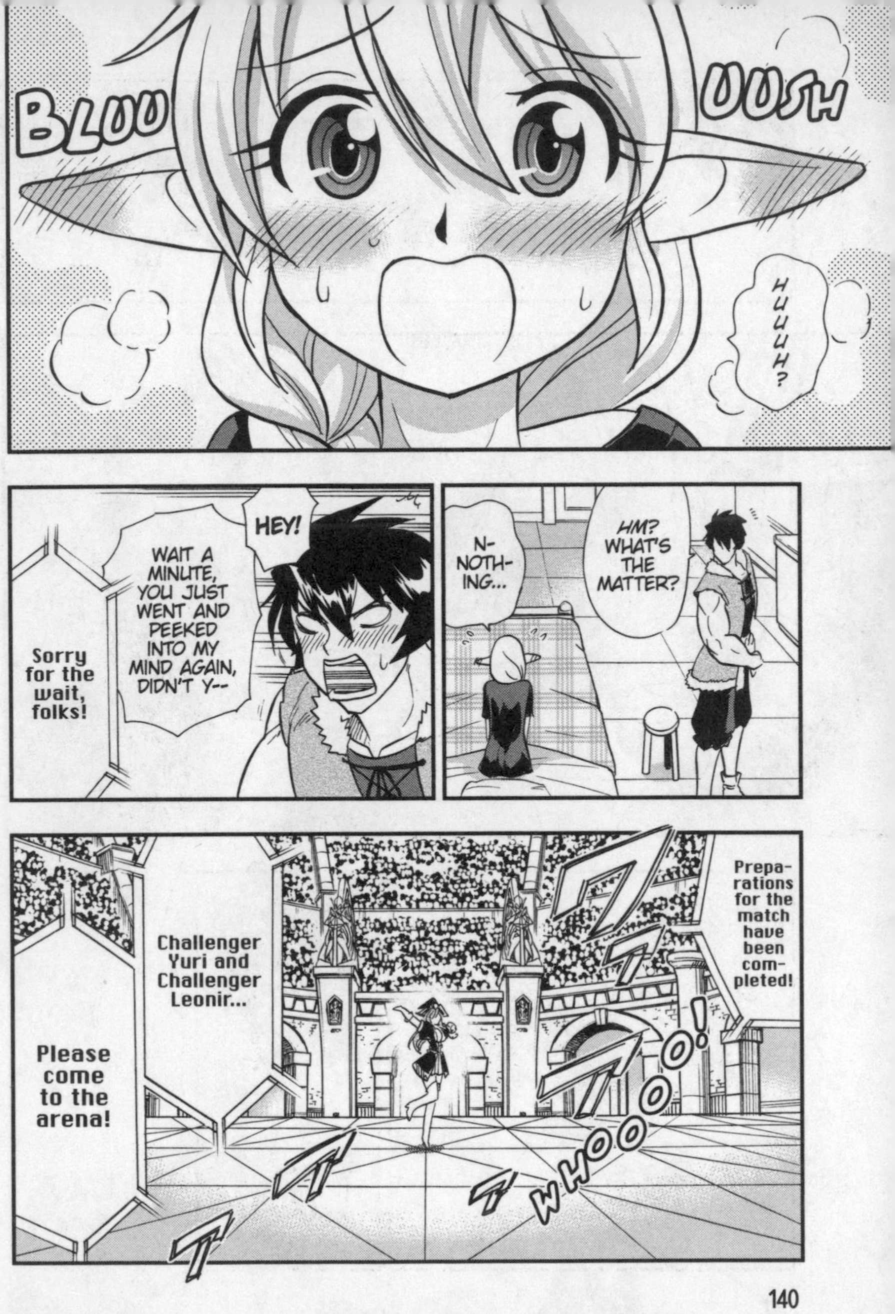
BLUU
UUSH
HUUUH?
HM? WHAT'S THE MATTER?
N-NOTHING...
HEY!
WAIT A MINUTE, YOU JUST WENT AND PEEKED INTO MY MIND AGAIN, DIDN'T Y--
Sorry for the wait, folks!
Preparations for the match have been completed!
Challenger Yuri and Challenger Leonir...
Please come to the arena!
WHOOOOO!

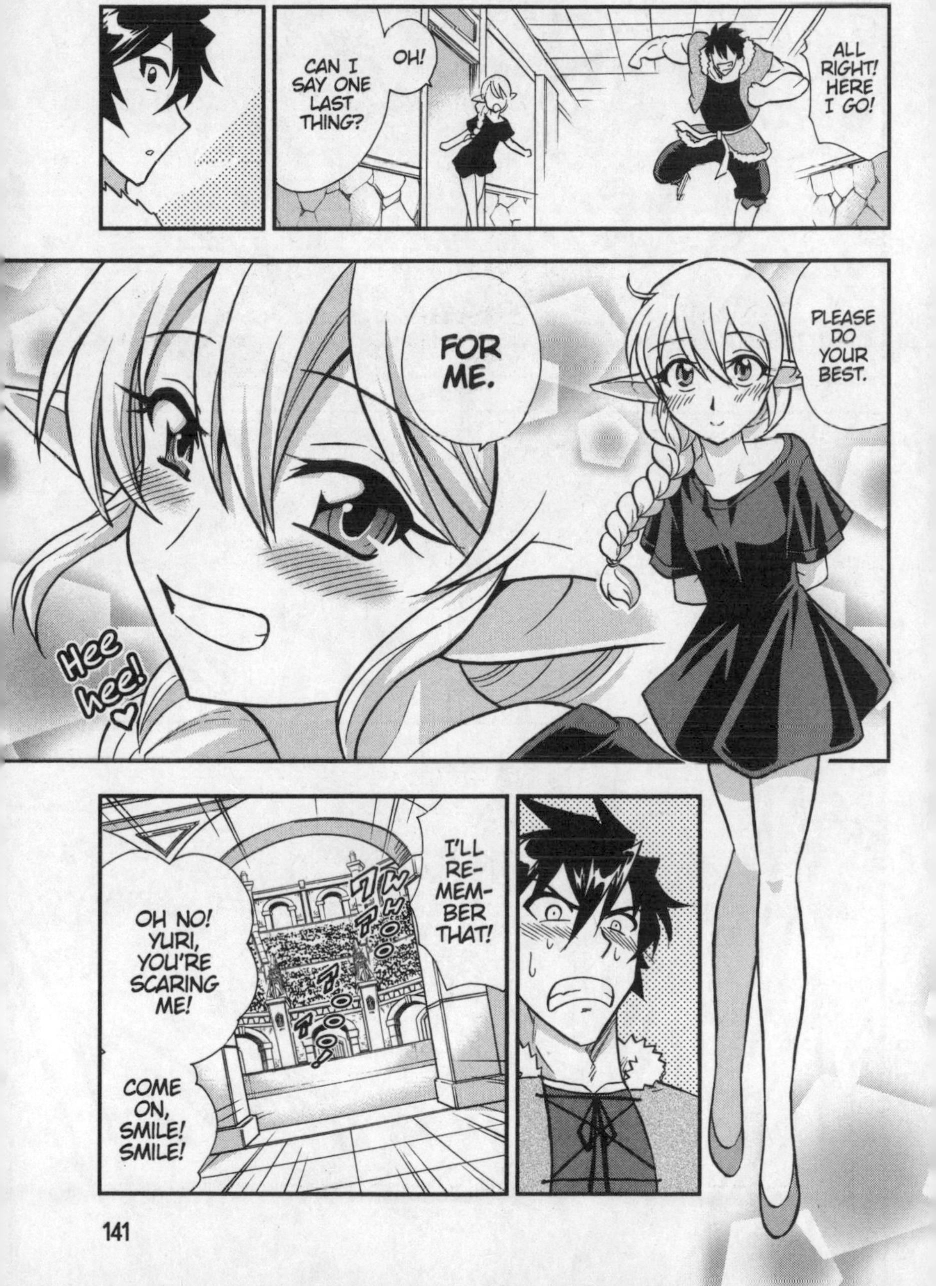
ALL RIGHT! HERE I GO!
OH!
CAN I SAY ONE LAST THING?
PLEASE DO YOUR BEST.
FOR ME.
Hee hee! ♥
I'LL RE-MEM-BER THAT!
OH NO! YURI, YOU'RE SCARING ME!
COME ON, SMILE! SMILE!

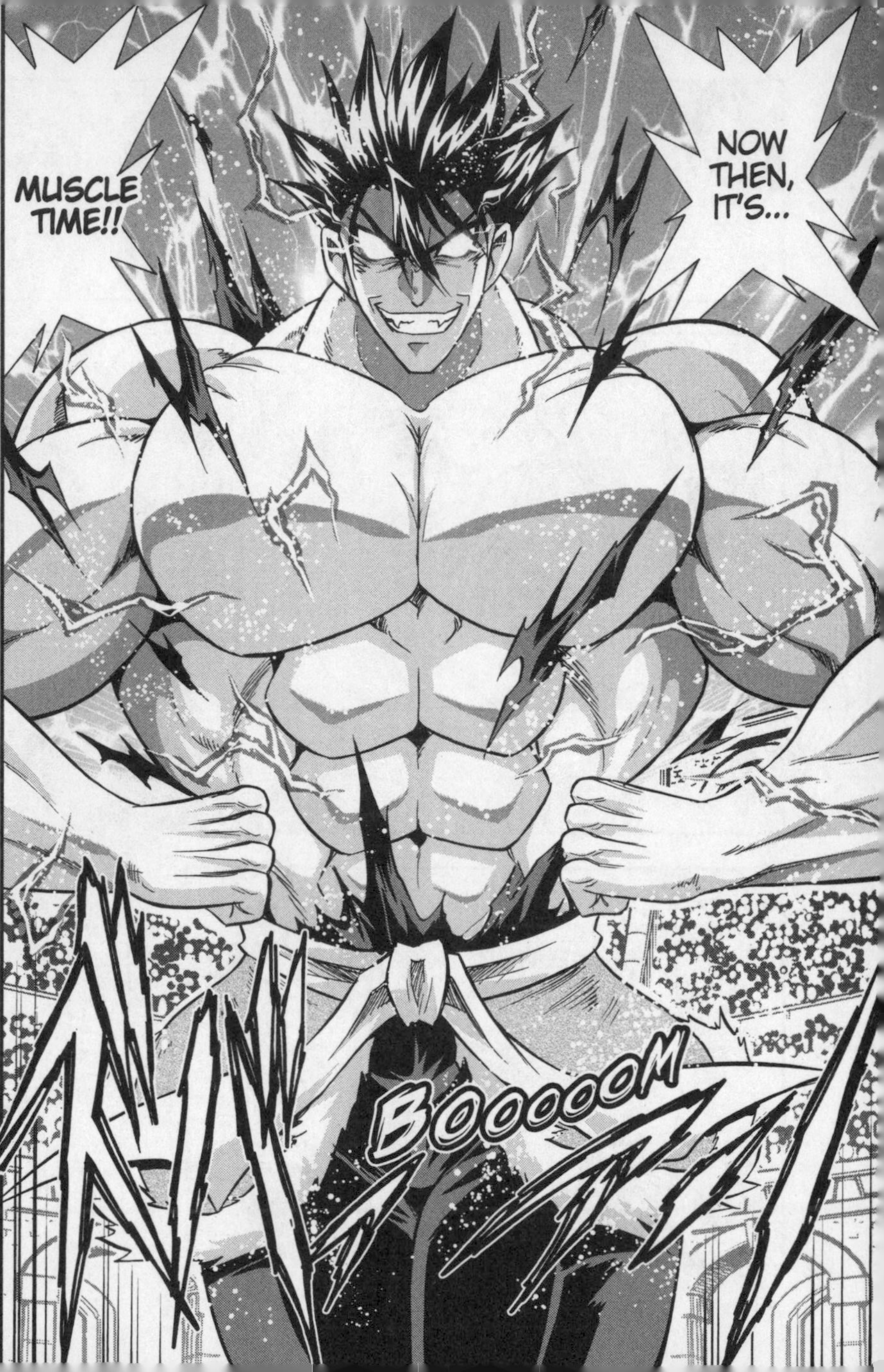
NOW THEN, IT'S...
MUSCLE TIME!!
BOOOOOOM

CHAPTER 14 END

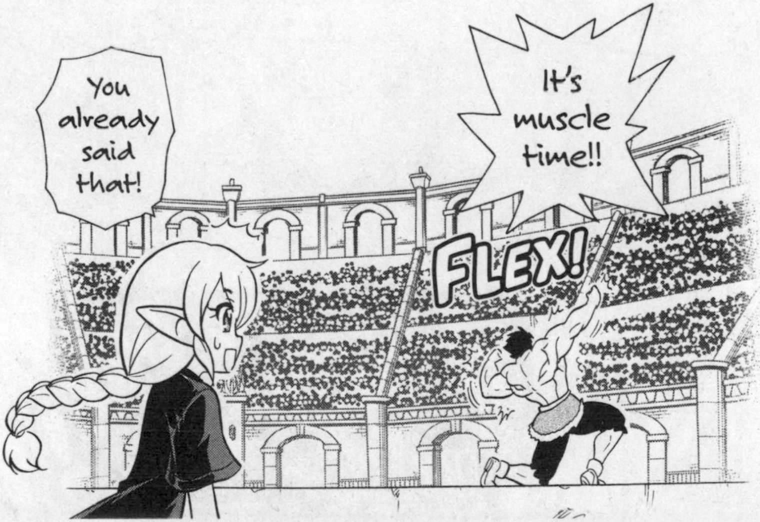
It's muscle time!!
FLEX!
You already said that!

MUSCLES ARE BETTER THAN MAGIC!

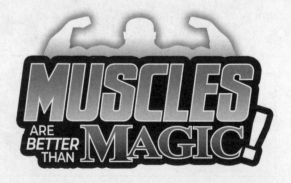

CHAPTER 15
Magic Battle Tournament (5)

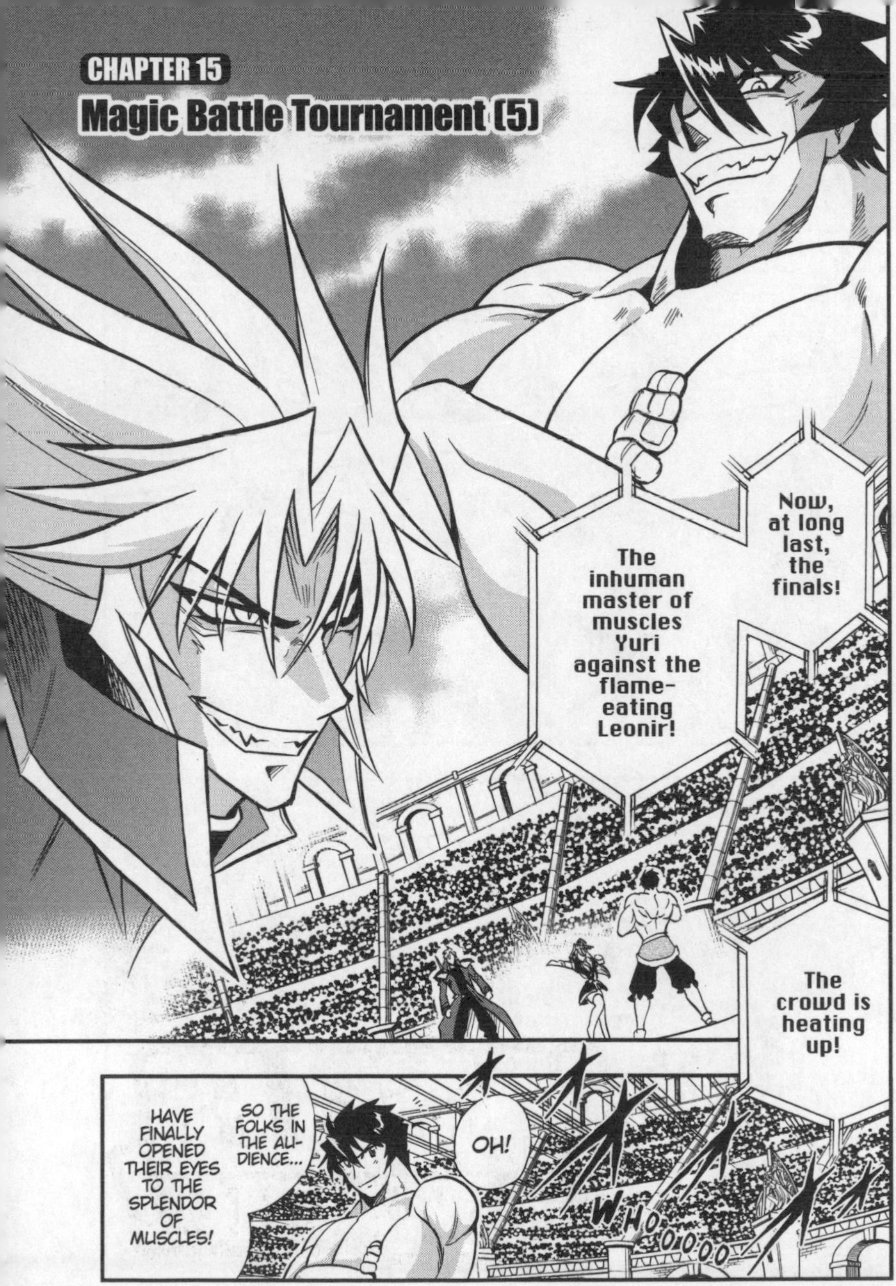
Now, at long last, the finals!
The inhuman master of muscles Yuri against the flame-eating Leonir!
The crowd is heating up!
OH!
SO THE FOLKS IN THE AU-DIENCE...
HAVE FINALLY OPENED THEIR EYES TO THE SPLENDOR OF MUSCLES!
WHOOOOOO

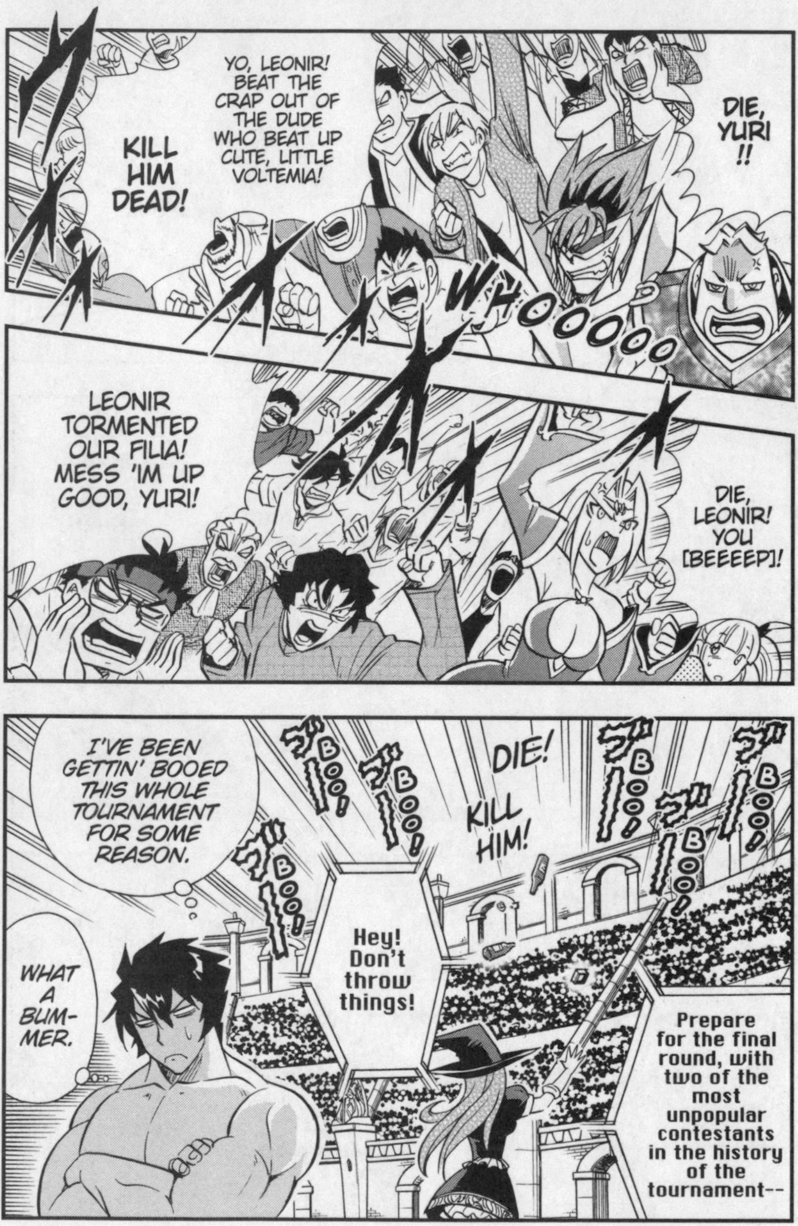
DIE, YURI!!
YO, LEONIR! BEAT THE CRAP OUT OF THE DUDE WHO BEAT UP CUTE, LITTLE VOLTEMIA!
KILL HIM DEAD!
WHOOOOOO
DIE, LEONIR! YOU [BEEEEP]!
LEONIR TORMENTED OUR FILIA! MESS 'IM UP GOOD, YURI!
Prepare for the final round, with two of the most unpopular contestants in the history of the tournament--
BOO!
BOO!
BOO!
DIE!
KILL HIM!
BOO!
BOO!
BOO!
Hey! Don't throw things!
I'VE BEEN GETTIN' BOOED THIS WHOLE TOURNAMENT FOR SOME REASON.
WHAT A BUM-MER.

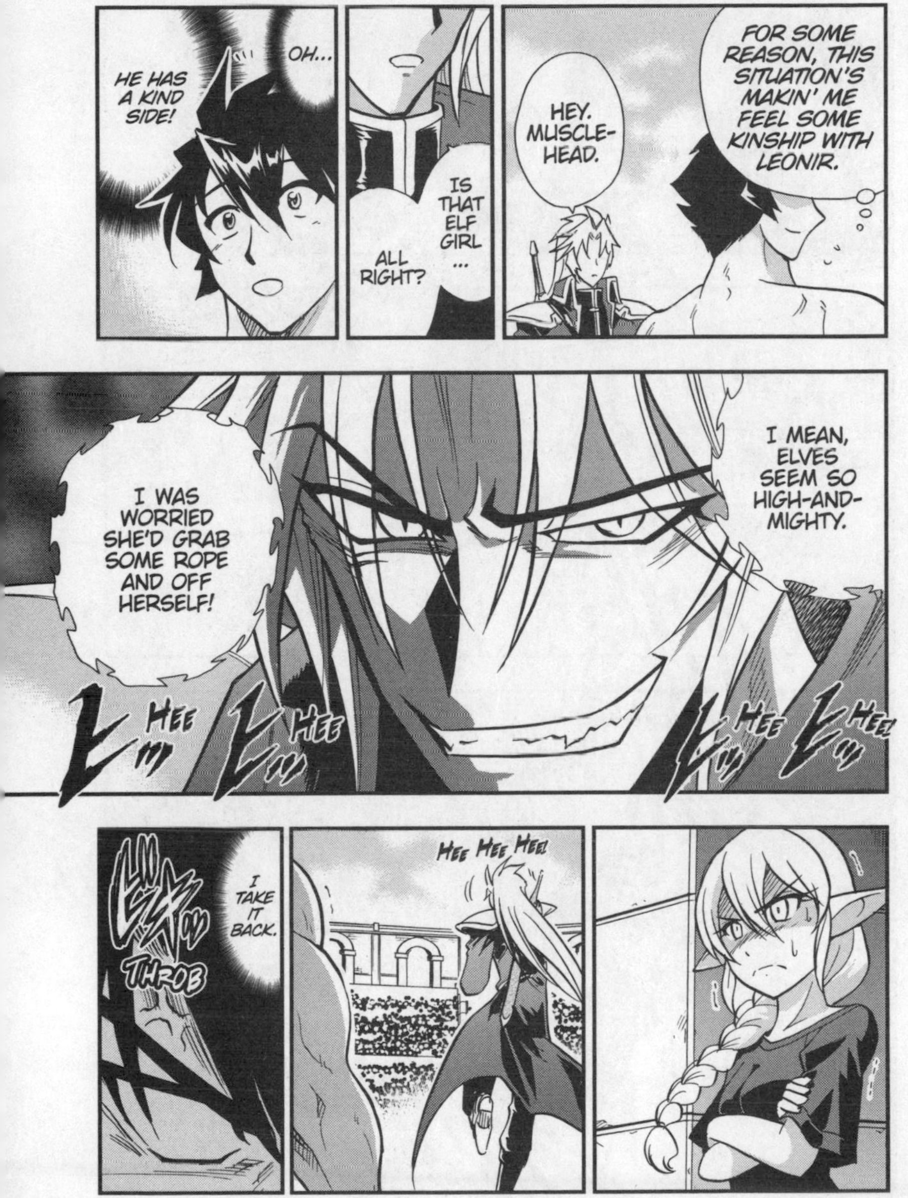
FOR SOME REASON, THIS SITUATION'S MAKIN' ME FEEL SOME KINSHIP WITH LEONIR.
HEY. MUSCLE-HEAD.
IS THAT ELF GIRL ...
ALL RIGHT?
OH...
HE HAS A KIND SIDE!
I MEAN, ELVES SEEM SO HIGH-AND-MIGHTY.
I WAS WORRIED SHE'D GRAB SOME ROPE AND OFF HERSELF!
ヒッ HEE
ヒッ HEE
ヒッ HEE
ヒッ HEE
HEE HEE HEE!
I TAKE IT BACK.
THROB

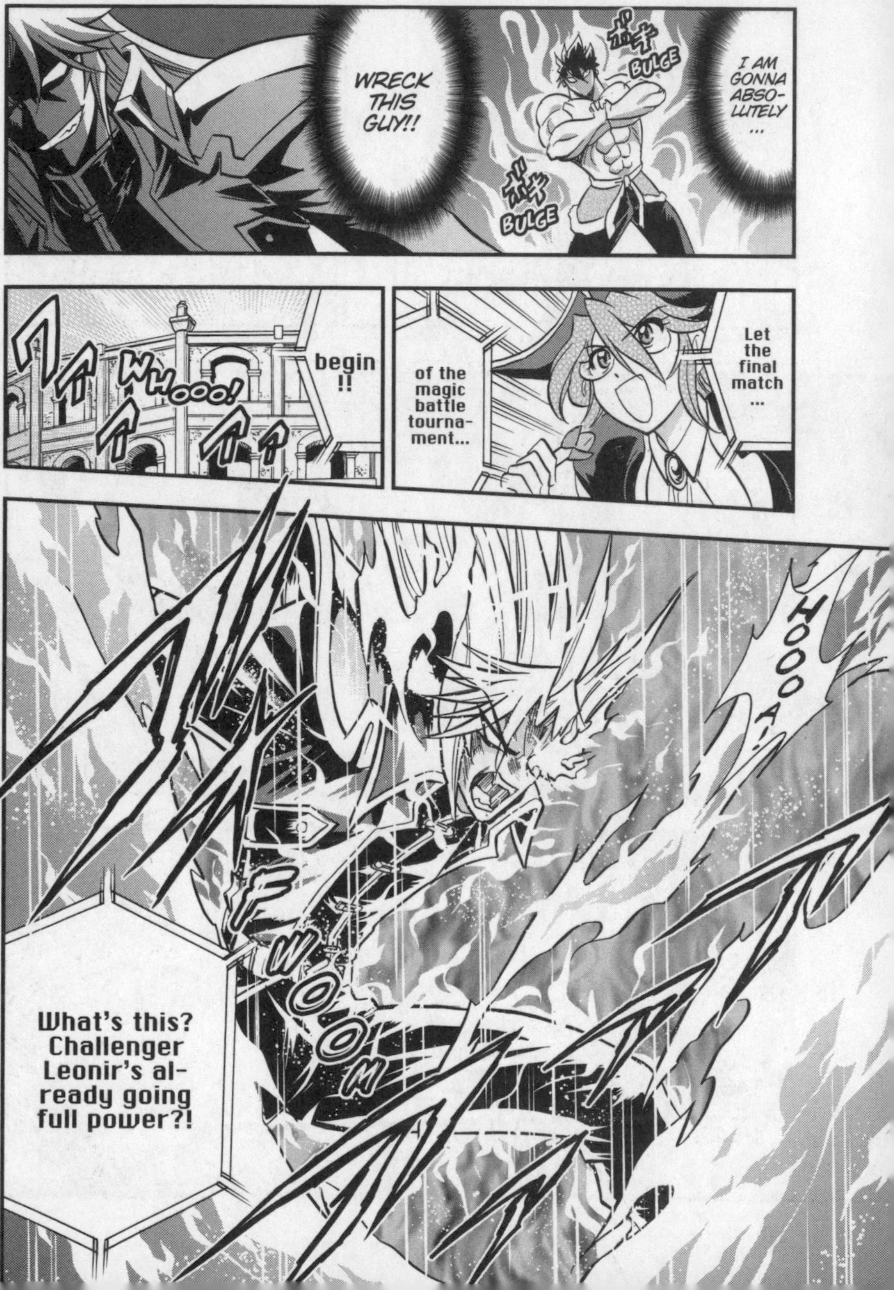
I AM GONNA ABSO-LUTELY ...
BULGE
BULGE
WRECK THIS GUY!!
Let the final match ...
of the magic battle tourna-ment...
begin !!
WHOOO!
HOOOA!!
FWOOOM
What's this? Challenger Leonir's al-ready going full power?!

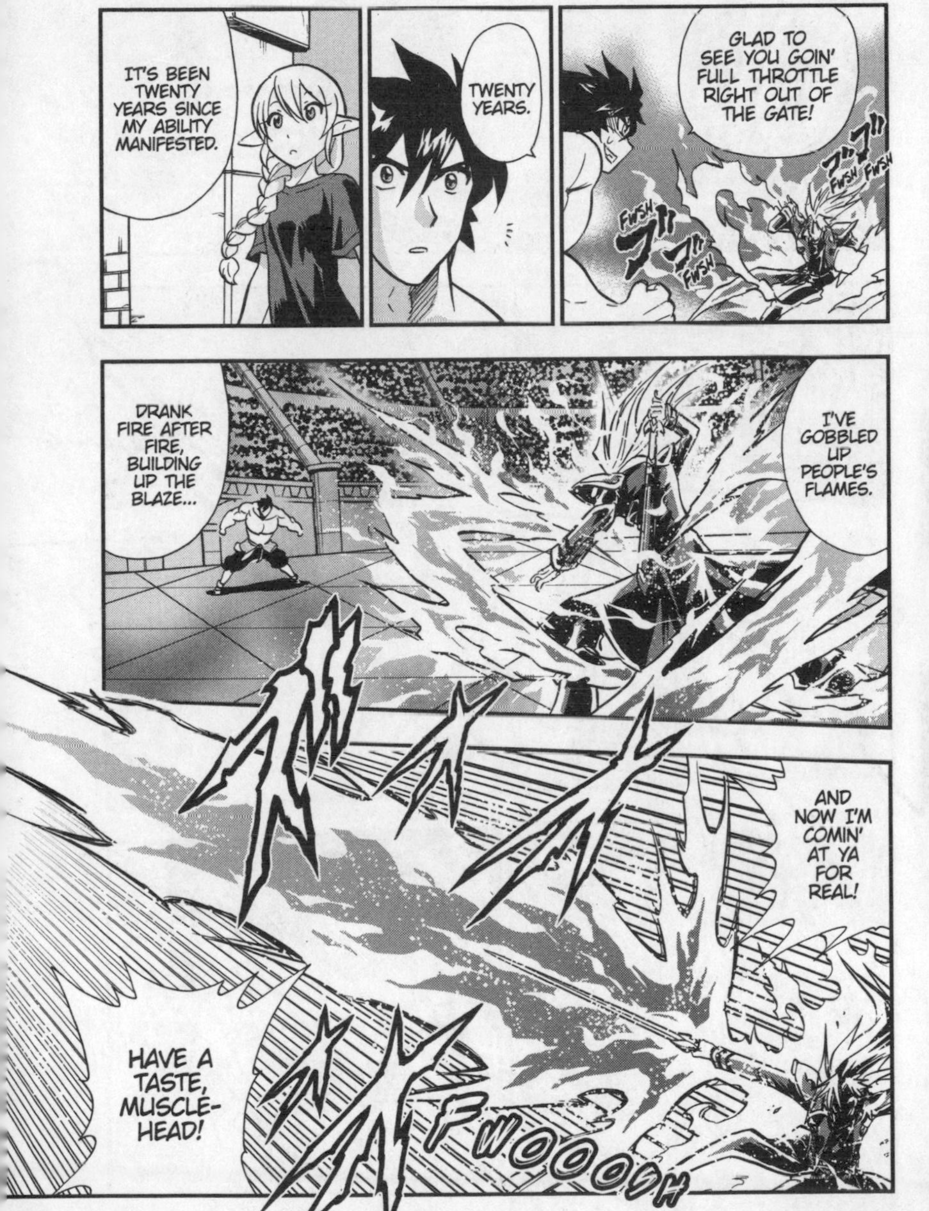
GLAD TO SEE YOU GOIN' FULL THROTTLE RIGHT OUT OF THE GATE!
FWSH FWSH
FWSH FWSH
TWENTY YEARS.
IT'S BEEN TWENTY YEARS SINCE MY ABILITY MANIFESTED.
I'VE GOBBLED UP PEOPLE'S FLAMES.
DRANK FIRE AFTER FIRE, BUILDING UP THE BLAZE...
AND NOW I'M COMIN' AT YA FOR REAL!
HAVE A TASTE, MUSCLE-HEAD!
FWOOOOSH

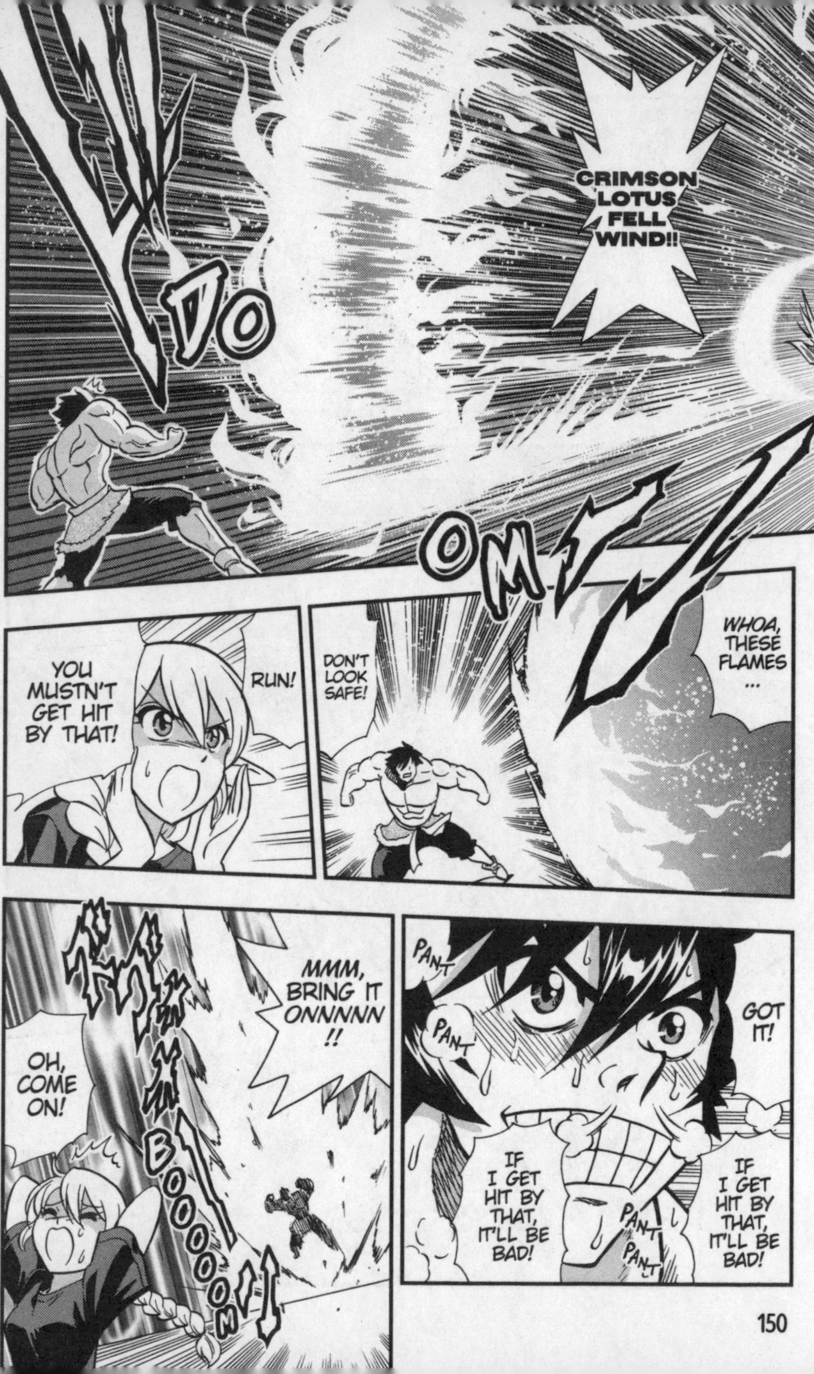
CRIMSON LOTUS FELL WIND!!
DO
OM
WHOA, THESE FLAMES ...
DON'T LOOK SAFE!
RUN!
YOU MUSTN'T GET HIT BY THAT!
GOT IT!
PANT PANT
IF I GET HIT BY THAT, IT'LL BE BAD!
IF I GET HIT BY THAT, IT'LL BE BAD!
PANT PANT
MMM, BRING IT ONNNNN!!
OH, COME ON!
BOOOOOOM!

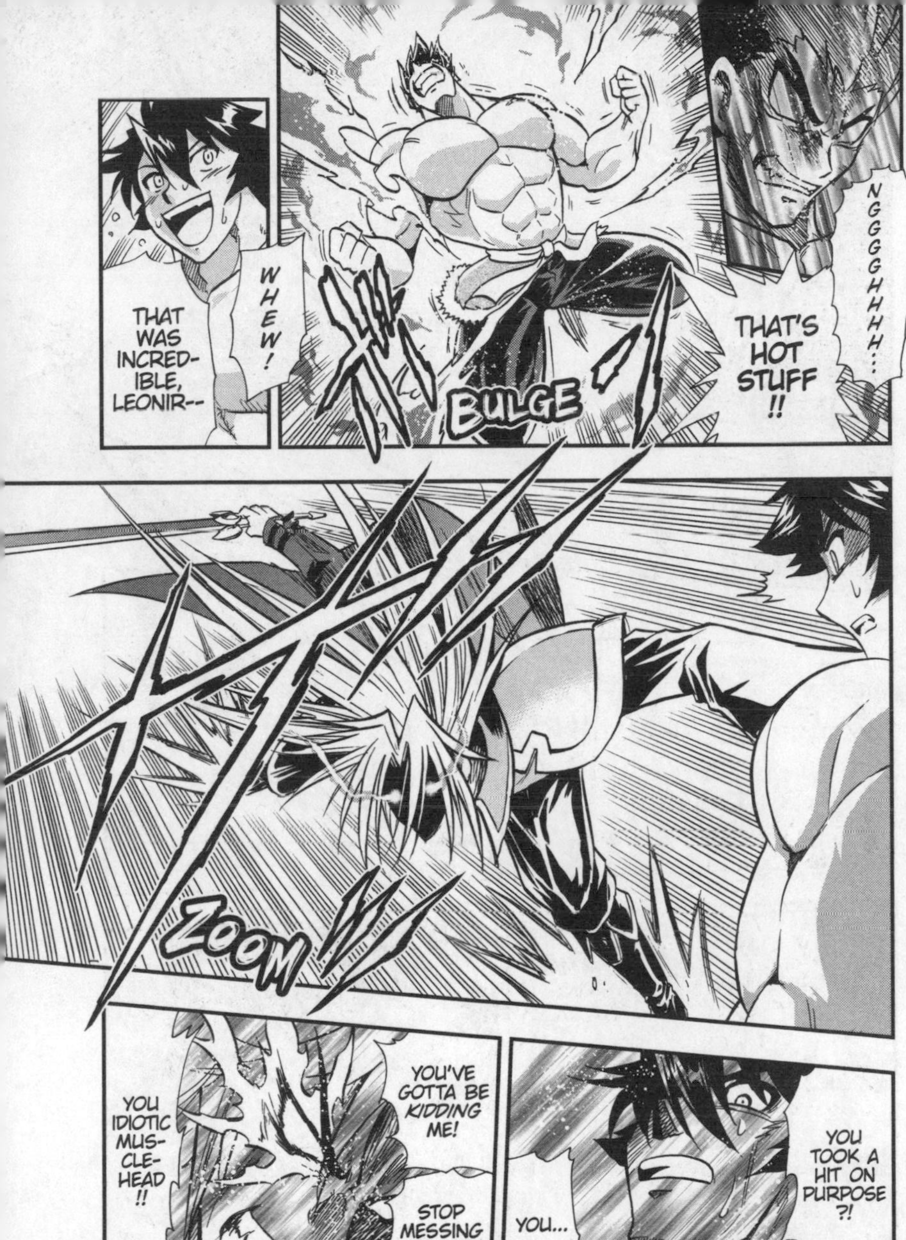
NGGGHHHH...
THAT'S HOT STUFF!!
BULGE
WHEW!
THAT WAS INCREDIBLE, LEONIR--
ZOOM
YOU TOOK A HIT ON PURPOSE?!
YOU...
YOU'VE GOTTA BE KIDDING ME!
STOP MESSING AROUND!
YOU IDIOTIC MUSCLE-HEAD!!

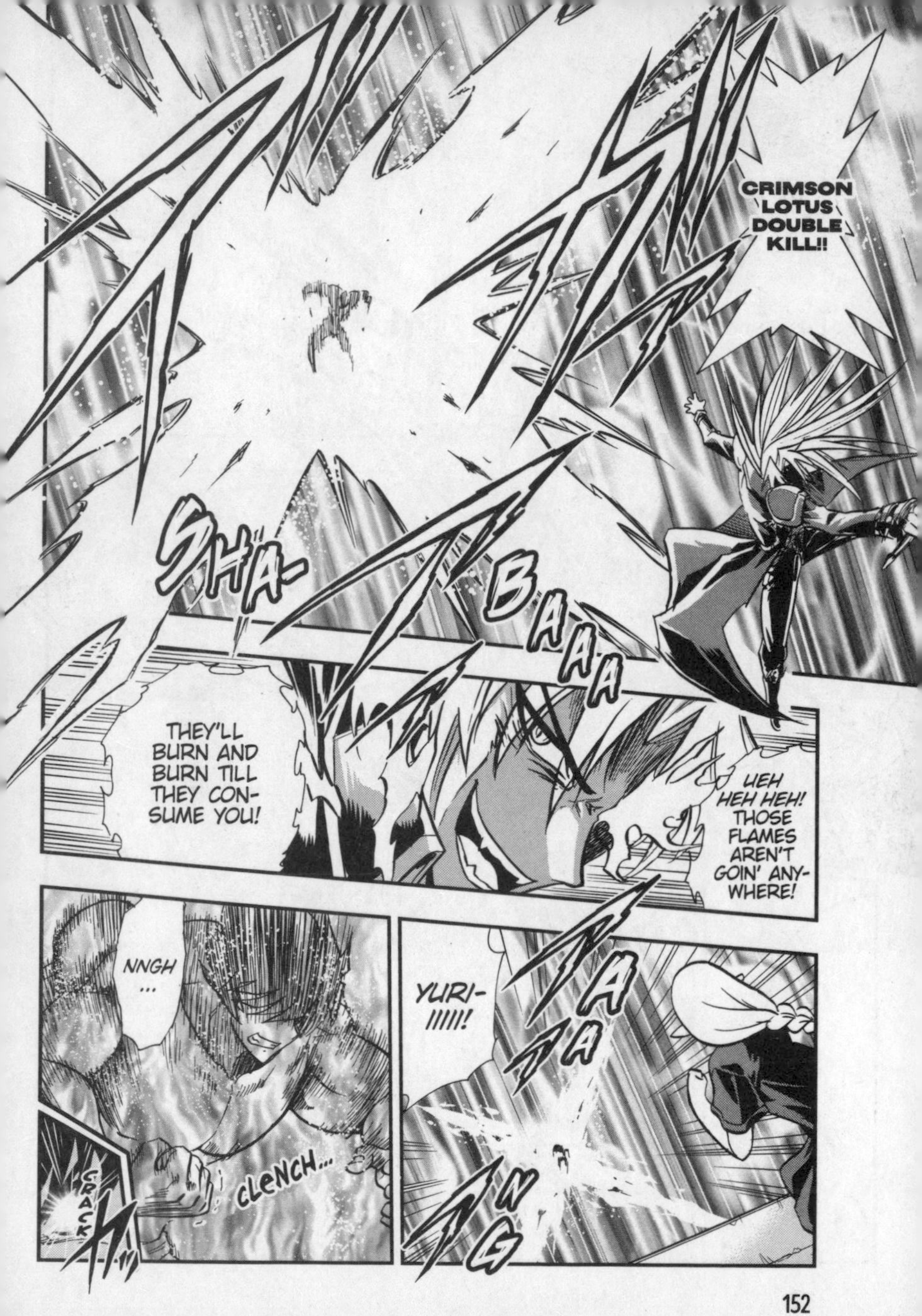
CRIMSON LOTUS DOUBLE KILL!!
SHA-
BAAAA
UEH HEH HEH! THOSE FLAMES AREN'T GOIN' ANY-WHERE!
THEY'LL BURN AND BURN TILL THEY CON-SUME YOU!
AAAA
NNG
YURI-IIIIII!
NNGH ...
CLENCH...
CRACK

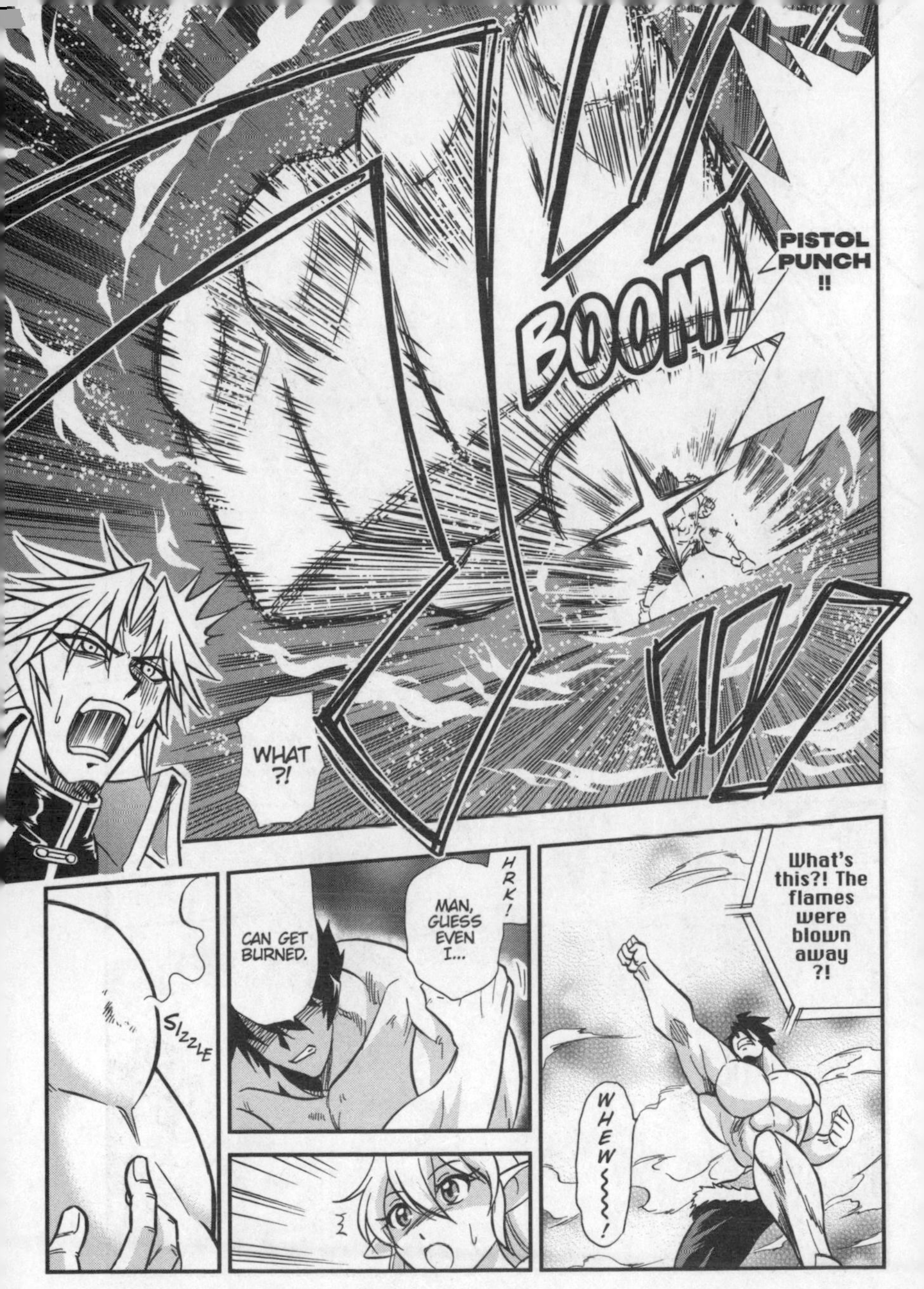
PISTOL PUNCH!!
BOOM
WHAT?!
What's this?! The flames were blown away?!
WHEW~~!
HRK!
MAN, GUESS EVEN I...
CAN GET BURNED.
SIZZLE

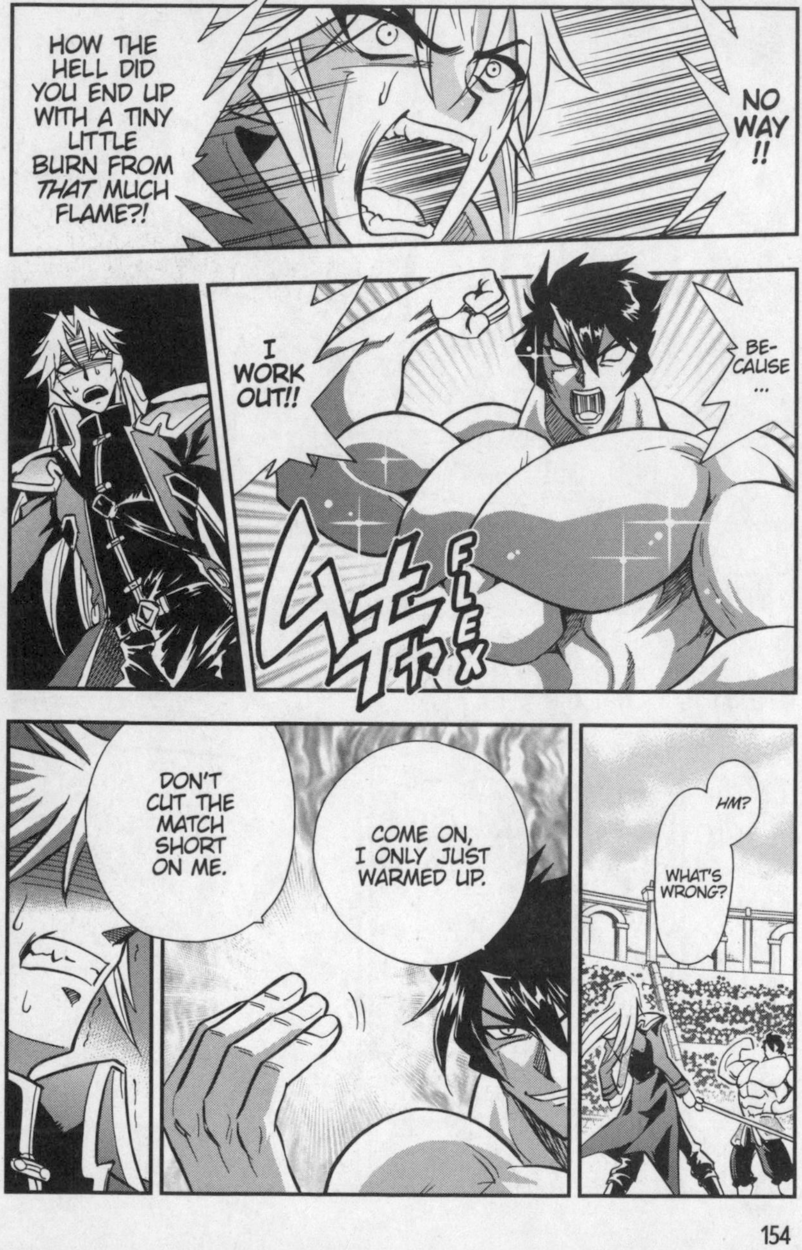
NO WAY!!
HOW THE HELL DID YOU END UP WITH A TINY LITTLE BURN FROM *THAT* MUCH FLAME?!
BE-CAUSE...
I WORK OUT!!
FLEX
HM?
WHAT'S WRONG?
COME ON, I ONLY JUST WARMED UP.
DON'T CUT THE MATCH SHORT ON ME.

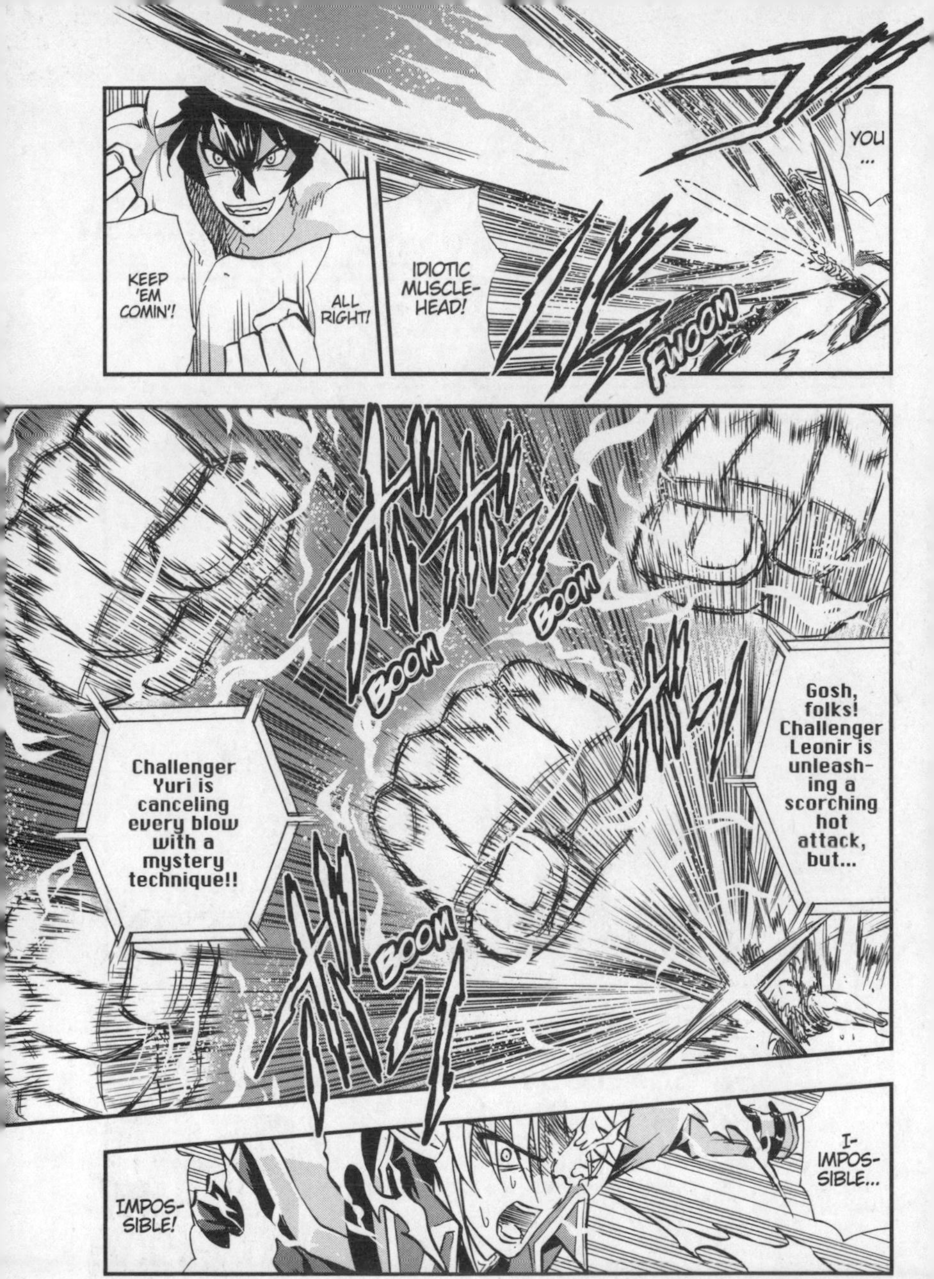
YOU ...
IDIOTIC MUSCLE-HEAD!
FWOOM
ALL RIGHT!
KEEP 'EM COMIN'!
Gosh, folks! Challenger Leonir is unleashing a scorching hot attack, but...
BOOM
BOOM
BOOM
Challenger Yuri is canceling every blow with a mystery technique!!
BOOM
I-IMPOSSIBLE...
IMPOSSIBLE!

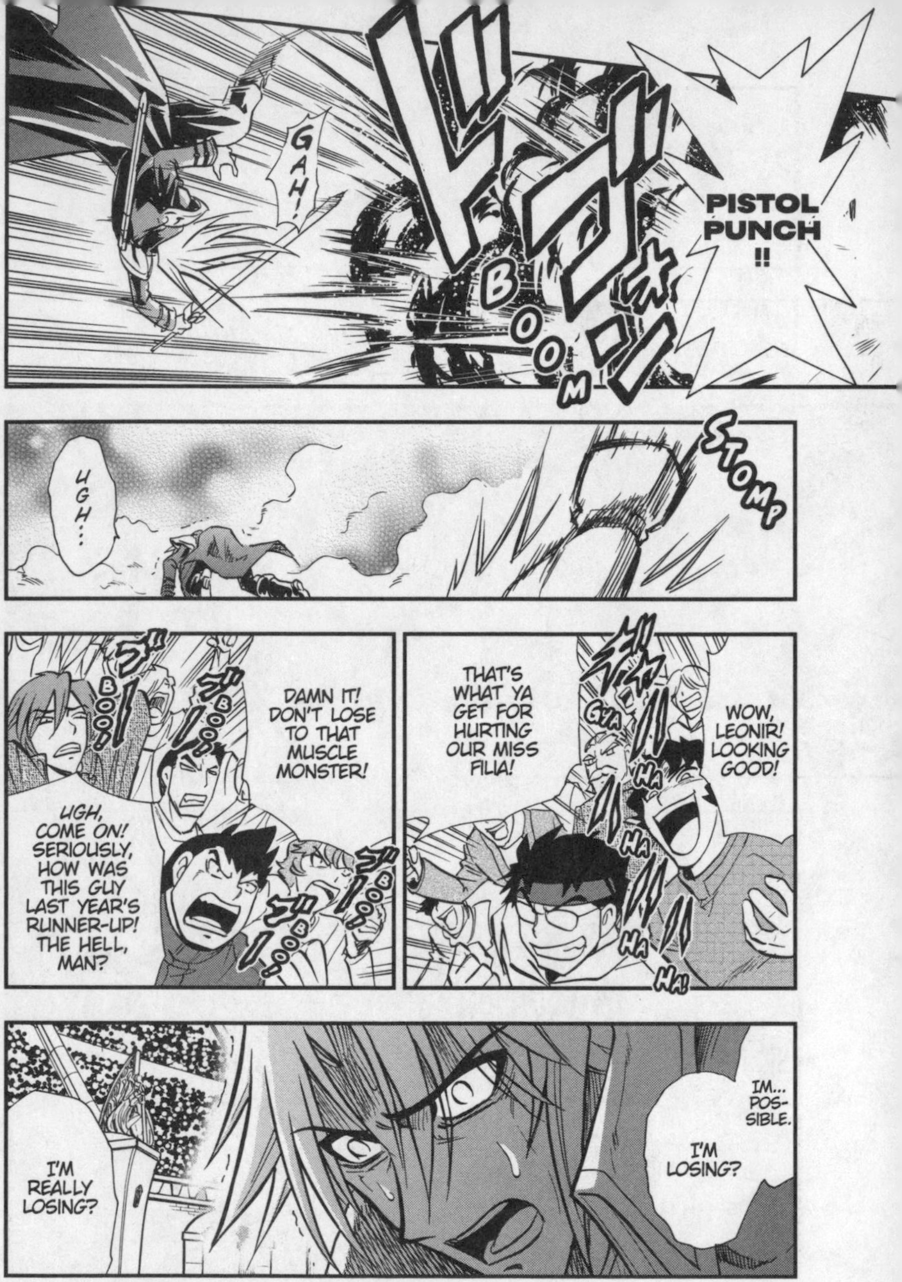
PISTOL PUNCH!!
BOOM
GAH!
STOMP
UGH...
WOW, LEONIR! LOOKING GOOD!
GYA HA HA HA HA HA!
THAT'S WHAT YA GET FOR HURTING OUR MISS FILIA!
DAMN IT! DON'T LOSE TO THAT MUSCLE MONSTER!
BOOO!
BOOO!
UGH, COME ON! SERIOUSLY, HOW WAS THIS GUY LAST YEAR'S RUNNER-UP! THE HELL, MAN?
BOOO!
BOOO!
IM... POS-SIBLE.
I'M LOSING?
I'M REALLY LOSING?

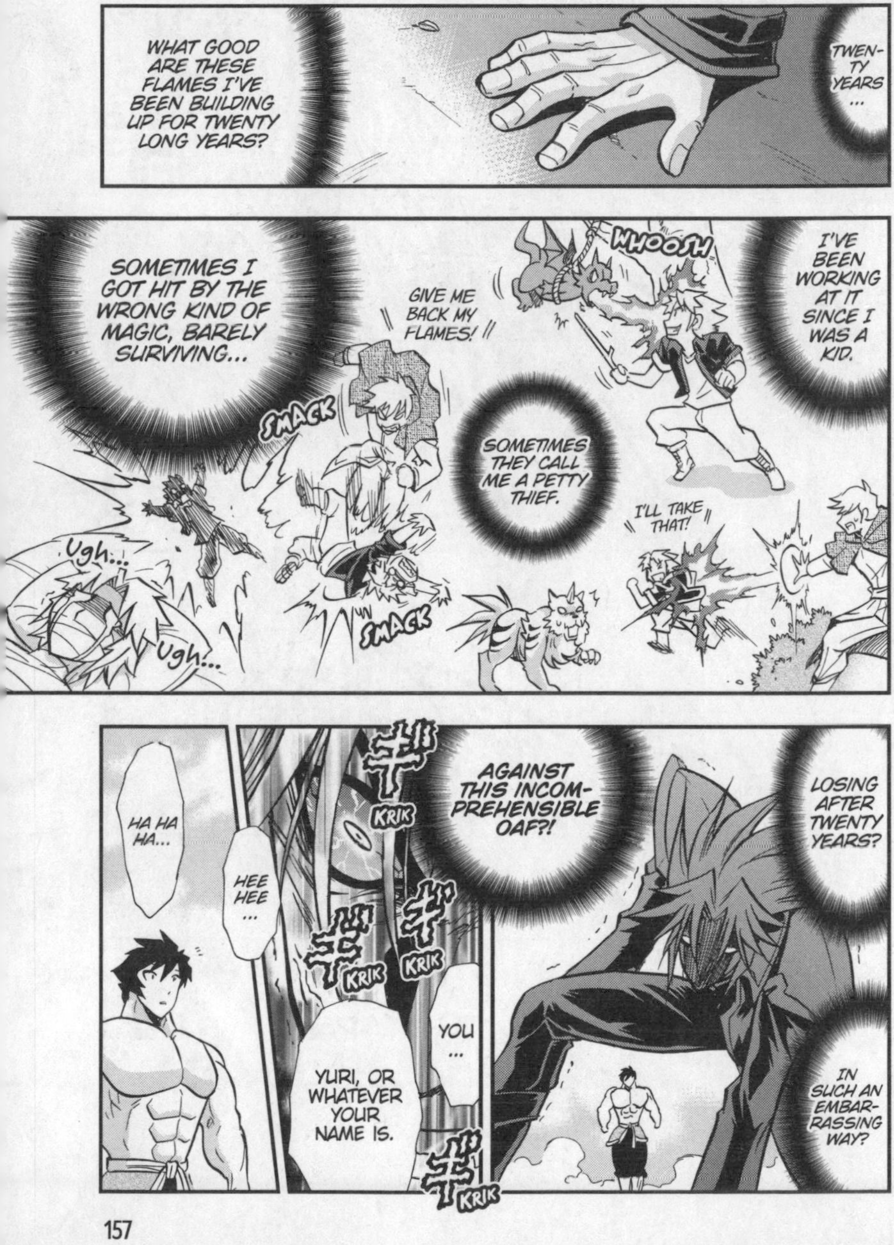
TWENTY-TY YEARS...
WHAT GOOD ARE THESE FLAMES I'VE BEEN BUILDING UP FOR TWENTY LONG YEARS?
I'VE BEEN WORKING AT IT SINCE I WAS A KID.
WHOOSH
GIVE ME BACK MY FLAMES!
SOMETIMES I GOT HIT BY THE WRONG KIND OF MAGIC, BARELY SURVIVING...
SMACK
SOMETIMES THEY CALL ME A PETTY THIEF.
I'LL TAKE THAT!
SMACK
Ugh...
Ugh...
LOSING AFTER TWENTY YEARS?
AGAINST THIS INCOM-PREHENSIBLE OAF?!
IN SUCH AN EMBAR-RASSING WAY?
KRIK
KRIK
KRIK
KRIK
KRIK
HEE HEE...
YOU...
YURI, OR WHATEVER YOUR NAME IS.
HA HA HA...

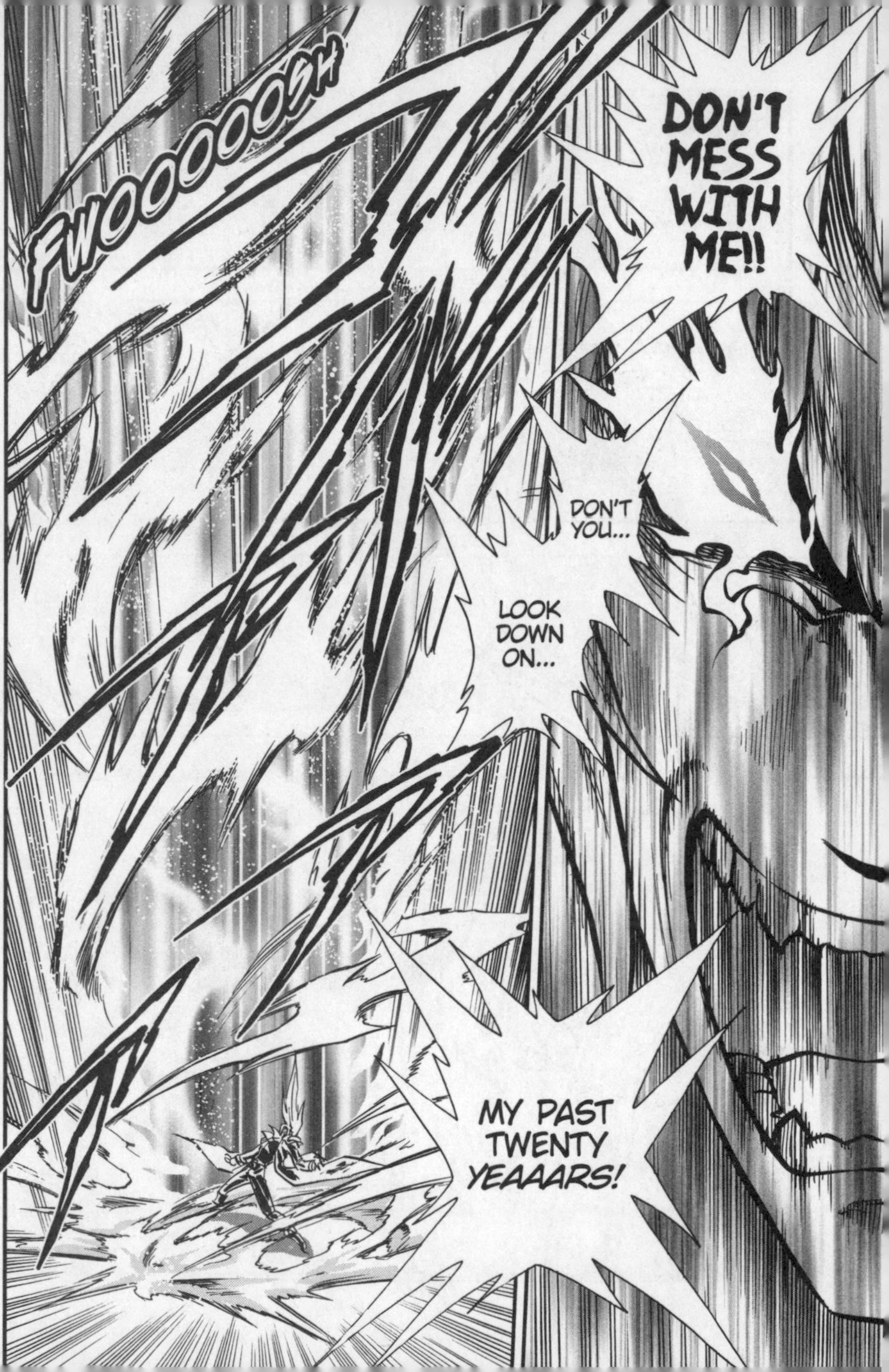
DON'T MESS WITH ME!!
FWOOOOOSH
DON'T YOU...
LOOK DOWN ON...
MY PAST TWENTY YEAAARS!

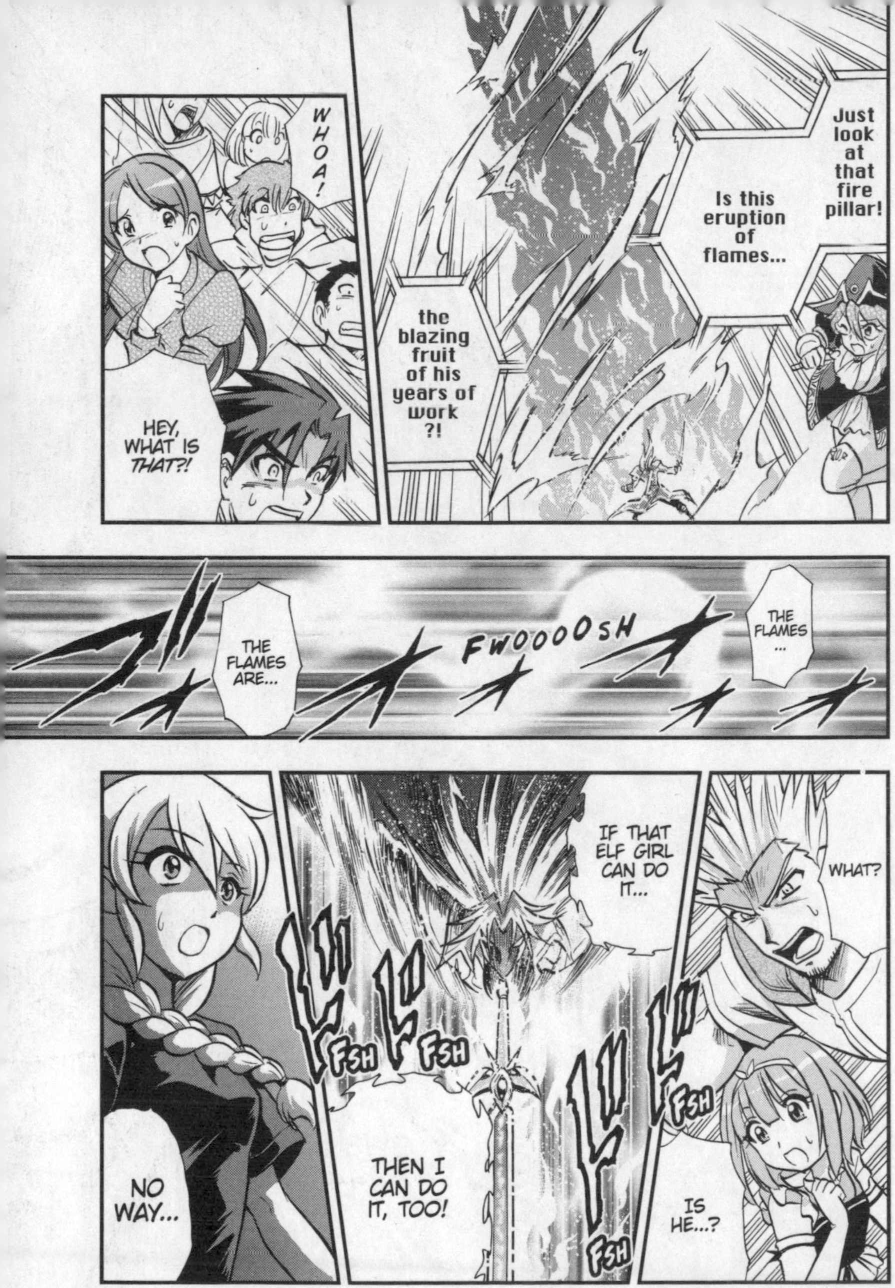

Just look at that fire pillar!
Is this eruption of flames...
the blazing fruit of his years of work ?!
WHOA!
HEY, WHAT IS THAT?!
THE FLAMES ...
FWOOOOSH
THE FLAMES ARE...
WHAT?
IS HE...?
IF THAT ELF GIRL CAN DO IT...
FSH
FSH
FSH
FSH
THEN I CAN DO IT, TOO!
NO WAY...

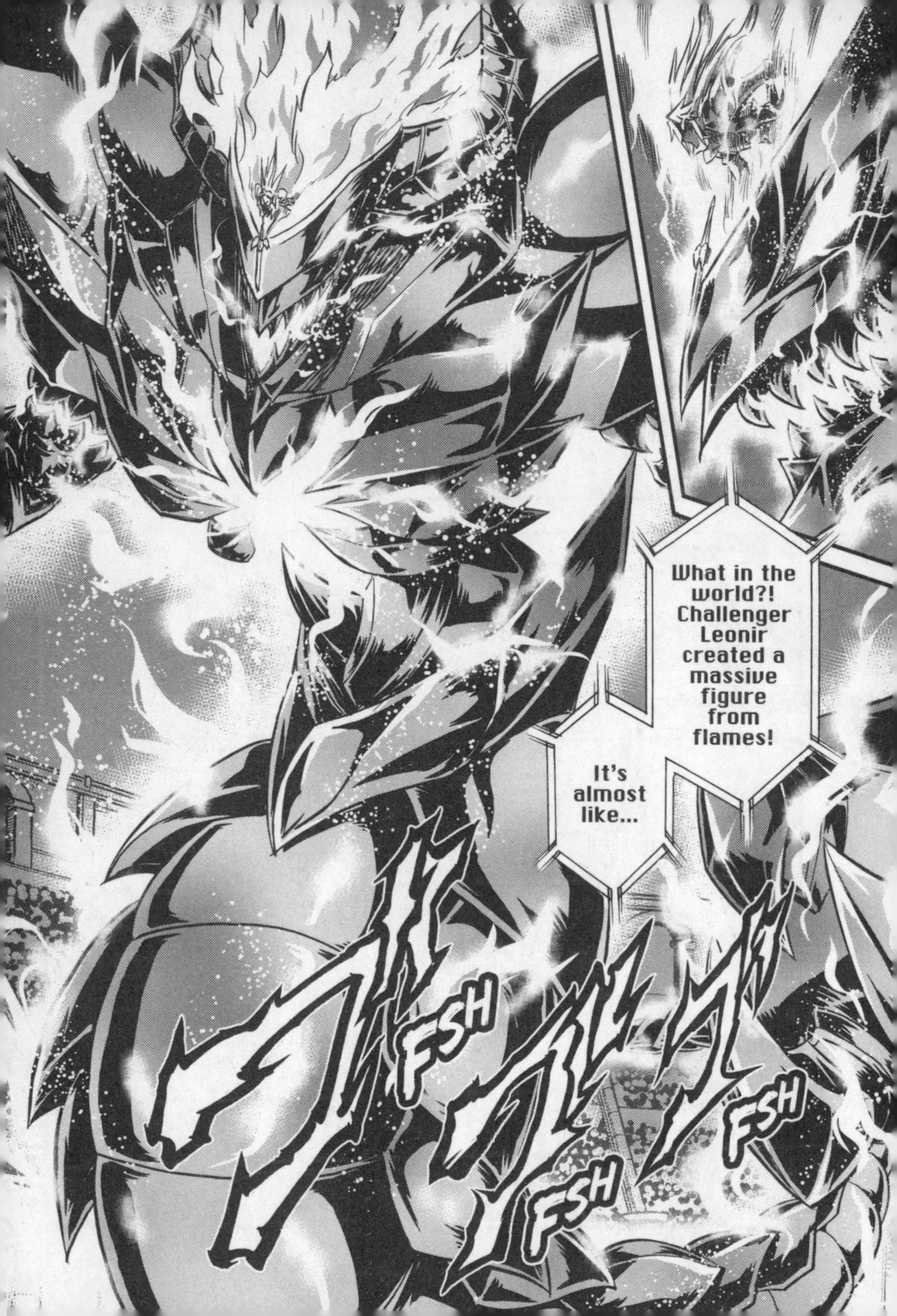
What in the world?! Challenger Leonir created a massive figure from flames!
It's almost like...
FSH
FSH
FSH

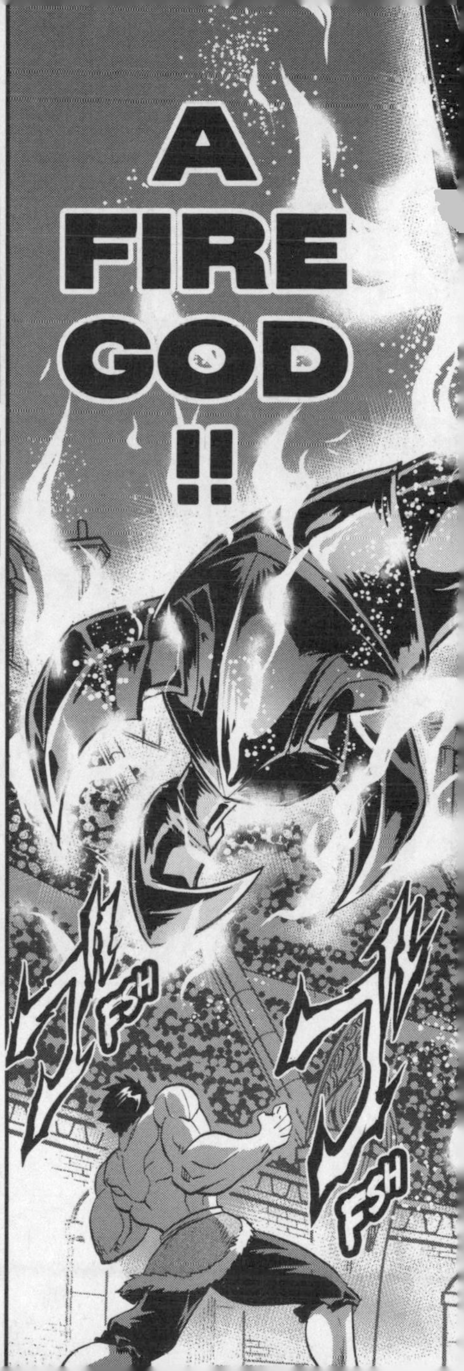
A FIRE GOD!!
FSH
FSH

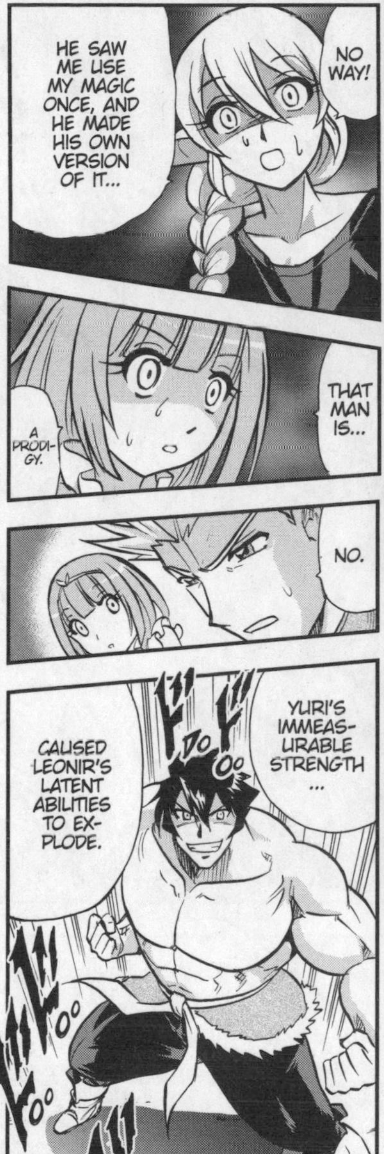
NO WAY!
HE SAW ME USE MY MAGIC ONCE, AND HE MADE HIS OWN VERSION OF IT...
THAT MAN IS...
A PRODIGY.
NO.
YURI'S IMMEASURABLE STRENGTH ...
CAUSED LEONIR'S LATENT ABILITIES TO EXPLODE.
OM

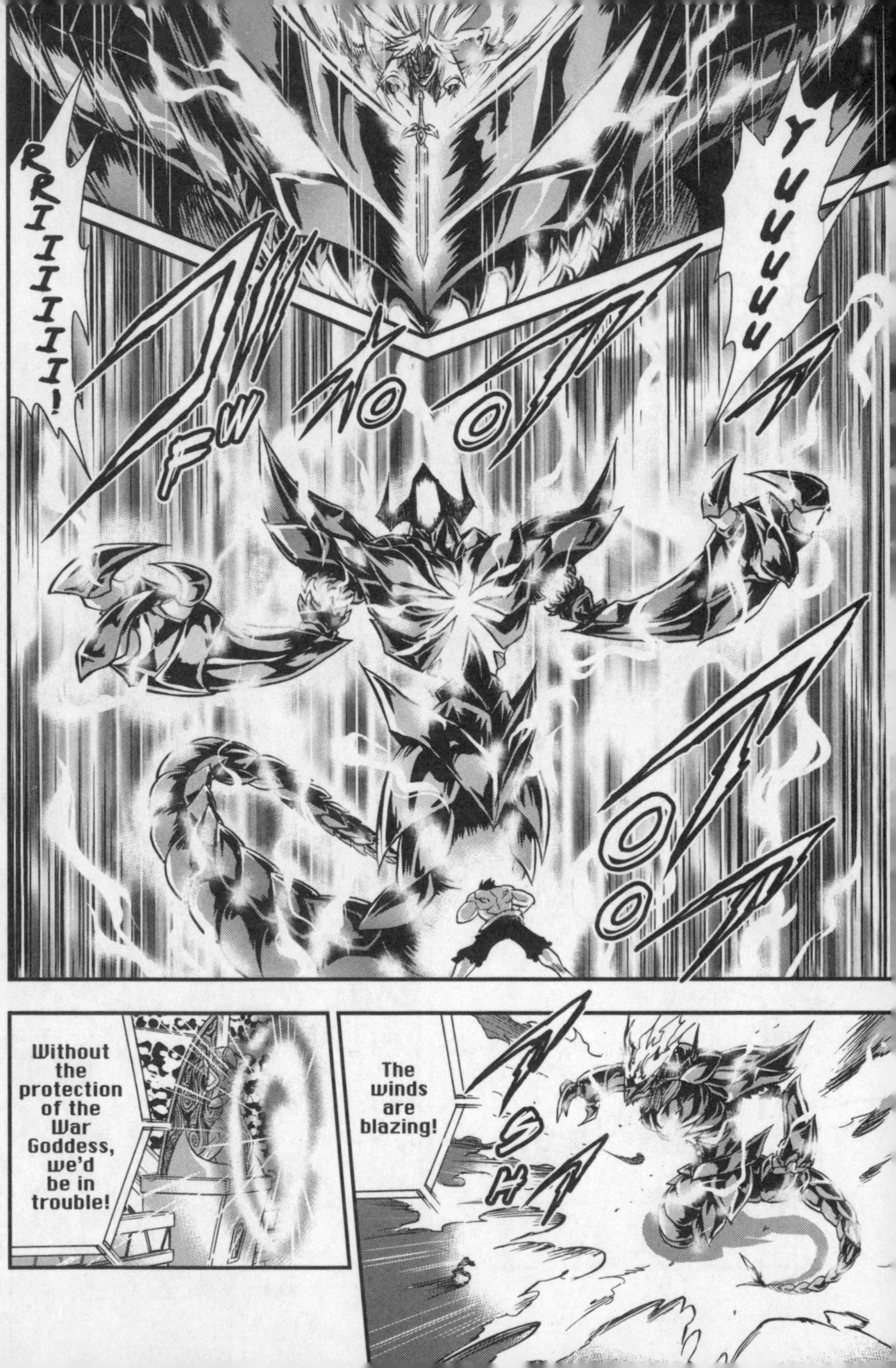
YUUUUUU
FWOOOO
RRIIIIIIII!
SH
The winds are blazing!
Without the protection of the War Goddess, we'd be in trouble!

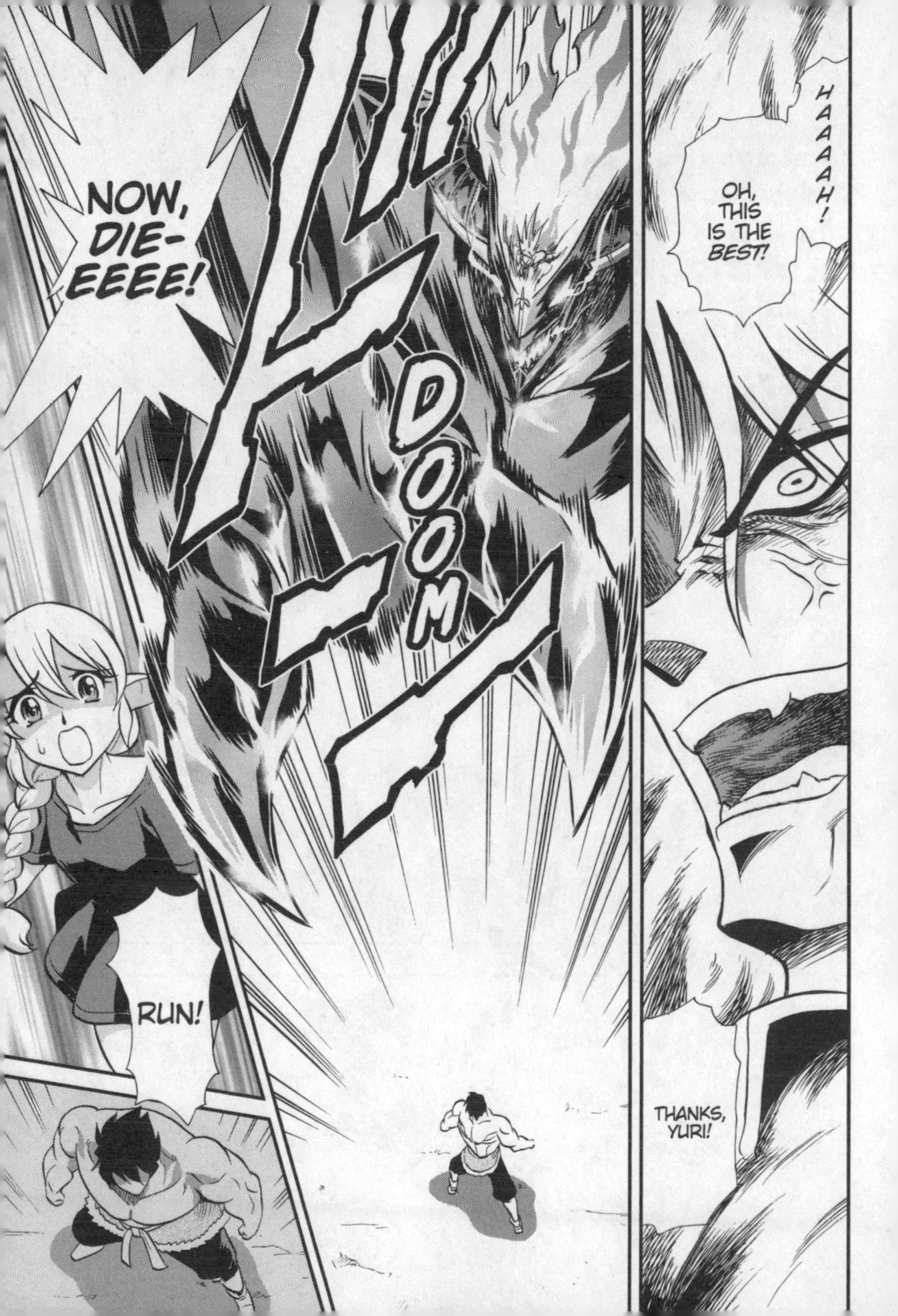
HAAAAAH!
OH, THIS IS THE BEST!
THANKS, YURI!
NOW, DIE-EEEEE!
DOOOM
RUN!

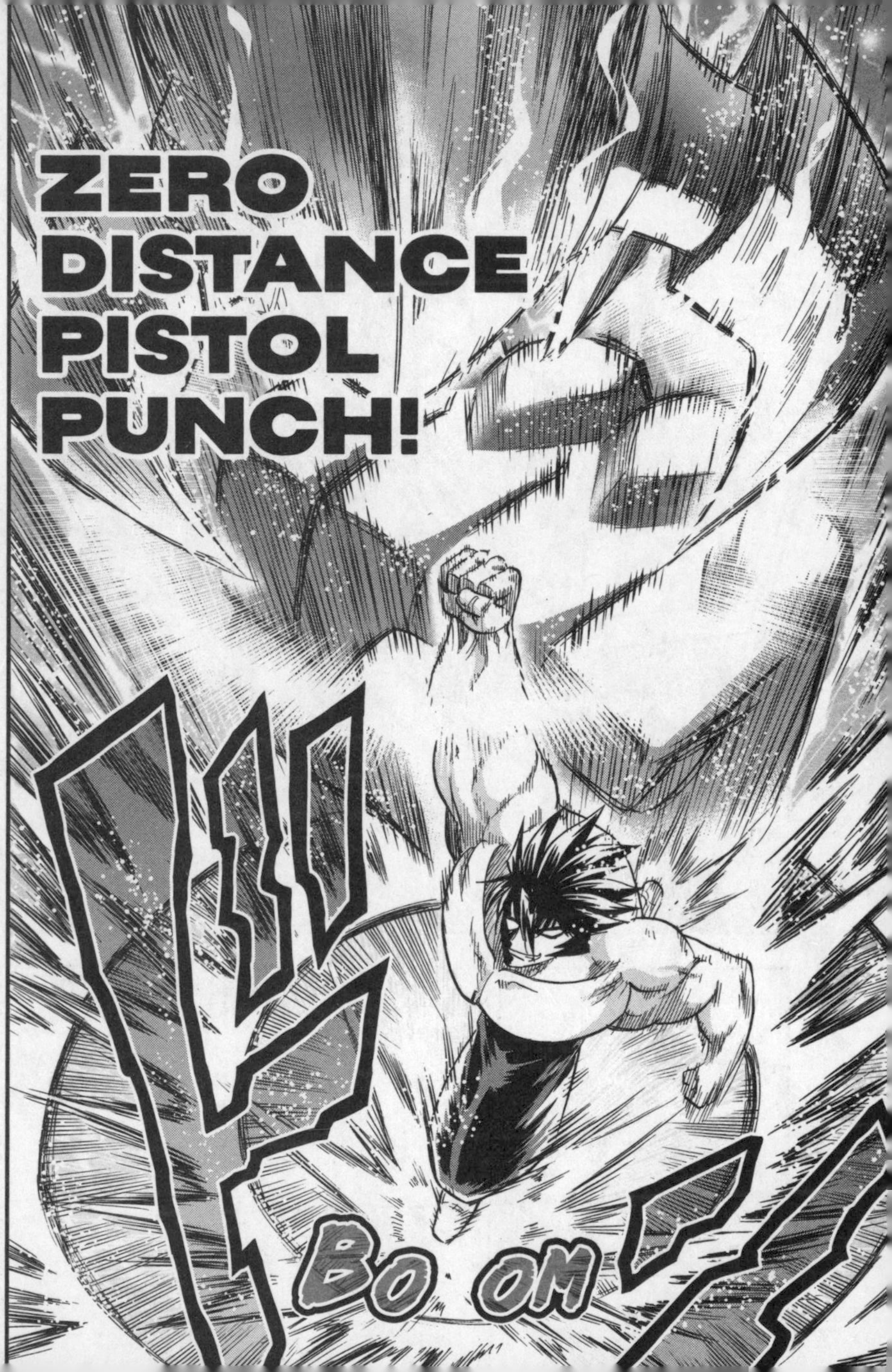
ZERO DISTANCE PISTOL PUNCH!
BOOM

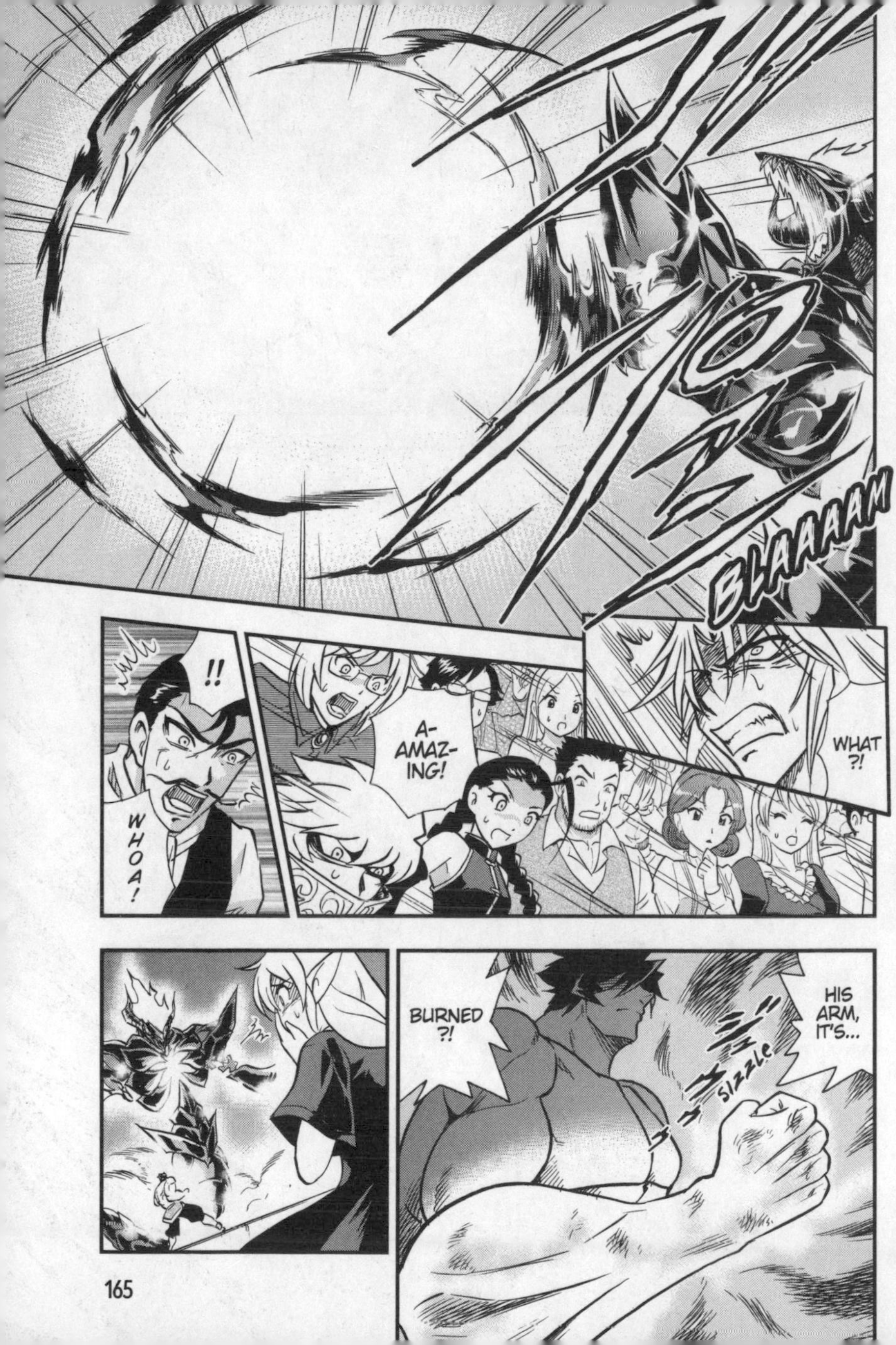
BLAAAAM
WHAT ?!
A-AMAZ-ING!
!!
WHOA!
HIS ARM, IT'S...
SIZZLE
BURNED ?!

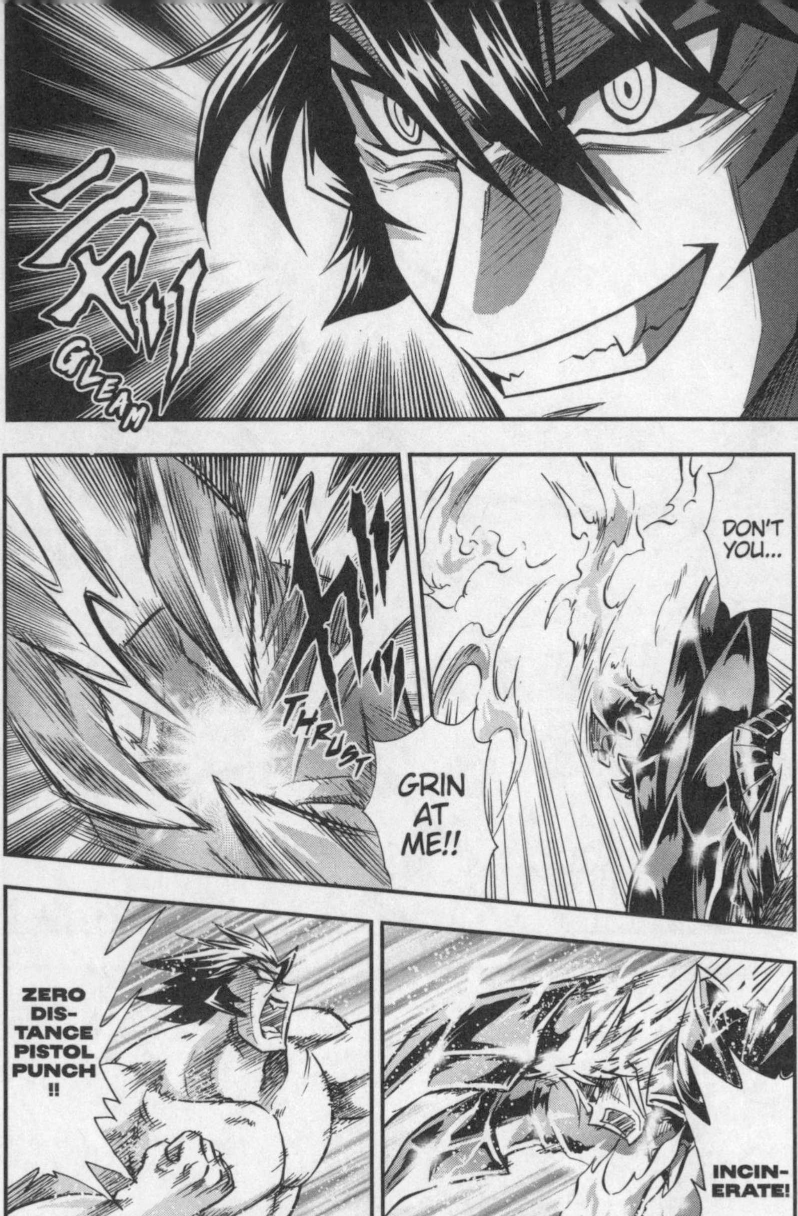
GLEAM
DON'T YOU...
GRIN AT ME!!
THRUST
INCIN-ERATE!
ZERO DIS-TANCE PISTOL PUNCH !!

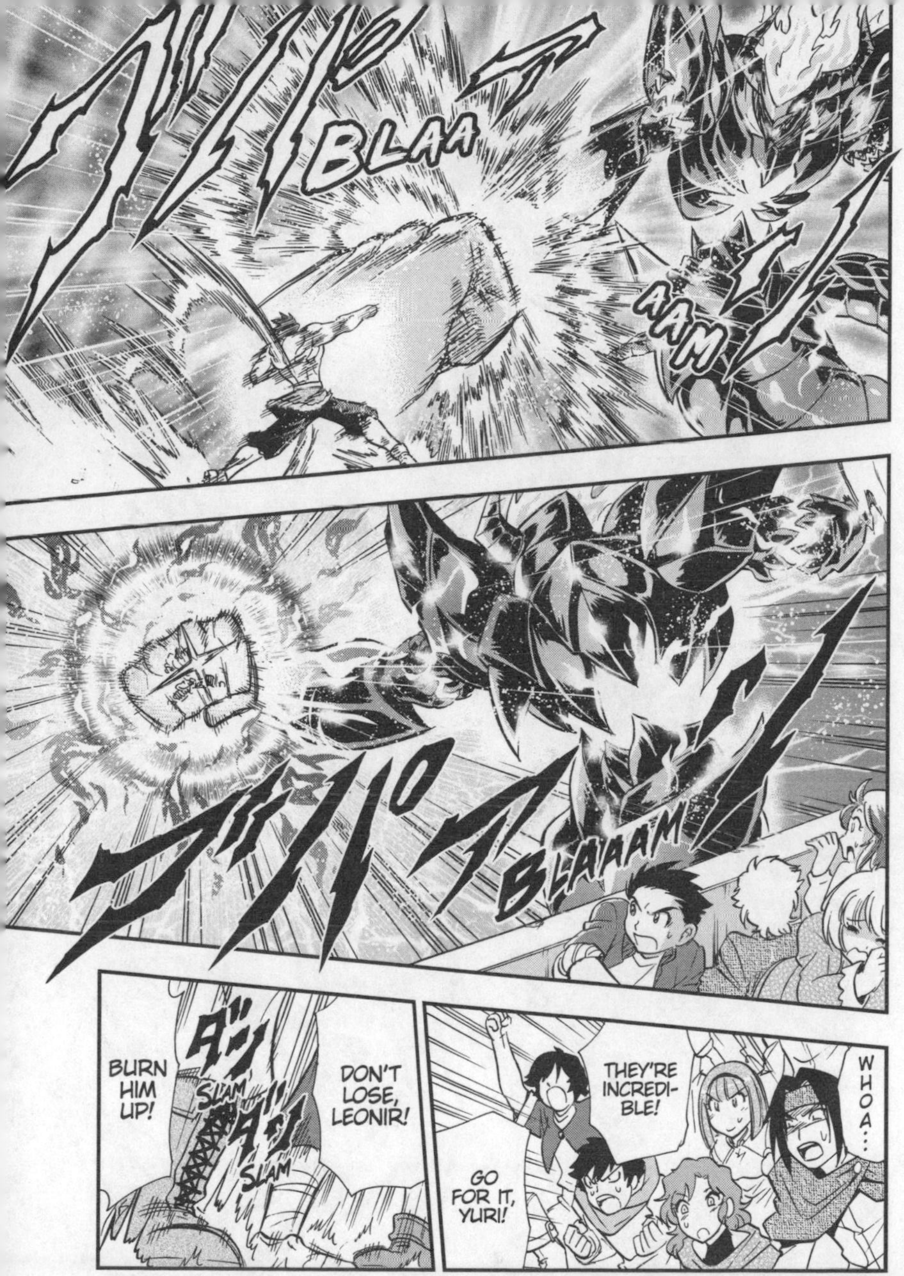
BLAA
AAM
BLAAAM
WHOA...
THEY'RE INCREDIBLE!
GO FOR IT, YURI!
DON'T LOSE, LEONIR!
SLAM
SLAM
BURN HIM UP!

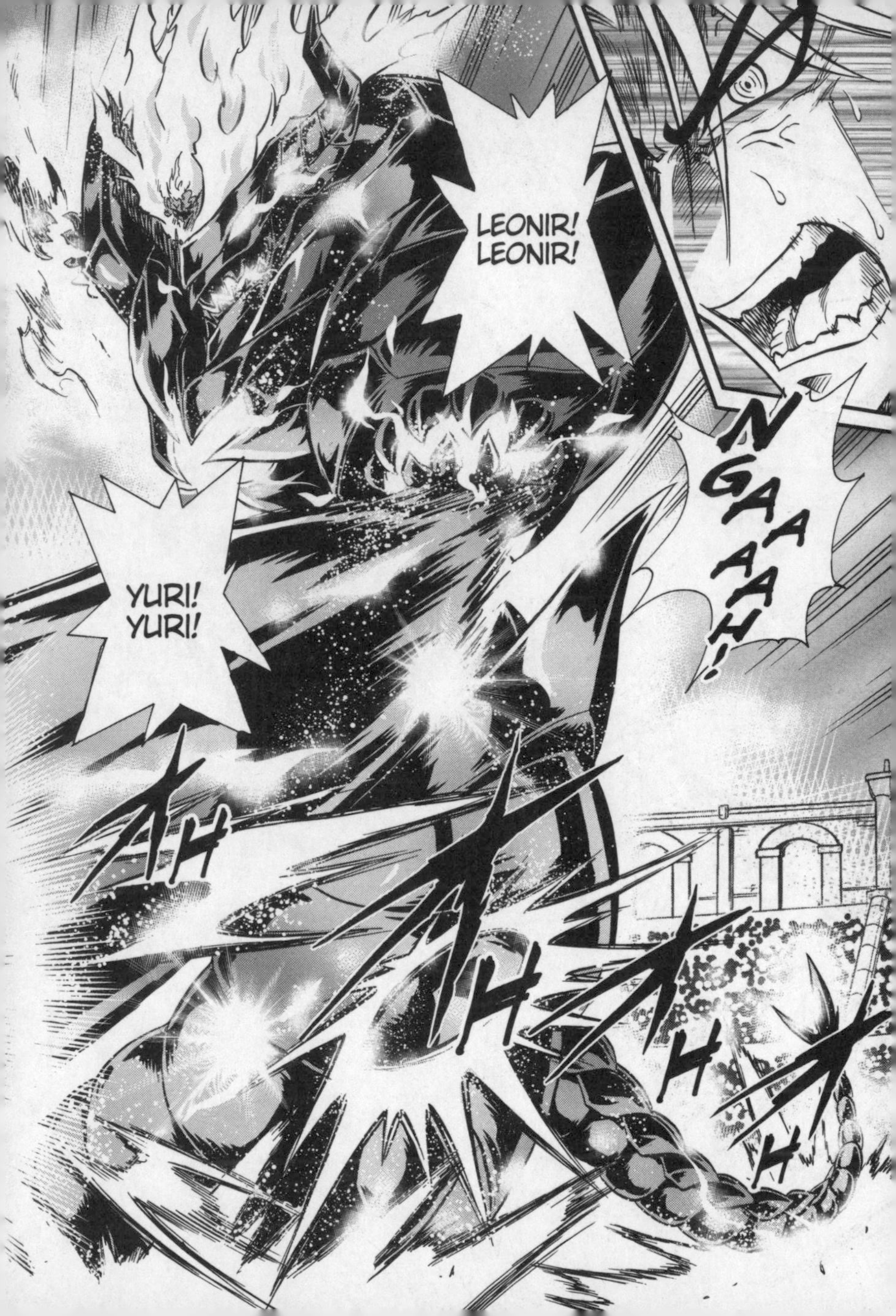
NGAAAAAH!
LEONIR! LEONIR!
YURI! YURI!
AH AH AH H H H

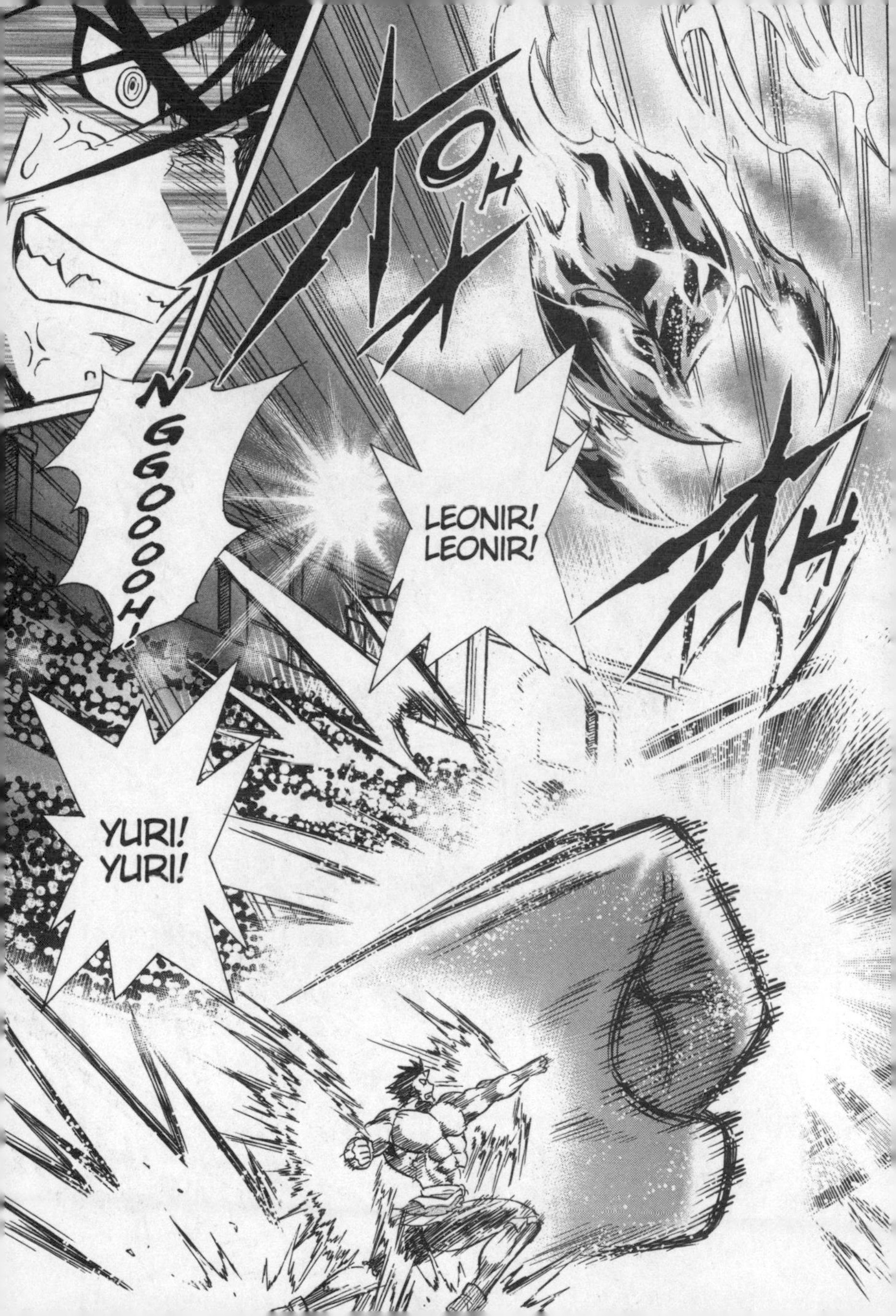
LEONIR! LEONIR!
NGGOOOOOH!
YURI! YURI!

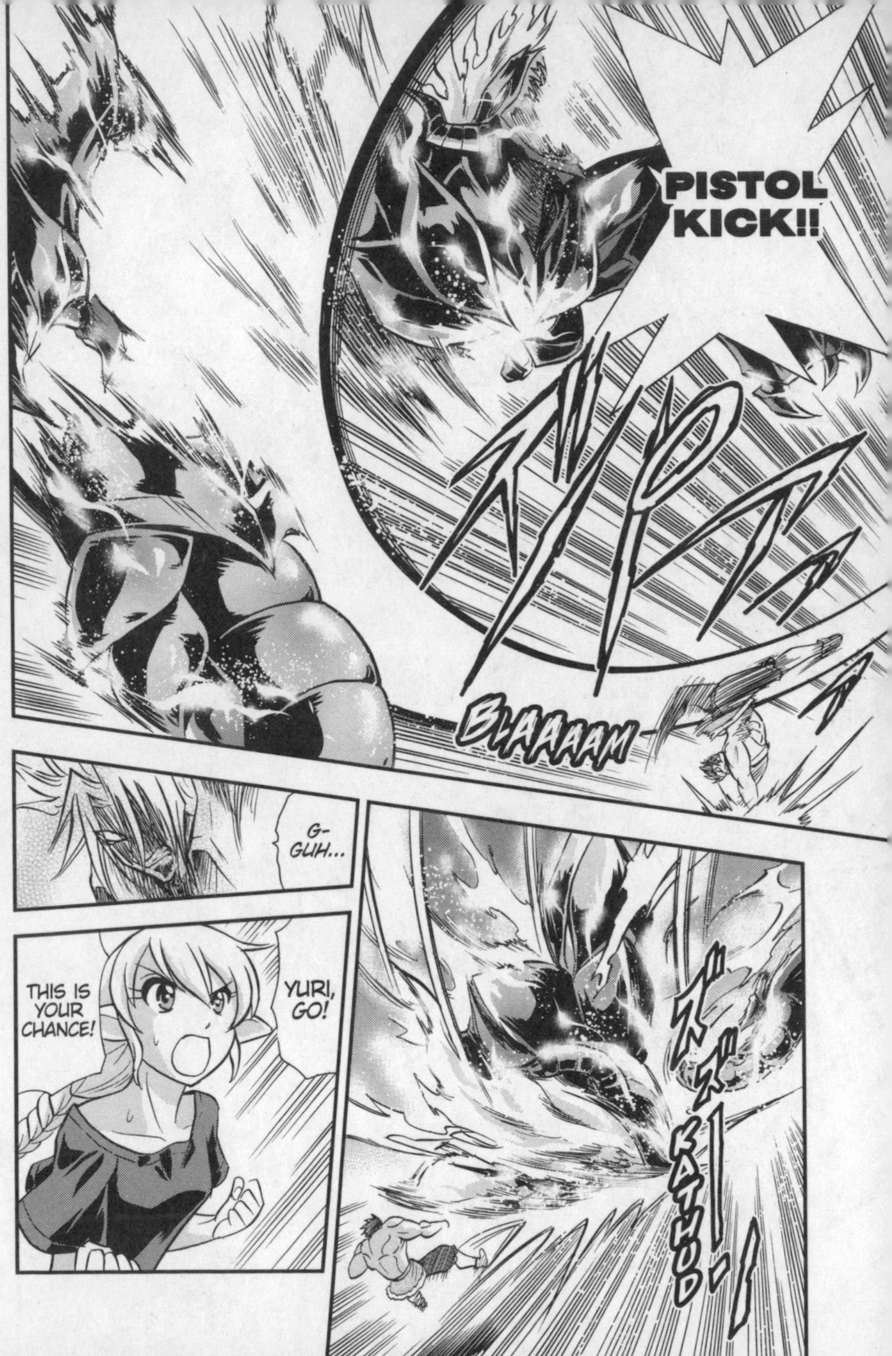
PISTOL KICK!!
BLAAAAAM
KATHUD
G-GUH...
YURI, GO!
THIS IS YOUR CHANCE!

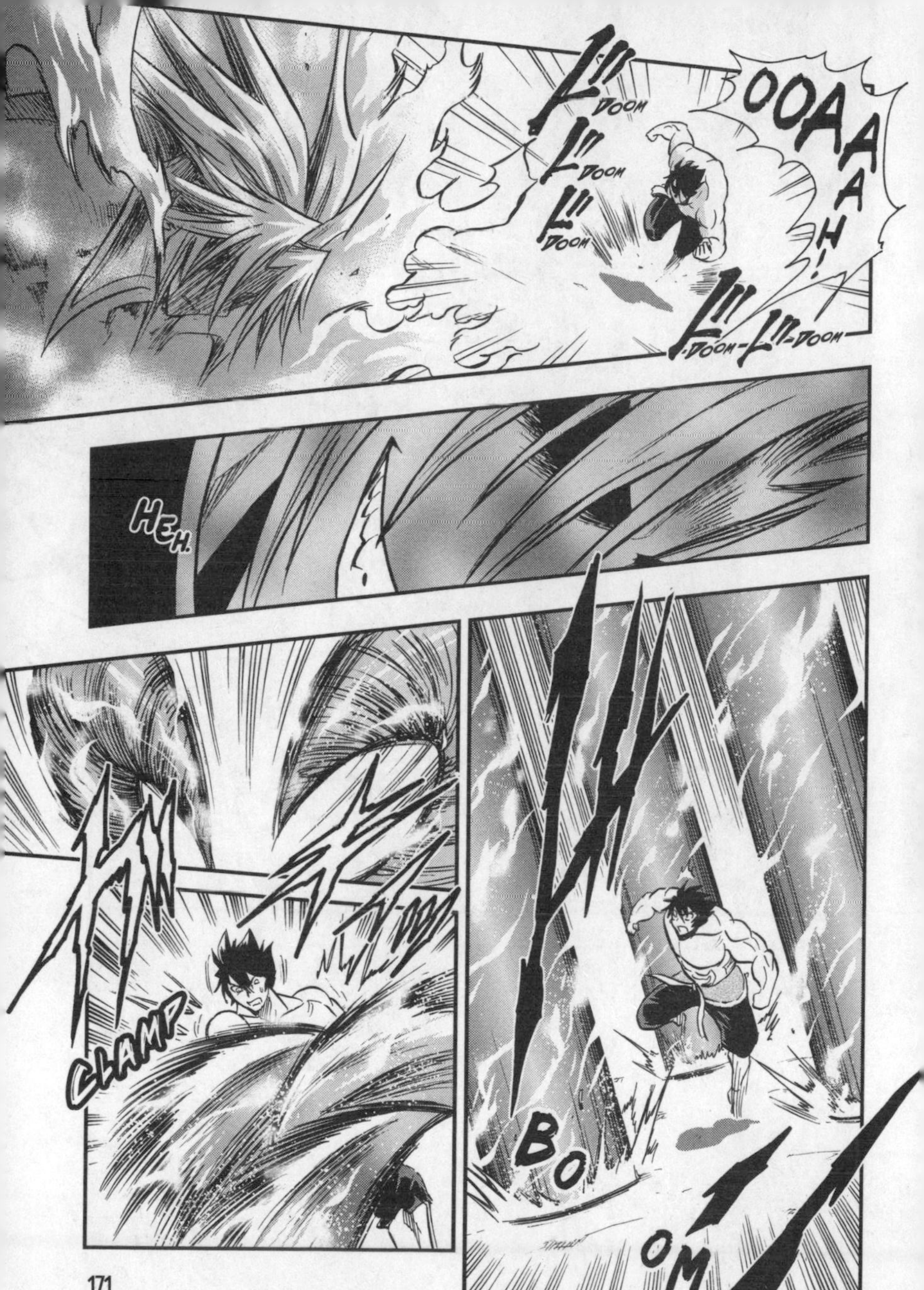
DOOM
DOOM
DOOM
OOAAAAH!
DOOM-DOOM
HEH.
BOOM
CLAMP

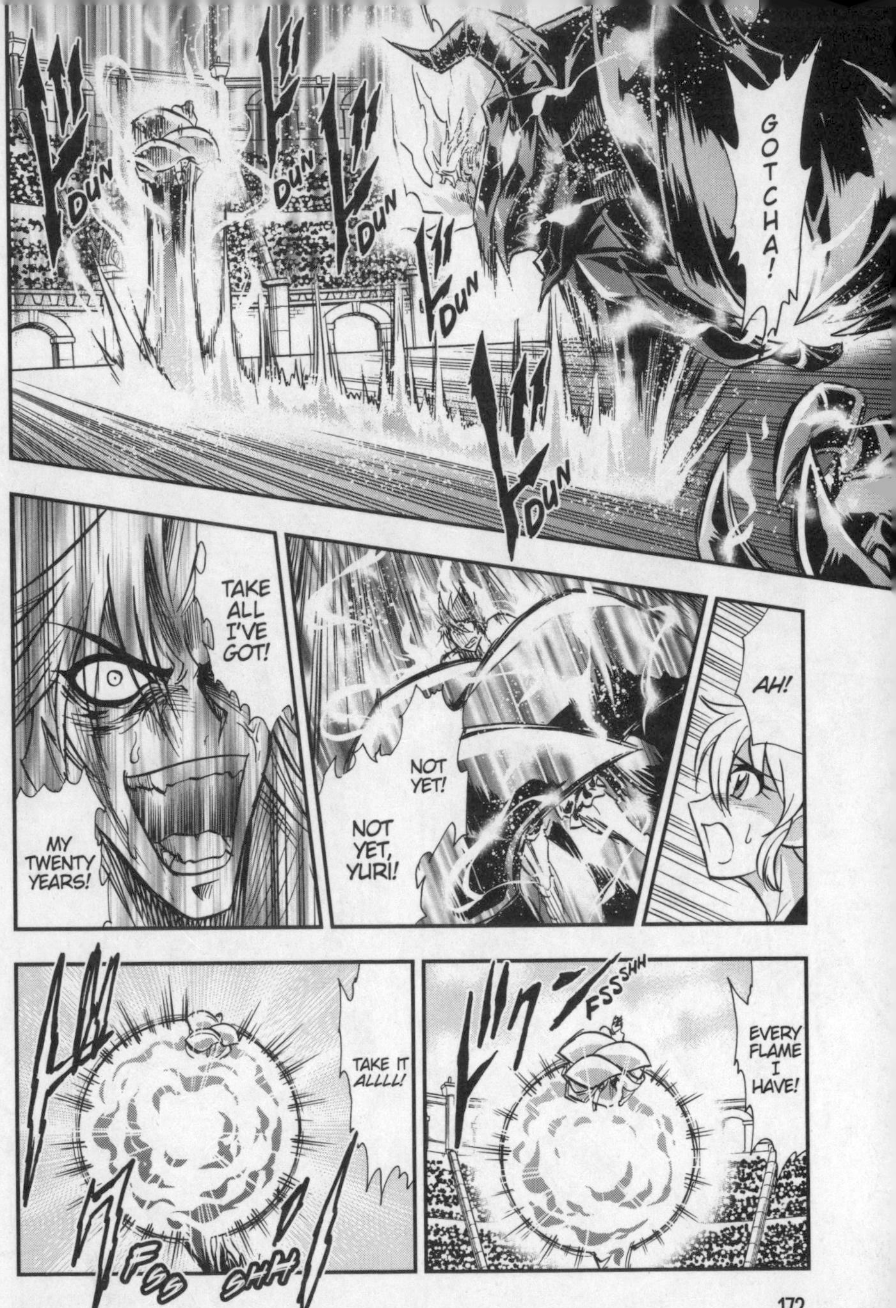
GOTCHA!
DUN
DUN
DUN
DUN
DUN
DUN
AH!
NOT YET!
NOT YET, YURI!
TAKE ALL I'VE GOT!
MY TWENTY YEARS!
EVERY FLAME I HAVE!
FSSSHH
TAKE IT ALLLL!
FSS SHH

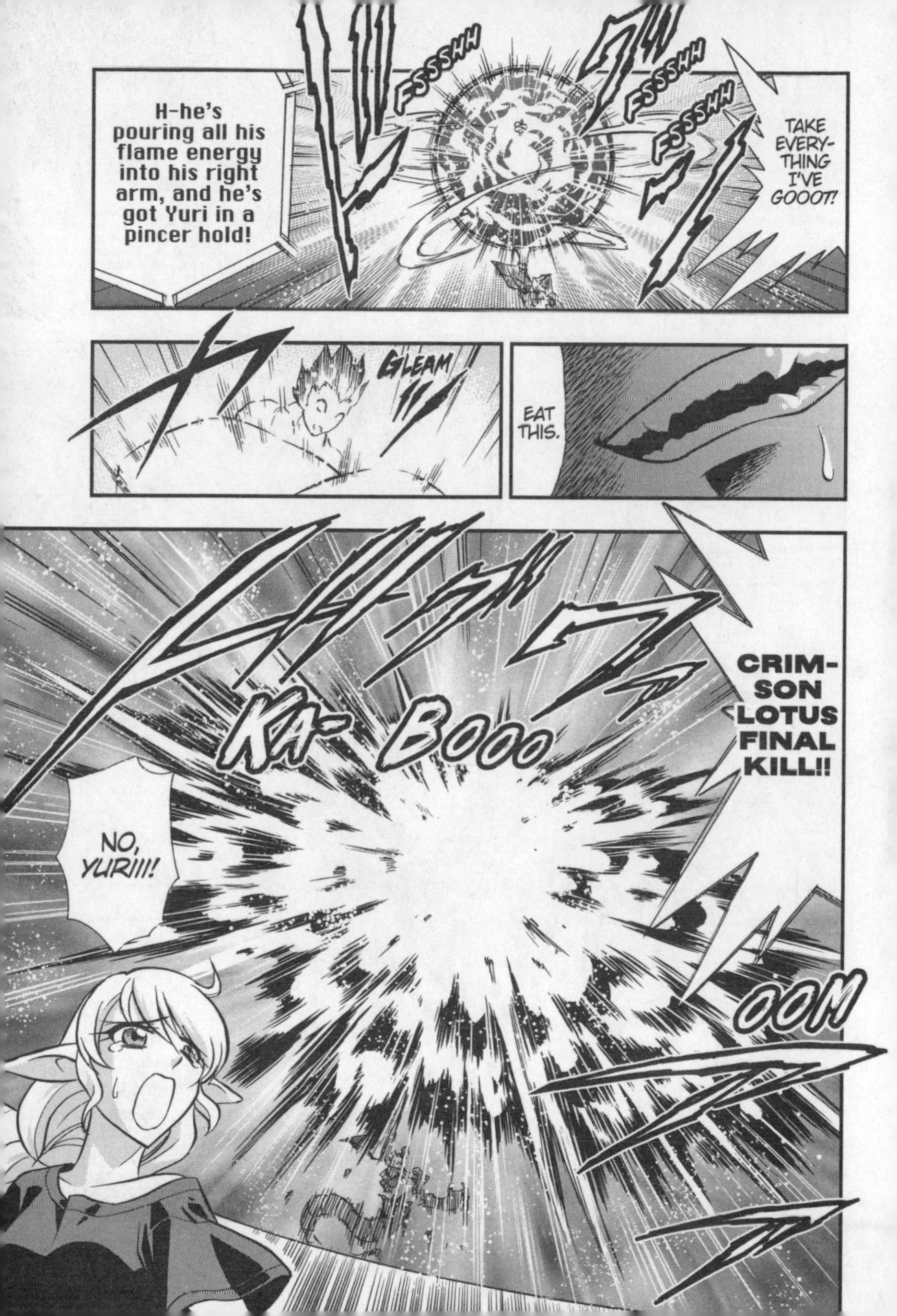
TAKE EVERY-THING I'VE GOOOT!
FS-SSHH
FS-SSHH
FS-SSHH
H-he's pouring all his flame energy into his right arm, and he's got Yuri in a pincer hold!
EAT THIS.
GLEAM
CRIM-SON LOTUS FINAL KILL!!
KA-BOOOOOM
NO, YURIII!

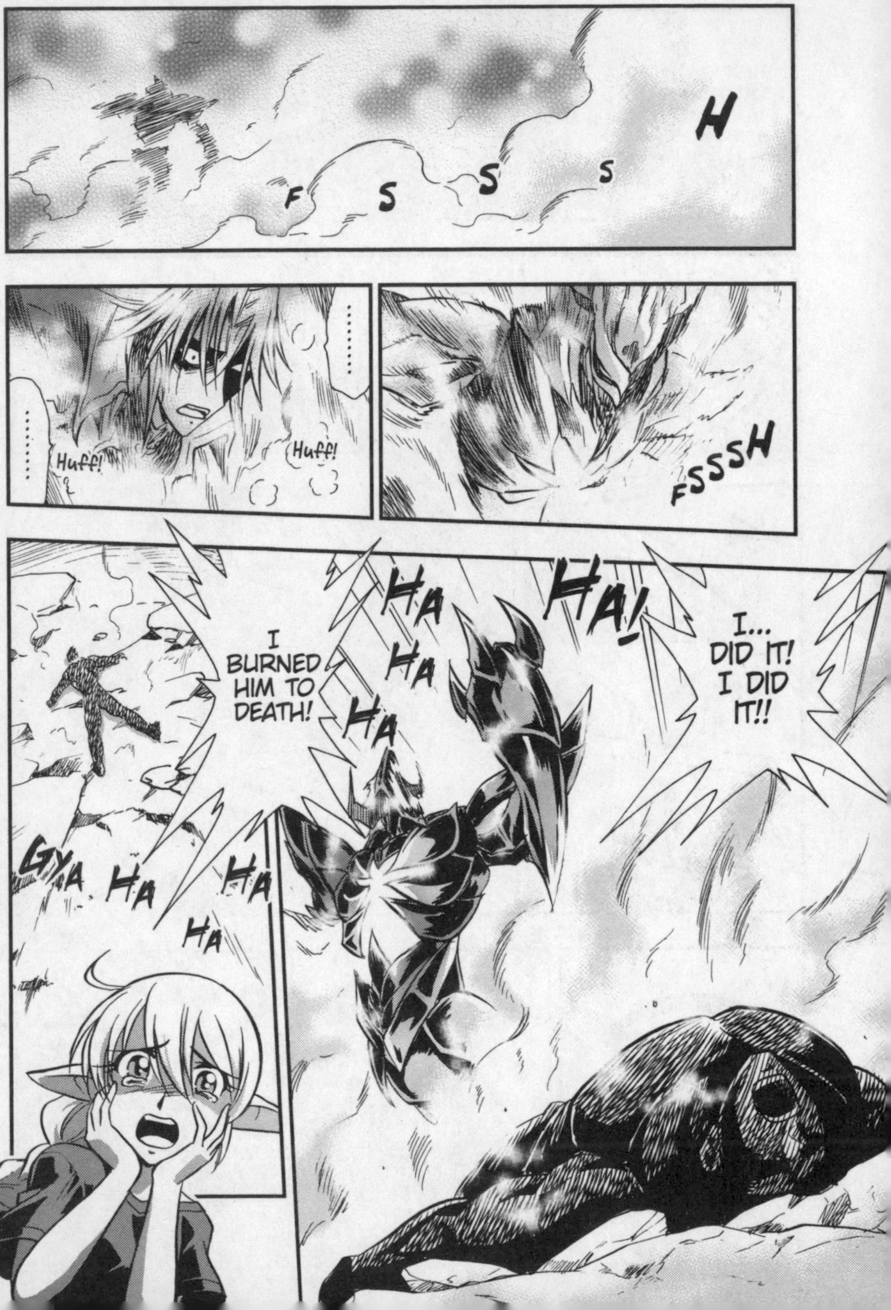
F S S S H
FSSSH
……
Huff!
Huff!
……
HA!
I... DID IT! I DID IT!!
HA HA HA
I BURNED HIM TO DEATH!
GYA HA HA HA
HA

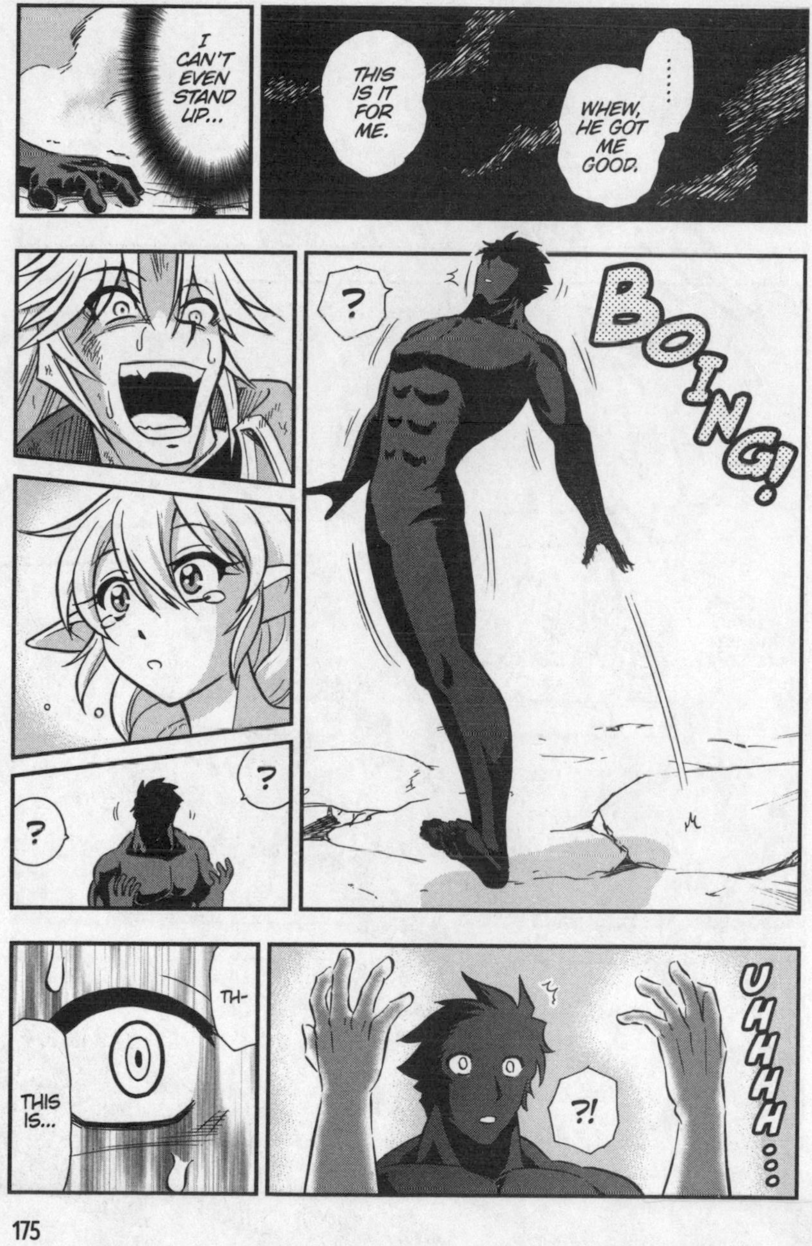
......
WHEW, HE GOT ME GOOD.
THIS IS IT FOR ME.
I CAN'T EVEN STAND UP...
BOING!
?
?
?
UHHHH...
?!
TH-
THIS IS...

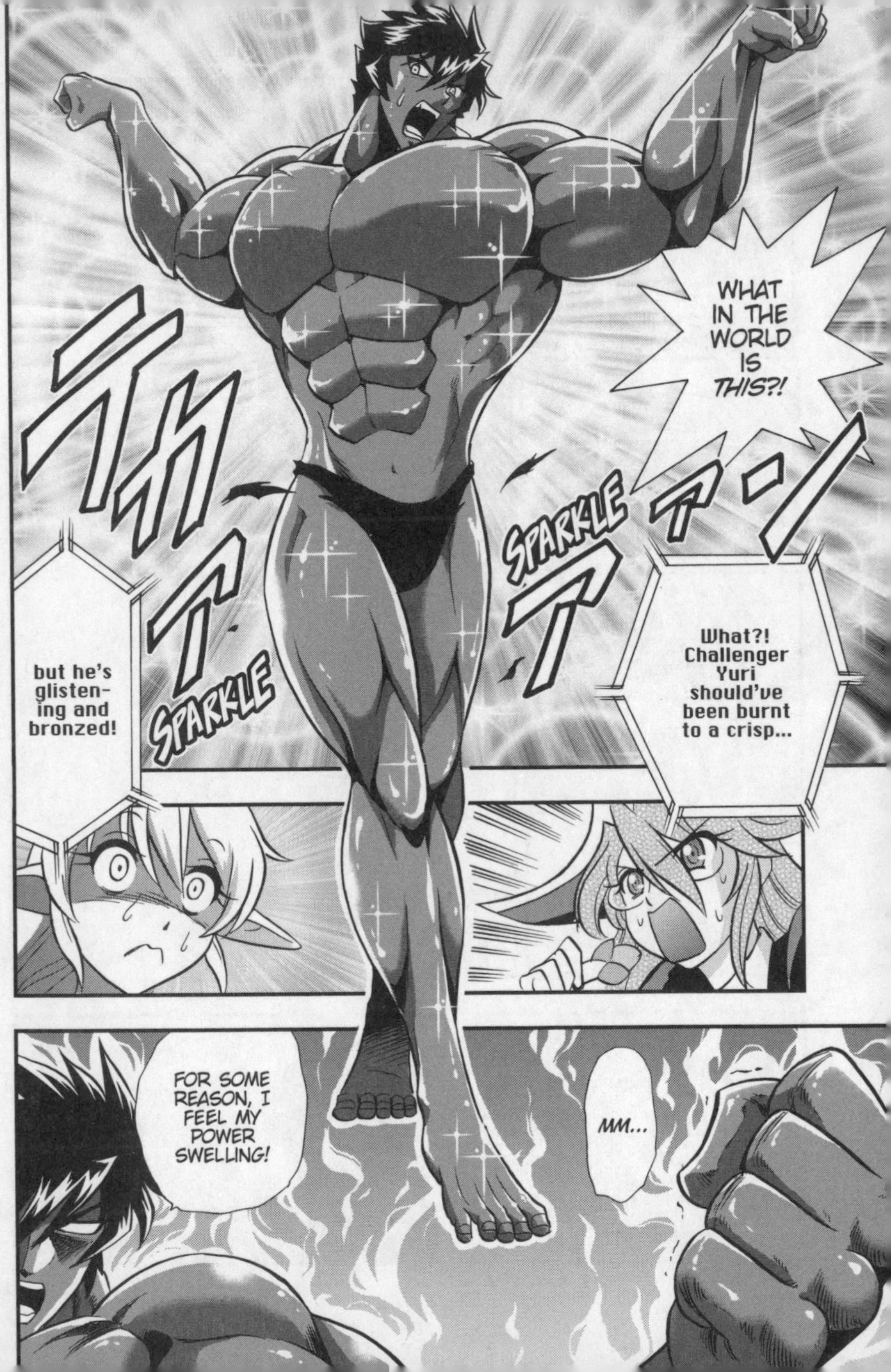

WHAT IN THE WORLD IS THIS?!
SPARKLE
SPARKLE
What?! Challenger Yuri should've been burnt to a crisp...
but he's glisten-ing and bronzed!
MM...
FOR SOME REASON, I FEEL MY POWER SWELLING!

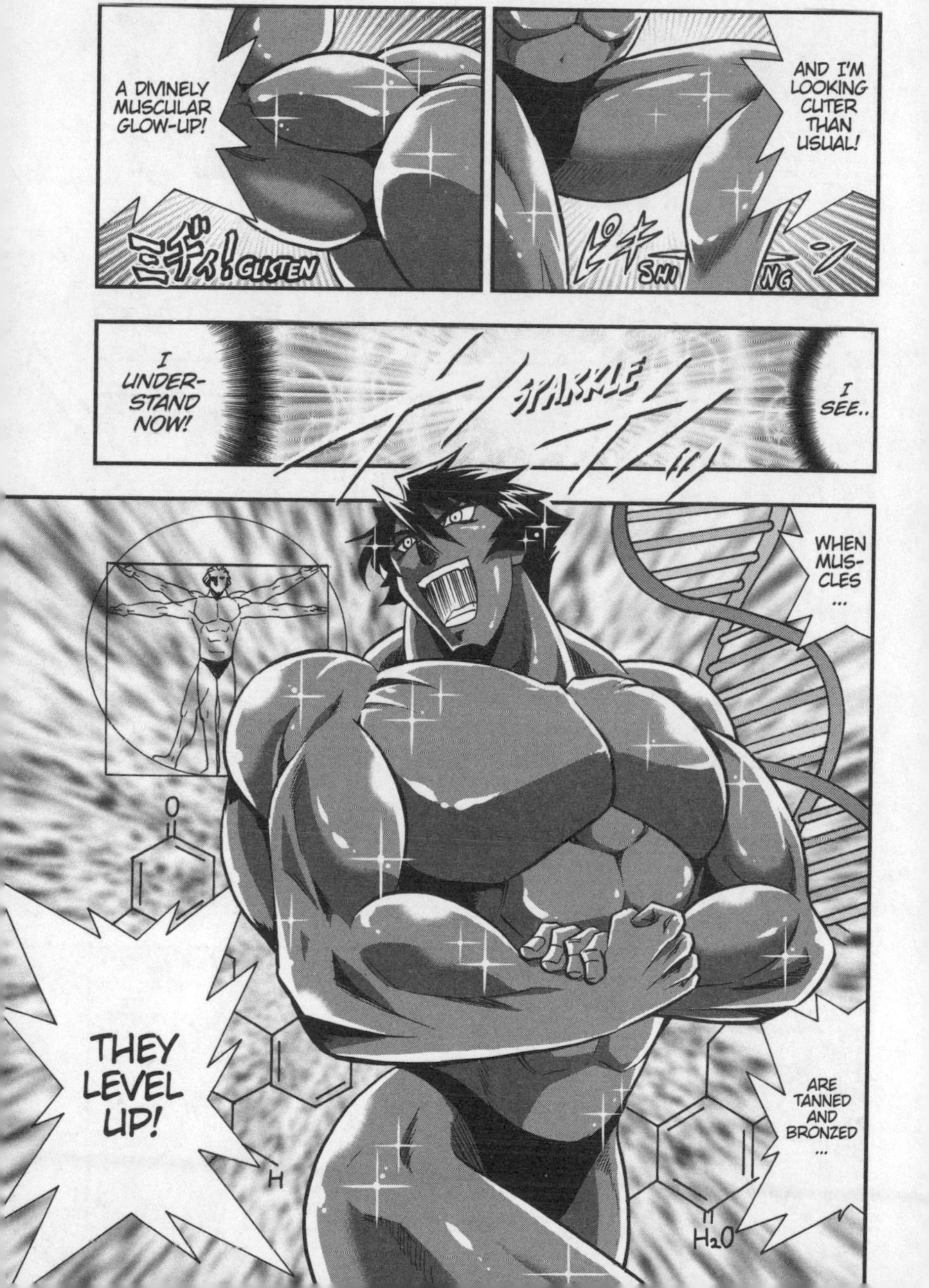
AND I'M LOOKING CUTER THAN USUAL!
SHI NG
A DIVINELY MUSCULAR GLOW-UP!
GLISTEN
I SEE..
SPARKLE
I UNDERSTAND NOW!
WHEN MUSCLES ...
ARE TANNED AND BRONZED ...
THEY LEVEL UP!

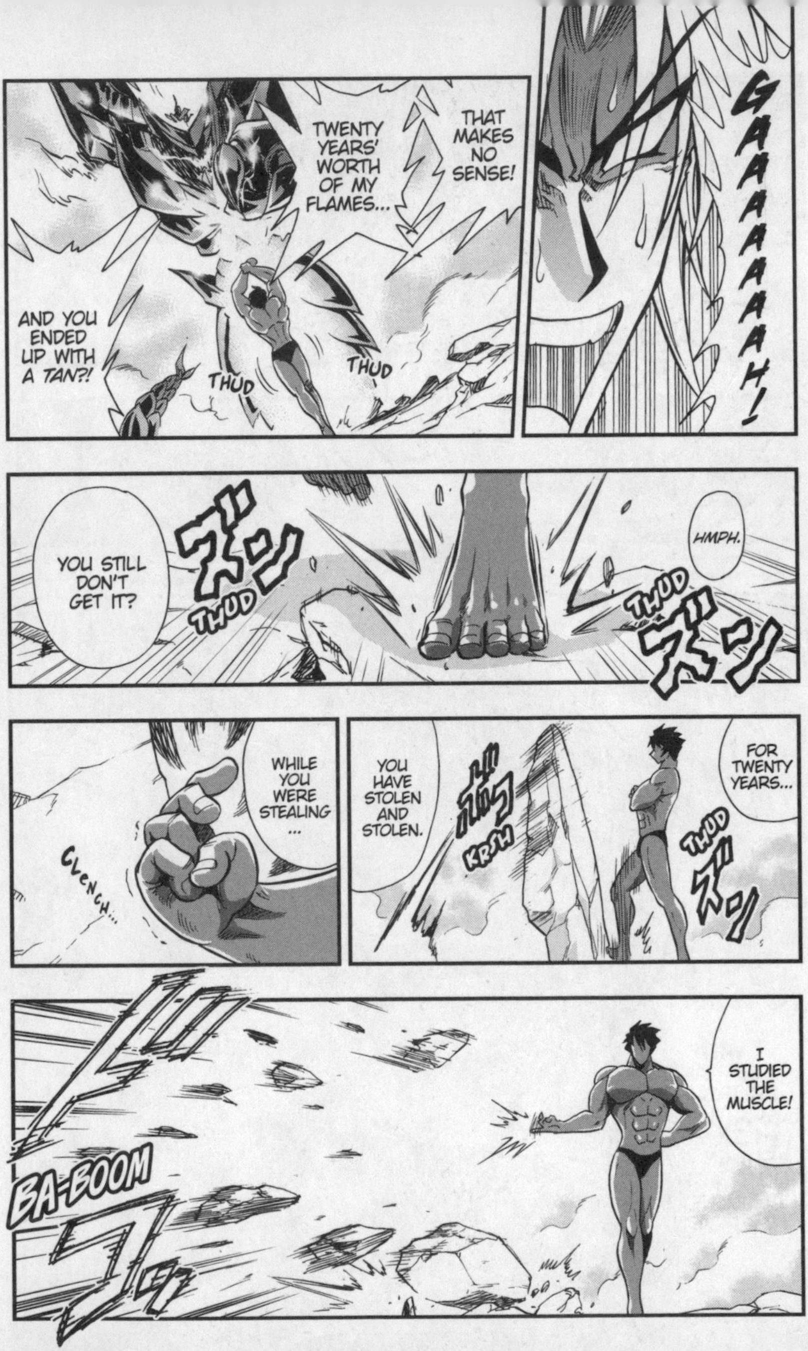
GAAAAAAAH!
THAT MAKES NO SENSE!
TWENTY YEARS' WORTH OF MY FLAMES...
THUD
AND YOU ENDED UP WITH A TAN?!
THUD
HMPH.
ズン
THUD
ズン
THUD
YOU STILL DON'T GET IT?
FOR TWENTY YEARS...
ズン
THUD
YOU HAVE STOLEN AND STOLEN.
ボコ
KRSH
WHILE YOU WERE STEALING ...
CLENCH...
I STUDIED THE MUSCLE!
BA-BOOM

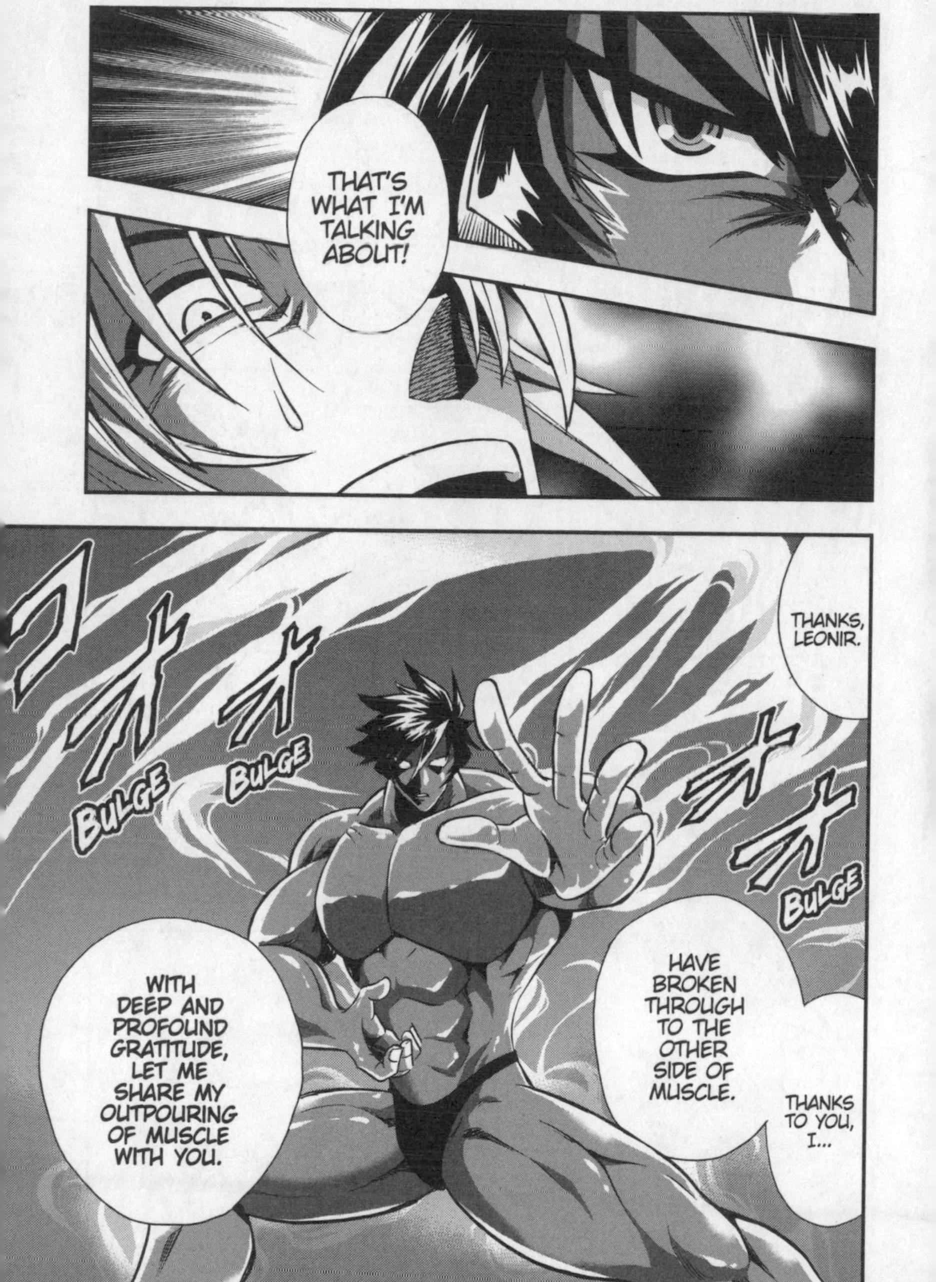
THAT'S WHAT I'M TALKING ABOUT!
THANKS, LEONIR.
BULGE
THANKS TO YOU, I...
HAVE BROKEN THROUGH TO THE OTHER SIDE OF MUSCLE.
BULGE
BULGE
WITH DEEP AND PROFOUND GRATITUDE, LET ME SHARE MY OUTPOURING OF MUSCLE WITH YOU.

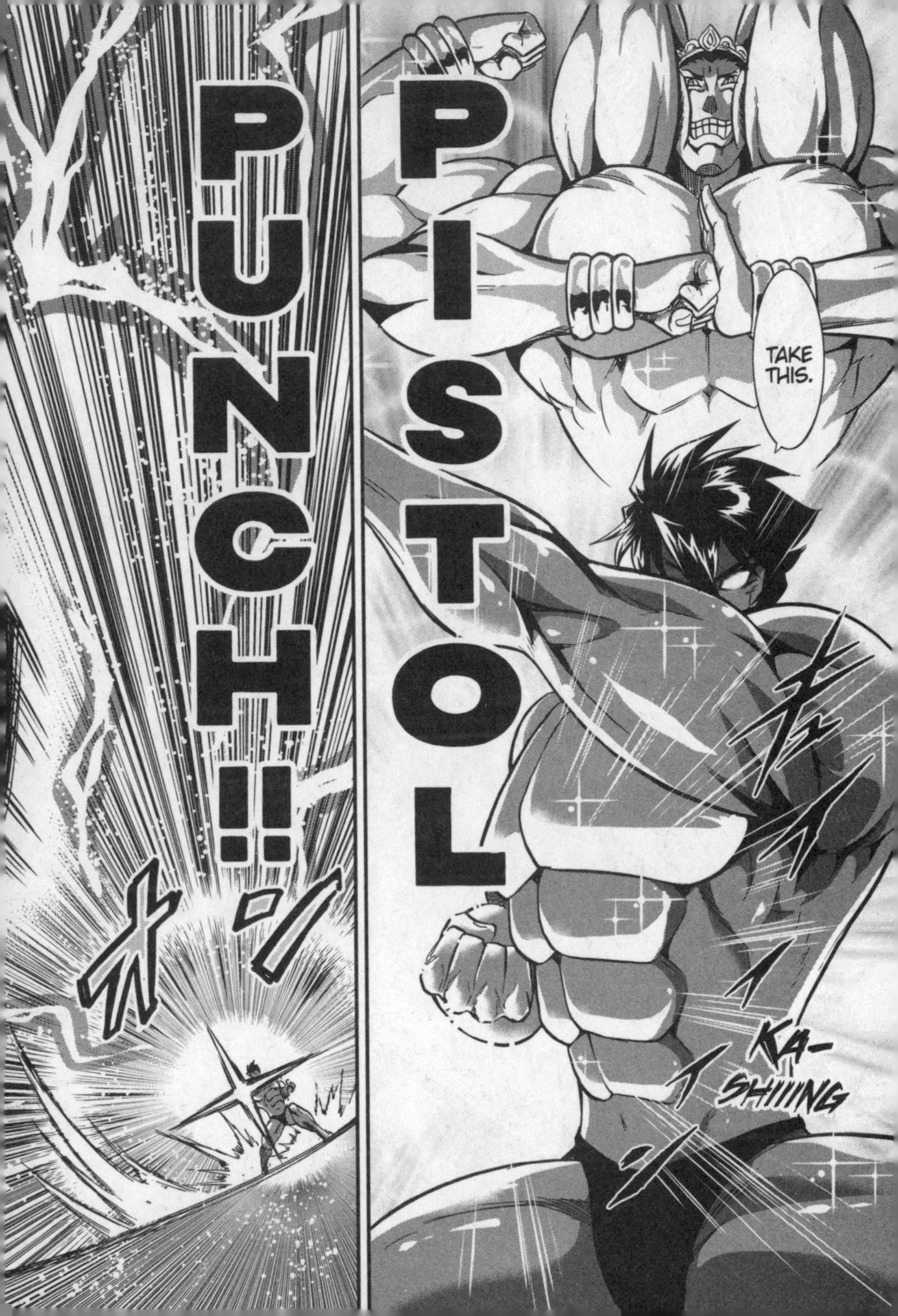
TAKE THIS.
PISTOL
KA-SHIIING
PUNCH!!

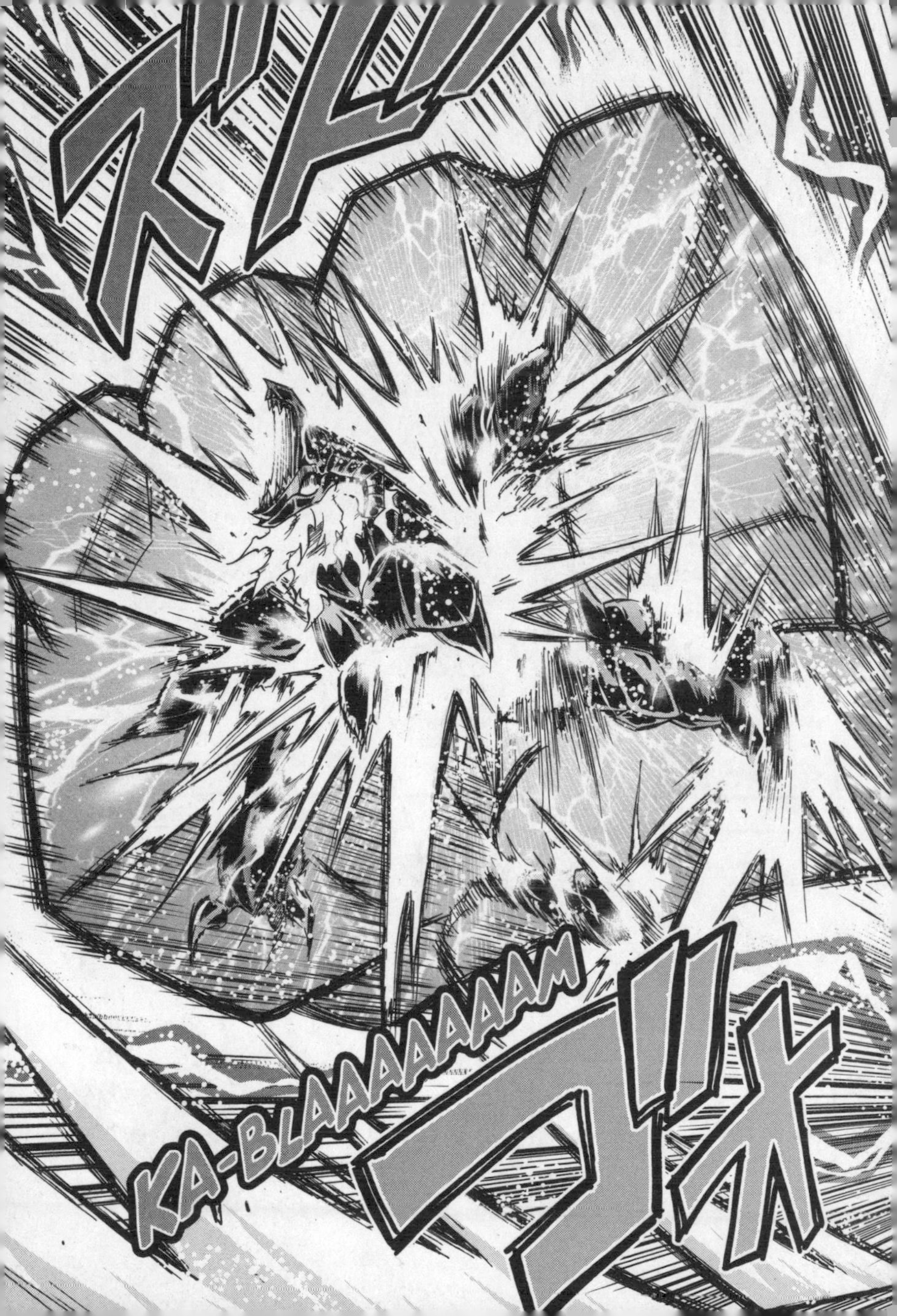
KA-BLAAAAAAAAM

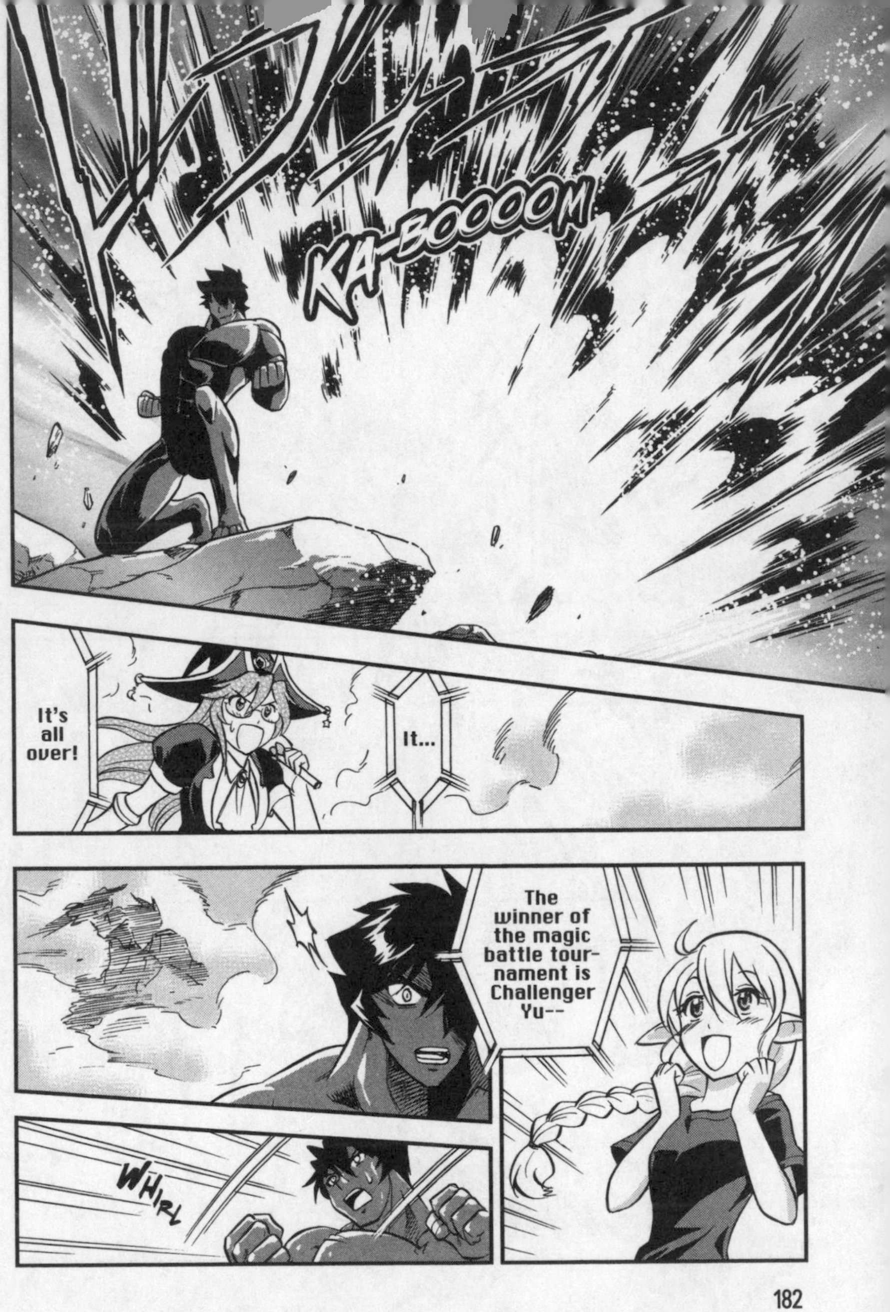
KA-BOOOOM
It...
It's all over!
The winner of the magic battle tour-nament is Challenger Yu--
WHIRL

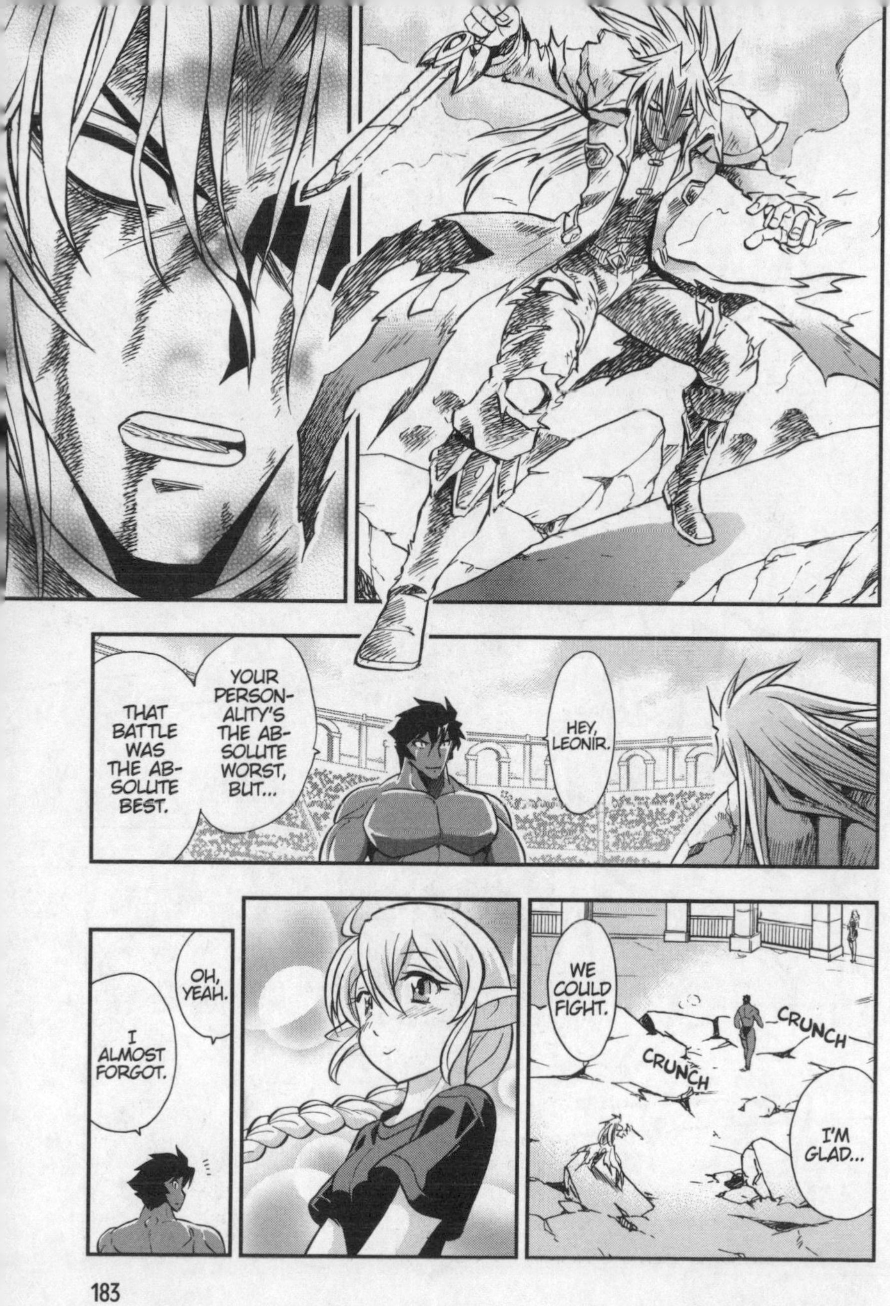
HEY, LEONIR.
YOUR PERSONALITY'S THE ABSOLUTE WORST, BUT...
THAT BATTLE WAS THE ABSOLUTE BEST.
I'M GLAD...
WE COULD FIGHT.
CRUNCH
CRUNCH
OH, YEAH.
I ALMOST FORGOT.

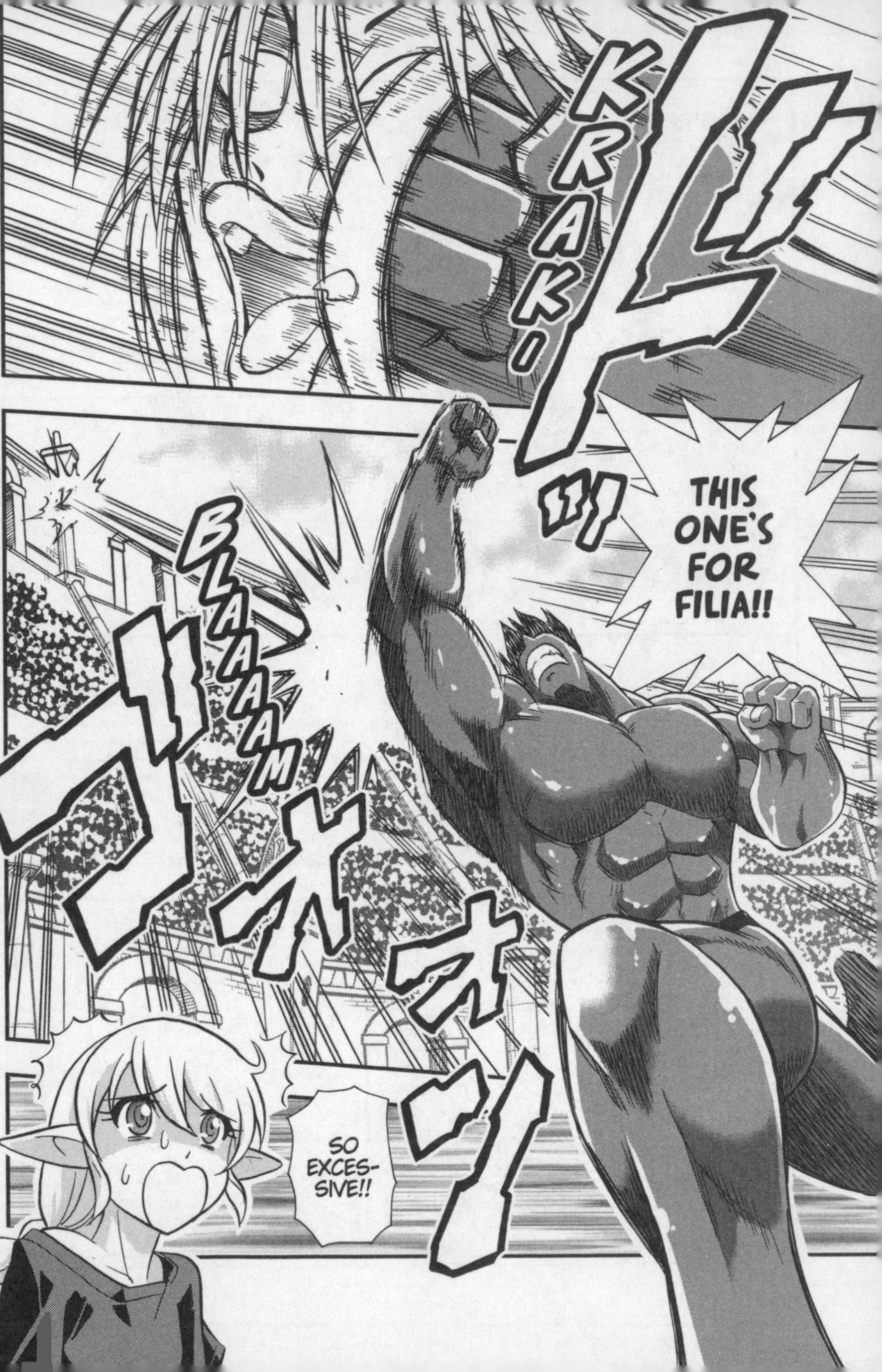
KRAK!
THIS ONE'S FOR FILIA!!
BLAAAAAM
SO EXCES-SIVE!!

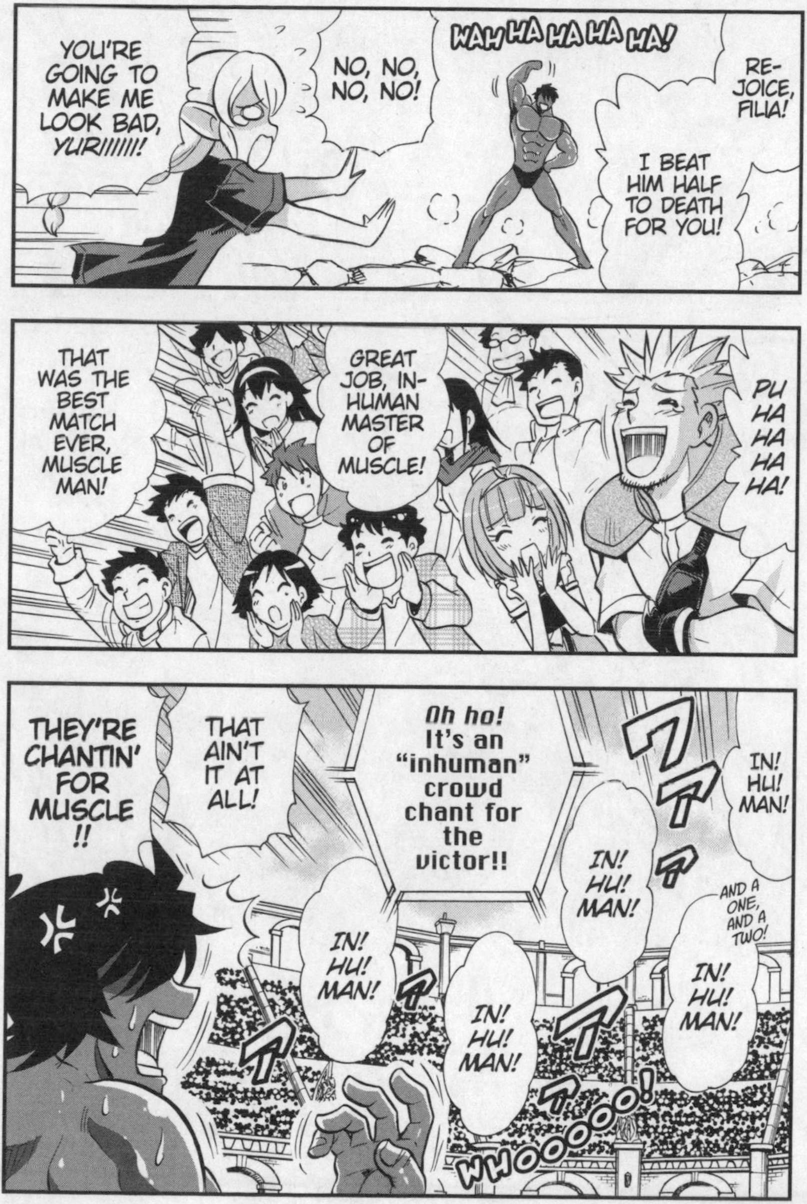
RE-JOICE, FILIA!
I BEAT HIM HALF TO DEATH FOR YOU!
WAH HA HA HA HA!
NO, NO, NO, NO!
YOU'RE GOING TO MAKE ME LOOK BAD, YURI!!!!!!!
PU HA HA HA HA HA!
GREAT JOB, IN-HUMAN MASTER OF MUSCLE!
THAT WAS THE BEST MATCH EVER, MUSCLE MAN!
IN! HU! MAN!
AND A ONE, AND A TWO!
IN! HU! MAN!
IN! HU! MAN!
IN! HU! MAN!
IN! HU! MAN!
WHOOOOOO!
Oh ho! It's an "inhuman" crowd chant for the victor!!
THAT AIN'T IT AT ALL!
THEY'RE CHANTIN' FOR MUSCLE!!

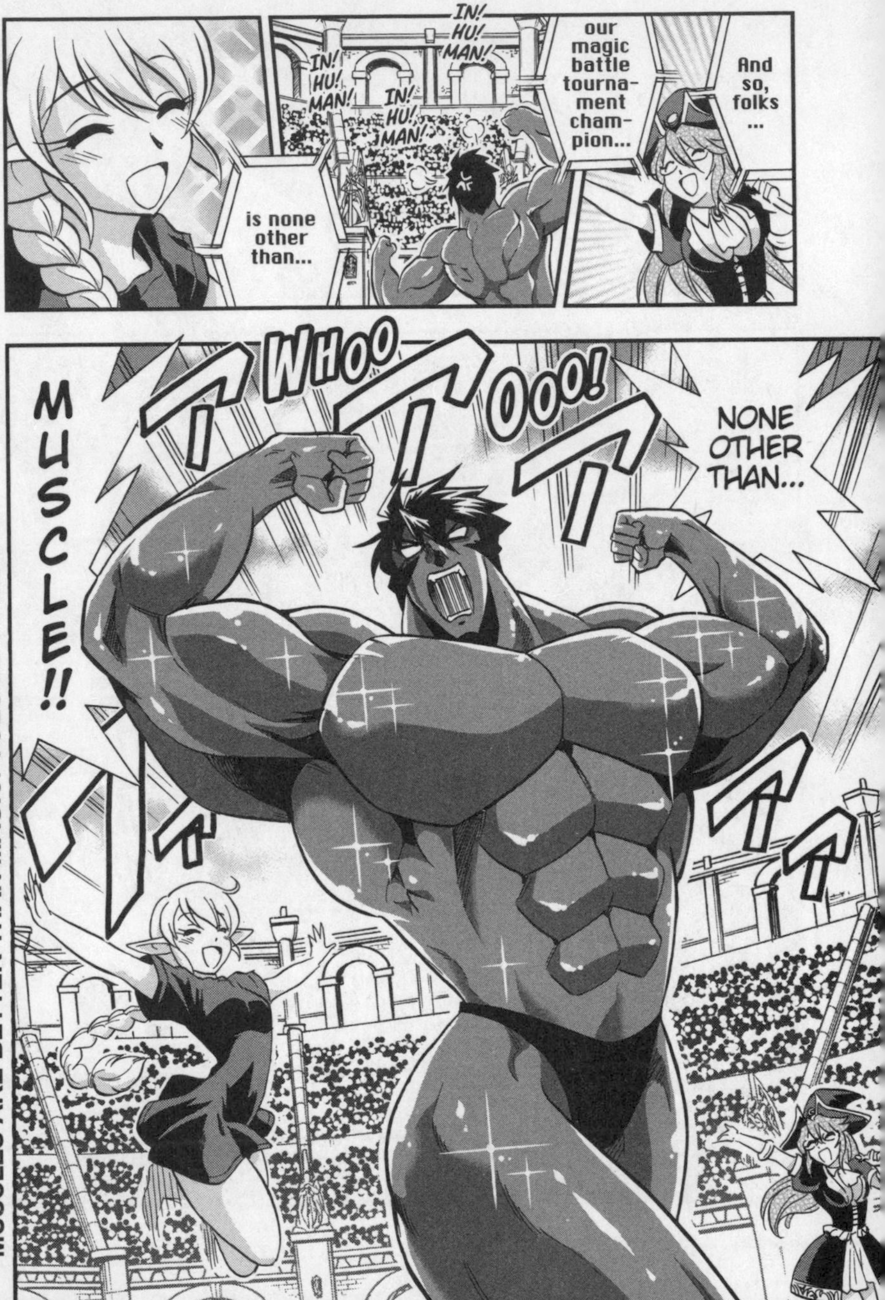

And so, folks ...
our magic battle tourna- ment cham- pion...
IN! HU! MAN!
IN! HU! MAN!
IN! HU! MAN!
is none other than...
WHOOOOO!
NONE OTHER THAN...
MUSCLE!!

MUSCLES ARE BETTER THAN MAGIC! VOLUME 3 END

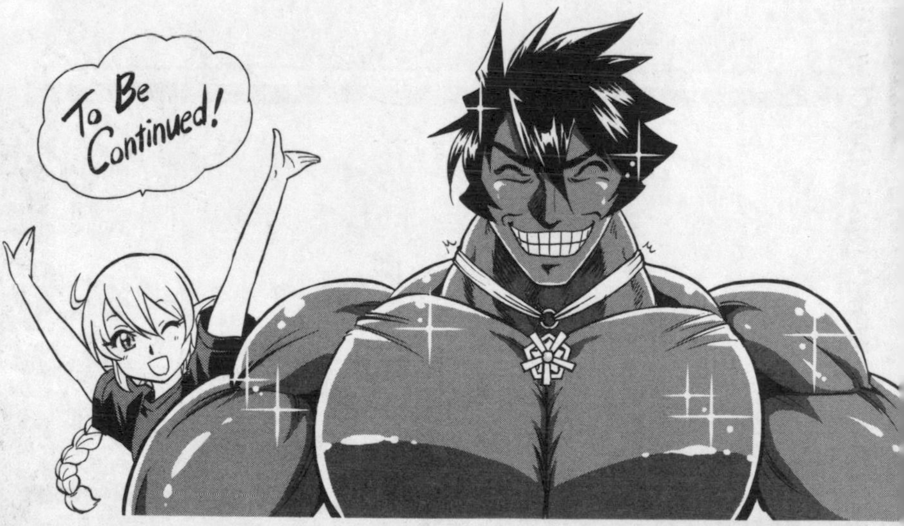
To Be Continued!

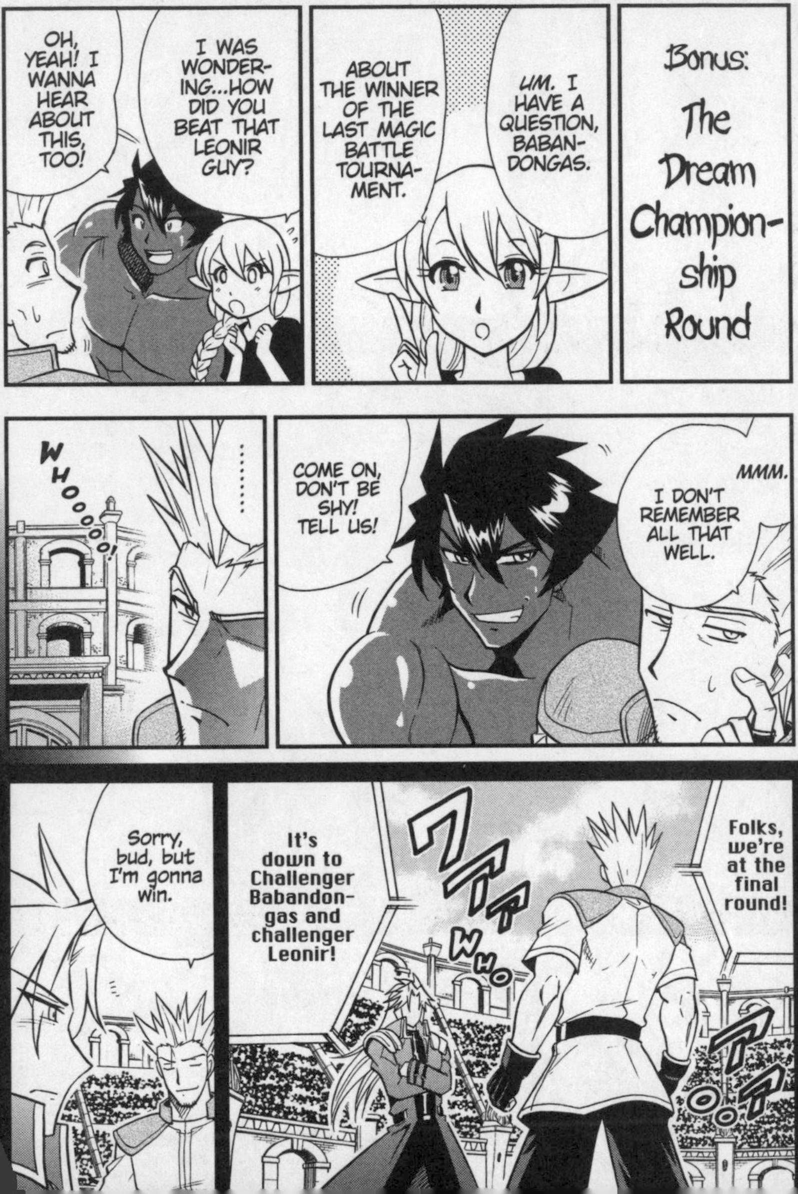
Bonus: The Dream Championship Round
UM. I HAVE A QUESTION, BABANDONGAS.
ABOUT THE WINNER OF THE LAST MAGIC BATTLE TOURNAMENT.
I WAS WONDERING...HOW DID YOU BEAT THAT LEONIR GUY?
OH, YEAH! I WANNA HEAR ABOUT THIS, TOO!
MMM.
I DON'T REMEMBER ALL THAT WELL.
COME ON, DON'T BE SHY! TELL US!
......
WHOOOOOO!
Folks, we're at the final round!
WHO
It's down to Challenger Babandongas and challenger Leonir!
Sorry, bud, but I'm gonna win.

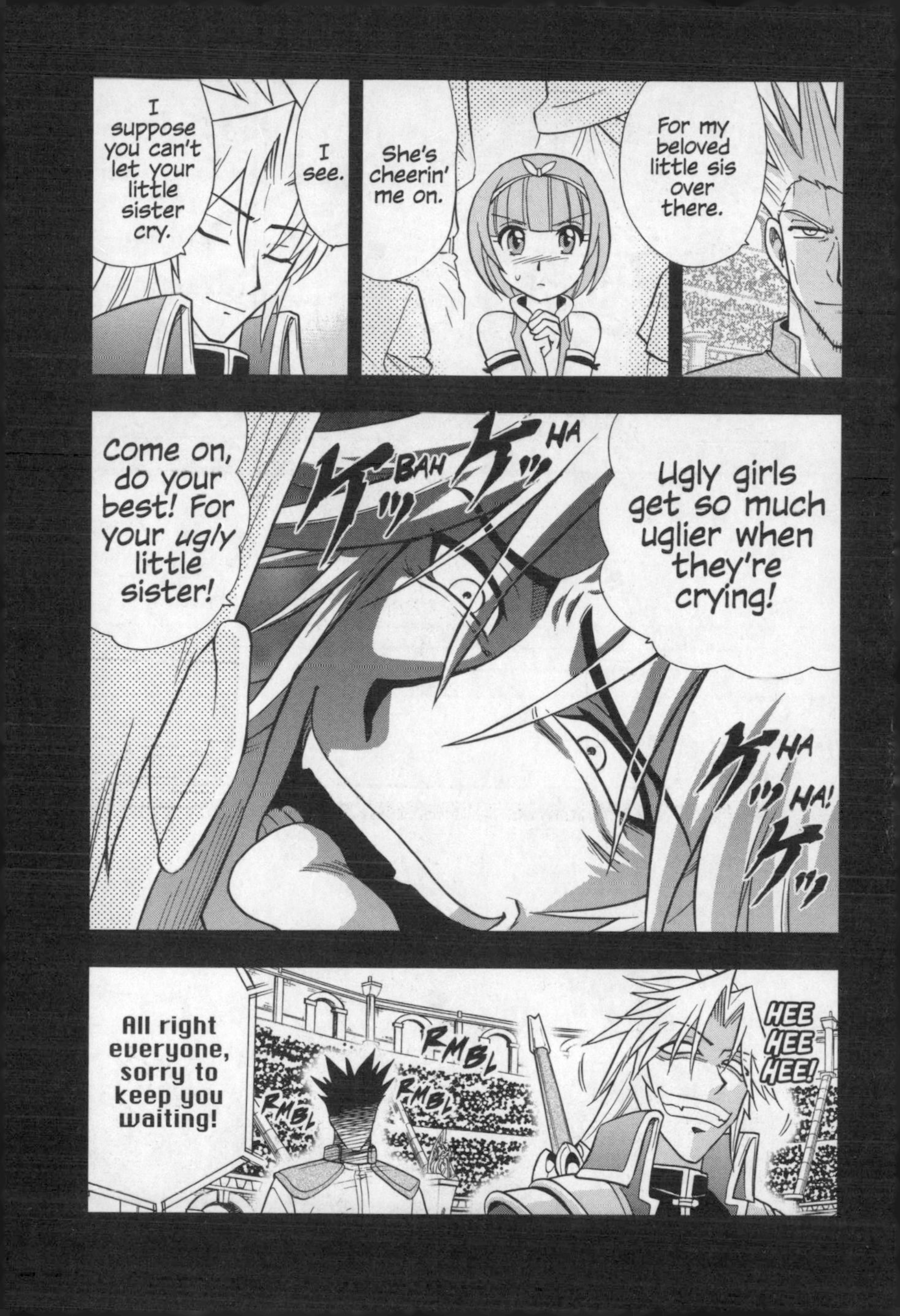
For my beloved little sis over there.
She's cheerin' me on.
I see.
I suppose you can't let your little sister cry.
Ugly girls get so much uglier when they're crying!
HA
BAH
Come on, do your best! For your *ugly* little sister!
HA
HA!
HEE HEE HEE!
RMBL
RMBL
RMBL
All right everyone, sorry to keep you waiting!

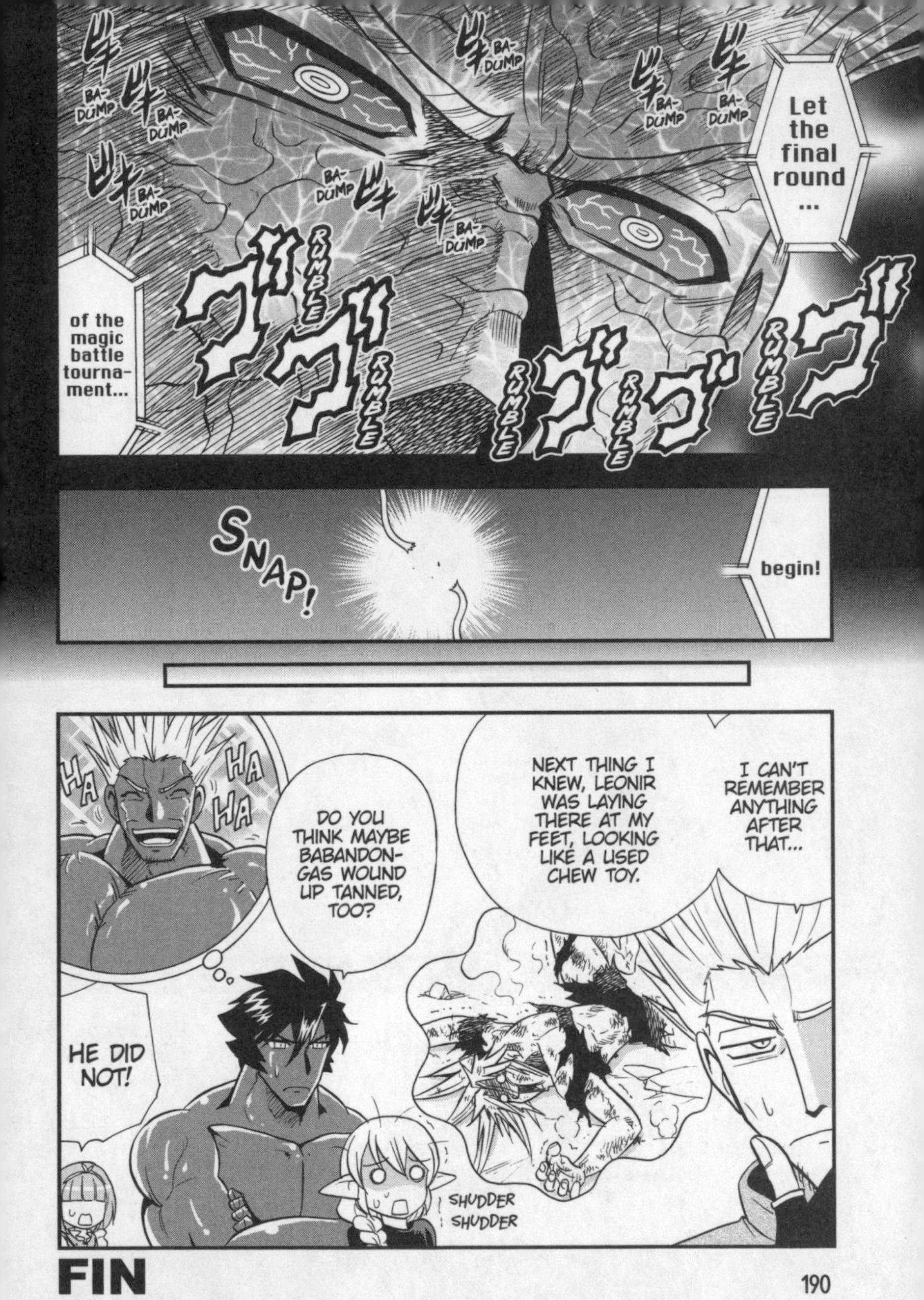
Let the final round ...
BA-DUMP
BA-DUMP
BA-DUMP
BA-DUMP
BA-DUMP
BA-DUMP
BA-DUMP
BA-DUMP
of the magic battle tournament...
RUMBLE
RUMBLE
RUMBLE
RUMBLE
RUMBLE
begin!
SNAP!
I CAN'T REMEMBER ANYTHING AFTER THAT...
NEXT THING I KNEW, LEONIR WAS LAYING THERE AT MY FEET, LOOKING LIKE A USED CHEW TOY.
DO YOU THINK MAYBE BABANDONGAS WOUND UP TANNED, TOO?
HA HA
HA HA
HE DID NOT!
SHUDDER SHUDDER

FIN

AFTERWORD

In battle manga, the tournament stories are the highlight!! That's why I tried to make the battle scenes even more exaggerated in the manga version. I hope that fans of the original books will really enjoy them, too.

I don't know why I love characters who lose all the time. Huh? You don't get it? Well, my favorite loser is Doch. I want him to be happy. He's not going to show up again though. (lol)

The next volume will be the start of a whole new chapter! Filia will become this and that, there's going to be a reunion with someone dearly missed, and an unbelievable enemy is going to appear...

There's no rest for the weary, and for well-trained muscles!

Welp, see ya again in Volume 4!

8/2019 小野寺浩二
Kouji Onodera

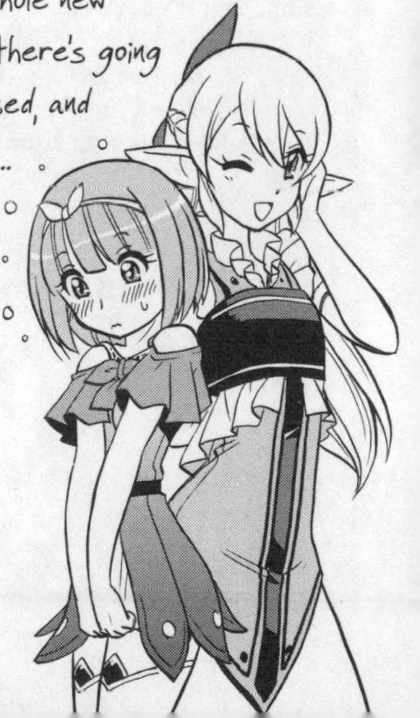

Congratulations on the release of Volume 3!
A year has already passed since this series started,
like the blink of an eye. Time sure does fly.

Every year seems to go faster than the last! Honestly
though, I'm extremely happy to see the manga version of *Muscles
are Better than Magic* entering its second year. Thanks to that, this
series has now become a part of my daily life. It's something I enjoy
each month.

This volume is all about the magic battle tournament, and the story
keeps heating up. Even though I know what's going to happen, my
hands start sweating and I'm overcome with excitement every time I
read it. I can feel the intensity through the art, and it's just fantastic.

And every time I write some comments at the end of the book, I
always think like where it ends! The main, overall plot remains the
same, but it's been restructured in a way that makes it more suitable
for manga. Every volume really ends on a high note.

Ugh, I can't wait to read the next one! I'll be looking forward to the
next volume and the stories in it with the same excitement as all of
you!

Doraneko

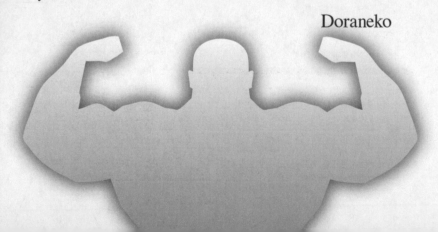

MUSCLES ARE BETTER THAN MAGIC!

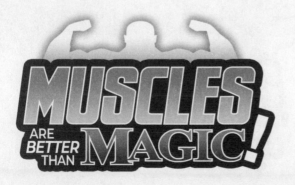

MUSCLES ARE BETTER THAN MAGIC!

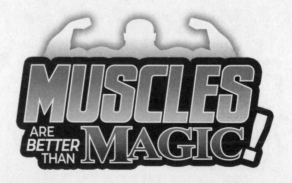

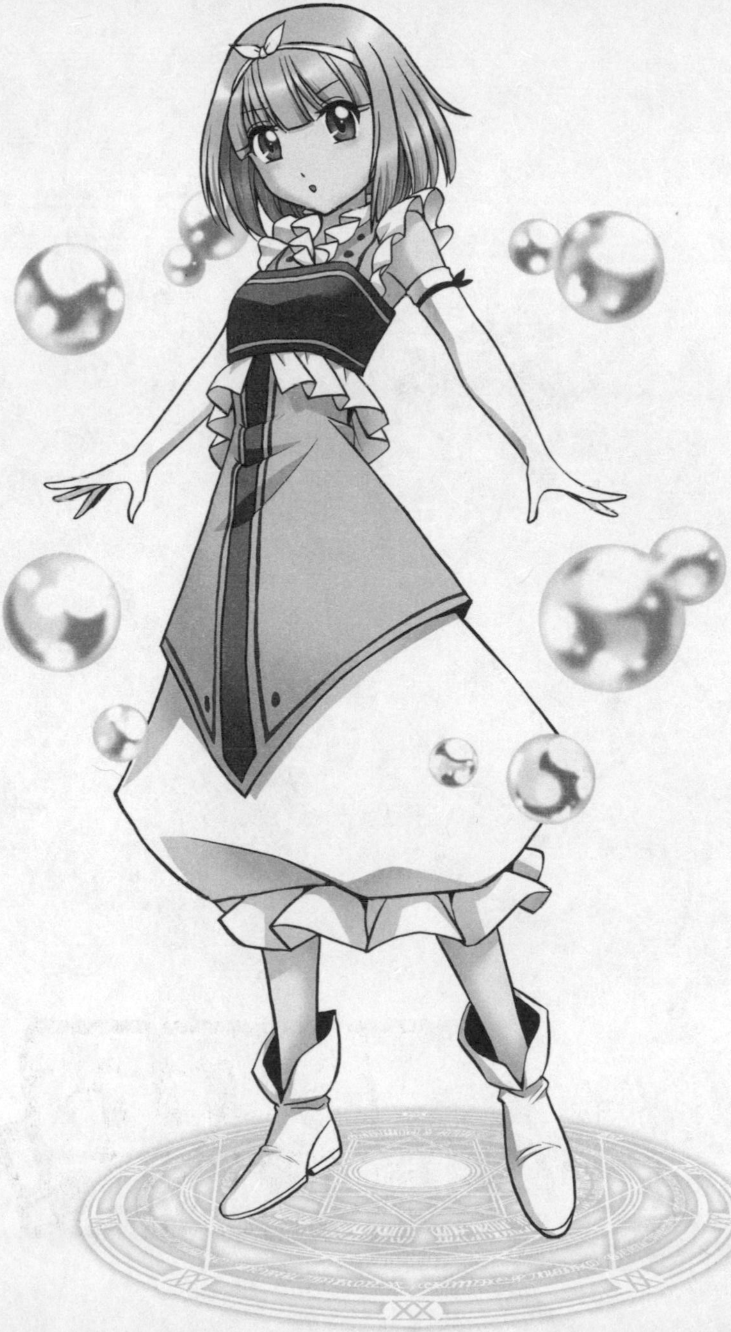

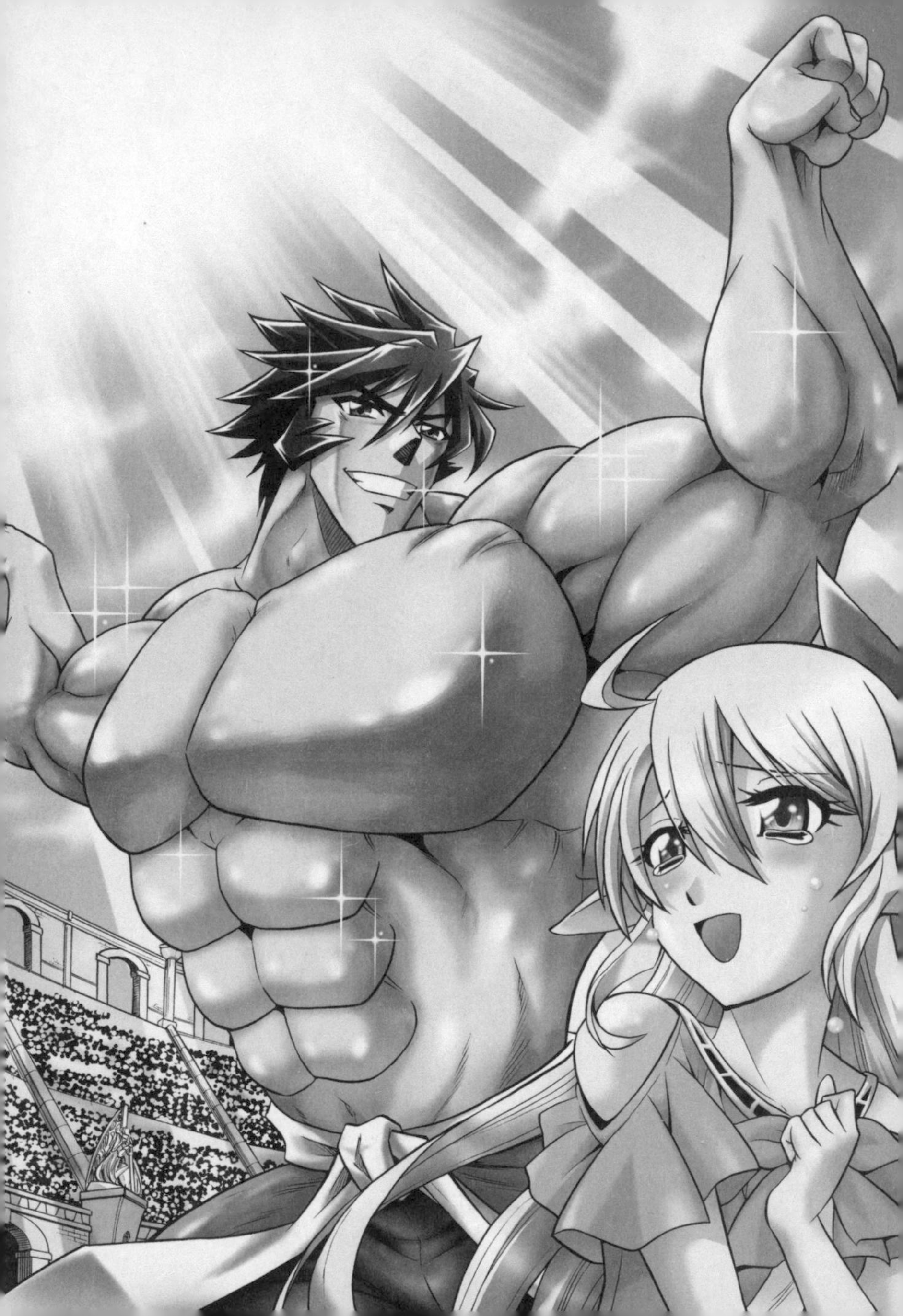

MUSCLES ARE BETTER THAN MAGIC!

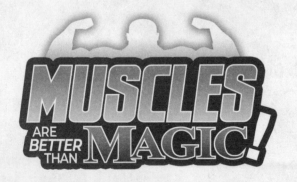

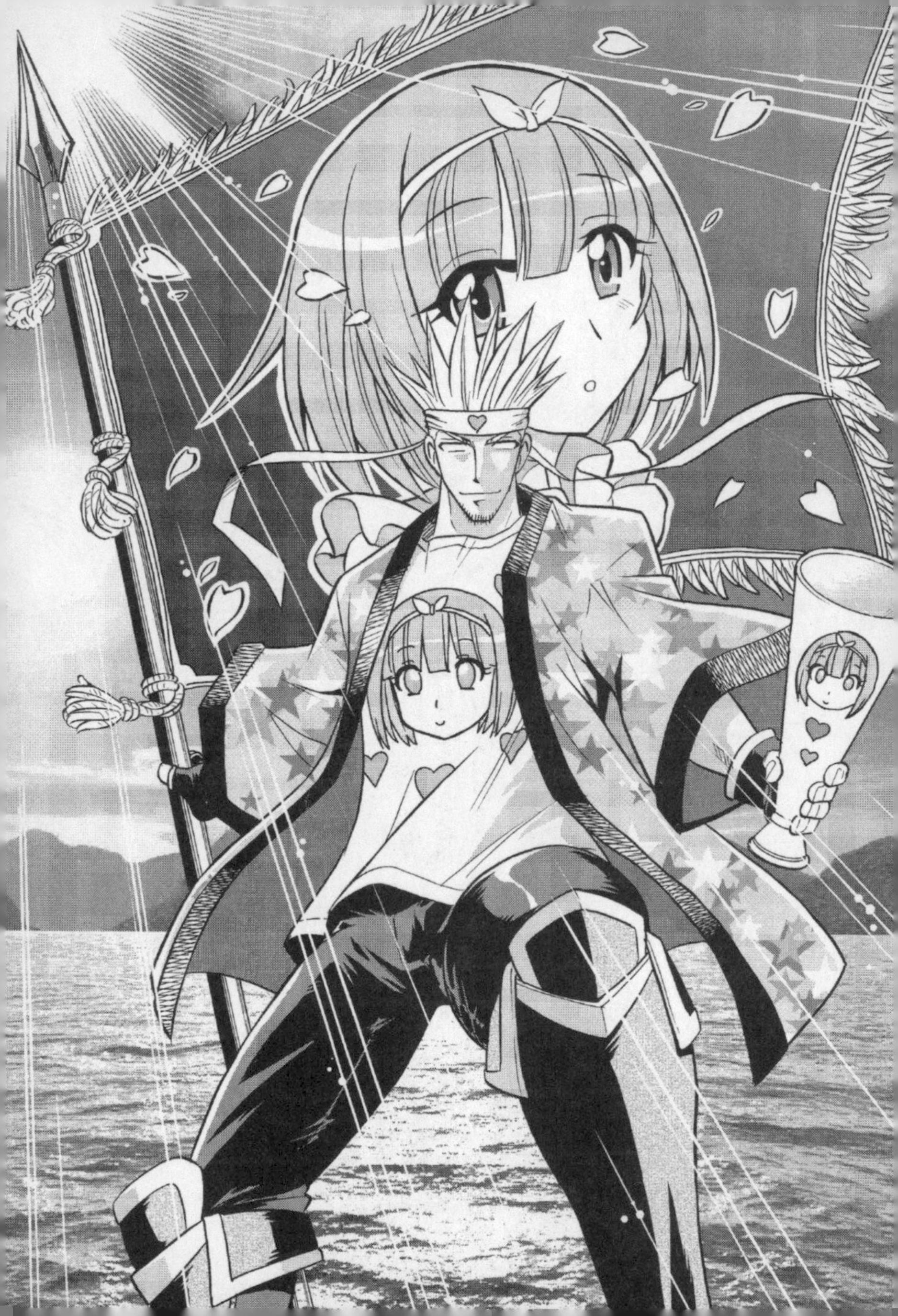

MUSCLES ARE BETTER THAN MAGIC!

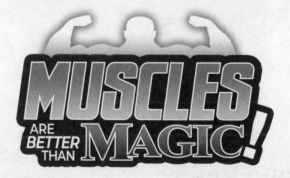